Reading STREET

Program Authors

Peter Afflerbach

Camille Blachowicz

Candy Dawson Boyd

Elena Izquierdo

Connie Juel

Edward Kame'enui

Donald Leu

Jeanne R. Paratore

P. David Pearson

Sam Sebesta

Deborah Simmons

Alfred Tatum

Sharon Vaughn

Susan Watts Taffe

Karen Kring Wixson

PEARSON

Glenview, Illinois • Boston, Massachusetts
Chandler, Arizona • Upper Saddle River, New Jersey

We dedicate Reading Street to
Peter Jovanovich.

~

His wisdom, courage,
and passion for education
are an inspiration to us all.

Accelerated Reader®

PEARSON

ISBN-13: 978-0-328-47009-9
ISBN-10:   0-328-47009-0
2 3 4 5 6 7 8 9 10 V064 14 13 12 11 10
CC1

Any Path, Any Pace

"Welcome to
Reading Street!
Bienvenidos too."

PEARSON

SCOTT FORESMAN

PEARSON

Find Your Place on Reading Street!

Who said so?

The Leading Researchers,

Program Authors

Peter Afflerbach, Ph.D.
Professor
Department of Curriculum
and Instruction
University of Maryland
at College Park

Camille L. Z. Blachowicz, Ph.D.
Professor of Education
National-Louis University

Candy Dawson Boyd, Ph.D.
Professor
School of Education
Saint Mary's College of California

Elena Izquierdo, Ph.D.
Associate Professor
University of Texas at El Paso

Connie Juel, Ph.D.
Professor of Education
School of Education
Stanford University

Edward J. Kame'enui, Ph.D.
Dean-Knight Professor of
Education and Director
Institute for the Development of
Educational Achievement and
the Center on Teaching and Learning
College of Education
University of Oregon

Donald J. Leu, Ph.D.
John and Maria Neag Endowed
Chair in Literacy and Technology
Director, The New Literacies
Research Lab
University of Connecticut

Jeanne R. Paratore, Ed.D.
Associate Professor of Education
Department of Literacy and
Language Development
Boston University

P. David Pearson, Ph.D.
Professor and Dean
Graduate School of Education
University of California, Berkeley

Sam L. Sebesta, Ed.D.
Professor Emeritus
College of Education
University of Washington, Seattle

Deborah Simmons, Ph.D.
Professor
College of Education and
Human Development
Texas A&M University

Alfred W. Tatum, Ph.D.
Associate Professor and Director
of the UIC Reading Clinic
University of Illinois at Chicago

Sharon Vaughn, Ph.D.
H. E. Hartfelder/Southland
Corporation Regents Professor
Director, Meadows Center for
Preventing Educational Risk
University of Texas

Susan Watts Taffe, Ph.D.
Associate Professor in Literacy
Division of Teacher Education
University of Cincinnati

Karen Kring Wixson, Ph.D.
Professor of Education
University of Michigan

Consulting Authors

Jeff Anderson, M.Ed.
Author and Consultant
San Antonio, Texas

Jim Cummins, Ph.D.
Professor
Department of Curriculum,
Teaching and Learning
University of Toronto

Lily Wong Fillmore, Ph.D.
Professor Emerita
Graduate School of Education
University of California, Berkeley

Georgia Earnest García, Ph.D.
Professor
Language and Literacy Division
Department of Curriculum
and Instruction
University of Illinois at
Urbana-Champaign

George A. González, Ph.D.
Professor (Retired)
School of Education
University of Texas-Pan American,
Edinburg

Valerie Ooka Pang, Ph.D.
Professor
School of Teacher Education
San Diego State University

Sally M. Reis, Ph.D.
Board of Trustees Distinguished
Professor
Department of Educational
Psychology
University of Connecticut

Jon Scieszka, M.F.A.
Children's Book Author
Founder of GUYS READ
Named First National Ambassador
for Young People's Literature 2008

Grant Wiggins, Ed.D.
Educational Consultant
Authentic Education
Concept Development

Lee Wright, M.Ed.
Pearland, Texas

Practitioners, and Authors.

Consultant

Sharroky Hollie, Ph.D.
Assistant Professor
California State University
Dominguez Hills, CA

Teacher Reviewers

Dr. Bettyann Brugger
Educational Support Coordinator–
Reading Office
Milwaukee Public Schools
Milwaukee, WI

Kathleen Burke
K–12 Reading Coordinator
Peoria Public Schools, Peoria, IL

Darci Burns, M.S.Ed.
University of Oregon

Bridget Cantrell
District Intervention Specialist
Blackburn Elementary School
Independence, MO

**Tahira DuPree Chase,
M.A., M.S.Ed.**
Administrator of Elementary
English Language Arts
Mount Vernon City School District
Mount Vernon, NY

Michele Conner
Director, Elementary Education
Aiken County School District
Aiken, SC

Georgia Coulombe
K–6 Regional Trainer/
Literacy Specialist
Regional Center for Training and
Learning (RCTL), Reno, NV

Kelly Dalmas
Third Grade Teacher
Avery's Creek Elementary, Arden, NC

Seely Dillard
First Grade Teacher
Laurel Hill Primary School
Mt. Pleasant, SC

Jodi Dodds-Kinner
Director of Elementary Reading
Chicago Public Schools, Chicago, IL

Dr. Ann Wild Evenson
District Instructional Coach
Osseo Area Schools, Maple Grove, MN

Stephanie Fascitelli
Principal
Apache Elementary, Albuquerque
Public Schools, Albuquerque, NM

Alice Franklin
Elementary Coordinator, Language
Arts & Reading
Spokane Public Schools, Spokane, WA

Laureen Fromberg
Assistant Principal
PS 100 Queens, NY

Kimberly Gibson
First Grade Teacher
Edgar B. Davis Community School
Brockton, MA

Kristen Gray
Lead Teacher
A.T. Allen Elementary School
Concord, NC

Mary Ellen Hazen
State Pre-K Teacher
Rockford Public Schools #205
Rockford, IL

Patrick M. Johnson
Elementary Instructional Director
Seattle Public Schools, Seattle, WA

Theresa Jaramillo Jones
Principal
Highland Elementary School
Las Cruces, NM

Sophie Kowzun
Program Supervisor, Reading/
Language Arts, PreK–5
Montgomery County Public Schools
Rockville, MD

David W. Matthews
Sixth Grade Teacher
Easton Area Middle School
Easton, PA

Ana Nuncio
Editor and Independent Publisher
Salem, MA

Joseph Peila
Principal
Chappell Elementary School
Chicago, IL

Ivana Reimer
Literacy Coordinator
PS 100 Queens, NY

Sally Riley
Curriculum Coordinator
Rochester Public Schools
Rochester, NH

Dyan M. Smiley
Independent Educational Consultant

Michael J. Swiatowiec
Lead Literacy Teacher
Graham Elementary School
Chicago, IL

Dr. Helen Taylor
Director of English Education
Portsmouth City Public Schools
Portsmouth, VA

Carol Thompson
Teaching and Learning Coach
Independence School District
Independence, MO

Erinn Zeitlin
Kindergarten Teacher
Carderock Springs Elementary School
Bethesda, MD

Any Path, Any Pace

UNIT 2

Working Together

Key

SI Strategic Intervention
OL On-Level
A Advanced
ELL ELL

In this Teacher's Edition Unit 2, Volume 2

Reader's & Writer's
NOTEBOOK

Grade 2

In the First Stop on Reading Street

 GO Digital!

See It!

- **Big Question Video**

- **Concept Talk Video**

- **Interactive Sound-Spelling Cards**

- **Envision It! Animations**

- **Sing with Me Animations**

Hear It!

- **Sing with Me Animations**

- **eSelections**

- **Grammar Jammer**

- **eReaders**

- **Leveled Reader Database**

Do It!

- **Vocabulary Activities**

- **Story Sort**

- **21st Century Skills Activities**

- **Online Assessment**

- **Letter Tile Drag and Drop**

UNIT 1

Exploration

Volume 1

Volume 2

UNIT **2**

Working Together

Key
- **SI** Strategic Intervention
- **OL** On-Level
- **A** Advanced
- **ELL** ELL

UNIT 3

Creative Ideas

Volume 1

Volume 2

Reader's & Writer's NOTEBOOK · Grade 2

UNIT 4

Our Changing World

Key

SI Strategic Intervention
OL On-Level
A Advanced
ELL ELL

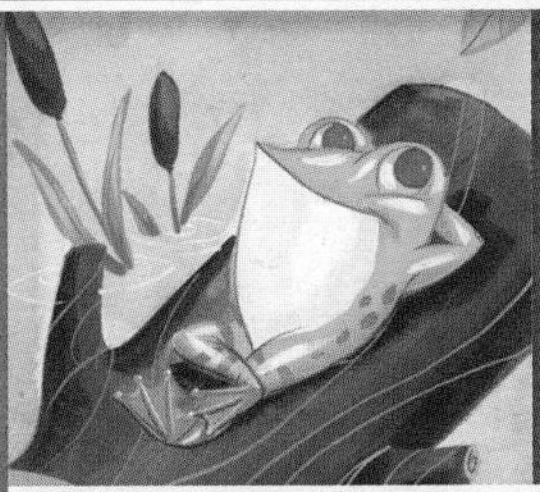

Volume 1

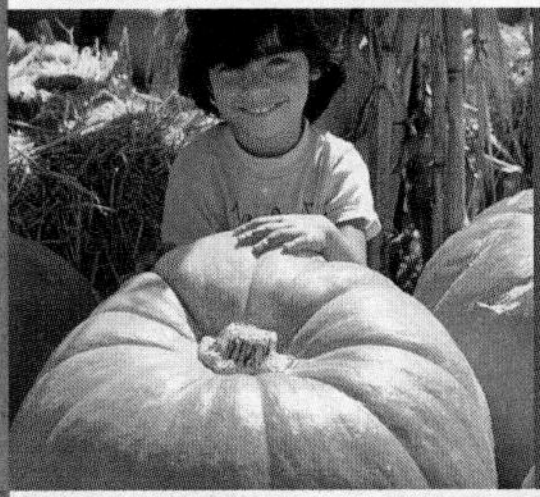

Volume 2

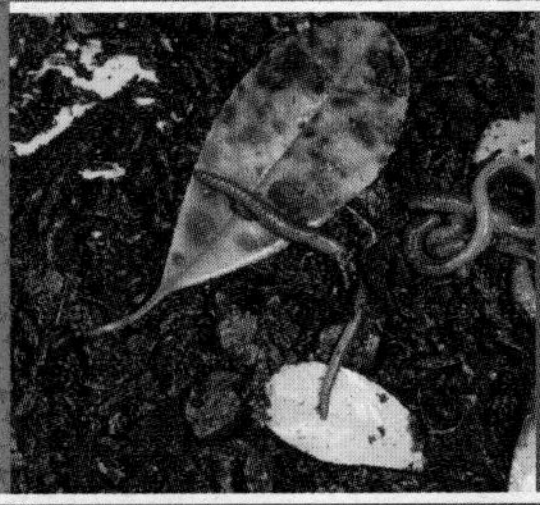

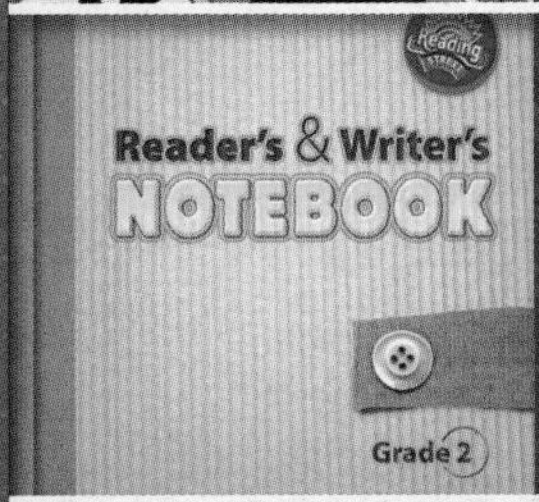

Reader's & Writer's
NOTEBOOK
Grade 2

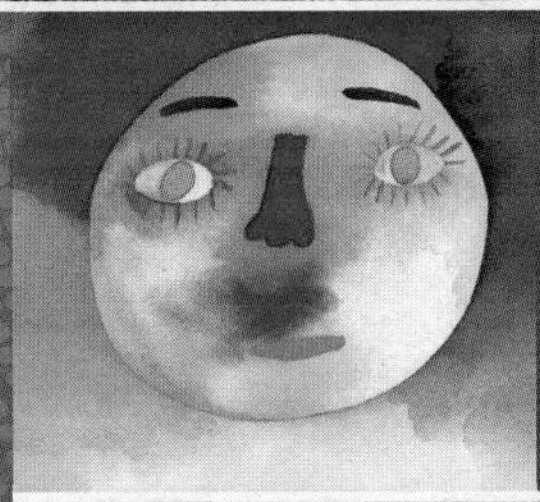

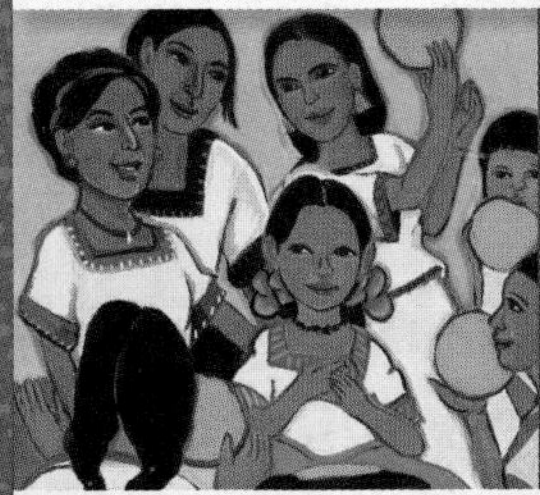

UNIT 5

Responsibility

Volume 1

Volume 2

Reader's & Writer's NOTEBOOK
Grade 2

UNIT 6

Traditions

Key
SI Strategic Intervention
OL On-Level
A Advanced
ELL ELL

Volume 1

WEEK 1 • Just Like Josh Gibson
Realistic Fiction 360a–391l
How Baseball Began Expository Text
Differentiated Instruction SI OL A ELL ....DI•1–DI•21

WEEK 2 • Red, White, and Blue: The Story of the American Flag Informational Text 392a–425l
"You're a Grand Old Flag" Poetry
Differentiated Instruction SI OL A ELL ....DI•22–DI•42

WEEK 3 • A Birthday Basket for Tía
Realistic Fiction 426a–457l
Family Traditions: Birthdays 21st Century Skills
Differentiated Instruction SI OL A ELL ....DI•43–DI•63

Volume 2

WEEK 4 • Cowboys Informational Text 458a–495l
Cowboy Gear Informational Text
Differentiated Instruction SI OL A ELL ....DI•64–DI•84

WEEK 5 • Grace for President Realistic Fiction....496a–529l
Home Sweet Home Informational Text
Differentiated Instruction SI OL A ELL ....DI•85–DI•105

Reader's & Writer's NOTEBOOK Grade 2

WEEK 6 • Interactive Review ....IR•1–IR•60
Are traditions and celebrations important in our lives?
Unit Wrap Up

Customize Writing ....CW•1–CW•20
Customize Literacy...CL•1–CL•47
Let's Learn Amazing Words ....OV•1–OV•3

UNIT 2

Skills Overview

Key

T Tested Skill

🔄 Target Skill

	WEEK 1	WEEK 2
	Tara and Tiree, Fearless Friends Literary Nonfiction pp. 192–207 **Rescue Dogs** Expository Text pp. 212–215	**Abraham Lincoln** Informational Text pp. 224–239 **"Lincoln"** Poetry pp. 244–245
Question of the Week	How can we help each other in dangerous situations?	How has working together changed history?
Amazing Words	*courageous, hazard, rescue, avalanche, instinct, skittish, blustery, fast-paced*	*identify, participate, significant, scour, ingenious, aloft, architect, tinker*
Phonemic Awareness	Substitute Initial Phonemes	Segment and Count Phonemes
Phonics	T 🔄 Vowels: *r*-Controlled *ar, or, ore, oar* Review Consonant Digraphs	T 🔄 Contractions Review Vowels: *r*-Controlled *ar, or, ore, oar*
Spelling	Vowels: *r*-Controlled *ar, or, ore*	Contractions
Comprehension	T 🔄 **Skill** Cause and Effect 🔄 **Strategy** Summarize Review **Skill** Fact and Opinion	T 🔄 **Skill** Author's Purpose 🔄 **Strategy** Text Structure Review **Skill** Facts and Details
High-Frequency Words	T *family, pull, listen, once, heard, break*	T *second, you're, either, laugh, worst, great, certainly*
Vocabulary	Unfamiliar Words	Dictionary/Glossary
Fluency	Accuracy and Appropriate Rate	Read with Expression
Writing	Narrative Nonfiction Trait: Voice	Biography Trait: Focus/Ideas
Conventions	T Nouns	T Proper Nouns
Speaking/Listening	Give and Follow Instructions	Purposes of Media
Research Skills	Taking Notes	Time Line

Get Ready to Read / *Read and Comprehend* / *Language Arts*

The Big Question
How can we work together?

WEEK 3	WEEK 4	WEEK 5	WEEK 6
Scarcity Expository Text pp. 254–267 **Goods and Services** 21st Century Skills pp. 272–275	**The Bremen Town Musicians** Drama/Fairy Tale pp. 284–301 **A Fool Goes Fishing** Folk Tale pp. 306–311	**One Good Turn Deserves Another** Folk Tale pp. 320–335 **The Lion and the Mouse** Fable pp. 340–343	**Interactive Review**
How can we work together to meet people's needs?	Why is it a good idea to work together?	How can we work together to solve problems?	How can we work together?
decision, producer, consumer, fiber, strand, extraordinary, lack, typical	*partnership, solution, survival, miserable, struggle, depend, familiar, insist*	*resolve, conflict, pursue, deserve, mope, coax, ramp, startle*	Review Unit 2 Amazing Words
Substitute Initial Phonemes	Substitute Initial Phonemes	Substitute Final Phonemes	
T Vowels: *r*-Controlled *er, ir, ur* Review Contractions	T Plurals Review Vowels: *r*-Controlled *er, ir, ur*	T Vowel Patterns *a, ai, ay* Review Plurals	Review Vowels: *r*-Controlled *ar, or, ore, oar;* Contractions, Plurals, Vowels: *r*-Controlled *er, ir, ur;* Vowel Patterns *a, ai, ay*
Vowels: *r*-Controlled *er, ir, ur*	Plurals	Vowel Digraphs *ai, ay*	Review Unit 2 Spelling Words
T **Skill** Facts and Details **Strategy** Background Knowledge Review **Skill** Cause and Effect	T **Skill** Cause and Effect **Strategy** Story Structure Review **Skill** Compare and Contrast	T **Skill** Compare and Contrast **Strategy** Inferring Review **Skill** Author's Purpose	Review Cause and Effect, Author's Purpose, Facts and Details, Compare and Contrast
T *enough, word, ago, whole, above, toward*	T *people, sign, bought, scared, probably, shall, pleasant*	T *brought, door, everybody, behind, promise, sorry, minute*	T Review Unit 2 High-Frequency Words
Time-Order Words	Homophones	Unfamiliar Words	Review Unfamiliar Words, Dictionary: Guide Words, Time-Order Words, Homophones
Appropriate Phrasing	Expression	Accuracy	Read for Fluency
Writing for Tests Trait: Word Choice	Fairy Tale Trait: Organization	Folk Tale Trait: Sentences	Writing Process: Directions
T Singular and Plural Nouns	T Plural Nouns	T Possessive Nouns	Review Unit 2 Conventions
Ask and Answer Questions	Purposes of Media	Give and Follow Instructions	
Chapter Headings	Encyclopedia	Reading a Web Page	

UNIT 2

Monitor Progress
Make Data-Driven Decisions

Data Management
- Assess
- Diagnose
- Prescribe
- Disaggregate

Classroom Management
- Monitor Progress
- Group
- Differentiate Instruction
- Inform Parents

Don't Wait Until Friday

SUCCESS PREDICTORS	WEEK 1	WEEK 2	WEEK 3	WEEK 4
Word Reading **Phonics**	T Vowels: *r*-Controlled *ar, or, ore, oar*	T Contractions	T Vowels: *r*-Controlled *er, ir, ur*	T Plurals
WCPM **Fluency**	Read with Accuracy and Appropriate Rate 48–58 WCPM	Read with Expression 48–58 WCPM	Read with Appropriate Phrasing 48–58 WCPM	Read with Expression 48–58 WCPM
Vocabulary **High-Frequency Words**	T family T pull T listen T once T heard T break	T second T you're T either T laugh T worst T great T certainly	T enough T word T ago T whole T above T toward	T people T sign T bought T scared T probably T shall T pleasant
Vocabulary **Oral Vocabulary/ Concept Development** (assessed informally)	courageous hazard rescue avalanche instinct skittish blustery fast-paced	identify participate significant scour ingenious aloft architect tinker	decision producer consumer fiber strand extraordinary lack typical	partnership solution survival miserable struggle depend familiar insist
Retelling **Text Comprehension**	T **Skill** Cause and Effect **Strategy** Summarize	T **Skill** Author's Purpose **Strategy** Text Structure	T **Skill** Facts and Details **Strategy** Background Knowledge	T **Skill** Cause and Effect **Strategy** Story Structure

Key

T Tested Skill

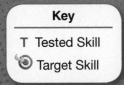 Target Skill

Key

T Tested Skill

 Target Skill

WEEK 5

T **Vowel Patterns** *a, ai, ay*
Read with Accuracy
48–58 WCPM
T brought
T door
T everybody
T behind
T promise
T sorry
T minute
resolve
conflict
pursue
deserve
mope
coax
ramp
startle
T **Skill** Compare and Contrast
Strategy Inferring

WEEK 6

T **Review Unit 2** Phonics
Reread for Fluency
48–58 WCPM
Review Unit 2 High-Frequency Words
Review Unit 2 Amazing Words
Review Skills Cause and Effect, Author's Purpose, Facts and Details, Compare and Contrast

Online ASSESSMENT
ReadingStreet.com

Online Classroom

Manage Data

- Assign the Unit 2 Benchmark Test for students to take online.

- Online Assessment records results and generates reports by school, grade, classroom, or student.

- Use reports to disaggregate and aggregate Unit 2 skills and standards data to monitor progress.

- Based on class lists created to support the categories important for AYP (gender, ethnicity, migrant education, English proficiency, disabilities, economic status), reports let you track adequate yearly progress every six weeks.

Group

- Use results from Unit 2 Benchmark Tests taken online through Online Assessment to measure whether students have mastered the English-Language Arts Content Standards taught in this unit.

- Reports in Online Assessment suggest whether students need Extra Support or Intervention.

Individualized Instruction

- Tests are correlated to Unit 2 tested skills and standards so that prescriptions for individual teaching and learning plans can be created.

- Individualized prescriptions target instruction and accelerate student progress toward learning outcome goals.

- Prescriptions include remediation activities and resources to reteach Unit 1 skills and standards.

UNIT 2

Assessment and Grouping

for Data-Driven Instruction

4-Step Plan for Assessment
1 Diagnose and Differentiate
2 Monitor Progress
3 Assess and Regroup
4 Summative Assessment

STEP 1 Diagnose and Differentiate

Baseline Group Tests

Diagnose

To make initial grouping decisions, use the Baseline Group Test, the Texas Primary Reading Inventory (TPRI), or another initial placement test. Depending on children's ability levels, you may have more than one of each group.

Differentiate

If... student performance is **SI** **then...** use the regular instruction and the daily **Strategic Intervention** small group lessons.

If... student performance is **OL** **then...** use the regular instruction and the daily **On-Level** small group lessons.

If... student performance is **A** **then...** use the regular instruction and the daily **Advanced** small group lessons.

Small Group Time

SI Strategic Intervention

- Daily small group lessons provide more intensive instruction, more scaffolding, more practice, and more opportunities to respond.
- Reteach lessons in the *First Stop on Reading Street* provide additional instructional opportunities with target skills.
- Leveled readers build background and provide practice for target skills and vocabulary.

OL On-Level

- Explicit instructional routines teach core skills and strategies.
- Daily On-Level lessons provide more practice and more opportunities to respond.
- Independent activities provide practice for core skills and extension and enrichment options.
- Leveled reader provides additional reading and practice for core skills and vocabulary.

A Advanced

- Daily Advanced lessons provide instruction for accelerated learning.
- Leveled reader provides additional reading tied to lesson concepts.

Additional Differentiated Learning Options

Reading Street Response to Intervention Kit
- Focused intervention lessons on the five critical areas of reading: phonemic awareness, phonics, vocabulary, comprehension, and fluency

My Sidewalks on Reading Street
- Intensive intervention for struggling readers

STEP 2 Monitor Progress

Don't Wait Until Friday

Use these tools during lesson teaching to **monitor student progress.**

- **Skill and Strategy** instruction during reading
- **Don't Wait Until Friday** boxes to check word reading, retelling, fluency, and oral vocabulary
- **Weekly Assessment** on Day 5 to check phonics and fluency
- **Reader's and Writer's Notebook** pages at point of use
- **Weekly Tests** to assess target skills for the week
- **Fresh Reads for Fluency and Comprehension**

Weekly Tests

Fresh Reads for Fluency and Comprehension

STEP 3 Assess and Regroup

Use these tools during lesson teaching to assess and regroup.

- **Weekly Assessments** Record results of weekly assessments in retelling, phonics, and fluency to track student progress.
- **Unit Benchmark Test** Administer this test to check mastery of unit skills.
- **Regroup** We recommend the first regrouping to be at the end of Unit 2. Use weekly assessment information and Unit Benchmark Test performance to inform regrouping decisions. Then regroup at the end of each subsequent unit.

First Stop on Reading Street Assessment Chart

Group Baseline Group Test	→ Regroup Units 1 and 2	→ Regroup Unit 3	→ Regroup Unit 4	→ Regroup Unit 5	→ End of Year
Unit 1 Weeks 1–6	Unit 2 Weeks 7–12	Unit 3 Weeks 13–18	Unit 4 Weeks 19–24	Unit 5 Weeks 25–30	Unit 6 Weeks 31–36

Outside assessments, such as DRA, TPRI, and DIBELS, may recommend regrouping at other times during the year.

STEP 4 Summative Assessment

Use these tools after lesson teaching to assess students.

- **Unit Benchmark Tests** Use to measure a student's mastery of unit skills.
- **End-of-Year Benchmark Test** Use to measure a student's mastery of program skill covered in all six units.

Unit and End-of-Year Benchmark Tests

Concept Launch

Understanding By Design

Grant Wiggins, Ed. D. Reading Street Author

"We need to go beyond questions answerable by unit facts to questions that burst through the boundaries of the topic. Deep and transferable understandings depend upon framing work around such questions."

Working Together

Reading Street Online

www.ReadingStreet.com
• Big Question Video
• eSelections
• Envision It! Animations
• Story Sort

How can we work together?

UNIT 2

Small Group Time
Flexible Pacing Plans

Small Group Time

Sometime you have holidays, programs, assemblies, or other interruptions to the school week. This plan can help you make Small Group Time decisions if you have less time during the week.

Key
- **SI** Strategic Intervention
- **OL** On-Level
- **A** Advanced
- **ELL** ELL

SI OL A

5 Day Plan
DAY 1	• Phonemic Awareness • Phonics • Reading Practice
DAY 2	• High-Frequency Words • Leveled Reader
DAY 3	• Phonics • Leveled Reader
DAY 4	• High-Frequency Words • Reading Practice
DAY 5	• Phonics • Comprehension

4 Day Plan
DAY 1	• Phonemic Awareness • Phonics • Reading Practice
DAY 2	• High-Frequency Words • Leveled Reader
DAY 3	• Phonics • Leveled Reader
DAY 4	• High-Frequency Words • Reading Practice

3 Day Plan
DAY 1	• Phonemic Awareness • Phonics • Reading Practice
DAY 2	• Phonics • Leveled Reader
DAY 3	• High-Frequency Words • Reading Practice

ELL

5 Day Plan
DAY 1	• Frontload Concept • Preteach Skills • Conventions/Writing
DAY 2	• Review Concept and Skills • Frontload and Read Main Selection • Conventions/Writing
DAY 3	• Review Concept and Skills • Reread Main Selection • Conventions/Writing
DAY 4	• Review Concept and Skills • Read ELL or ELD Reader • Conventions/Writing
DAY 5	• Review Concept and Skills • Reread ELL or ELD Reader • Conventions/Writing

4 Day Plan
DAY 1	• Frontload Concept • Preteach Skills • Conventions/Writing
DAY 2	• Review Concept and Skills • Frontload and Read Main Selection • Conventions/Writing
DAY 3	• Review Concept and Skills • Reread Main Selection • Conventions/Writing
DAY 4	• Review Concept and Skills • Read ELL or ELD Reader • Conventions/Writing

3 Day Plan
DAY 1	• Frontload Concept • Preteach Skills • Conventions/Writing
DAY 2	• Review Concept and Skills • Frontload and Read Main Selection • Conventions/Writing
DAY 3	• Review Concept and Skills • Read ELL or ELD Reader • Conventions/Writing

This Week on Reading Street!

 Question of the Week

Why is it a good idea to work together?

Working Together

Daily Plan

 Don't Wait Until Friday

Whole Group
- Plurals
- Cause and Effect
- Fluency
- Vocabulary

MONITOR PROGRESS | **Success Predictor**

Day 1	Day 2	Day 3	Day 4	Day 5
Check Word Reading	Check High-Frequency Words	Check Retelling	Check Fluency	Check Oral Vocabulary

Small Group

Teacher-Led
- Reading Support
- Skill Support
- Fluency Practice

Practice Stations

Independent Activities

Customize Literacy More support for a Balanced Literacy approach, see pp. CL•1–CL•45.

Customize Writing More support for a customized writing approach, see pp. CW•11–CW•20.

Whole Group
- Writing: Fairy Tale
- Conventions: Plural Nouns That Change Spelling
- New Literacies

Assessment
- Weekly Tests
- Day 5 Assessment
- Fresh Reads

You Are Here! Unit 2 Week 4

This Week's Reading Selections

Main Selection
Genre: **Drama/Fairy Tale**

Paired Selection

Decodable Practice Readers

Leveled Readers

ELL and ELD Readers

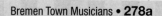

Resources on Reading Street!

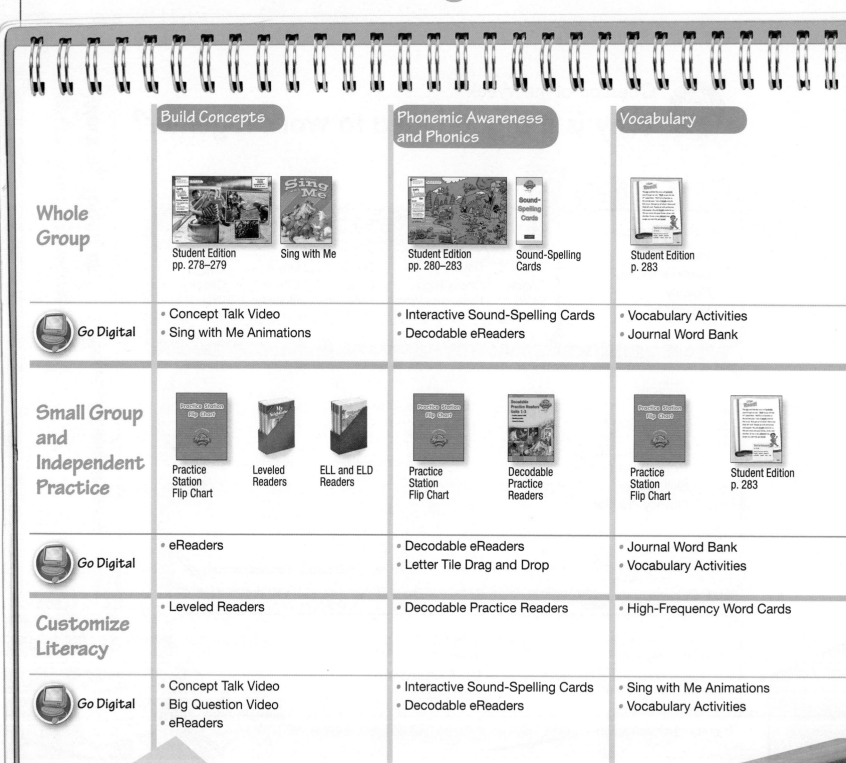

	Build Concepts	Phonemic Awareness and Phonics	Vocabulary
Whole Group	Student Edition pp. 278–279 / Sing with Me	Student Edition pp. 280–283 / Sound-Spelling Cards	Student Edition p. 283
Go Digital	• Concept Talk Video • Sing with Me Animations	• Interactive Sound-Spelling Cards • Decodable eReaders	• Vocabulary Activities • Journal Word Bank
Small Group and Independent Practice	Practice Station Flip Chart / Leveled Readers / ELL and ELD Readers	Practice Station Flip Chart / Decodable Practice Readers	Practice Station Flip Chart / Student Edition p. 283
Go Digital	• eReaders	• Decodable eReaders • Letter Tile Drag and Drop	• Journal Word Bank • Vocabulary Activities
Customize Literacy	• Leveled Readers	• Decodable Practice Readers	• High-Frequency Word Cards
Go Digital	• Concept Talk Video • Big Question Video • eReaders	• Interactive Sound-Spelling Cards • Decodable eReaders	• Sing with Me Animations • Vocabulary Activities

Question of the Week
Why is it a good idea to work together?

Week 4

Comprehension	Fluency	Conventions and Writing
 Student Edition pp. 284–301	 Decodable Practice Readers	 Student Edition pp. 304–305
• Envision It! Animations • eSelections	• eSelections • eReaders	• Grammar Jammer
 Practice Station Flip Chart / Leveled Readers / ELL and ELD Readers	 Practice Station Flip Chart / Decodable Practice Readers	 Practice Station Flip Chart / Reader's and Writer's Notebook
• eReaders • Story Sort	• Decodable eReaders	• Grammar Jammer
• Envision It! Skills and Strategies Handbooks • Leveled Readers	• Leveled Readers	• Reader's and Writer's Notebook
• Envision It! Animations • eReaders	• eReaders	• Grammar Jammer

You Are Here! Unit 2 Week 4

My 5-Day Planner for Reading Street!

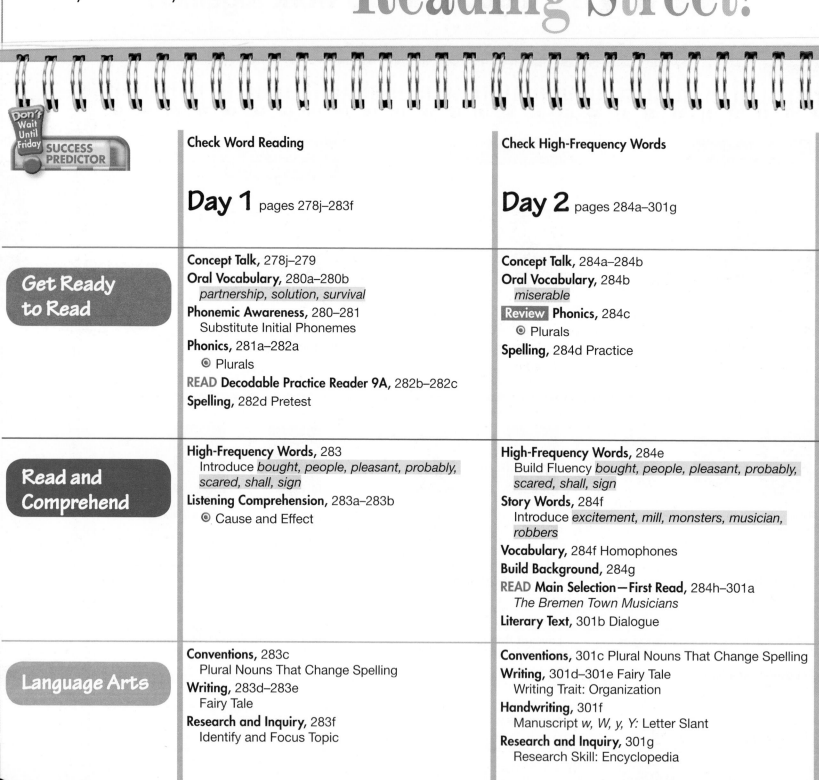

SUCCESS PREDICTOR
Don't Wait Until Friday

	Check Word Reading **Day 1** pages 278j–283f	Check High-Frequency Words **Day 2** pages 284a–301g
Get Ready to Read	**Concept Talk,** 278j–279 **Oral Vocabulary,** 280a–280b *partnership, solution, survival* **Phonemic Awareness,** 280–281 Substitute Initial Phonemes **Phonics,** 281a–282a ◉ Plurals **READ Decodable Practice Reader 9A,** 282b–282c **Spelling,** 282d Pretest	**Concept Talk,** 284a–284b **Oral Vocabulary,** 284b *miserable* Review **Phonics,** 284c ◉ Plurals **Spelling,** 284d Practice
Read and Comprehend	**High-Frequency Words,** 283 Introduce *bought, people, pleasant, probably, scared, shall, sign* **Listening Comprehension,** 283a–283b ◉ Cause and Effect	**High-Frequency Words,** 284e Build Fluency *bought, people, pleasant, probably, scared, shall, sign* **Story Words,** 284f Introduce *excitement, mill, monsters, musician, robbers* **Vocabulary,** 284f Homophones **Build Background,** 284g **READ Main Selection—First Read,** 284h–301a *The Bremen Town Musicians* **Literary Text,** 301b Dialogue
Language Arts	**Conventions,** 283c Plural Nouns That Change Spelling **Writing,** 283d–283e Fairy Tale **Research and Inquiry,** 283f Identify and Focus Topic	**Conventions,** 301c Plural Nouns That Change Spelling **Writing,** 301d–301e Fairy Tale Writing Trait: Organization **Handwriting,** 301f Manuscript *w, W, y, Y:* Letter Slant **Research and Inquiry,** 301g Research Skill: Encyclopedia

You Are Here!
Unit 2
Week 4

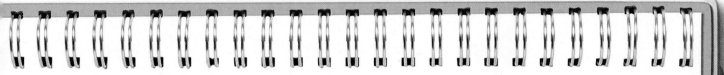

Check Retelling	**Check Fluency**	**Check Oral Vocabulary**
Day 3 pages 302a–305b	**Day 4** pages 306a–311g	**Day 5** pages 312a–313k
Concept Talk, 302a–302b **Oral Vocabulary,** 302b *struggle* **Phonics,** 302c ⊚ Plurals **READ Decodable Practice Passage 9B,** 302d **Spelling,** 302e Dictation	**Concept Talk,** 306a–306b **Oral Vocabulary,** 306b *depend, familiar, insist* Review **Phonics,** 306c Vowels: *r*-controlled *er, ir, ur* Review **Fluent Word Reading,** 306d **READ Decodable Practice Reader 9C,** 306e–306f **Spelling,** 306g Partner Review	**Concept Wrap Up,** 312a Review **Oral Vocabulary,** 312b Review **Phonics,** 312c Plurals **Spelling,** 312d Test
Fluency, 302f Expression Review **High-Frequency Words,** 302g *bought, people, pleasant, probably, scared, shell, sign* Review **Story Words,** 302g *excitement, mill, monsters, musician, robbers* **READ Main Selection—Second Read,** 284–301, 302h–303a	**Social Studies in Reading,** 306h **READ Paired Selection,** 306–311a "A Fool Goes Fishing" **Fluency,** 311b Expression	**Vocabulary,** 312–313 Homophones **Fluency,** 313a Expression **Media Literacy,** 313a Review **Comprehension,** 313b Cause and Effect Review **Vocabulary,** 313b High-Frequency and Story Words **Literary Text,** 313c Folk Tale **Assessment,** 313d–313f Monitor Progress
Conventions, 303b Plural Nouns That Change Spelling **Writing,** 304–305a Fairy Tale Writer's Craft: Beginning, Middle, and End **Research and Inquiry,** 305b Gather and Record Information	**Conventions,** 311c Plural Nouns That Change Spelling **Writing,** 311d–311e Fairy Tale Revising Strategy **Media Literacy,** 311f Recognize and Explain Purposes of Media **Research and Inquiry,** 311g Review and Revise Topic	Review **Conventions,** 313g Plural Nouns That Change Spelling **Writing,** 313h–313i Fairy Tale Writer's Craft: Plural Nouns **Research and Inquiry,** 313j Communicate **Wrap Up Your Week,** 313k Why is it a good idea to work together?

Grouping Options for Differentiated Instruction
Turn the page for the small group time lesson plan.

Week 4

Planning Small Group Time on Reading Street!

SMALL GROUP TIME RESOURCES

Look for this Small Group Time box each day to help meet the individual needs of all your children. Differentiated Instruction lessons appear on the DI pages at the end of each week.

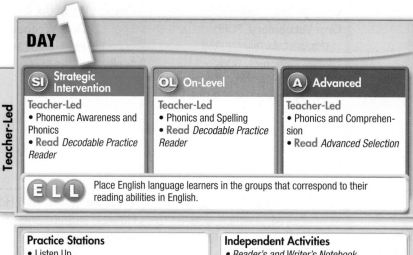

DAY 1

Teacher-Led

SI Strategic Intervention	OL On-Level	A Advanced
Teacher-Led	**Teacher-Led**	**Teacher-Led**
• Phonemic Awareness and Phonics	• Phonics and Spelling	• Phonics and Comprehension
• **Read** *Decodable Practice Reader*	• **Read** *Decodable Practice Reader*	• **Read** *Advanced Selection*

ELL Place English language learners in the groups that correspond to their reading abilities in English.

Practice Stations	**Independent Activities**
• Listen Up	• *Reader's and Writer's Notebook*
• Word Work	• Concept Talk Video

ELL Reader Advanced Advanced-High

ELD Reader Beginning Intermediate

ELL Poster

You Are Here!
Unit 2
Week 4

Day 1

SI Strategic Intervention	**Phonemic Awareness and Phonics,** DI•64 **Read Decodable Practice Reader 9A,** DI•64
OL On-Level	**Phonics and Spelling,** DI•69 **Read Decodable Practice Reader 9A,** DI•69
A Advanced	**Phonics and Comprehension,** DI•72 **Read Advanced Selection,** DI•72
ELL English Language Learners	DI•75–DI•84 **Concepts and Oral Vocabulary** **Listening (Read Aloud)**

Reading Street Response
to Intervention Kit

Reading Street Leveled
Practice Stations Kit

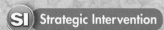

SI Strategic Intervention

Below-Level Reader

Decodable Practice Readers

Concept Literacy Reader

OL On-Level

On-Level Reader

A Advanced

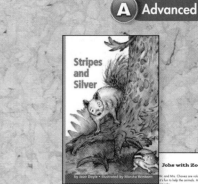

Advanced
Reader

Advanced Selection

Small Group Weekly Plan

Day 2	Day 3	Day 4	Day 5
High-Frequency Words, DI•65 **Read Concept Literacy Leveled Reader,** DI•65	**Phonics,** DI•66 **Read Below-Level Leveled Reader,** DI•66	**High-Frequency Words,** DI•67 **Read Decodable Practice Reader 9C,** DI•67	**Phonics and Comprehension,** DI•68 **Reread Main Selection,** DI•68
High-Frequency Words, DI•69 **Reread Decodable Practice Reader 9A,** DI•69	**Read On-Level Leveled Reader,** DI•70	**Conventions,** DI•71 **Read Leveled Reader,** DI•71	**Phonics Review,** DI•71 **Reread On-Level Leveled Reader,** DI•71
Comprehension, DI•72 **Read Main Selection,** DI•72	**Read Advanced Leveled Reader,** DI•73	**Comprehension,** DI•74 **Read Paired Selection,** DI•74	**Fluency and Comprehension,** DI•74 **Reread Advanced Selection,** DI•74
DI•75–DI•84 Concepts Vocabulary Phonics and Spelling Conventions	DI•75–DI•84 Concepts Vocabulary Comprehension Skill Main Selection	DI•75–DI•84 Concepts Vocabulary ELL/ELD Readers ELL Workshop	DI•75–DI•84 Concepts Vocabulary

Practice Stations for Everyone on Reading Street!

Listen Up!
Substitute initial phonemes.

Objectives
• Substitute initial phonemes.

Materials
• *Listen Up!* Flip Chart
• paper
• pencils

Differentiated Activities

🔵 Write the word *cap.* Circle the *c.* Change the /k/ to another letter sound to make a new word. Do it again to make another word ending in *-ap.* Say both new words.

🔺 Write the word *late.* Circle the *l.* Then change the /l/ to another letter sound to make a new word. Do it twice more to make three words ending in *-ate.* Say each new word.

🟥 On paper folded in three columns, write *-and, -ir,* and *-ite* atop each column. Say a letter sound before each phoneme to form all the words you can.

Technology
• Modeled Pronunciation Audio CD

Words To Know
Identify time and order sequence words.

Objectives
• Identify time and order sequence words.
• Follow directions that include time and order sequence words.

Materials
• *Words to Know* Flip Chart
• High-Frequency Word Cards with sequence words
• Teacher-made cards with Unit 2 Week 3 Story Words
• paper, pencils, crayons

Differentiated Activities

• **Time and order sequence words** explain the order in which events happen. *Before, first, next,* and *last* are sequence words.

🔵 First, take the sequence cards *first* and *next.* Next, draw a picture showing what you do *first* and *next* to get ready for school. Then label each drawing "first" and "next."

🔺 First, choose three story word cards. Next, take the sequence cards *first, next,* and *last.* Last, write three sentences using one story word and one sequence word.

🟥 Write a paragraph to teach the reader how to do something. Try to use at least four time and order sequence words.

Technology
• Online Tested Vocabulary Activities

Word Work
Identify *r*-controlled vowels *er, ir,* and *ur.*

Objectives
• Identify the *r*-controlled vowels *er, ir,* and *ur.*
• Create new words using the *r*-controlled vowels *er, ir,* and *ur.*

Materials
• *Word Work* Flip Chart
• Sound-Spelling Cards: 67, 72, 104
• Letter Tiles
• paper
• pencils, crayons

Differentiated Activities

🔵 Look at the Sound-Spelling Cards. Say the words quietly. Use Letter Tiles to spell them. Now write the words. Use a different-colored crayon to circle each *r*-controlled vowel.

🔺 Look at the Sound-Spelling Cards. Say each word quietly, and spell it using the Letter Tiles. Write a new word for each vowel-*r* pattern. Say each word.

🟥 Look at the Sound-Spelling Cards. Say each word quietly. Now think of two new words for each *r*-controlled vowel. Use the words to write a silly poem.

Technology
• Interactive Sound-Spelling Cards

You Are Here!
Unit 2
Week 4

Use this week's materials from the
Reading Street Leveled Practice Stations
Kit to organize this week's stations.

Key

 Below-Level Activities

△ On-Level Activities

■ Advanced Activities

Practice Station
Flip Chart

Let's Write!
Write an expository nonfiction story.

Objectives
• Write an expository nonfiction story.
• Use words that clearly express information.

Materials
• *Let's Write!* Flip Chart
• paper
• pencils

Differentiated Activities
• **Expository nonfiction** explains or describes something true.

 Think of when you got a job done with teamwork. Write two sentences about it. Draw a picture.

△ Think of a time when teamwork helped to get a job done. Write an expository nonfiction story about it. Give information. Write at least three sentences.

■ Recall a time when working with others helped get a job done. Write an expository nonfiction article about the experience. Use words that give information about the event.

Read For Meaning
Identify the facts and details in a story.

Objectives
• Identify the facts and details in a story.

Materials
• *Read for Meaning* Flip Chart
• 2.2.3 Leveled Readers
• paper
• pencils
• crayons

Differentiated Activities

 Read *The Barn Raising*. Write one fact. Then write one detail that tells about that fact.

△ Read *Farming Families.* Write two facts. Then write two or more details that help explain or add interest to those facts.

■ Read *Many Types of Energy*, and write two facts. Write two or more details that expand on those facts. Then write a paragraph about a science fact. Include two details that enrich the fact.

Technology
• Online Student Edition
• Leveled eReaders

Get Fluent
Practice fluent reading.

Objectives
• Read aloud with appropriate phasing.

Materials
• *Get Fluent* Flip Chart
• 2.2.3 Leveled Readers

Differentiated Activities

 Work with a partner. Take turns reading pages from *The Barn Raising*. As you read, look at how words are grouped and read with appropriate phrasing. Punctuation can help you read with appropriate phrasing. Give your partner feedback.

△ Work with a partner. Take turns reading pages from *Farming Families*. As you read, look at how words are grouped and read with appropriate phrasing. Punctuation can help you read with appropriate phrasing. Give your partner feedback.

■ Work with a partner. Take turns reading pages from *Many Types of Energy*. As you read, look at how words are grouped and read with appropriate phrasing. Punctuation can help you read with appropriate phrasing. Give your partner feedback.

Technology
• Reading Street Readers CD-ROM

My Weekly Work Plan

week 4

Objectives

- Introduce concept: working together.
- Share information and ideas about the concept.

Today at a Glance

Oral Vocabulary
partnership, solution, survival

Phonemic Awareness
Substitute Initial Phonemes

Phonics and Spelling
◎ Plurals

Fluency
Oral Rereading

High-Frequency Words
bought, people, pleasant, probably, scared, shall, sign

Comprehension
◎ Cause and Effect

Conventions
Plural Nouns That Change Spelling

Writing
Fairy Tale: Key Features

Research and Inquiry
Identify and Focus Topic

Concept Talk

Question of the Week

? **Why is it a good idea to work together?**

Introduce the concept

To build concepts and to focus children's attention, tell them that this week they will talk, sing, read, and write about why working together is a good idea. Write the Question of the Week and track the print as you read it.

ROUTINE **Activate Prior Knowledge** **Team Talk**

1. **Think** Have children think for a minute about why working together is a good idea.
2. **Pair** Have pairs of children discuss the question.
3. **Share** Have children share their ideas with the group.

Guide discussion and encourage elaboration with prompts such as:
What are some ways you have worked with classmates?

Routines Flip Chart

Anchored Talk

Develop oral language

Have children turn to pages 278–279 in their Student Editions. Read the title and look at the photos. Use these questions to guide discussion and create the "Why is it good to work together?" concept map.

- Why are all the children paddling the canoe in a kind of *partnership*? (Possible response: If they paddle together, it's easier for everyone to get where they want to go.)

- The bees are making honey. How does working together help bees *survive*? (Possible response: Each bee does a little of the work.)

- What *solution* have the people found to help everyone cross the stream? (Possible response: They join hands to help the whole group get across.) We've talked about how working together makes it easier to get to a destination in a canoe or to get across a stream. We've talked about how it helps bees survive. Let's add *We reach a goal more easily* to our map.

Oral Vocabulary

Objectives
• Listen closely to speakers and ask questions to help you better understand the topic. • Share information and ideas about the topic. Speak clearly and at a correct pace.

Let's Talk About

Working Together
● Share information about working together to solve problems.
● Share ideas about working together to help get the job done.

READING STREET ONLINE
CONCEPT TALK VIDEO
www.ReadingStreet.com

You've learned
0 6 4
Amazing Words
so far this year!

278   279

Student Edition pp. 278–279

Amazing Words

You've learned 0 6 4 words so far.

You'll learn 0 0 8 words this week!

partnership	struggle
solution	depend
survival	familiar
miserable	insist

 Writing on Demand

Develop Writing Fluency
Ask children to write about a time when they got help by working with others. Have them write for two to three minutes. Children should write as much as they can. Tell them to try to do their best writing. You may want to discuss what children wrote during writing conferences.

Connect to reading

Explain that tomorrow children will read a play about a group of animals that work together to reach a goal.

Why is it a good idea to work together?

We reach a goal more easily.

We combine our strengths.

ELL Preteach Concepts Use the Day 1 instruction on ELL Poster 9 to assess and build background knowledge, develop concepts, and build oral vocabulary.

ELL

English Language Learners

ELL Support Additional support and modified instruction is provided in the *ELL Handbook* and in the ELL Support lessons on pp. DI•75–DI•84.

Listening Comprehension
English learners will benefit from visual support to understand the key terms in the concept map. Use the pictures on pages 278–279 to scaffold understanding; e.g., when talking about bees working together, point to the picture of the bees.

ELL Poster 9

Objectives
- Build oral vocabulary.
- Discuss the concept to develop oral language.
- Share information and ideas about the concept.

Oral Vocabulary
Amazing Words

Introduce Amazing Words

Display page 9 of the *Sing with Me* Big Book. Tell children they are going to sing about working with others. Ask children to listen for the Amazing Words *partnership, solution,* and *survival* as you sing. Sing the song again and have children join you.

 Sing with Me Big Book Audio

A Partnership with You

Had a problem,
Had a problem.
Tried to solve it on my own.
Couldn't find a good solution,
So I called you on the phone.

Solved my problem,
Solved my problem.
Thank you, Friend, for all you do.
What is good for my survival
Is a partnership with you.

Sing with Me Big Book p. 9

Teach Amazing Words

Amazing Words — Oral Vocabulary Routine

1 Introduce Relate the word *partnership* to the song: In the song, a problem is solved through partnership. Supply a child-friendly definition: *Partnership* means that two or more people have joined together and become partners. Have children say the word.

2 Demonstrate Provide examples to show meaning: My best friend and I have a *partnership*—we are partners when we play our favorite game. Our class joined in a *partnership* with another class to sponsor a craft show.

3 Apply Have children demonstrate their understanding: Is a *partnership* like a dog and a cat barking and hissing at each other or like two squirrels gathering nuts together?

See p. OV•1 to teach *solution* and *survival*.

Routines Flip Chart

Amazing Words

partnership	struggle
solution	depend
survival	familiar
miserable	insist

Check understanding of Amazing Words

Have children look at the picture of the girl talking with the boy over the phone on page 9. How might the girl and boy be in a *partnership*? Use the word *partnership* in your answer. (Possible response: They may be in *partnership* to work out a homework problem over the phone.)

How could a *partnership* with a friend be good for someone's *survival*? (Possible response: A partnership can make a person's life easier because a friend can help with problems.)

How would calling a friend help find a *solution* to a problem? Use *solution* in your answer. (Possible response: Two friends can talk about a problem and work together to figure out a solution to a problem.)

Apply Amazing Words

Have children demonstrate their understanding of the Amazing Words by completing these sentences orally.

My dad and uncle formed a **partnership** to sell _____.

Raccoons hunt to find _____ for **survival**.

When I can't find a **solution**, I ask _____.

Corrective feedback

If... children have difficulty using the Amazing Words,

then... remind them of the definitions. Then provide opportunities for children to use the words in sentences.

Preteach Academic Vocabulary

Write the following on the board:

- **cause and effect**
- **drama**
- **plural nouns that change spelling**

Have children share what they know about this week's Academic Vocabulary. Use children's responses to assess their prior knowledge. Preteach the Academic Vocabulary by providing a child-friendly description, explanation, or example that clarifies the meaning of each term. Then ask children to restate the meaning of the Academic Vocabulary in their own words.

Differentiated Instruction

 Advanced

Amazing Words Remind children of the bees making honey. Have them brainstorm ways other animals work together in a *partnership* for *survival*. (Possible response: Two robins feed their babies. Herds of elephants migrate together in search of food and water.)

SI **Strategic Intervention**

Understand Meaning Help children recognize the meaning of the words *problem* and *solution* by asking them which comes first, the solution or the problem. Then provide opportunities for children to use the words in sentences.

English Language Learners

Pronunciation If children have difficulty with the pronunciation of *survival,* say the word slowly, emphasizing the long vowel sound /ī/ in the accented syllable and have children repeat the word.

Student Edition pp. 280–281

Phonemic Awareness
Substitute Initial Phonemes

Introduce

Have children look at the picture on pages 280–281 of the Student Edition. We can see two or more animals and things that are the same kind. I see two birds. Can you point to them? How many foxes do you see? (four foxes) We would say *fox* for one of them but we say *foxes* for more. Have children identify two or more animals and things that are the same.

Model

Now we can change a sound in these words to say a different word. Read and follow the first bulleted point on the page with children. Let's change the beginning sound in more words. We can change /h/ in *hats* to /m/—*mats.* I'll change /s/ /t/ in *sticks* to /k/—*kicks.*

Guide practice

Read and follow the remaining points on the page with children. (Possible responses: beavers, birds, building, boards) Guide children as they substitute initial phonemes: /b/ in *boards* to /k/ (*cords*), /n/ in *nails* to /r/ (*rails*), /l/ in *logs* to /b/ (*bogs*), /n/ in *knees* to /t/ /r/ (*trees*), /s/ /k/ in *skunks* to /t/ /r/ (*trunks*).

Corrective feedback

If... children make an error,
then... model by segmenting and blending the starting word and have them repeat. Do the same for the changed word. Then say both words.

Phonics—Teach/Model
Plurals -s, -es, -ies

plural -s

Sound-Spelling
Card 141

plural -es

Sound-Spelling
Card 139

-ies

Sound-Spelling
Card 142

Word Parts Strategy

1 Connect Write *wagged* and *skating*. Point out to children that they have already studied words like these. Ask them to read the words and identify the base words, endings, and spelling changes. (*Wagged* has the base word *wag* and the ending *-ed;* the final consonant was doubled. *Skating* has the base word *skate* and the ending *-ing;* the *e* was dropped.) Explain that today children will learn about endings for plurals.

2 Use Sound-Spelling Cards A **plural** is a word that means "more than one." Display Card 141. Point to the word *dogs* and read it. The ending *-s* is added to make most words plural. Display Card 139. Point to *peaches* and read it. The ending *-es* is added to words that end in *sh, ch, tch, s, ss,* or *x* to make plurals. Display Card 142. Point to *babies* and read it. When a word ends in consonant-*y*, the *y* is changed to *i* before adding *-es* to make a plural.

3 Model Write *cars* and *porches.* When I see a word ending with *-s* or *-es,* I look for the base word and read it; then I read the ending. Cover the ending of each word, read it, and then uncover and read the ending: *car, /z/—cars; porch, /ez/—porches.*

Write *parties.* When I see a word ending with *ies,* I know a *y* changed to *i* before *-es* was added. The *i* has the same sound that the *y* did. Write *party* under *parti: party, /z/—parties.*

4 Guide Practice Have children read cars, *porches,* and *parties* with you. Write the plurals below. Have the group read them with you. Then identify the base word, ending, and spelling change, if any, of each plural.

thorns	pennies	boxes	buddies	ashes
picnics	ditches	stories	parties	glasses

5 Review What do you know about reading plurals? (Read the base word, read the ending, and then say the two parts together. A final *y* may change to *i* before *-es* is added.)

Routines Flip Chart

Differentiated Instruction

 **Strategic Intervention**
Use Plurals in Sentences
Have children use objects and pictures in the classroom to make up sentences with plurals. For example: *There are three books on the table. I see a picture of a mother dog with her puppies.*

ELL

English Language Learners
Pronunciation Point out that the final s in plurals is often pronounced /z/ as in *stars, wishes,* and *cities.* Help children articulate the sound /z/ at the end of these words.

Language Transfer In Spanish, plurals are formed by adding *-s* to words ending in a vowel (*madre/madres*) and *-es* to words ending in a consonant (*arbol, arboles*). So Spanish speakers may add *-es* to any words ending in a consonant, for example, *girles* instead of *girls.* Give children additional practice writing plural endings for words ending in consonants.

Objectives

◎ Read plurals with endings *-s, -es,* and *-ies* (change of *y* to *i*).

• Decode words in context and independent of context.

Check Word Reading

SUCCESS PREDICTOR

Phonics—Build Fluency

🔊 Plurals

Model

Envision It!

Have children turn to page 282 in their Student Editions. Look at the pictures on this page. I see pictures of dogs, peaches, and babies. The word *dogs* has the ending *-s* that means "more than one." Continue with the other Envision It! pictures, explaining the plural ending in each word.

Guide practice

For each word in *Words I Can Blend,* have children identify the base word and the ending. Then have children read the whole word.

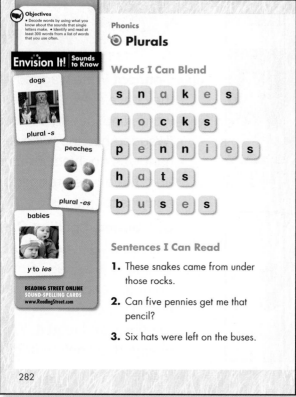

Student Edition p. 282

Corrective feedback

If... children have difficulty reading a word,

then... model identifying the plural ending. Read the base word and then read the ending. Have children read the word with you.

Word Analysis

Decode words independent of context

After children can successfully combine the word parts to read the plurals on page 282 in their Student Editions, point to words in random order and ask children to read them naturally.

Decode words in context

Have children read each of the sentences on page 282. Have them identify words in the sentences that are plurals.

Team Talk Pair children and have them take turns reading each of the sentences aloud.

On their own

Use *Reader's and Writer's Notebook* p. 133.

Reader's and Writer's Notebook, p. 133

Don't Wait Until Friday

MONITOR PROGRESS | Check Word Reading ⟳ Plurals

Write the following words and have the class read them. Notice which words children miss during the group reading. Call on individuals to read some of the words.

foxes	buses	insects	lilies	dishes
swirls	stories	gerbils	armies	perches
germs	roses	centers	pages	traces

Spiral Review
Row 2 reviews *r*-controlled vowels.

Row 3 reviews /s/*c*, /j/*g*, /z/*s*.

If... children cannot read plurals at this point,

then... use the Small Group Time Strategic Intervention lesson, p. DI•64, to reteach plurals. Continue to monitor children's progress using other instructional opportunities during the week. See the Skills Trace on p. 280–281.

Day 1 Check Word Reading	**Day 2** Check High-Frequency Words	**Day 3** Check Retelling	**Day 4** Check Fluency	**Day 5** Check Oral Vocabulary

Success Predictor

Differentiated Instruction

A **Advanced**

Extend plurals Provide children who can identify and read plurals correctly with more challenging plurals to read, such as: *addresses, libraries, companies*, and *sunglasses*.

Spelling Pattern

For base words ending with consonant-*y*, the *y* changes to *i* before adding -*es*.

Extend Spelling Pattern

The same spelling rule about changing *y* to *i* to form plurals also applies to adding inflected endings to third-person verbs, such as *she tries* and *they hurried*. Point this out to children, and give practice in reading and writing such verbs.

Vocabulary Support

You may wish to explain the meaning of this word.

gerbils small furry animals often kept as pets

Decodable Practice Reader 9A

 Plurals

Decode words independent of context	Have children turn to the first page and decode each word.
Read high-frequency words	Have children identify and read the high-frequency words *are, together, go, give, won't,* and *after* on the first page.
Preview Decodable Reader	Have children read the title and preview the story. Tell them they will decode plurals, words for more than one person or thing.
Decode words in context	Pair children for reading and listen as they decode. One child begins. Children read the entire story, switching readers after each page. Partners reread the story. This time the other child begins.

Things to Do
Written by Tina Johannsen

Decodable Practice Reader 9A

Plurals -s, -es, ies, change f to v
places   things   lots   lunches   notes
passes   bases   stands   tunes   classes
puppies   leaves   crafts

High-Frequency Words
are   together   go
give   won't   after

145

Fletch and Fran are pals.
They do things together.
Fletch and Fran go places
and see lots of things.
146

At lunch, Fletch and Fran
trade sack lunches.
Fran's dad packs snacks.
Fletch likes them.
147

Fran and Fletch give nice notes.
Fran hopes Fletch passes his test.
Fletch tells her about a fun plan he
has.
148

Fletch hit a home run.
Fran is glad.
When Fletch runs bases,
Fran likes to sit in the stands
and yell for him.
149

Fran got a prize for singing.
When Fran sings tunes,
Fletch won't miss it.
He thinks her singing is nice.
150

Fletch's mom drives them
home after classes.
They do work for class.
Then they spend time in the park.
151

Fletch and Fran visit with
puppies at the park.
They grab stuff
and make crafts.
Fletch and Fran have fun.
152

Corrective feedback

If... children have difficulty reading a word, **then...** refer them to the Sound-Spelling Cards to identify the sounds in a decodable word; prompt them to blend the word. If the word is a plural with an ending *-s* or *-es*, tell children to chunk the word and say the parts of the word, first separately and then together.

- What is the new word?
- Is the new word a word you know?
- Does it make sense in the story?

Check decoding and comprehension

Have children retell the story to include characters, settings, and events. Then have children find plurals in the story. Children should supply *pals, things, places, lots, lunches, snacks, notes, bases, stands, tunes, classes, puppies,* and *crafts.*

Review print awareness

Point out the comma on the fourth page of the story. Remind children that a comma means to pause briefly. Have children look through the story for another sentence with a comma and read that sentence aloud.

Reread for Fluency

Have children reread Decodable Practice Reader 9A to develop automaticity decoding plurals.

 ROUTINE **Oral Rereading**

1 **Read** Have children read the entire book orally.

2 **Reread** To achieve optimal fluency, children should reread the text three or four times.

3 **Corrective Feedback** Listen as children read. Provide corrective feedback regarding their fluency and decoding.

Routines Flip Chart

English Language Learners
Plurals
Beginning Preview pages that have plurals pictured: *pals* (p. 146), *lunches* (p. 147), *notes* (p. 148), *puppies* (p. 152). For each plural, point to each of the two in the picture at a time, say the singular word, and have children repeat. Write the singular word. Then point to both in the picture, say the plural, and have children repeat. Write it and circle the plural change. Have children find and point to the plural word on the page. Read the page aloud and tell children to raise their hand when they hear the plural.

Intermediate Write the list of plurals in the book on the board in mixed order. Read each page of the story aloud as children follow along in their books. Pause after each sentence that has a plural. Ask children to point to the word on the board so everyone can repeat it together.

Advanced/Advanced-High After reading, have children take turns summarizing the text on each page. Have listeners identify any plural word that the speaker said. Have children point to the plural if they find it in the text and use it in a new sentence.

Objectives
- Spell plurals -s, -es, -ies.
- Read high-frequency words.

Spelling Pretest
Plurals -s, -es, -ies

Dictate spelling words

Dictate the words. Read the sentences. Have children write the words. If needed, segment into meaningful parts, clarify pronunciations, and give meanings. Have children check their pretests and correct misspelled words.

1. **lunch**	We had sandwiches for **lunch**.	
2. **lunches**	The children's **lunches** are on the table.	
3. **story**	I just read a **story** about a rabbit.	
4. **stories**	My uncle tells funny **stories**.	
5. **tune**	Can you whistle a happy **tune**?	
6. **tunes***	Jack sang three **tunes** at the show.	
7. **switch**	The light **switch** is by the door.	
8. **switches**	Turn off all the light **switches**.	
9. **baby**	The **baby** plays with her toes.	
10. **babies**	There are two **babies** in one stroller.	
11. **note**	I taped a **note** on the refrigerator.	
12. **notes**	I wrote thank-you **notes** to my friends.	

*Word marked with asterisk comes from the selection *The Bremen Town Musicians*.

Let's Practice It!
TR DVD•93

On their own Use Let's Practice It! p. 93 on the *Teacher Resource DVD-ROM*.

Small Group Time

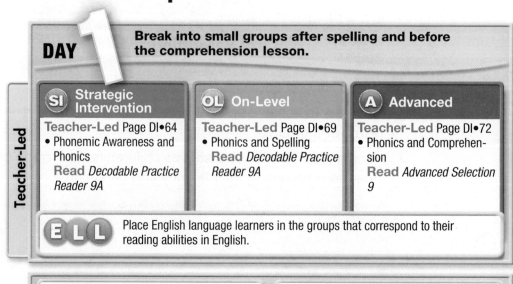

DAY 1 Break into small groups after spelling and before the comprehension lesson.

Teacher-Led

SI Strategic Intervention	OL On-Level	A Advanced
Teacher-Led Page DI•64	Teacher-Led Page DI•69	Teacher-Led Page DI•72
• Phonemic Awareness and Phonics	• Phonics and Spelling	• Phonics and Comprehension
Read *Decodable Practice Reader 9A*	**Read** *Decodable Practice Reader 9A*	**Read** *Advanced Selection 9*

ELL Place English language learners in the groups that correspond to their reading abilities in English.

Practice Stations
- Listen Up
- Word Work

Independent Activities
- Read independently/Reading Log on *Reader's and Writer's Notebook* p. RR2
- Concept Talk Video

High-Frequency Words

Differentiated Instruction

Introduce

ROUTINE Nondecodable Words

1 **Say and Spell** Look at page 283. Some words we have to learn by remembering the letters rather than saying the sounds. We will say and spell the words to help learn them. Point to the first word in the High-Frequency Words list. This word is *bought*. The letters in *bought* are b-o-u-g-h-t, *bought*. Have children say and spell each word, first with you, and then without you.

2 **Identify Familiar Letter-Sounds** Point to the first letter in *bought*. This letter stands for a sound. What is the letter and what is its sound? (*b/b/*) Point to the last letter in *bought*. What is the letter and what is its sound? (*t/t/*)

3 **Demonstrate Meaning** Tell me a sentence using the word *bought*. Follow this routine with the other High-Frequency Words.

Routines Flip Chart

SI **Strategic Intervention**
Check Spelling Have children choose the correct spelling of each word from three random spellings.

A **Advanced**
Extend Spelling Challenge children who spell words correctly to spell more difficult words such as: *crumbs, centuries, classes, supplies, libraries,* and *houses.*

Phonics/Spelling Generalization

Each spelling word is a plural formed by adding the ending *-s, -es,* or *-ies.*

Read words independent of context

Have children read the high-frequency words on page 283 aloud. Add the words to the Word Wall.

Read words in context

Chorally read the **I Can Read!** passage along with the children. Then have them read the passage aloud to themselves. When they are finished, ask children to reread the high-frequency words.

On their own

Use *Reader's and Writer's Notebook* p. 134.

Student Edition p. 283

Reader's and Writer's Notebook p. 134

ELL

English Language Learners
Spelling Clarify the meaning of each spelling word with examples, such as saying *tunes* are songs or other pieces of music. For *switches,* point to any light switches in the classroom, and say These are switches.

Frontload for Read Aloud Use the modified Read Aloud in the *ELL Support Lessons* to prepare students to listen to "Three Little Mice" (page 283b).

Objectives
◎ Identify cause and effect in drama.

Skills Trace
◉ **Cause and Effect**
Introduce U2W1D1; U2W4D1; U5W2D1
Practice U2W1D2; U2W1D3; U2W1D4; U2W4D2; U2W4D3; U2W4D4; U5W2D2; U5W2D3; U5W2D4
Reteach/Review U2W1D5; U2W3D3; U2W4D5; U3W4D3; U5W2D5; U6W3D3
Assess/Test Weekly Tests U2W1; U2W4; U5W2
Benchmark Tests U2; U5

KEY:
U=Unit   W=Week   D=Day

Listening Comprehension
🎯 Cause and Effect

Introduce

When an author tells what happened and why it happened, the author is using **cause and effect**. Display the words *so* and *because*. Sometimes authors use **clue words** such as *so* and *because* to help readers figure out what happened and why.

Envision It!

Have children turn to p. EI•3 in their Student Editions. These pictures show an example of what happened and why it happened. Discuss these questions using the pictures:

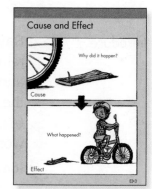
Student Edition p. EI•3

• What happened to the child's bike? (It got a flat tire.) A flat tire is the effect.

• Why did it happen? (The child rode over a nail.) A nail is the cause.

Model

Today we will read a story about three mice. Read **"Three Little Mice."** Use Graphic Organizer 19 to model cause and effect.

 Think Aloud When I read, I look for what happened. In the story, the three mice built a new home. I ask myself, "Why did this happen?" It is because the mice were afraid of the big, orange cat. Add *The three mice were afraid of the big, orange cat* to the first cause box. Then add *They built a safe home* to the Effect box following the arrow. Children can add examples to the chart. Guide them to find other causes and effects in the story.

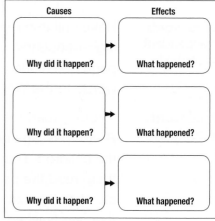
Graphic Organizer 19

Guide practice

Have children draw a picture to show an effect, or what happened, in "Three Little Mice." Then have children use the clue word *because* or *so* to write a sentence under the picture to tell the cause, or why this happened.

On their own

Use *Reader's and Writer's Notebook* p. 135.

Reader's and Writer's Notebook p. 135

Read Aloud

Three Little Mice

Once upon a time, there were three little mice that lived in a beautiful park in the city. The three mice lived peacefully in the park, sunning themselves on the park benches and cooling themselves in the fountains. Then one day something changed. A big orange alley cat moved in. The cat was feared by all of the mice and birds in the park. It was said that the big orange alley cat could swallow a mouse whole!

One day the three little mice got together to talk about the big orange alley cat.

"The big orange alley cat will eat us up!" cried the first little mouse.

"We must do something!" cried the second little mouse.

"Our survival depends on it!" cried the third little mouse.

The three little mice worked together to find a solution to their problem. They decided that the best way to stay safe from the big orange alley cat was to find a place where they could hide.

"We can hide under a bush," suggested the first little mouse. They began digging under a lilac bush, but the big orange alley cat found them and chased them away, crying, "Meow…meow….

Come back here, little mice!"

"We could build a nest beneath a statue," suggested the second little mouse. They found a large stone statue and began building their nest. Soon, however, the big orange alley cat found them and chased them away, crying, "Meow… meow…. Come back here, little mice!"

The three little mice thought and thought. They looked around the park. Finally the third little mouse spotted a small hole in the bottom of one of the drinking fountains. "Let's go hide there," he yelled. They scurried about, working in partnership, gathering old bottle caps, twigs, and small pieces of broken clay to hide the opening to their new home.

At last it was built. "It's lovely," said one of the three little mice. "And just in time. Hurry! Run into our new home. Here comes the alley cat!"

"Meow…meow…where are you, little mice?" cried the cat.

The three little mice were safely inside their new home, peeking at the cat from behind the new door. They giggled to themselves as the big alley cat walked away, and the three little mice lived happily ever after.

Academic Vocabulary

cause why something happened

effect what happened

clue words words and phrases that signal causal relationships, such as *because, so,* and *since*

Objectives

- Identify and use plural nouns that change spelling.
- Understand and recognize the features of a fairy tale.

MINI-LESSON

5 Day Planner
Guide to Mini-Lessons

DAY 1	Read Like a Writer
DAY 2	Organization/ Sequence
DAY 3	Writing the Parts of a Story
DAY 4	Revising Strategy: Adding Phrases
DAY 5	Proofread for Plural Nouns

Conventions
Plural Nouns That Change Spelling

Model

Explain that some **nouns** change spelling when they are made **plural nouns**. *Children, geese,* and *wolves* are examples of nouns that change spelling.

Display Grammar Transparency 9. Read the definition aloud and the noun under each picture. Then read the directions and model number 1.

- Look at the picture above *man*. There is one person, a man. Look at the picture above the blank. There are three people. I see a word in the word box that means "more than one man." The plural of *man* is *men*.

- I write *men* on the line.

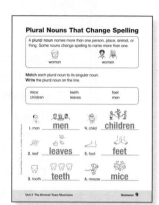

Grammar Transparency 9
TR DVD

Guide practice

Continue with items 2–6, having children identify how the spelling of each noun changes to form the plural.

Connect to oral language

Have the class complete these sentence frames orally using plural nouns that change spelling.

1. One mouse is bigger than the other three _____. (mice)

2. One child is sitting, and two _____ are standing. (children)

3. I lost one tooth, but she lost five _____. (teeth)

On their own

Team Talk Write these singular nouns on the board: *ox, goose, wolf, mouse,* and *calf.* Pair children and have them talk about the name for more than one of each animal. Then have them spell the plural form of each animal name.

Writing—Fairy Tale
Introduce

MINI-LESSON

Read Like a Writer

■ **Introduce** You know many fairy tales, such as *The Three Little Pigs* and *Cinderella*. This week you will write a fairy tale. A fairy tale is a story about magical characters and events.

Prompt Think about a fairy tale in which the characters work together. Now write your own fairy tale about characters who work together.

Trait Organization

Mode Narrative

Reader's and Writer's Notebook p. 136

■ **Examine Model Text** Let's listen to a fairy tale. Track the print as you read aloud "The Farmer's Daughters" on *Reader's and Writer's Notebook* p. 136. Have children follow along.

■ **Key Features** Who are the characters in the fairy tale? (a farmer, three daughters, a troll) Have children find and circle the magical character (the troll). Have them identify the good characters (farmer, three daughters) and the bad character (the troll). Then have children write 1's before the sentences that tell what the troll did at the beginning of the story. (second paragraph, first three sentences) Next, have them write 2's before the sentences that tell what the daughters did next. (third paragraph, both sentences) Then have children write a 3 before the sentence that tells what the troll does at the end of the tale. (He howled and ran away!)

This fairy tale tells about a magical character and events. The beginning tells that the troll ate the plants. The middle tells what the three daughters did to stop him. The end tells that the troll ran away and never came back.

Write Guy
Jeff Anderson

Writers Write!

Young writers succeed in classrooms where they write. Children need to read every day and to write every day. Teachers do not need to read and assess everything that children write.

Academic Vocabulary

plural noun a noun that names more than one person, place, animal, or thing

Daily Fix-It

1. The donkey didnt have any food
The donkey didn't have any food.

2. He mised his lunchs.
He missed his lunches.

Discuss the Daily Fix-It corrections with children. Review sentence punctuation, using an apostrophe to write contractions, and the spelling of *missed* and *lunches.*

English Language Learners
Options for Conventions Support To provide children with practice on plural nouns that change spelling, use the modified conventions lessons in the *ELL Handbook.*

Objectives

- Understand and recognize the features of a fairy tale.
- Identify a topic connected to this week's concept.
- Narrow the focus of the topic by formulating inquiry questions related to the topic.
- Discuss people and animals that work together.

Writing—Fairy Tale
Introduce, continued

Review key features

Review key features of a fairy tale with children. You may want to post these key features in the classroom to allow children to refer to them as they work on their fairy tales.

Key Features of a Fairy Tale

- It tells a story about magical characters and events.
- The characters usually are either very good or very bad.

Connect to familiar texts

Use examples from this week's Read Aloud, *Three Little Mice,* or another fairy tale that children have read. In *Three Little Mice,* the mice are the good characters and the cat is the bad character. At the beginning of the story, the mice lived peacefully in the park until the cat moved in and wanted to eat them. In the middle of the story, the mice worked together to solve their problem. They tried a few things, but the cat kept finding them. At the end of the story, the mice found a small hole at the bottom of a fountain. At last, they were safe.

Look ahead

Tell children that tomorrow they will plan their own fairy tales.

ROUTINE Quick Write for Fluency Team Talk

 Talk Read these questions aloud, and have children respond with plural nouns.

What other fairy tale has mice as characters?

Can you name another fairy tale that has three animal characters?

 Write Have children write short sentences to answer the questions. Make sure their sentences include plural nouns that name animals.

 Share Partners can read their answers to one another.

Routines Flip Chart

Research and Inquiry
Identify and Focus Topic

Teach

Display and review this week's concept web that explores the question: *Why is it a good idea to work together?*

Model

Think Aloud I've seen different kinds of birds working together. Only one bird waits in a tree to signal others when I put out bird food. It sings loudly before others will come to eat. I'd like to research the topic Birds and ask *Are there different ways birds work together?*

Guide practice

Have children tell about people or animals they've seen working together either in person or pictures. Ask what they would like to learn more about this week. Help them clarify: What is your topic? What is your question? Record children's topics and questions in a list.

On their own

Use *Reader's and Writer's Notebook* p. 141.

Reader's and Writer's Notebook p. 141

Wrap Up Your Day

✔ **Word Analysis: Plurals** Write *lunches* and *stories*. Ask children how the words are alike. (both plural) Have children read the words.

✔ **Spelling** Have children write the word *tune* and then write *tunes*. Continue with *switch, switches* and *baby, babies*.

✔ **Build Concepts** Ask children to recall the Read Aloud, "Three Little Mice." Why were the mice looking for a new home? (Possible response: They needed to be safe from the cat.)

✔ **Homework** Send home this week's Family Times Newsletter from Let's Practice It! pp. 89–90 on the *Teacher Resource DVD-ROM*.

Let's Practice It!
TR DVD • 89–90

Preview DAY 2

Tell children that tomorrow they will read about some friends and how they worked together.

Objectives
- Discuss the concept to develop oral vocabulary.
- Build oral vocabulary.

Today at a Glance

Oral Vocabulary
miserable

Phonics and Spelling
◉ Plurals

High-Frequency Words
bought, people, pleasant, probably, scared, shall, sign

Story Words
excitement, mill, monsters, musician, robbers

Vocabulary
Homophones

Fluency
Oral Rereading

Comprehension
◉ Cause and Effect
◉ Story Structure

Conventions
Plural Nouns That Change Spelling

Writing
Fairy Tale

Handwriting
Letters *Ww, Yy*, Letter Slant

Research and Inquiry
Research Skill: Encyclopedia

Concept Talk

 Question of the Week
Why is it a good idea to work together?

Build concepts

To reinforce concepts and to focus children's attention, have children sing "A Partnership with You" from the *Sing with Me* Big Book. If your goal is to solve a problem, what can you do? (You can call a friend and ask for help.)

🔘 *Sing with Me* Big Book Audio

Introduce Amazing Words

Display the Big Book, *From Me to You.* Read the title and identify the author. In the story, the author uses the word *miserable* in place of the word *unhappy.* Have children listen to the story to find out who is *miserable.*

From Me to You
Big Book

ⒺⓁⓁ Reinforce Vocabulary Use the Day 2 instruction on ELL Poster 9 to reinforce the meanings of high-frequency words and discuss the lesson concept.

ⒺⓁⓁ Poster 9

Go Digital!   Sing With Me Animations   Concept Talk Video

Whole Group

Oral Vocabulary
Amazing Words

Teach Amazing Words

Amazing Words — Oral Vocabulary Routine

1 Introduce the Word Relate the word *miserable* to the book. Rat feels *miserable* because he is lonely. Supply a child-friendly definition. *Miserable* means "very unhappy." Have children say the word.

2 Demonstrate Provide examples to show meaning. The boy was *miserable* about missing school. The girl feels *miserable* because she is sick.

3 Apply Have children demonstrate their understanding. Show me how you would look if you were *miserable*. What could make you *miserable*?

Routines Flip Chart

Anchored Talk

Add to the concept map

Discuss why working together is a good idea.

- The three little mice in the story you listened to yesterday are afraid of the cat. How do they solve their problem and get the job done? (They work together to hide the opening of their new home.) Let's add *We solve problems* to our map.

- In the *From Me to You* story, Rat feels *miserable*. How do others help him? (Friends show they care about him.) Let's add *Working together can make us feel better* and *Friends make us feel less miserable* to our map.

ELL

English Language Learners
Physical Response Teach the word *miserable* by acting it out and having children join you. To reinforce understanding, use the word in the day's activities. For example, have children show *miserable* faces if it rains at recess time.

Objectives

- Apply knowledge of letter-sound correspondences and syllable patterns to decode words in context and independent of context.
- Spell plurals -s, -es, -ies.

Phonics
Inflected Endings; Plurals

Review Review inflected endings -s, -ed, and -ing using Sound-Spelling Cards 129, 118, 119, 126, and 127 and plurals -s, -es, and -ies using Sound-Spelling Cards 141, 139, and 142.

Decode words independent of context Display these words. Have the class combine meaningful word parts to read the words. Then point to the words in random order and ask children to decode them quickly.

dresses	poppies	riding
waved	insects	stopping
stirs	stories	rushes

Corrective feedback Model combining base words and endings to read the words and then ask children to combine and read them with you.

Decode words in context Display these sentences. Have the class read the sentences.

Team Talk Then have pairs take turns reading the sentences naturally.

I **saved lots** of **pennies** as one of my **hobbies**.

People are **sitting** on the **benches** and **munching** on their **lunches**.

The **puppies** and **kittens napped** in the **boxes**.

Spelling
Plurals *-s, -es, -ies*

Guide practice

Tell children that you will segment the sounds in each spelling word or break the word into meaningful word parts. They should repeat the sounds or word parts in each word as they write them. Check the spelling of each word before saying the next word.

1. /n/ /ō/ /t/ /s/ **notes**
2. /s/ /t/ /ôr/ /ē/ **story**
3. bab, ies **babies**
4. /s/ /w/ /i/ /ch/ **switch**
5. /t/ /ü/ /n/ **tune**
6. /n/ /ō/ /t/ **note**

7. /b/ /ā/ /b/ /ē/ **baby**
8. /t/ /ü/ /n/ /z/ **tunes**
9. stor, ies **stories**
10. /l/ /u/ /n/ /ch/ **lunch**
11. lunch, es **lunches**
12. switch, es **switches**

On their own

Use *Reader's and Writer's Notebook,* p. 137.

Small Group Time

Reader's and Writer's Notebook p. 137

DAY 2

Break into small groups after spelling and before the comprehension lesson.

SI Strategic Intervention	**OL On-Level**	**A Advanced**
Teacher-Led Page DI•65	Teacher-Led Pages DI•69	Teacher-Led Page DI•72
• High-Frequency Words	• High-Frequency Words	• Comprehension
Read *Let's Clean Up the Park*	Reread *Decodable Practice Reader, 9A*	Read *The Bremen Town Musicians*

ELL Place English language learners in the groups that correspond to their reading abilities in English.

Practice Stations	**Independent Activities**
• Words to Know	• Read independently/Reading Log on *Reader's and Writer's Notebook* p. RR2
• Get Fluent	• AudioText of Main Selection

English Language Learners

Pronounce Plurals *-s, -es, -ies* In English, the *s* in plural endings *-s, -es,* and *-ies* is pronounced /s/ in some words *(notes, gifts)* and /z/ in others *(tunes, lunches, stories).* Speakers of other languages may have difficulty pronouncing words that end with the sound /z/ and may also spell them with the letter *z.* Give children extra practice with words, such as *frogs, switches,* and *cities,* that end with the letter *s* and the sound /z/.

Objectives
- Learn story words: *mill, musician, excitement, robbers, monsters.*
- Review high-frequency words.
- Identify and use homophones.

Check High-Frequency Words

SUCCESS PREDICTOR

High-Frequency Words

Read words independent of context

Point to the words *bought, people, pleasant, probably, scared, shall,* and *sign* on the Word Wall. Remind children that there are some words we learn by remembering the letters, rather than saying the sounds. Then have them read each of the high-frequency words aloud.

Team Talk Have children choose two high-frequency words and give them time to create a sentence in which both words are used properly. Then have them share their sentence with a partner.

MONITOR PROGRESS | **Check High-Frequency Words**

Point to these words on the Word Wall and have the class read them. Listen for children who miss words during the reading. Call on those children to read some of the words individually.

people	sign	bought	scared	
probably	shall	pleasant		**Spiral Review** Rows 3 and 4 review previously taught high-frequency words.
above	toward	whole	world	←
enough	ago			←

If... children cannot read these words,

then... use the Small Group Time Strategic Intervention lesson, p. DI•65, to reteach the words. Monitor children's fluency with these words during reading, and provide additional practice.

Day 1	Day 2	Day 3	Day 4	Day 5
Check Word Reading	Check High-Frequency Words	Check Retelling	Check Fluency	Check Oral Vocabulary

Success Predictor

Story Words
The Bremen Town Musicians

Introduce story words

Use Vocabulary Transparency 9 to introduce this week's story words. Read each sentence as you track the print. Frame each underlined word and explain its meaning.

Vocabulary Transparency 9
TR DVD

mill	a building where grain is crushed into flour
monsters	scary creatures
robbers	people who steal
excitement	a feeling of being very happy
musician	someone who plays music

Have children read each sentence with you.

Vocabulary
Homophones

Model homophones

Explain that **homophones** are words that sound the same but are spelled differently and have different meanings. Draw a web or display Graphic Organizer 15. In the middle circle, write *homophones.* In six outer circles, write: *night, be, road, seen, heard,* and *here.* Explain that each word has a homphone.

 Think Aloud I see the word *night*. The word *knight* sounds the same but is spelled differently and has a different meaning. So *night* and *knight* are homophones. I'll write *knight* in the circle next to *night*.

Guide practice

Have a volunteer give the homophone for *be* and write it in the circle *(bee)*. Repeat for the remaining words.

On their own

Have children choose a pair of homophones and draw and label a picture that shows the meanings for each word.

Use *Reader's and Writer's Notebook,* p. 138.

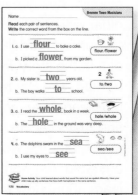

Reader's and Writer's Notebook p. 138

Objectives
- Build background on jobs farm animals do.
- Preview and predict.
- Use key features of drama to improve understanding of text.
- Set a purpose for reading text.

Build Background
The Bremen Town Musicians

Background Building Audio

Have children listen to the CD. Tell them to listen for the jobs the different farm animals do and why the animals think they are losing their jobs.

 Background Building Audio

Team Talk Have children turn to a partner and use these questions for discussion:

- What job do roosters do on the farm?
- What farm jobs do cats, dogs, and donkeys do?
- Why do Farmer Brown's animals think they are losing their jobs?

Organize information in a web

Draw a web or display Graphic Organizer 15. Write *Work done by farm animals* in the center circle. Have children recall what they learned about the jobs farm animals do. To complete the web, have children name the jobs performed by different farm animals.

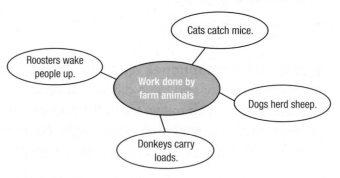

Graphic Organizer 15

Connect to selection

We learned about the jobs farm animals do for their owners. As animals grow older, often they are not able to work as hard they once did. In the story we are about to read, *The Bremen Town Musicians,* four animals find that they are no longer needed for the work they once did. As we read, we'll learn about how the animals work together to solve their problems.

Student Edition pp. 284–285

Double Day Read!

Main Selection—First Read
The Bremen Town Musicians

Practice the skill

⏱ **Cause and Effect** Remind children that a cause is why something happened, and an effect is what happened. For more practice, use Let's Practice It! p. 97 on the *Teacher Resource DVD-ROM.*

Introduce the strategy

⏱ **Story Structure** Explain that good readers look for the problem in a story. They also follow the **sequence**, or order, of events in a story from beginning to end to see how the problem is solved. Have children turn to page EI•24 in their student Edition.

Envision It!

Think Aloud Look at these pictures. What is happening at the beginning? (a girl strikes out) What happens in the middle? (She strikes out again.) What happens in the end? (She makes a home run.) When I read a story, I look for the **story structure** or how the story is organized. I look for the problem that the characters face.

Introduce genre

Let's Read A **drama** is a story written to be acted out. It has characters, setting, and plot. Most of the story is told through the characters' **dialogue** or conversation. As they read *The Bremen Town Musicians,* ask children to look for the names of the characters in bold letters. These names tell which character says the words that follow.

Preview and predict

Have children identify the title, the author, and the illustrator. Help them look through pp. 286–288 and use key words (repeating words, such as *old, ran away, go to Bremen, be a musician)* to predict what might happen in the drama.

Set a purpose

Good readers read for a purpose. Setting a purpose helps us to think and understand more as we read. Guide children to set a purpose for reading the drama.

Tell children that today they will read *The Bremen Town Musicians* for the first time. Use the Day 2 Guide Comprehension notes to help children develop their comprehension of the selection.

Double Day Read!
First Read

Continue to DAY 2
For the First Read, use **Guide Comprehension** across the top of pages 284–301.

 INTERACT with TEXT

Strategy Response Log

Genre Before reading, have children use p. RR15 in their *Reader's and Writer's Notebook* to identify the characteristics of drama.

Academic Vocabulary

dialogue a conversation, either written out or spoken

drama a story written to be acted out for an audience

sequence the order of events

story structure the organization of a story, with a chain of events leading to the solution of a problem

Let's Practice It!
TR DVD•97

Student Edition
p. EI•24

ELL

English Language Learners
Build Background Before children listen to the CD, build background and elicit prior knowledge. On the CD, you will hear about the jobs farm animals do and why they think they are losing their jobs. What do you think a rooster might do? Use the picture of the animals on pages 284–285 to give visual support for the words *donkey* and *rooster.*

Frontload Main Selection Take a picture walk to frontload the selection, then review the selection summary (*ELL Handbook,* pp. 79–81). Use the Retelling Cards to provide visual support for the summary.

Objectives

- ◎ Use a variety of strategies to understand drama.
- ◎ Identify and use cause and effect to understand dialogue in drama.
- • Determine word meaning and use newly acquired vocabulary.
- • Discuss ideas related to, but not expressed in the literature.

DAY 2

Guide Comprehension

Skills and Strategies

Connect to Concept

Working Together How might these four animals work together? (Possible response: The title includes the word *musicians,* and the animals look like they are singing. Maybe they will work as musicians.)

Amazing Words

Have children continue discussing the concept using the Amazing Words *partnership, solution, survival,* and *miserable* as they read.

The Bremen Town
Musicians

retold as a play by Carol Pugliano-Martin
illustrated by Jon Goodell

Genre

Drama/Fairy Tale
Drama is a story written to be acted out for others. A **Fairy Tale** usually takes place long ago and far away and has fantastic characters. Next you will read about four animals that become friends and travel to a faraway town.

284

Question of the Week
Why is it a good idea to work together?

285

Student Edition pp. 284–285

DAY 3

Extend Thinking

Think Critically

Higher-Order Thinking Skills

Analysis Use what you know from reading this story before to tell if this picture comes from the beginning, the middle, or the end of the story.

If... children cannot explain that this picture comes from the middle of the story,
then... ask them to retell what happened in the beginning and middle of the story.

Strategies

Story Structure Remind children that good readers look for the problem and solution. Have children explain the donkey's problem and tell whether or not they agree that his solution is a good one.

If... children have difficulty deciding if the donkey's solution is a good one,
then... have them first explain what the donkey believes is the solution.

NARRATOR 1: Once there was a donkey. He worked hard for his owner for many years. Day after day he carried heavy bags of grain to the mill.

NARRATOR 2: But the donkey grew old. He could no longer work hard. One day he heard his owner talking about him. He said he was going to get rid of the donkey. The donkey was worried.

DONKEY: Oh, no! What will happen to me? I must run away. I'll go to Bremen. There I can be a fine musician. (The donkey sings this song:)

Off I go to Bremen Town.
It's the place to be!
I will play my music there.
People will love me!
With a hee-haw here,
And a hee-haw there.
Here a hee, there a haw,
Everywhere a hee-haw.
Off I go to Bremen Town.
It's the place to be!

286

287

Student Edition pp. 286–287

Review **Compare and Contrast**
Analysis Compare the way the donkey feels when he hears his owner's plan to the way he feels walking to Bremen Town. (Possible response: At first the donkey is worried what will happen, but along the road he feels better. He sings and is hopeful about becoming a musician.)

Higher-Order Thinking Skills
Evaluation Judge the author's use of two narrators in the drama. Is it effective? Why or why not? (Possible response: The author's use of two narrators works well because the narrators give background information and they describe the series of events that make up the plot.)

Skills and Strategies, continued

DAY 2

Skills

🔊 **Cause and Effect** Why did the dog run away? What clue word in the dialogue helps you find the cause and effect? (The dog ran away because his owner wanted to get rid of him. The clue word is *so.*)

Vocabulary

Homophones Point out the word *weak* on p. 288. The word *weak* sounds like another word. That word is spelled *w-e-e-k* and has a different meaning. If I say, "The dog walked for a *week*," what do I mean? (seven days) If I say, "The dog is *weak*," what do I mean? (not strong)

 NARRATOR 1: So the donkey left that night. He had not gone far when he saw a dog lying on the ground.

 NARRATOR 2: The dog looked weak. He also looked sad. The donkey knelt down to speak to the dog.

DONKEY: What is the matter, my friend?

DOG: Ah, me. Now that I am old and weak, I can no longer hunt. My owner wants to get rid of me. I got scared, so I ran away. Now I don't know what I will do.

DONKEY: You can come with me to Bremen. I am going to be a musician. Will you join me?

DOG: I'd love to! I can bark very pleasant tunes.

DOG AND DONKEY: Off we go to Bremen Town. It's the place to be! We will play our music there. We'll be filled with glee!

DONKEY: With a hee-haw here, and a hee-haw there. Here a hee, there a haw, everywhere a hee-haw.

DOG: With a bow-wow here and a bow-wow there. Here a bow, there a wow, everywhere a bow-wow.

DOG AND DONKEY: Off we go to Bremen Town. It's the place to be!

288

289

Student Edition pp. 288–289

Think Critically, continued

DAY 3

Higher-Order Thinking Skills

Analysis Explain why the donkey understands how the dog feels.

If... children have trouble explaining how the donkey relates to the dog's problem,
then... ask them to recall and compare what similar thing happened to the donkey to make him start out for Bremen Town.

Word Reading

Decoding Have children check their reading of new words using these questions:

- Did I blend the sounds to read the word?
- Did I put the new word in the sentence to make sure it made sense?
- Did I look for word parts to help me understand the word?

Vocabulary

Story Words Have children locate the story word *musicians* on page 290. What does the donkey mean when he says, "We are going to become *musicians?*" (They are going to make music with their singing.)

NARRATOR 1: So, the donkey and the dog set off for Bremen. Soon, they saw a cat sitting by the road.

NARRATOR 2: The cat had the saddest face the donkey and the dog had ever seen. They stopped to find out what was wrong.

DOG: Hello there. Why so glum?

CAT: Ho, hum. Now that I am old and my teeth are not sharp, I cannot catch mice. My owner wants to get rid of me. I don't know what I will do.

DONKEY: You'll come to Bremen with us, that's what! We are going to become musicians. Won't you join us?

CAT: Sure I will! I love to meow.

DONKEY, DOG, AND CAT: Off we go to Bremen Town. It's the place to be! We will play our music there. We're a gifted three!

DONKEY: With a hee-haw here, and a hee-haw there. Here a hee, there a haw, everywhere a hee-haw.

DOG: With a bow-wow here, and a bow-wow there. Here a bow, there a wow, everywhere a bow-wow.

CAT: With a meow-meow here, and a meow-meow there. Here a meow, there a meow, everywhere a meow-meow.

ALL: Off we go to Bremen Town. It's the place to be!

290

291

Student Edition pp. 290–291

Higher-Order Thinking Skills

Synthesis Suppose a pig, a cow, or a sheep were to join the group. What might the new animal sing to add lines to the song?

If... children have trouble creating new lines, **then...** have them use the sound the animal makes, such as *oink-oink* or *baa-baa,* in place of the donkey's *hee-haw.*

Skills and Strategies, continued

Skills

DAY 2

⊙ Cause and Effect Use the dialogue to tell what happened when the animals met the rooster. (The dog said, "Come with us…." and the cat said, "We'll make a wonderful group…." The rooster crowed, "Let's go" and joined the group.)

If… children have difficulty using the dialogue to find the effect,
then… remind them to look for the words the animals used and ask themselves what happened.

NARRATOR 1: The three musicians walked along some more. They came to a farmyard. There they heard a rooster crowing sadly.

ROOSTER: Cock-a-doodle-doo! Cock-a-doodle-doo!

DONKEY: My, you sound so sad. What is wrong?

ROOSTER: I used to crow to wake up the farmer each morning. But he just bought an alarm clock. Now he doesn't need my crowing so he wants to get rid of me. Now I'm a cock-a-doodle-*don't!* Oh, what will I do?

DOG: Come with us to Bremen. We're going to be musicians.

CAT: With your fine crowing, we'll make a wonderful group!

ROOSTER: I *cock-a-doodle-do* think that's a wonderful idea! Let's go!

Student Edition pp. 292–293

Think Critically, continued

DAY 3

Higher-Order Thinking Skills
Evaluation Do animals become less useful to their owners when they are older?

If… children have difficulty responding,
then… ask what happens to animals' bodies when they get older.

Connect to Science
Dogs and Aging As dogs get older, they may lose some hearing and vision. They may be less able to fight off disease and have less energy.

Team Talk Have pairs talk about older pets they have had or know about.

Strategies

Story Structure This drama is based on an old fairy tale. In fairy tales, there is often a pattern in the events. What pattern can you see in this story? (The animals meet another animal and the animal joins the group to become a musician. The new animal adds a new verse to the song.)

If... children have difficulty explaining the pattern, **then...** ask children who donkey meets first, who is next, and how the events are alike.

DONKEY, DOG, CAT, AND ROOSTER:
Off we go to Bremen Town. It's the place to be!
We will play our music there. We're a sight to see!

DONKEY: With a hee-haw here, and a hee-haw there.
Here a hee, there a haw, everywhere a hee-haw.

DOG: With a bow-wow here, and a bow-wow there.
Here a bow, there a wow, everywhere a bow-wow.

CAT: With a meow-meow here, and a meow-meow there. Here a meow, there a meow, everywhere a meow-meow.

ROOSTER: With a cock-a-doodle here, and a cock-a-doodle there. Here a doodle, there a doodle, everywhere a cock-a-doodle.

ALL: Off we go to Bremen Town. It's the place to be!

294

295

Student Edition pp. 294–295

Higher-Order Thinking Skills

Synthesis Compare the animals' song with the words and music for the song "Old MacDonald Had a Farm." How does knowing "Old MacDonald Had a Farm" make the text easier to read?

If... children have trouble explaining the connection between the song and the text,
then... have children sing a verse of "Old MacDonald Had a Farm."

Skills and Strategies, continued

Skills

Cause and Effect What happened when the animals sang? Why did it happen? (The robbers ran from the house because they were frightened by the noise.)

Word Reading
High-Frequency Words Point out the words *sign* and *shall*. Have children practice reading these words.

NARRATOR 2: The four musicians walked until it got dark. Finally, they saw a sign that said Bremen Town. They danced with excitement, but they were also very tired. They wanted to rest.

NARRATOR 1: They saw light coming from a little house up the road. They walked up to the window, but none of the animals was tall enough to see inside. So, the dog stood on the donkey's back, the cat stood on the dog's back, and the rooster stood on the cat's back and peeked inside.

DOG: What do you see, rooster?

ROOSTER: I think there are three robbers in there! They are sitting at a table full of delicious-looking food!

CAT: Food? I'm starving! What shall we do? We must get them out of that house!

ROOSTER: I have a plan. Listen closely.

NARRATOR 2: The rooster whispered his plan to the others.

296

NARRATOR 1: All of a sudden, the four began singing. They made quite a noise. When the robbers heard the animals, they ran out of the house screaming!

NARRATOR 2: The four musicians went inside the house. There they ate and ate until they were full. Then, it was time for bed.

297

Student Edition pp. 296–297

Think Critically, continued

Higher-Order Thinking Skills
Analysis Classify the characters in this drama into two categories: good characters and bad characters.

If... children have difficulty identifying the bad characters,
then... ask them what robbers do and how they dress to prevent others from identifying them.

Strategies

⏺ **Story Structure** What happens first, next, and last to Robber 3 after he goes inside the house? (First the cat scratches his face, next the dog bites his leg, and last the donkey kicks him.)

If... children can't put the events in order,
then... have them look at the illustration on p. 298 to see where the animals are sleeping and then at the order of illustrations on p. 299.

NARRATOR 1: The donkey slept in the soft grass in the yard. The dog slept behind the front door. The cat slept near the warmth of the fireplace. And the rooster slept high on a bookshelf.

NARRATOR 2: After a while, the robbers returned to finish eating their feast.

ROBBER 1: That noise was probably just the wind. Besides, I can't wait to eat the rest of that roast beef!

ROBBER 2: I can taste those mashed potatoes now!

ROBBER 3: I'll go first just to make sure it's safe.

NARRATOR 1: So the robber went inside. He was cold, so he went to the fireplace to warm himself. There he surprised the cat, who scratched his face.

NARRATOR 2: The robber ran to the front door. The dog was startled and bit his leg. The robber ran outside. He tripped over the donkey, who kicked him.

298

299

Student Edition pp. 298–299

Higher-Order Thinking Skills

Synthesis Invent another way for the animals to get Robber 3 to leave them alone. (Possible responses: They might have locked the door; they might begin singing again.)

Higher-Order Thinking Skills

Evaluation Do you think it was right for the animals to act the way they did? Why or why not?

If... children have difficulty evaluating whether it was right,
then... ask them what the robbers might have done to them and discuss how creatures have the right to protect themselves.

Skills and Strategies, continued

DAY 2

Strategies

Story Structure How is the problem in the beginning of *The Bremen Town Musicians* solved at the end of the story? (Possible response: The animals, who had no home or way to survive, find a home and are successful as musicians in Bremen.)

Strategy Self-Check

Have children discuss what happens in the beginning, middle, and end of this fairy tale. Then have them explain how using sequence helped them understand the story.

Continue to DAY 2

Comprehension Check p. 301a

NARRATOR 1: All this noise woke the rooster up. He started screeching, "Cock-a-doodle-doo!" The robber ran back to his friends.

ROBBER 3: There are four horrible monsters in there! One scratched me with its long nails. Another bit me. Another kicked me. And the fourth one screamed, "Coming to get yooouuuuu!"

ROBBER 1: Four monsters! Let's get out of here!

NARRATOR 2: And the robbers ran off, never to be heard from again.

NARRATOR 1: But the four musicians stayed there. They sang every night in Bremen, where they became the famous Bremen Town Musicians!

300

301

Student Edition pp. 300–301

Think Critically, continued

DAY 3

Review **Compare and Contrast**

Analysis Compare how the animals felt in the beginning of the story to how they feel at the end. (Possible response: Each of the animals was sad and alone in the beginning, but at the end they are happy and working successfully together.)

Connect to Social Studies

Importance of Work Have children discuss how work helps people survive. Bring out that people exchange their skills and talents for money that buys food and shelter.

Team Talk Have pairs talk about the kinds of work people do.

Comprehension Check

Have children discuss each question with a partner.
Ask several pairs to share their responses.

☑ **Drama** How do you know that this selection is a drama? (Possible response: It is a story with characters, setting, and plot to be acted out. The story is told through the words, or dialogue, of the characters. The speeches are labeled with the names of the characters.)

☑ **Confirm predictions** What prediction that you made using a key word on the first three pages of the story was confirmed? (Possible response: I used the key words old, get rid of, musicians, and Bremen to predict that despite being old the animals would become successful musicians in Bremen.)

☑ **Make judgments** What do you think made it possible for the animals to survive? (Possible response: Each animal was willing to change and work with the others. By forming a partnership and working together, they combined their strengths to defeat the robbers and become famous musicians.)

☑ **Main idea** What is the main idea in this drama? (Possible response: Friends can help each other and work together to solve problems.)

☑ **Connect text to world** Why do you think different versions of this story have been popular for a long time in different places in the world? (Possible response: People in different times and places face the problem of growing old or losing their jobs when things change.)

Differentiated Instruction

 Advanced
Have small groups choose two pages from the drama, assign the parts, and practice reading the lines as they act out what the animals are doing.

English Language Learners
Support Discussion Provide additional context for the questions. For example: A drama is a story with characters, a setting, and a plot to be acted out in front of an audience. How do you know this selection is a drama? (It has a plot, characters, and a setting and is supposed to be acted out.) Extend language opportunities by asking follow-up questions, such as: Who are the characters? Where does the story take place? What happens?

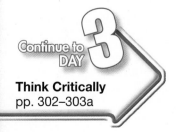
Continue to DAY 3
Think Critically
pp. 302–303a

Objectives
- Identify elements of dialogue in a drama.
- Identify and use plural nouns that change spelling.

Literary Text
Dialogue

Identify elements of dialogue

Use *The Bremen Town Musicians* to teach the elements of dialogue.

- *The Bremen Town Musicians* is a **drama**, or a play meant to be performed for an audience. In a play, the story is told mostly through the characters' dialogue. **Dialogue** is conversation that is spoken by characters. Each character has a particular way of speaking.

- What do you think the donkey is like? What are his traits? How do you think he might sound as he speaks? (The donkey is friendly and wants to help others. He might have a deep voice and "hee-haw" a lot.)

Guide practice

Together, write the name of each character in the first column of a chart. Then write the traits of each character and how the character might speak.

Characters	Traits	How They Speak
Donkey	friendly	deep voice, hee-haw
Dog	weak	thin voice, bow-wow
Cat	sad	high voice, meow

Graphic Organizer 26

On their own

Team Talk Give each child a character from the play, or have pairs take turns reading the dialogue of one character. Have children read the dialogue aloud, speaking like the character might speak, in an informal performance of the play *The Bremen Town Musicians*.

Reread for Fluency

Have children reread pp. 296–297 of *The Bremen Town Musicians*.

ROUTINE Paired Reading

1. **Reread** To achieve optimal fluency, have partners reread the text three or four times.

2. **Corrective Feedback** Listen as children read. Provide corrective feedback regarding their fluency and decoding.

Routines Flip Chart

Conventions
Plural Nouns That Change Spelling

Model plural nouns that change spelling

Write *child* and *mouse* on the board. Point to each word as you read it. Ask children to identify the plural of each word. *(children, mice)* Some nouns change their spelling when they are made plural. What is another example of a singular noun that changes spelling when it is made plural? (Possible response: *wolf/wolves*)

Guide practice

Write the following sentences on the board. Have children read the sentences and identify the plural noun in each sentence and the singular noun that changes its spelling when the plural is formed.

1. The oxen are working.	(oxen, ox)
2. I saw two mice trying to hide.	(mice, mouse)
3. The shelves are too high to reach.	(shelves, shelf)
4. The men are talking.	(men, man)

Connect to oral language

Have the class complete these sentence frames orally using plural nouns that change spelling.

1. I lost two loose _____ when I bit into an apple.

2. In the fall, all the _____ on this tree turn red.

3. The playground is filled with parents and their _____.

On their own

Use *Reader's and Writer's Notebook,* p. 139.

 INTERACT with TEXT

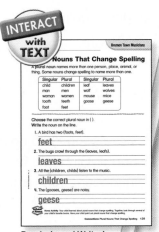

Reader's and Writer's Notebook p. 139

Daily Fix-It

3. He at good food on the fam.
He <u>ate</u> good food on the <u>farm</u>.

4. But he was'nt at the farm now
But he <u>wasn't</u> at the farm now<u>.</u>

Discuss the Daily Fix-It corrections with children. Review sentence punctuation, the *ar* spelling of /är/, contractions, and the VC*e* generalization.

ELL English Language Learners

Support Grammar If children have difficulty with the plural form of nouns that change spelling, then say the singular and plural forms in the form of a silly rhyme, and have children clap as they repeat it after you; for example: *One mouse and two mice sat down on the ice! One man and five men stand by the pen. One goose and ten geese each ate a piece.*

Objectives
- Generate ideas for a fairy tale.
- Recognize features of a fairy tale.

Writing—Fairy Tale
Writing Trait: Organization

Introduce the prompt

Review with children the key features of a fairy tale. Point out that *The Bremen Town Musicians* is a fairy tale. Assure them that they can make up a fairy tale with magical characters and events. Explain that today children will plan their own fairy tale. It will have a beginning, a middle, and an end. Read aloud the writing prompt.

Writing Prompt

> Think about a fairy tale in which the characters work together. Now write your own fairy tale about characters who work together.

Help children generate ideas

Sharing the Writing

 Think Aloud To plan a fairy tale, the first thing we will do is choose characters to write about. Let's make a chart that lists good and bad fairy tale characters. The bad characters cause problems for the good characters. **Display a T-chart.** I'll start by writing *mice* in the Good Characters column and *cat* in the Bad Characters column.

Guide children in identifying other good and bad characters from fairy tales. Possible ideas are shown. Record the responses, and keep the chart, so that children can refer to it as they plan and draft their fairy tale.

Good Characters	Bad Characters
mice	cat
princess or prince	mean woman or man
elf	troll
girl or boy	evil king
unicorn	dragon
pigs	fox

Have each child choose good and bad characters to write a fairy tale about. Circulate to guide them. Tell them to select characters that are interesting to them.

Differentiated Instruction

SI Strategic Intervention

Planning a Setting If children find it difficult to choose a setting for their fairy tale, make a list of possible settings. For example: *castle, field, forest, farm, bridge, country road,* and *house.*

MINI-LESSON

Organization/Sequence

■ **Introduce** Use *Reader's and Writer's Notebook* p. 140 to model story planning. To plan a fairy tale, I can use a chart. I don't need a title yet, but I've chosen my characters and setting. The good characters are a girl and two elves, the bad character is a troll, and the setting is the forest. I'll write this in the boxes. Now I'll plan what happens in the beginning, middle, and end of my story.

Story Chart

Reader's and Writer's Notebook p. 140

■ **Model** At the beginning, the girl and two elves were walking in the forest. A troll took them and put them in a hole. I'll write that in the Beginning box. In the middle, the girl and elves had an idea. One elf stood on the other's shoulders. Then the girl stood on top and climbed out. I'll write that in the Middle box. At the end, the girl used a long stick to pull the elves out. Then they ran home and lived happily ever after. I'll write that in the End of Story box. Now plan your fairy tale. **Circulate to guide and assist children.**

ROUTINE   Quick Write for Fluency   Team Talk

1. **Talk** Have children take two minutes to tell their story events to a partner.
2. **Write** Each child briefly writes about the events in the beginning, middle, and end of the planned fairy tale.
3. **Share** Each child reads the story ideas to the partner.

Routines Flip Chart

ELL

English Language Learners

Support Prewriting
Beginning Have children draw pictures of story events, label them, and share them with a partner.

Intermediate Have children write words or phrases to express story events. Have them describe the plan to a partner.

Advanced/Advanced-High Have children write short sentences in their story charts. Have them read their sentences to partners and clarify their ideas.

Objectives

- Write letters legibly and with proper slant.
- Write plural words with *-s*, *-es*, and *-ies*.
- Understand how to use an encyclopedia to locate information.

Handwriting

Letters *W, w* and *Y, y*/Letter Slant

Model letter formation

Display upper- and lower-case letters: *Ww* and *Yy*. Use the stroke instructions pictured below to model proper letter formation. Have children write the letters several times and circle their best ones.

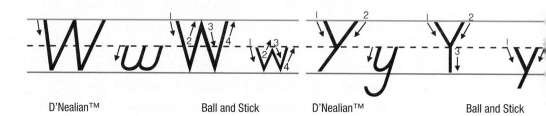

D'Nealian™   Ball and Stick   D'Nealian™   Ball and Stick

Model letter slant

Explain that when we write a word, all the letters in that word should have the same slant. Some writers slant their letters to the right. Write the word *yellow* with a right slant and show the slant with a ruler. Other writers slant their letters to the left. Demonstrate again. Still others make their letters straight up and down. Use the same method to demonstrate. The important thing is to avoid slanting your letters in different ways. Write *yellow* with an inconsistent letter slant; have children identify which sample is easiest to read and explain why.

Guide practice

Write the following sentence, using letters with an inconsistent slant. *What are your spelling words this week?*

Team Talk Have children work in pairs to discuss what is wrong with the sentence and how it needs to be fixed. Have them write the sentence correctly. As part of their discussion, have them identify whether they would write the sentence using a left slant, a right slant, or straight up and down letters.

Research and Inquiry
Research Skill: Encyclopedia

Academic Vocabulary

encyclopedia a book or set of books that provides information about many subjects arranged in alphabetical order

Teach

Explain that an **encyclopedia** is a book or set of books that provides information about many subjects. The subjects are arranged in alphabetical order. Print encyclopedias are usually sets of many books, called volumes. Each volume contains information about things that begin with a specific letter of the alphabet. If you wanted to find out about crocodiles, you would select the *C* volume in a set of encyclopedias and look for the word *crocodile*.

Model

Think Aloud Display Research Transparency 9 and point as you explain how to look up a topic. This looks like a page from an encyclopedia. The guide words at the top tell me that this page has information about words that come alphabetically between *corn* and *crow*. I'm looking for information about crocodiles, so I will look at the guide words to see if the word *crocodile* fits alphabetically between *corn* and *crow*. "Croc" in *crocodile* comes after "co" in *corn* and before "crow," so I know I have found the right page. Now I look at the topics on the page. They are arranged in alphabetical order so I can find the word *crocodile*.

Research Transparency 9
TR DVD

Guide practice

Use the transparency to help children answer the questions. As children respond, record their responses on the transparency. Then review and discuss the information.

Wrap Up Your Day

✔ **High-Frequency Words** Write: *I think people will probably like the play.* Have children read the sentence. Point to *people* and *probably,* and have children read them.

✔ **Build Concepts** Recall *The Bremen Town Musicians.* Ask: What is one reason the animals were miserable before they got together? (Their owners no longer needed them.) Was their partnership for survival? (no, for happiness)

Preview DAY 3

Tell children that tomorrow they will reread *The Bremen Town Musicians.*

Objectives
- Build oral vocabulary.
- Identify details in text.
- Share information and ideas about the concept.

Today at a Glance

Oral Vocabulary
struggle

Phonics and Spelling
◉ Plurals

Fluency
Read with Expression

High-Frequency Words
bought, people, pleasant, probably, scared, shall, sign

Story Words
excitement, mill, musician, monsters, robbers

Comprehension
Compare and Conrast

Conventions
Plural Nouns That Change Spelling

Writing
Fairy Tale: Draft

Research and Inquiry
Gather and Record Information

Concept Talk

 Question of the Week
Why is it a good idea to work together?

Build concepts

To reinforce concepts and to focus children's attention, have children sing "A Partnership with You" from the *Sing with Me* Big Book. How could you help a friend with a problem? (Possible response: You could listen to your friend and suggest a solution.)

💿 *Sing with Me* Big Book Audio

Monitor listening comprehension

Display the Big Book, *From Me to You*. As children listen to the story, have them think about friendship and who is struggling to be a friend. Then read the book aloud.

- How does Bat feel when Rat goes to see him? (Possible answer: Bat is miserable and doesn't want to talk to Rat.)

- Why is Rat struggling to help Bat? (He knows how Bat feels because he was miserable before he got the letter, and he wants to help Bat.)

From Me to You
Big Book

ELL Expand Vocabulary Use the Day 3 instruction on ELL Poster 9 to expand children's use of English vocabulary to communicate about lesson concepts.

ELL Poster 9

Oral Vocabulary
Amazing Words

Teach Amazing Words

 **Amazing Words** Oral Vocabulary Routine

1. **Introduce the Word** Relate the word *struggle* to the book. Rat *struggles* to help Bat. That means Rat does all he can to help. Supply a child-friendly definition. *Struggle* means "to try hard" or "to fight hard." If you *struggle*, you work hard to do something difficult. Have children say the word.

2. **Demonstrate** Provide examples to show meaning. The swimmer *struggled* against the big waves. It is a *struggle* for me to save money.

3. **Apply** Have children demonstrate their understanding. Show how you would *struggle* to carry a heavy pile of books from one table to another. Show how you would *struggle* not to laugh at a time you are supposed to be quiet.

Routines Flip Chart

Anchored Talk

Add to the concept map

Use these questions to discuss why working together is a good idea as you add to the map.

- In the drama *The Bremen Town Musicians,* what problem do the animals share? (Their owners no longer want them.)

- Why did the animals need to combine their strengths to scare the robbers? (Each animal was not strong enough alone, and they needed to use their strengths together.)

- How do the animals' *struggles* change when they work together? (When they work together, their struggles are easier.) Let's add *It makes a struggle easier* to the map.

 Amazing Words

partnership	struggle
solution	depend
survival	familiar
miserable	insist

Differentiated Instruction

SI **Strategic Intervention**
Listen and Respond Help children demonstrate the actions conveyed by the words *knocked* and *winked* in *From Me to You.*

A **Advanced**
Amazing Words Have children share examples of problems that cause people to struggle and solutions for the problems.

ELL **English Language Learners**
Vocabulary Help children understand that *struggle* can mean a physical struggle (a swimmer *struggles* against waves) or a mental struggle (Rat *struggles* to help Bat).

Bremen Town Musicians • 302b

Objectives
- ◉ Read and sort plurals with -s, -es, and -ies.
- • Decode contractions in context and independent of context.

Phonics
Sort Words

Model word sorting

Write *-s, -es,* and *-ies* as headings for a three-column chart, as children do the same on their own papers. Now we are going to sort words with plurals *-s, -es,* and *-ies.* Write the word *benches* and read it aloud. The word *benches* is plural. There is more than one bench. I see that *benches* ends with *-es.* I will add *benches* to the chart under the *-es* and we will read it together. Model writing *benches* under the heading *-es* and reading the parts, first alone and then with children: *bench, es—benches.*

-s	-es	-ies
orders	kisses	bunnies
tunes	lunches	stories
shirts	patches	puppies

Guide practice

I will write some plurals. When I write a word, read it in your head. Then hold up one finger if the plural is a base word with *-s* added. Hold up two fingers if the plural is a base word with *-es* added. And hold up three fingers if the plural is a base word that has *y* that changed to *i* before the ending *-es.* Then we will write the words on the charts, and you will read each word together when I point to it. Write the following plurals near the chart for children to sort: *orders, bunnies, stories, kisses, tunes, lunches, puppies, shirts,* and *patches.* When the sort is complete, have children reread each column as you point to the words.

Corrective feedback

For corrective feedback, model reading the word and identify any spelling changes in the base word.

Fluent Word Reading

Model

Write *copies.* I know how to read the parts for plurals, so I can read this word. I put the parts together, *cop, ies,* and read the plural *copies*

Guide practice

Write the words below. Look for word parts you know, and say them in your head. When I point to the word, we'll read it together. Allow one second per sound previewing time for the first reading.

parks	batches	armies	brushes	girls	parties

On their own

Have children read the list above three or four times, until they can read one word per second.

Word Analysis

Decode words independent of context

Have children turn to page 153 in *Decodable Practice Readers* 2.1 and find the first list of words. Each word in this list is a plural with *-s, -es,* or *-ies.* Let's read these words. Be sure that children identify the base word and ending that form each plural.

Next, have children read the high-frequency words.

Yard Sale

Decodable Practice Passage 9B

Plurals
boxes · shelves · benches
glasses · dishes · dresses
books · brushes · waxes
crutches · soles · parties
pennies · dimes

High-Frequency Words
people · after · bought

Mom and Dad had a yard sale. Dad got boxes of stuff from attic shelves. One box had an odd red jar. "We will use this for cash at the sale," said Dad.

At nine in the morning, Mom and Dad set sale stuff on benches in the yard. The benches had glasses, dishes, dresses, comic books, brushes, waxes for cars, used crutches, and much more.

At ten, the yard was filled with people. Dad and Mom had fun with them. "Yard sales are like parties," said Dad.

After five, Dad's red jar was filled with pennies, dimes, and more. People had bought a lot. Then a man spotted Dad's red jar. "Is that jar for sale?" he asked.

Dad dumped the cash in a bag and said, "Yes!"

Mom and Dad had a great yard sale!

153   154

Decodable Practice
Readers 2.1, pp. 153–154

Decode words in context

Chorally read the story along with the children. Have children identify plurals in the story with *-s, -es,* and *-ies.*

Team Talk Pair children and have them take turns reading the story aloud to each other. Monitor children as they read to check for proper pronunciation and appropriate pacing.

On their own

To further develop automaticity, have children take the story home to reread.

Differentiated Instruction

SI Strategic Intervention

Plurals with -s, -es, -ies Draw a T-chart on the board with the headings *One* and *More Than One.* Write the following list of words near the chart: *buses, fox, lunches, stories, berry, dogs, bus, foxes, lunch, story, berries,* and *dog.* Have children say each word and write it under the correct heading. After all the words are written, have children draw a line to connect each word with its plural.

Objectives
- Spell plurals with -s, -es, and -ies.
- Read aloud fluently with expression.

Spelling
Plurals -s, -es, -ies

Spell high-frequency words

Write *people* and *scared* and point them out on the Word Wall. Have children say and spell the words with you and then without you.

Dictation

Have children write these sentences. Say each sentence. Then repeat it slowly, one word at a time

1. Some people didn't eat their lunches.
2. We got scared when she turned off the lamp switches.
3. Which stories did the people like?

Proofread and correct

Write each sentence, spelling words one at a time. Have children circle and rewrite any misspelled words.

On their own

Use *Reader's and Writer's Notebook*, p. 142.

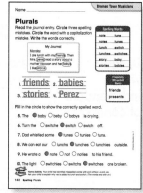

Reader's and Writer's Notebook p. 142

Small Group Time

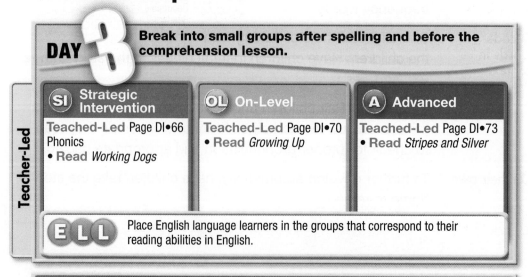

DAY 3 Break into small groups after spelling and before the comprehension lesson.

Teacher-Led

SI Strategic Intervention
Teached-Led Page DI•66
Phonics
• Read *Working Dogs*

OL On-Level
Teached-Led Page DI•70
• Read *Growing Up*

A Advanced
Teached-Led Page DI•73
• Read *Stripes and Silver*

ELL Place English language learners in the groups that correspond to their reading abilities in English.

Practice Stations
• Read for Meaning
• Let's Write

Independent Activities
• Read independently/Reading Log on *Reader's and Writer's Notebook* p. RR2
• AudioText of Main Selection

Model Fluency
Read with Expression

Model fluent reading

Have children turn to Student Edition page 290. Follow along as I read this page. Question marks and exclamation marks let us know how to express characters' words. We can read a character's words with the expression we think that animal would use.

Guide practice

Have children read the page with you. Then have them reread the page as a group without you until they read with appropriate expression. Continue in the same way with page 291.

Corrective feedback

If... children have difficulty reading with appropriate expression,

then... prompt:

• What do you do when you see a question mark or exclamation mark?

• How do you think these characters would talk?

Reread for Fluency

ROUTINE   Choral Reading

1. **Select a Passage** For *The Bremen Town Musicians,* use pages 292–293.

2. **Model** First, have children track the print as you read.

3. **Guide Practice** Then have children read along with you.

4. **Corrective Feedback** Have the class read aloud without you. Monitor progress and provide feedback. For optimal fluency, children should reread three to four times.

Routines Flip Chart

Check comprehension

Have children retell the story to show the causes and effects.

Spelling Words

Plurals -s, -es, -ies

1. note	7. tune
2. notes	8. tunes
3. lunch	9. switch
4. lunches	10. switches
5. story	11. baby
6. stories	12. babies

High-Frequency Words

13. people	14. scared

Options for Oral Rereading

Use The *Bremen Town Musicians* or the Day 1 Decodable Practice Reader.

Professional Development

Fluency As children become more fluent oral readers, they comprehend better. A study by the National Assessment of Educational Progress has found a correlation between reading with fluency and comprehending the text.

Objectives
- Read high-frequency words.
- Establish purpose for reading text.
- Review key features of drama.

High-Frequency and Story Words

Read words independent of context

Display and review this week's high-frequency words and story words. Have children read the words aloud.

Read words in context

Display the following sentence frames. Have children complete the sentences using high-frequency and story words. Have the children read each completed sentence with you.

> 1. The police officer *scared* the _____ away. (robbers)
>
> 2. Most of the _____ who live in town work at the *mill*. (people)
>
> 3. We _____ costumes and dressed up as *monsters*. (bought)
>
> 4. If the weather is _____, we'll *probably* have a picnic. (pleasant)
>
> 5. A great *musician* creates a lot of _____ . (excitement)
>
> 6. We *shall* put up a _____ that our house is for sale. (sign)

On their own

Use *Reader's and Writer's Notebook*, p. 143.

Reader's and Writer's
Notebook p. 143

Main Selection—Second Read
The Bremen Town Musicians

Review
Compare and contrast

Tell children that today they will read the drama again. Remind children that they can **compare** two or more things by telling how the things are alike, and they can **contrast** the things by telling how the things are different. The clue words *like* and *as* show likenesses, and the clue words *but* and *unlike* show differences. Comparing and contrasting characters and events can help us better understand drama. For more practice with compare and contrast, use Let's Practice It! p. 92 on the *Teacher Resource DVD-ROM*.

Let's Practice It!
TR DVD•92

Review
Genre: drama

Let's Read Remind children that drama is a story written for acting out in front of an audience. Have children recall the elements of a drama. (It has characters, a setting, a plot, and dialogue following the characters' names that is meant to be acted out.)

Set a purpose

Remind children that good readers read for a purpose. Guide children to set a new purpose for reading *The Bremen Town Musicians* today, such as finding out how the animal characters are alike and different.

Extend thinking

Tell children they will now read *The Bremen Town Musicians* for the second time. Use the Day 3 Extend Thinking notes to encourage children to use higher-order thinking skills to go beyond the details of the drama.

Continue with DAY **3**

For the Second Read, use **Extend Thinking** across the bottom of pages 284–301.

Second Read

Differentiated Instruction

A Advanced

Compare and Contrast Ask children who understand compare and contrast to use a Venn Diagram, or Graphic Organizer 17, to show how two of the animals are alike and different. Have children explain their diagrams to a partner or small group.

Story Words

excitement something that causes strong, lively feelings

mill a building where grain is crushed or ground into flour

monsters scary, make-believe creatures

musician someone who sings, plays an instrument, or conducts music

robbers people who steal

Academic Vocabulary

compare and contrast the ways two or more things are alike and different

ELL

English Language Learners
Words in Context Provide support by supplying a word bank for children during the sentence frames review activity on p. 302g.

Objectives
- Retell a narrative.
- ◎ Identify cause and effect in a drama.
- ◎ Identify story structure in a drama.
- Write clear, coherent sentences.

Check Retelling
SUCCESS PREDICTOR

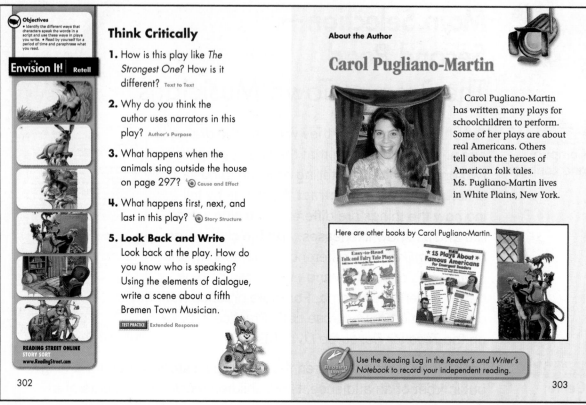

Envision It! | Retell

Think Critically

1. How is this play like *The Strongest One*? How is it different? Text to Text

2. Why do you think the author uses narrators in this play? Author's Purpose

3. What happens when the animals sing outside the house on page 297? ◎ Cause and Effect

4. What happens first, next, and last in this play? ◎ Story Structure

5. **Look Back and Write** Look back at the play. How do you know who is speaking? Using the elements of dialogue, write a scene about a fifth Bremen Town Musician. TEST PRACTICE Extended Response

READING STREET ONLINE
STORY SORT
www.ReadingStreet.com

302

About the Author

Carol Pugliano-Martin

Carol Pugliano-Martin has written many plays for schoolchildren to perform. Some of her plays are about real Americans. Others tell about the heroes of American folk tales. Ms. Pugliano-Martin lives in White Plains, New York.

Here are other books by Carol Pugliano-Martin.

Use the Reading Log in the *Reader's and Writer's Notebook* to record your independent reading.

303

Student Edition pp. 302–303

Retelling

Envision It! Have children work in pairs, retelling the story to one another. Remind children that their partners should include the characters, setting, and events from the beginning, middle, and end of the story. Children should use the retelling strip in the Student Edition. Monitor children's retelling.

Scoring rubric

> **Top-Score Response** A top-score response makes connections beyond the text, elaborates on the author's purpose, and describes in detail the characters, setting, and plot.

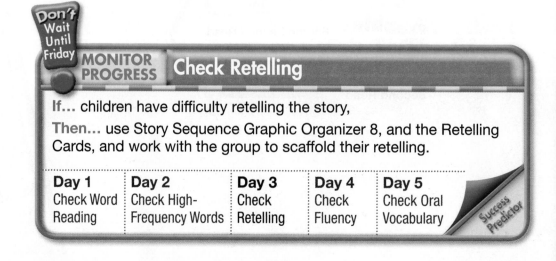

Don't Wait Until Friday

MONITOR PROGRESS Check Retelling

If... children have difficulty retelling the story,

Then... use Story Sequence Graphic Organizer 8, and the Retelling Cards, and work with the group to scaffold their retelling.

Day 1	Day 2	Day 3	Day 4	Day 5
Check Word Reading	Check High-Frequency Words	Check Retelling	Check Fluency	Check Oral Vocabulary

Success Predictor

Think Critically

Text to Text

1. Possible response: Both plays have narrators and, like the ant, the donkey meets others along the way. This play is different because the ant asks questions of each animal he meets but the donkey brings the other animals with him along on his journey.

Author's Purpose

2. Possible response: The author uses narrators because they tell the background information and help tell the story and keep it moving along.

⦿ Cause and Effect

3. When the animals sing outside the house, the robbers run out of the house screaming.

⦿ Story Structure

4. First the animals run away and go together to the town of Bremen. Next they sing to scare away the robbers and scratch, bite, kick, and screech at the robbers when they return. Last, the robbers run away and the animals become the famous Bremen Town Musicians.

5. **Look Back and Write** For writing fluency, assign a five-minute time limit. As children finish, encourage them to reread their response and proofread for errors.

Scoring rubric

> **Top-Score Response** A top-score response uses details from the text and the pictures to tell how you know who is speaking and create a scene with a new musician. For example:
>
> The name of the character who is speaking is in bold print at the beginning of each piece of dialogue. The Bremen Town Musicians are the donkey, dog, cat, and rooster. As they walked to Bremen they came to a dairy where they met a sad cow.
>
> **Cow:** Moooo! Moooo!
> **Donkey:** Why are you so sad, cow?
> **Cow:** I can't give any more milk so the dairy farmer doesn't need me anymore.
> **Dog, Cat, and Rooster:** Come with us!
> **Cow:** That's a wonderful idea! Moooooo! Let's go!

Meet the author

Read aloud page 303 as children follow along. Ask children what kind of plays the author writes.

Differentiated Instruction

A **Advanced**

Look Back and Write Ask children who show proficiency with the writing prompt to explain why the donkey invites the other animals he meets along the way to join him.

Strategy Response Log

Genre Have children revisit p. RR15 in their *Reader's and Writer's Notebook* where they identified the characteristics of drama. After reading, have them describe one characteristic of drama from the play and how it helped tell the story.

Plan to Assess Retelling

☐ Week 1: Strategic Intervention
☐ Week 2: Advanced
☐ Week 3: Strategic Intervention
☑ This week assess On-Level children.
☐ Week 5: Strategic Intervention
☐ Week 6: Assess any children you have not yet checked during this unit.

Retelling

Success Predictor

Objectives
- Identify and use plural nouns that change spelling in reading, writing, and speaking.
- Write a draft of a fairy tale.

Conventions
Plural Nouns That Change Spelling

Review
Plural nouns that change spelling

Remind children that some nouns change spelling when the plural is formed: *The* child *saw* a goose *at the farm*; *The* children *saw* geese *at the farm*.

Guide practice

Write this sentence on the board. Have children read it aloud and identify the singular nouns that change spelling when the plural is formed. (man, woman, child, ox)

> **The man, woman, and child petted the ox.**

How would the sentence change if you used the plural form of each noun? (The men, women, and children petted the oxen.)

Team Talk Pair children and have one child say an oral sentence containing plural nouns. Have the partner clap each time he or she hears a noun that changes its spelling when the plural is formed. Then have children switch roles.

Connect to oral language

Have the class use plural nouns that change spelling to complete these sentence frames orally.

> 1. We read a story about Snow White and the seven _____.
> 2. Then we sang the song "Three Blind _____."
> 3. Most of the _____ in our class like fairy tales.

On their own

Use Let's Practice It! p. 95 on the *Teacher Resource DVD-ROM*.

Let's Practice It!
TR DVD•95

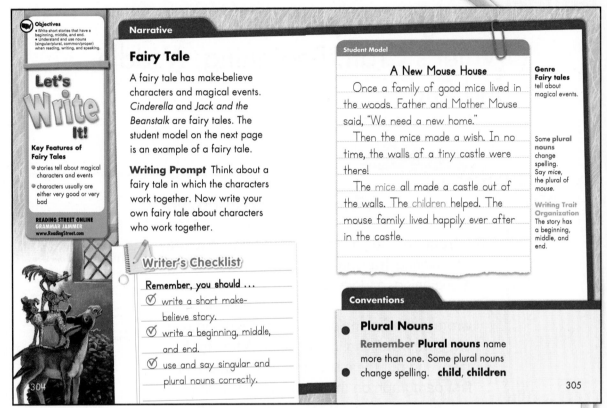

Student Edition pp. 304–305

Objectives
• Write short stories that have a beginning, middle, and end.
• Understand and use nouns (singular/plural, common/proper) when reading, writing, and speaking.

Let's Write It!

Key Features of Fairy Tales
• stories tell about magical characters and events
• characters usually are either very good or very bad

READING STREET ONLINE
GRAMMAR JAMMER
www.ReadingStreet.com

Narrative

Fairy Tale

A fairy tale has make-believe characters and magical events. *Cinderella* and *Jack and the Beanstalk* are fairy tales. The student model on the next page is an example of a fairy tale.

Writing Prompt Think about a fairy tale in which the characters work together. Now write your own fairy tale about characters who work together.

Writer's Checklist

Remember, you should . . .
☑ write a short make-believe story.
☑ write a beginning, middle, and end.
☑ use and say singular and plural nouns correctly.

304

Student Model

A New Mouse House

Once a family of good mice lived in the woods. Father and Mother Mouse said, "We need a new home."

Then the mice made a wish. In no time, the walls of a tiny castle were there!

The mice all made a castle out of the walls. The children helped. The mouse family lived happily ever after in the castle.

Genre
Fairy tales tell about magical events.

Some **plural nouns** change spelling. Say *mice*, the plural of *mouse*.

Writing Trait Organization The story has a beginning, middle, and end.

Conventions

● **Plural Nouns**
Remember Plural nouns name more than one. Some plural nouns
● change spelling. **child, children**

305

Daily Fix-It

5. He red a dog storie.
   He <u>read</u> a dog stor<u>y</u>.

6. He new other storys too.
   He <u>k</u>new other stor<u>ies</u> too.

Discuss the Daily Fix-It corrections with children. Review the short *e* vowel sound and its spellings, forming plurals with words that end in *y*, and the spelling of *knew*.

Let's Write It!

Teach

Use pp. 304–305 in the Student Edition. Read aloud the Key Features of Fairy Tales and the definition of a fairy tale. Help children better understand the Writing Prompt by reading it aloud and discussing the Writer's Checklist with children.

Review the student model

Then read "A New Mouse House" on page 305 to children. Point out the magical characters and events. Explain to children that the three paragraphs tell the beginning, middle, and end of the story. Read aloud and briefly discuss the side notes about Genre, the Writing Trait, and plural nouns that change spelling.

Scoring rubric

Top-Score Response Help children understand that a top-score response tells about magical characters and events, has a beginning, a middle, and end, and uses plural nouns correctly. For a complete rubric see Writing Rubric 9 from the *Teacher Resource DVD-ROM.*

Connect to conventions

Read to children the Conventions note about Plural Nouns. Point out the plural nouns that change spelling in the model fairy tale (*mice* and *children*).

Objectives
- Write a draft of a fairy tale.
- Use strong verbs in writing.
- Gather information about a topic.

Writing—Fairy Tale
Writer's Craft: Beginning, Middle, and End

MINI-LESSON

Writing the Parts of a Story

■ **Introduce** Use your story chart from yesterday and Writing Transparency 9A to model writing a beginning, middle, and end. When I wrote my fairy tale, I used my chart. Yesterday, I wrote in the Beginning box that a girl and two elves were walking in the forest. A troll took them and put them in a hole. **Read aloud the first paragraph on the Transparency. Point out that you replaced the words** *took* **and** *put* **with** *grabbed* **and** *threw*. **Point out that strong words make the beginning of the story exciting.**

The Girl and the Elves

Once upon a time, a girl and two elfs were walking in the forest. A troll grabbed them and threw them in a hole!

The hole was deep. But the girl and elves had an idea. First, one elf stood on the other's shoulders. Then the girls stood on top of their shoulders and climbed out of the hole

The girl found a long stick near some bushs. she used it to pull the elves out. Then they ran home and lived happily ever after.

Unit 2: The Bremen Team Musicans   Writing Model **9A**

Writing Transparency 9A
TR DVD

■ Explain how children can use the story events they planned yesterday to draft their fairy tale: beginning, middle, and end. Tell them to think of words that give a clear picture of what is happening in each part. Discuss how fairy tales often end and what words are used to end the story (lived happily ever after).

Guide story writing

Now it is time to write your fairy tale. Tell how your characters work together. Have children use their story charts. Help them finish the ideas. Then guide children as they draft their fairy tales.

ROUTINE **Quick Write for Fluency** **Team Talk**

1 **Talk** Have partners take one minute to talk about how the characters in their fairy tale worked together.

2 **Write** Each child writes a sentence that tells what the characters did.

3 **Share** Partners point out plural nouns in the others' sentences.

Routines Flip Chart

Research and Inquiry
Gather and Record Information

Teach

Display the topics and questions list from Day 1. Tell children that the first thing to do today is to decide which sources might help them answer their question. We need sources with information about the topic so we can look for parts about our question.

Model

 Think Aloud My topic is Birds. Some possible sources might be an encyclopedia, nonfiction books with *Birds* in the title, and Web sites. These are the sources I will start with. I can also think of other useful keywords. Birds are animals. Birds are wildlife. Sources about animals or wildlife *might* have parts just about birds. When I look at any source, I will look for information and pictures about birds working together.

Guide practice

Go through the list of children's topics; have children tell how they will find relevant sources. Help with possible keywords.

Use your Day 1 example to start a chart. Have children start a chart and begin their research.

Topic: Birds

Question: Are there different ways that birds work together?

Fact I saw: One bird waits and signals about food.	Another fact: _____
Why it's good:	Why it's good:

✔ **Cause and Effect** Why does thinking about how a character feels help you to understand more about a story? (Possible response: I can better understand the character's motivations and actions.)

✔ **Story Structure** Have children recall why it is helpful to see a pattern of events while reading.

SI Strategic Intervention

Topics If needed, help children select appropriate keywords for their topic search. Guide children to recall where they saw information about interesting people or animals working together. If in a book, what was the whole book about?

Preview DAY 4

Tell children that tomorrow they will read a selection about animals helping animals.

Objectives

- Discuss the concept to develop oral vocabulary.
- Build oral vocabulary.
- Identify details in text.

Today at a Glance

Oral Vocabulary
depend, familiar, insist

Phonics and Spelling
Review Vowels: *r*-controlled *er, ir, ur*

High-Frequency Words
Review

Comprehension
◉ Story Structure

Fluency
Read with Expression

Conventions
Plural Nouns That Change Spelling

Writing
Fairy Tale: Revise

Media Literacy
Recognize and Explain Purposes of Media

Research and Inquiry
Review and Revise Topic

Concept Talk

Question of the Week

 Why is it a good idea to work together?

Build concepts

To reinforce concepts and to focus children's attention, have children sing "A Partnership with You" from the *Sing with Me* Big Book. How can an animal be in partnership with another animal? (Sometimes animals work together as a team. Bees work together to make honey.)

💿 *Sing with Me* Big Book Audio

Review Genre: animal fantasy

Have children tell the key features of animal fantasy: it tells about made-up people, animals, things, and events. The animals in the story do things real animals do not do. Explain that today you will read a story about two dogs that work together.

Monitor listening comprehension

Recall that the animals in *The Bremen Town Musicians* worked together to help one another solve a problem. Have children listen to "Down Girl and Sit Save the Day" to find out how the dogs, Down Girl and Sit, work together to find their masters. Read the selection.

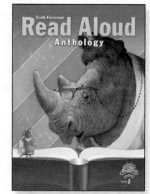

Read Aloud Anthology "Down Girl and Sit Save the Day"

ELL Produce Oral Language Use the Day 4 instruction on ELL Poster 9 to extend and enrich language.

ELL Poster 9

Oral Vocabulary
Amazing Words

Teach Amazing Words

 **Oral Vocabulary Routine**

1. **Introduce the Word** Relate the word *depend* to the story. Down Girl thinks her master *depends* on her to get them home. Supply a child-friendly definition. *Depend* means "to count on." When you depend on someone, you trust that person. Have children say the word.

2. **Demonstrate** Provide examples to show meaning. I *depend* on my alarm clock to wake me up in the morning. A kitten *depends* on its mother for food and protection.

3. **Apply** Have children demonstrate their understanding. What do you *depend* on?

See p. OV•1 to teach *familiar* and *insist*.

Routines Flip Chart

Anchored Talk

Add to the concept map

Discuss animals working together.

• Why did the dogs work together in "Down Girl and Sit Save the Day"? (Down Girl and Sit worked together because they wanted to help each other find their masters.) Let's add *Friends help each other* to our map.

• People often depend on each other for protection. How did Down Girl want to protect her master? (Down Girl thought Rruff was forgetful and wanted to protect him from getting lost.) Let's add *Friends protect each other* and *Friends depend on each other* to the map.

Amazing Words

partnership	struggle
solution	depend
survival	familiar
miserable	insist

ELL

English Language Learners

Frontload Comprehension Use ELL Poster 9 to review things people do in the winter, such as build a snowman, make an angel in the snow, and shovel snow. Before reading, ask children How does snow look? How does it feel when you touch it?

Cognates The words *insist* and *depend* have cognates Spanish. The words *insistir* and *depender* may help Spanish speakers learn the English words.

Objectives

• Read and identify words with *r*-controlled vowels *er, ir,* and *ur.*
• Read words fluently in context and independent of context.

Phonics Review
r-Controlled *er, ir, ur*

Review Sound-spellings

To review last week's phonics skill, write *clerk, thirst,* and *curb.* You studied words like these last week. What do you know about the vowel sounds in these words? (They are *r*-controlled vowels. The sound /ėr/ is spelled *er* in *clerk, ir* in *thirst,* and *ur* in *curb.*)

Write *sister.* What do you know about dividing this longer word into syllables? (The word is divided between the two middle consonants, *s* and *t.*) How do you read the syllables of this word? (*sis/ter*) What is the word? (*sister*)

Corrective feedback

If children are unable to answer the questions about *r*-controlled *er, ir,* and *ur,* refer them to Sound-Spelling Cards 67, 72, and 104.

Guide practice

Write *er, ir,* and *ur* as headings in a three-column chart. I will write some words. When I write a word, read it in your head. Pay attention to the spelling for /ėr/. Then tell me under what heading the word belongs: *burn, perch, nurse, chirp, after, survive, birth, winter, twirl, burst, third, monster.* Write each word in the appropriate column. Then have children read the words. Have them identify words that have two syllables. (*winter, after, monster, survive*).

er	ir	ur
perch	chirp	burn
winter	twirl	nurse
after	birth	survive
monster	third	burst

On their own

Use *Let's Practice It!* p. 91 on the *Teacher Resource DVD-ROM.*

Let's Practice It!
TR DVD•91

Fluent Word Reading
Spiral Review

Read words independent of context

Display these words. Tell children that they can blend or chunk some words on this list and others are Word Wall words.

Have children read the list three or four times until they can read at the rate of two to three seconds per word.

ago	we'll	I'm	snacks	while
haven't	whole	children	word	puppies
benches	pennies	plates	with	above
enough	dishes	shelf	it's	toward

Word Reading

Corrective feedback

If... children have difficulty reading whole words,
then... have them use sound-by-sound blending or combine word parts for decodable words or have them say and spell high-frequency words.
If... children cannot read fluently at a rate of two to three seconds per word,
then... have pairs practice the list until they can read it fluently.

Read words in context

Display these sentences. Call on individuals to read a sentence. Then randomly point to review words and have children read them. To help you monitor word reading, high-frequency words are underlined and decodable words are italicized.

> The *children haven't* put <u>enough</u> *dishes* out.
>
> *I'm* going to spell the <u>whole</u> <u>word</u>.
>
> *We'll* race <u>toward</u> the *benches* *with* the *puppies*.
>
> *It's* <u>above</u> the first *shelf* next to the *plates*.
>
> The *pennies* were spent on *snacks* a *while* <u>ago</u>.

Sentence Reading

Corrective feedback

If... children are unable to read an underlined high-frequency word,
then... read the word for them and spell it, having them echo you.
If... children have difficulty reading an italicized decodable word,
then...guide them in blending or combining word parts.

Differentiated Instruction

Ⓐ Advanced

Create and Read Sentences
Challenge children to create sentences of their own with three plurals: one with -s, one with -es, and one with -ies. Have children exchange sentences with partners and read each other's sentence.

Spiral Review

These activities review
- previously taught high-frequency words *above, ago, enough, toward, whole, word*.
- plurals spelled -s, -es, and -ies.
- contractions spelled with *n't, 's, 'll,* and *'m*.
- consonant digraph sounds /ch/ spelled *ch*, /sh/ spelled *sh*, /th/ and /ᴛʜ/ spelled *th*, and /hw/ spelled *wh*.

ⒺⓁⓁ

English Language Learners
Fluent Word Reading Have children listen to a more fluent reader model the words or have pairs read the words together.

Objectives

- Apply knowledge of sound-spellings and word parts to decode unknown words when reading.
- Decode and read words in context and independent of context.
- Practice fluency with oral rereading.

Decodable Practice Reader 9C
Plurals

Decodable Practice Reader 9C

Decode words independent of context

Have children turn to the first page and decode each word.

Read high-frequency words

Have children identify and read the high-frequency words, *remember, people, bought, door, probably,* and *seemed* on the first page.

Preview

Have children read the title and preview the story. Tell them they will read plurals.

Decode words in context

Pair children for reading and listen as they decode. One child begins. Children read the entire story, switching readers after each page. Partners reread the story. This time the other child begins.

Stan forgets his lunches.
Stan forgets his bag.
His buddies are
probably sad for him.
156

It isn't fun to forget.
"People remember better
with notes,"
Stan's mom said.
She bought cards
and made notes for Stan.
157

It seemed like elves left notes.
This note on his cup
tells Stan to put dishes away.
Stan takes them to the sink.
158

This note at the sink
tells Stan to grab lunch.
Stan stuffs his lunch
in his bag.
159

This note on the clock
tells Stan to grab
his big bag.
Stan slips it on his back.
160

This note by Stan's door
tells him to flip these switches.
Stan turns off lamps.
161

This is a big day for Stan!
Stan did not forget things—
thanks to Mom's notes.
162

Corrective feedback

If... children have difficulty decoding a word, **then...** refer them to the Sound-Spelling Cards to identify the sounds in a decodable word; prompt them to blend the word. If the word is a plural with an ending *-s* or *-es*, tell children to chunk the word and say the parts of the word, first separately and then together.

- What is the new word?
- Is the new word a word you know?
- Does it make sense in the story?

Check decoding and comprehension

Have children retell the story to include characters, settings, and events. Then have children find plurals in the story. Children should supply *lunches, buddies, notes, cards, elves, dishes, switches, lamps,* and *things.*

Review Print awareness

Point out the periods at the end of each sentence on the first page of the story. Remind children that sentences that tell something end with a period. Have children point out other statements in the story and read them aloud.

Reread for Fluency

Have children reread Decodable Practice Reader 9C to develop automaticity decoding plurals.

 ROUTINE **Oral Rereading**

(1) **Read** Have children read the entire book orally.

(2) **Reread** To achieve optimal fluency, children should reread the text three or four times.

(3) **Corrective Feedback** Listen as children read. Provide corrective feedback regarding their fluency and decoding.

Routines Flip Chart

ELL

English Language Learners
Leveled Support
Beginning After reading, write and read the singular form of a plural story word on the board, for example, *note, lamp, lunch, dish, buddy,* or *elf.* Tell children that you will say the word for more than one and they will put their finger under it in the story. When all have found it, read the word on the page together two times. Ask a volunteer to change the word on the board so the group can read it again.

Intermediate After reading, have one child choose a plural word from the story and say it aloud. Tell other children to find the word and put their finger under it. When all children have located the correct word, read it aloud together. Use the plural in a short sentence about the picture and have children repeat. Guide children to use the word in another sentence. If needed, provide a stem such as *We write [on cards].*

Advanced/Advanced-High Pair children. Have them use the list on the first page to write plural words on small pieces of paper. Tell them to work together to sort the words into two groups: those showing a spelling change of *y* to *i* or *f* to *v* and those that do not. Have them practice reading the words.

Objectives
- Spell plural words.
- Spell high-frequency words.
- Recognize structure and elements of a folk tale.
- Relate prior knowledge to new text.

Spelling
Plurals

Partner Review

Supply pairs of children with index cards on which the spelling words have been written. Have one child read a word while the other writes it. Then have children switch roles. Have them use the cards to check their spelling and correct any misspelled words.

On their own

Use Let's Practice It! p. 94 on the *Teacher Resource DVD-ROM.*

Let's Practice It!
TR DVD • 94

Small Group Time

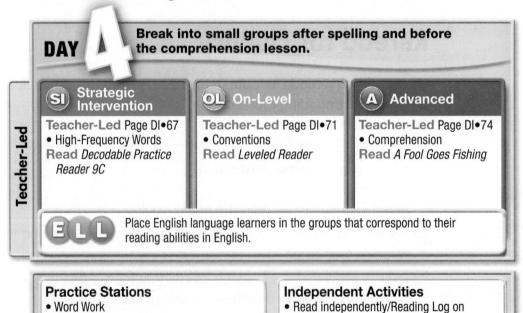

DAY 4 Break into small groups after spelling and before the comprehension lesson.

Teacher-Led

SI Strategic Intervention	OL On-Level	A Advanced
Teacher-Led Page DI•67 • High-Frequency Words **Read** Decodable Practice Reader 9C	Teacher-Led Page DI•71 • Conventions **Read** Leveled Reader	Teacher-Led Page DI•74 • Comprehension **Read** A Fool Goes Fishing

ELL Place English language learners in the groups that correspond to their reading abilities in English.

Practice Stations
- Word Work
- Get Fluent

Independent Activities
- Read independently/Reading Log on *Reader's and Writer's Notebook* p. RR2
- AudioText of Paired Selection

Social Studies in Reading

Preview and predict

Read the title and the first sentence of the selection on pages 306–311. Have children look through the selection and predict what they might learn. (Possible response: They might learn what happens when two men go fishing together.) Ask them what clues helped them make that prediction. (Possible response: The title "A Fool Goes Fishing" and the pictures show two men fishing.)

 Genre

Folk Tale Tell children that they will read a folk tale. Review the key features of a **folk tale:** it is a story that has been handed down over many years. Folk tales often have a **moral**, or lesson, as the theme. Explain that this selection is a folk tale because it is an old story with a lesson learned at the end.

Activate prior knowledge

Ask children to recall how the animals in *The Bremen Town Musicians* worked together. (They stood on each other's backs to see in the window of the house.) Today children will read about two men who do *not* work together to help each other.

Set a purpose

As children read "A Fool Goes Fishing" use Let's Think About in the Student Edition to help them focus on the features and structure of a folk tale.

Academic Vocabulary

folk tale a story handed down over the years, usually containing a moral at the end

moral a lesson taught by means of a story

Objectives

◉ Use story structure to comprehend text.

◉ Analyze cause and effect in literature.

Student Edition pp. 306–307

Guide Comprehension

Guide practice

🔵 Story Structure

Think Aloud I know that a story has characters, a setting, and a plot with a problem to be solved. These elements make up the **structure** of the story. When I read the first pages of "A Fool Goes Fishing," I look for the story structure. I see that the story happens near the West African forest. That is the **setting.** I see that the main **characters** are Anansi and Anene. I know there will be a conflict between Anansi and Anene because they are very different. I will read further to find out what kind of problem they have.

Monitor and Clarify

Think Aloud Good readers monitor and clarify to help understand what they read. I wonder why Anene is sitting while Anansi is cutting branches? I reread the part where Anene says, "I'll cut the branches, and you can get tired for me." That's silly, but Anansi falls for it. He decides to cut the branches and let Anene get tired. As I continue reading, I will stop and reread if I don't understand something.

Let's Think About Folk Tale

Possible response: We know that Anansi is not good at hunting, fighting, or working, but he is good at being clever. We also know he's really not that smart, since he fell for Anene's trick.

Later, it was time to make the traps. Anene said, "Somebody must do the work, and somebody must get tired. Let me do the work."

But Anansi was too clever for Anene. "Certainly not! I'm no fool. I'll be the one to do the work, and you can be the one to get tired." So Anene sat while Anansi made the traps.

Anene tried once more when it was time to put the traps in the water. "There are sharks in this water, Anansi," he said. "I'll wade in with the traps, and you can die for me."

"You expect *me* to die for *you*!" Anansi cried. "You must be a fool! I'll put the traps in the water. If I am bitten, you must die for me!"

The next day, Anansi and Anene found a few fish in the traps. Anene said, "Look, Anansi. There will probably be more fish tomorrow. You take these. I'll wait for tomorrow's catch."

"What!" cried Anansi. "You think I'd fall for that! I'll wait for tomorrow's catch. You can have the fish today." So Anene took the fish and sold them at the market.

Each day after that, Anansi was fooled by Anene into waiting for a better catch.

Let's Think About
Why does Anansi do all the work? **Folk Tale**

Let's Think About
What is the conflict in the story? Who is involved? **Folk Tale**

Let's Think About
How is the conflict building up? **Folk Tale**

308 | 309

Student Edition pp. 308–309

Academic Vocabulary

conflict a disagreement or problem

Guide Comprehension, continued

Sequence What do Anansi and Anene do after they cut the branches? (They make the traps to catch the fish.)

Let's Think About Folk Tale

Possible response: Anansi thinks if he works, he won't get tired. He thinks this because Anene tricks him into believing it.

Cause and Effect Why does Anansi agree to wade into the water with the traps? (Anene convinces him that one of them can wade in with the traps and the other one can die if a shark attacks. Anansi decides to be the one to wade, not the one to die.)

Let's Think About Folk Tale

Possible response: The conflict is between Anene and Anansi. Each wants to trick the other.

Let's Think About Folk Tale

Possible response: Every day Anene tricks Anansi again. We wonder if Anansi will ever catch on that he's being tricked.

Objectives

- Use story structure to comprehend text.
- Analyze cause and effect in literature.

Finally, the traps rotted. Anene said, "Anansi, it's your turn. I'll take the traps to sell at the market. You can have the last of the fish."

Anansi thought, "I'll bet those traps are worth a lot of money." He told Anene, "No, I'll take the traps. You can have the fish."

But when Anansi tried to sell the traps, the villagers became angry. "Who wants rotten traps?" they cried. "How foolish do you think we are?"

Anansi suddenly didn't feel so clever. He was very tired. He had no money, no fish, and rotten traps. What, he wondered, had gone wrong?

Anene said, "Anansi, remember how you wanted a fool to go fishing with you? Well, the only person you fooled was yourself."

Let's Think About How do you think Anansi will respond? Folk Tale

Let's Think About What do you think the theme of this story is? Why do you think so? Folk Tale

Reading Across Texts Both selections use repetition. What parts are repeated in *The Bremen Town Musicians* and *"A Fool Goes Fishing"*?

Writing Across Texts Write a short paragraph telling why you think the stories use repetition.

310

311

Student Edition pp. 310–311

Guide Comprehension, continued

Let's Think About Folk Tale

Possible response: Just as before, Anansi likely will decide to do the opposite of what Anene suggests, so he will want to take the traps to sell at the market.

Cause and Effect What causes the villagers to become angry? (They become angry because they think Anansi is trying to fool them into buying rotten traps.)

Story Structure How does the story end? (Possible response: Anansi finally realizes he has been tricked by Anene all along.)

Let's Think About Folk Tale

Possible response: I think the **theme** is that working together is important and people need to share the work. If Anansi had shared the work with Anene, they both would have benefited.

Guide Comprehension, continued

Cause and Effect Why do you think this story was passed down over the years? (To help people learn a lesson about working together and how to treat others.)

Story Structure What lesson do you think Anansi learned? (I think that Anansi learned to beware of trying to trick someone else because it might be you who is tricked instead.)

Reading Across Texts Have children find the parts of the songs in *The Bremen Town Musicians* that are repeated throughout the play. Ask children to point out the repetition of Anene offering to do the work but Anansi refusing in "A Fool Goes Fishing."

Writing Across Texts Children might write that the stories use repetition to help readers better understand the theme or to make it easier to remember the stories.

Academic Vocabulary

theme the lesson or meaning of a story

ELL

English Language Learners
Writing Across Texts Provide a graphic organizer for children to complete, on which they can write the events that repeat in each story.

Objectives

- Read aloud fluently with expression.
- Recognize that some plural nouns change spelling.
- Use plural nouns in written and spoken sentences.

Check Fluency WCPM
SUCCESS PREDICTOR

Fluency
Read with Expression

Guide practice

- Have children turn to page 296 in *The Bremen Town Musicians.*
- Have children follow along as you read the page with expression.
- Have the class read the page with you and then reread the page as a group until they read with no hesitation. Remind children to read the words the way characters would say them. To provide additional fluency practice, pair nonfluent readers with fluent readers.

ROUTINE Paired Reading

1. **Select a Passage** For *The Bremen Town Musicians,* use pages 300–301.
2. **Model** First, have children track the print as you read.
3. **Guide Practice** Then have children read along with you.
4. **On Their Own** For optimal fluency, have partners reread three or four times.

Routines Flip Chart

MONITOR PROGRESS Check Fluency WCPM

As children reread, monitor their progress toward their individual fluency goals. Current Goal: 48–58 words correct per minute. Mid-Year-Goal: 65 words correct per minute.

If... children cannot read fluently at a rate of 48–58 words correct per minute,

then... have children practice with text at their independent level.

Day 1	Day 2	Day 3	Day 4	Day 5
Check Word Reading	Check High-Frequency Words	Check Retelling	Check Fluency	Check Oral Vocabulary

Conventions
Plural Nouns That Change Spelling

Test practice

Use *Reader's and Writer's Notebook* p. 144 to help children identify and use plural nouns that change spelling. Recall that most plural nouns are formed by adding *-s* or *-es*, but some plural nouns like *wolves* and *children* are formed by a change in their spelling. Model identifying plural nouns that change spelling by writing this sentence on the board, reading it aloud, and underlining the plural nouns with spelling changes.

> **This book is about <u>elves</u> and <u>dwarves</u>.**

Then read the *Reader's and Writer's Notebook* p. 144 directions. Guide children as they mark the answer for number 1.

On their own

Use *Reader's and Writer's Notebook*, p. 144.

Connect to oral language

After children mark the answers to numbers 1–6, review the correct choices aloud, and have children read each sentence aloud. Tell them to clap as they read each plural noun that changes spelling.

Name _____
Plural Nouns That Change Spel...
Mark the letter of the word that correctly completes each sentence.

1. A flock of ____ flew by.
   ○ A goose
   ○ B geeses
   ⊗ C geese
2. All the ____ ate the cheese.
   ⊗ A mice
   ○ B mices
   ○ C mouse
3. The three ____ wear hats.
   ⊗ A men
   ○ B man
   ○ C mens
4. People tapped their ____.
   ○ A foots
   ⊗ B feet
   ○ C feets
5. Men and ____ danced.
   ⊗ A women
   ○ B woman
   ○ C womans
6. Does a rooster have ____?
   ○ A tooth
   ○ B tooths
   ⊗ C teeth

Choose a plural noun. Say a sentence for the noun.

144 Conventions Plural Nouns That Change Spelling

Reader's and Writer's Notebook, p. 144

INTERACT with TEXT

Fluency WCPM

Success Predictor

Objectives
• Revise a draft by adding phrases to clarify the sequence.

Writing—Fairy Tale
Revising Strategy

MINI-LESSON

Revising Strategy: Adding Phrases

■ Yesterday we wrote fairy tales about characters who worked together. Today we will revise. We can make our stories clearer by adding phrases that tell when things happen

Writing Transparency 9B
TR DVD

■ Display the Revising Tips. Explain that this is a time for making the fairy tale clear for anyone who will read it. Tomorrow children will proof-read to correct any errors such as misspellings, missing capital letters, or misplaced sentence periods.

Revising Tips
☐ Make sure your tale has a beginning, a middle, and an end.
☐ Add phrases to make the sequence of events clear.

■ Use Writing Transparency 9B to model adding phrases to clarify sequence. In my fairy tale, "The Girl and the Elves," I begin by saying that the girl and elves were walking in the forest. If I add the phrase, "All of a sudden," to the next sentence, it tells the reader how quickly the troll grabbed them. If I add the phrase, "after a while" to the sentence "But the girl and elves had an idea," it shows that it took time for them to get the idea. Add the two phrases on the transparency. Tell children they can add phrases to make the sequence clear in their fairy tale as they revise.

Peer conferencing

Peer Revision Pair up children and have them read the partner's fairy tale. Children should spend a minute or so telling their partner one thing they would change in their partner's story to make it clearer. Circulate to assist children planning to revise their fairy tales. As appropriate, suggest adding phrases to clarify the sequence.

Guide practice

Have children revise their fairy tales. For those not sure how to revise, have children refer to the Revising Tips or the Key Features of Fairy Tales.

Corrective feedback

Circulate to monitor and conference with children as they write. Remind them that they will have time to proofread and edit tomorrow. Today they can add phrases to make the sequence of events clear. Help them understand the benefits of adding phrases to improve their writing. Encourage them to explain why they want to add a phrase to a specific sentence.

ROUTINE — **Quick Write for Fluency** — Team Talk

1. **Talk** Read these sentences aloud, and have children identify a phrase that should be added to the second sentence to make the sequence clear.

   The girl was tired and went to bed early.

   She got up and felt great!

2. **Write** Have children write two sentences about two things that happen in sequence.

3. **Share** Partners can read the sentences to one another and orally add a phrase to the second sentence to make the sequence clear.

Routines Flip Chart

Differentiated Instruction

A Advanced

Reading Sentences Aloud Tell children that they may find it very helpful to read their sentences aloud to themselves after they write them. Explain that the best writers often use this technique to help them decide if a sentence is unclear and whether a word or phrase needs to be added.

Write Guy
Jeff Anderson

Life in a Fishbowl

When a teacher can't conference with every child, a "fishbowl conference" with one willing student can allow other children to observe, listen, and learn. It's important to reflect what the child is doing well and how a draft might be revised and improved.

Objectives
- Recognize and explain purposes of media.
- Ask relevant questions and make appropriate contributions.
- Listen attentively when others are speaking.
- Review answers to inquiry questions.

Media Literacy
Recognize and Explain Purposes of Media

Teach purposes of media

Tell children that they view, read, or listen to various media every day. Media include television, newspapers, magazines, radio and other means of communication. The purpose of media may be to inform, to persuade, or to entertain. When media amuses or interests us, it is entertainment. Discuss the entertainment purpose of media.

Model

Use the passage below to model recognizing the entertainment purpose in media.

 Suppose I view a television performance of *The Bremen Town Musicians*. I identify the topic and purpose. The topic is *working together* because the story is about animals forming a partnership. One purpose must be entertainment because it would be amusing to hear the animals sing their song and interesting to see how the animals outsmart the robbers. This TV show is entertaining because it is amusing and tells an interesting story.

Guide practice

Work with children to list various ways *The Bremen Town Musicians* could be presented through media, such as a stage performance, radio program, video, or print. Ask children the following questions:

1. How would a video be different from a stage performance?

2. What would be important in presenting the drama on the radio? What special sound effects might be used?

3. What would make this drama entertaining for someone reading the words without any pictures?

On their own

Have small groups of children work together to gather various entertainment media resources and view/read/listen to them. Have the groups share a media source with another group, identify the topic, and explain why its purpose is entertainment. Listeners should direct questions to the group that is presenting and respond whether they agree. Remind children to follow agreed-upon rules for discussion.

- Remember that good speakers contribute ideas in a discussion.
- Good listeners pay attention when others are speaking.

Research and Inquiry
Review and Revise Topic

Teach

Tell children that the next step in the inquiry project is to review their topic and see if the information they're finding tells about that topic. Sometimes our answers or the information available leads to a different idea about the topic.

Model

 Think Aloud I first thought about my topic *Birds* as meaning one kind helping several other kinds, because that's what I saw— chickadees, juncos, wrens, and more. When I researched, I could not find other facts or examples exactly about that. But I did find out that some birds of the *same kind* work together to build nests. That helps answer my question *Are there different ways that birds work together?* Now I think about my topic as meaning any birds, the same or different. I expect to learn more.

Guide practice

Have children review their topic and what they are discovering before they continue research. Ask if they need to change their idea about their topic, and if so, how. Assist children who have not recorded information or recorded something that doesn't support the topic and question. Remind children that tomorrow they will present their findings.

Wrap Up Your Day

✔ **Phonics** List singular words and plural words in mixed order. Point to each word and have children read aloud only the words for more than one. Have them tell how they know which words are plural.

✔ **Fluency** Display *My friends and I put peaches and berries on dishes.* Have children read the sentence three or four times until they can do so fluently.

Differentiated Instruction

A Advanced

Research Recording
Encourage children to record more facts or examples answering their question. Tell them to wait until tomorrow to draw conclusions about the facts they are gathering. Good researchers make conclusions after they think about all the collected facts.

Preview DAY 5

Remind children that they heard about two dogs helping their masters find the way home. Tomorrow they will hear the story again.

Objectives

- Review the concept: working together.
- Build oral vocabulary.
- Identify details in text.

Today at a Glance

Oral Vocabulary
Review

Phonics
◉ Review Plurals

Comprehension
◉ Cause and Effect

High-Frequency Words
Review

Story Words
Review

Conventions
Plural Nouns That Change Spelling

Writing
Fairy Tale: Edit

Research and Inquiry
Share Information

Check Oral Vocabulary
SUCCESS PREDICTOR

Concept Wrap Up

Question of the Week

Why is it a good idea to work together?

Review the concept

This week we have read and listened to stories about why it is a good idea to work together. Today you will listen to find out at what point Down Girl works alone and why. **Read the story.**

- Why does Down Girl take off with the bag of doughnuts? (Possible response: Down Girl thinks it is time to go home.)

Review Amazing Words

Orally review the meaning of this week's Amazing Words. Then display this week's concept map. Have children use Amazing Words such as *partnership* and *solution*, as well as the concept map, to answer the question, "Why is it a good idea to work together?"

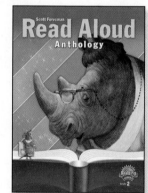

Read Aloud Anthology "Down Girl and Sit Save the Day"

Why is it a good idea to work together?

- Working together can make us feel better.
  - Friends can make us feel less miserable.
    - It makes a struggle easier.
- We reach a goal more easily.
  - We solve problems.
- We combine our strengths.
  - Friends help each other.
    - Friends protect each other.
      - Friends depend on each other.

ELL Check Concepts and Language Use the Day 5 instruction on ELL Poster 9 to monitor children's understanding of the lesson concept.

ELL Poster 9

Oral Vocabulary
Amazing Ideas

Connect to the Big Question

Team Talk Pair children and have them discuss how the Question of the Week connects to this unit's Big Question, "How can we work together?" Tell children to use the concept map and what they've learned from this week's Anchored Talks and reading selection to form an Amazing Idea—a realization or "big idea" about **working together**. Then ask each pair to share their Amazing Idea with the class.

Amazing Ideas might include these key concepts:

• We can help each other reach a goal or solve problems when we work together.

• Working together makes us stronger than we are alone.

It's Friday

MONITOR PROGRESS | **Check Oral Vocabulary**

Call on individuals to use this week's Amazing Words to talk about what we can learn by working together. Prompt discussion with the questions below. Monitor children's ability to use the Amazing Words and note which words children are unable to use.

• **When is a *partnership* better than working alone?**
• **Why would people *struggle* if they work alone?**
• **How can working with others help us become *familiar* with new ideas?**
• **When is it not good to *insist* on your own ideas?**
• **If you are *miserable*, what can make you feel better?**
• **How is friendship important to our *survival*?**
• **Who would you *depend* on for a *solution* to a problem?**

If... children have difficulty using the Amazing Words,

then... reteach the unknown words using the Oral Vocabulary Routines, pp. 280a, 284b, 302b, 306b.

Day 1	Day 2	Day 3	Day 4	Day 5
Check Word Reading	Check High-Frequency Words	Check Retelling	Check Fluency	Check Oral Vocabulary

Success Predictor

Amazing Words

partnership	struggle
survival	depend
solution	familiar
miserable	insist

E L L

English Language Learners
Amazing Words Rephrase the questions so children have the opportunity to produce oral language.

Oral Vocabulary

Success Predictor

Objectives
◎ Review plurals with *-s, -es, -ies.*

Assess
• Spell plurals with *-s, -es, -ies.*
• Spell high-frequency words.

Phonics
◉ Plurals *-s, -es, -ies*

Review
Target phonics skill

Write the following sentences on the board. Have children read each one, first quietly to themselves and then aloud as you track the print.

1. **The girls in dresses ate grapes and jellies.**

2. **Dad packed the dishes and cups in the boxes.**

3. **My buddies and I sang tunes and read stories.**

4. **The bunnies ran past the lilies and into the ditches.**

Team Talk Have children discuss with a partner which words are plurals. Have them name the base word and ending that form each plural. Then call on individuals to share with the class.

Spelling Test

Dictate spelling words

Say each word, read the sentence, repeat the word, and allow time for children to write the word.

1. **baby**	The **baby** is napping.
2. **lunch**	We will eat **lunch** at home.
3. **notes**	I wrote two **notes** to Mom.
4. **stories**	He liked the **stories** I made up.
5. **tunes**	She can hum many **tunes**.
6. **babies**	Those **babies** are so cute!
7. **story**	Dad will tell me a bedtime **story**.
8. **switches**	The **switches** were all shut off.
9. **tune**	I like that lively **tune**.
10. **note**	I wrote a **note** to my teacher.
11. **lunches**	Did you hand out the **lunches**?
12. **switch**	Please turn on the light **switch**.

High-Frequency Words

13. **people**	Many **people** are standing in line.
14. **scared**	A little cat **scared** the big dog.

Differentiated Instruction

SI Strategic Intervention

Check Spelling Have children choose the correct spelling of each word from three random spellings.

A Advanced

Extend Spelling Have children who have demonstrated proficiency in spelling individual words spell each word in a self-made sentence.

Small Group Time

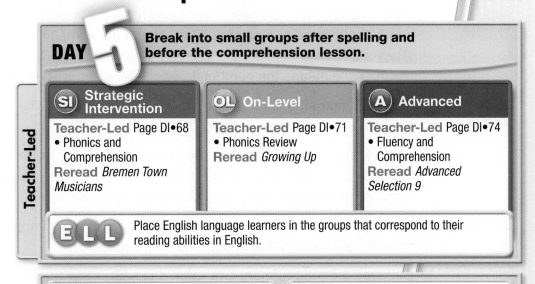

DAY 5 Break into small groups after spelling and before the comprehension lesson.

Teacher-Led

SI Strategic Intervention	**OL** On-Level	**A** Advanced
Teacher-Led Page DI•68	Teacher-Led Page DI•71	Teacher-Led Page DI•74
• Phonics and Comprehension	• Phonics Review	• Fluency and Comprehension
Reread *Bremen Town Musicians*	Reread *Growing Up*	Reread *Advanced Selection 9*

ELL Place English language learners in the groups that correspond to their reading abilities in English.

Practice Stations
• Words to Know
• Read for Meaning

Independent Activities
• Read independently/Reading Log on
• *Reader's and Writer's Notebook* p. RR2
• Concept Talk Video

DAY 5 Wrap Up your Week
40–45 min.

Objectives
- Identify homophones.
- Read aloud fluently with expression.
- Identify purposes of media.
- Participate in class discussion.
- Listen attentively.

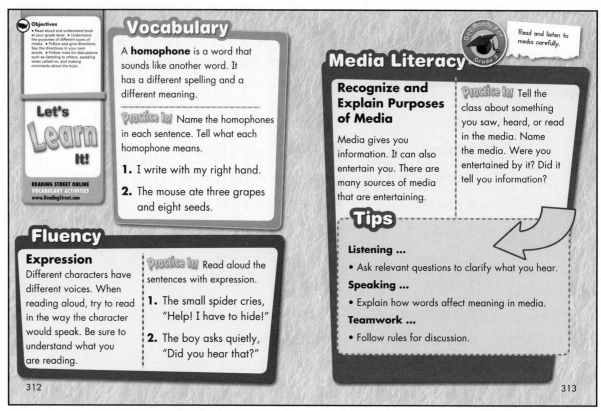

Objectives
• Read aloud and understand texts at your grade level. • Understand the purposes of different types of media. • Follow and give directions. Say the directions in your own words. • Follow rules for discussions such as listening to others, speaking when called on, and making comments about the topic.

Vocabulary

A **homophone** is a word that sounds like another word. It has a different spelling and a different meaning.

Practice It! Name the homophones in each sentence. Tell what each homophone means.

1. I write with my right hand.
2. The mouse ate three grapes and eight seeds.

Let's Learn It!
READING STREET ONLINE
VOCABULARY ACTIVITIES
www.ReadingStreet.com

Fluency

Expression
Different characters have different voices. When reading aloud, try to read in the way the character would speak. Be sure to understand what you are reading.

Practice It! Read aloud the sentences with expression.

1. The small spider cries, "Help! I have to hide!"
2. The boy asks quietly, "Did you hear that?"

Media Literacy

Read and listen to media carefully.

Recognize and Explain Purposes of Media

Media gives you information. It can also entertain you. There are many sources of media that are entertaining.

Practice It! Tell the class about something you saw, heard, or read in the media. Name the media. Were you entertained by it? Did it tell you information?

Tips

Listening ...
• Ask relevant questions to clarify what you hear.

Speaking ...
• Explain how words affect meaning in media.

Teamwork ...
• Follow rules for discussion.

312

313

Student Edition pp. 312–313

Vocabulary
Homophones

Teach

Read and discuss the Vocabulary lesson on page 312 of the Student Edition. Explain that homophones are words that sound the same but are spelled differently and have a different meaning.

Model

Write *one* and *won.* Say each word and have children repeat it. What is the same about these two words? (They sound the same.) What is different? (They are spelled differently and mean different things.) What do the words mean? (*One* means the number 1; *won* means succeeded over others.)

Guide practice

Read the instructions for the Vocabulary Practice It! activity. Read the first sentence and then have children repeat after you.

When I read this sentence, I know that *write* and *right* are homophones because they sound the same but are spelled differently. *Write* means to form words on paper, and *right* means the opposite of *left.*

On their own

Have the pairs read the next sentence and name the homophones. Ask them to tell the meaning of each homophone.

Corrective feedback

Circulate around the room and listen as children say the homophones and give their meaning. Provide assistance as needed.

312–313 Working Together • Unit 2 • Week 4

Fluency
Read with Expression

Teach Read and discuss the Fluency instructions.

Read words in context Give children a moment to look at the sentences. Then have them read each sentence three or four times until they can read each sentence with the expression appropriate to each character.

Media Literacy
Recognize and Explain Purposes of Media

Teach Have children turn to page 313 of the Student Edition. Read and discuss the information together. Remind children that some media resources provide information and some provide entertainment.

Ask children what kinds of media resources they find entertaining. List their ideas on the board.

Introduce prompt Read the Practice It! prompt with the class. Remind children to think about different types of media they use and whether it provides information or entertainment. Point out some various kinds of media, such as books, newspapers, magazines, and advertisements. Explain that in print media they will find nouns that change in spelling when the singular form is made plural.

Team Talk Have pairs take turns telling what they saw, heard, or read in the media. Tell children to share with their partners what was entertaining about the media they've chosen and what information they may have gotten from it, if any. Remind children to follow agreed-upon rules for discussion.

Differentiated Instruction

SI **Strategic Intervention**

Visualize Skills Some children might find it helpful to see additional visual representations of the vocabulary skill, homophones. Write various homophones on the board, such as *blue* and *blew; red* and *read;* and *two* and *to*. Read the words aloud together and review the differences in spelling and meaning of each set of homophones.

Recognize and Explain Purposes of Media

In addition to recognizing and explaining media purposes, children at Grade 3 should also be able to give an opinion about the effectiveness of a media presentation.

English Language Learners

Homophones Provide sentence frames to help children structure their understanding of homophones by filling in the appropriate words. Read the sentences with children.

I _____ my bicycle on the _____. (rode, road)

Did you _____ the huge waves by the _____? (see, sea)

Objectives
- ◎ Identify cause and effect in drama.
- • Read story words.
- • Identify the features of a folk tale.

Comprehension
↻ Cause and Effect

Review
Cause and effect

As you read, remember to think about things that happen and why those things happen. What questions can you ask to better understand the cause and effect? (What happened? Why did it happen?)

To check understanding of cause and effect, read aloud the following story and have children answer the questions that follow.

> Dakota was teaching her puppy, Pax, to fetch a ball, so they played in the backyard every Saturday. Dakota's mother warned her always to make sure the gate was shut tight. One day Pax bolted away and ran off because Dakota forgot to check the gate. Dakota and her mother searched the neighborhood. Finally, Dakota spotted Pax under Mrs. Harrison's porch. Dakota never forgot to check that gate again!

1. What happened? (Pax ran off.)

2. Why did it happen? (Dakota forgot to check the gate.)

3. What clue word helped you figure out why it happened? (*because*)

Vocabulary
High-Frequency and Story Words

Review
High-frequency words

Review this week's high-frequency words: *bought, people, pleasant, probably, scared, shall,* and *sign*. Provide an example of a riddle for one of the words for the class to solve, such as: I am the opposite of *sold*. I have six letters. (*bought*)

Team Talk Have children orally give riddles for the remaining six words to a partner to solve.

Review
Story words

Write the words *excitement, mill, musician, monsters,* and *robbers*. Read them aloud together. Then have children pantomime an action or expression to illustrate the meaning of each word. Classmates can identify the word.

Corrective feedback

For corrective feedback, review the definitions on p. 302h.

 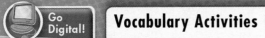
Literary Text
Features of a Folk Tale

Review
Genre

Use *The Bremen Town Musicians* and "A Fool Goes Fishing" to review the basic elements of a folk tale.

- A **folk tale** is an old story that has been told for many years. It may have animals that act like people.

- A folk tale often has **repetition,** sentences or events that repeat over and over again.

- A folk tale always has a simple problem, and often the characters learn a lesson at the end of the story.

Features of a Folk Tale If children have difficulty answering the questions about folk tales, read aloud the repetitive scenes with children, making them aware of how similar they are as they read.

Model

 Think Aloud I know that both *The Bremen Town Musicians* and "A Fool Goes Fishing" are old tales. One story has animals that acted like people. Both stories have a lot of repetition. All of these are things I've noticed about other folk tales too.

Guide practice

Ask the following questions to guide children in describing the features of a folk tale.

- What parts of "A Fool Goes Fishing" are repeated? (Possible response: Anene offers to do the work and let Anansi get tired, but Anansi thinks he's tricking him, so he always does the work.)

- What do you think is the moral of the story? (Possible response: Be careful who you try to trick, because they may trick you.)

On their own **Team Talk** Have children work in small groups to make up another story about Anansi and Anene. Their stories should include features of a folk tale, such as repetition and a moral.

English Language Learners
Answering Questions Provide English Learners with support for answering the questions by having them look back at the pictures in the selection to find clues. Have children work with a partner to match the question with a picture and then reread the page.

Objectives

◉ Plurals with -s, -es, -ies
• High-Frequency Words
• Fluency: WCPM
◉ Cause and Effect

Fluency Goals

Set individual fluency goals for children to enable them to reach the end-of-the-year goal.

• **Current Goal:** 48–58 WCPM
• **End-of-Year Goal:** 90 WCPM

Assessment
Monitor Progress

For a written assessment of plurals with -s, -es, -ies; high-frequency words; and cause and effect, use Weekly Test 9, pp. 49–54.

Assess words in context

Sentence reading Use the following reproducible page to assess children's ability to read words in context. Call on children to read two sentences aloud. Start over with sentence one if necessary.

MONITOR PROGRESS | **Sentence Reading**

If... children have trouble reading plurals with -s, -es, -ies,
then... see the Reteach Lesson in *First Stop.*

If... a child cannot read all the high-frequency words,
then... mark the missed words on a high-frequency word list and have the child practice reading the words with a fluent reader.

Success Predictor

Assess

Fluency Take a one-minute sample of children's oral reading. Have children read the fluency passage on p. 313f.

Comprehension Have the child read the entire passage. (If the child had difficulty with the passage, you may read it aloud.) Then have the child state a cause-and-effect relationship from the passage.

MONITOR PROGRESS | **Fluency and Comprehension**

If... a child does not achieve the fluency goal on the timed reading,
then... copy the passage and send it home with the child for additional fluency practice, or have the child practice with a fluent reader.

If... a child cannot state a cause and its effect,
then... see the Reteach Lesson in *First Stop.*

Success Predictor

Monitor accuracy

Record scores Have children monitor their accuracy by recording their scores using the Sentence Reading Chart and by recording the number of words read correctly per minute on their Fluency Progress Chart in *First Stop.*

Read the Sentences

1. People sat on park benches and ate sandwiches.

2. I shall get nice dishes and glasses for Mom and Dad.

3. The red roses and pink pansies had a pleasant smell.

4. When foxes scared them, five smart bunnies hid.

5. Mike bought bunches of grapes for his picnic with us.

6. Her sign read that Kate is selling puppies and kittens.

7. Thunder probably woke up her fillies and mules.

MONITOR PROGRESS

- Fluency
- Plurals with -s, -es, -ies
- High-frequency Words

Name _____

Read the Story

Animal Wishes

    Owl asked her friends to gather around. Summer   8
had almost arrived, and she wanted to hear their   17
wishes. "Bees, what is your wish?" asked Owl.   25
    "We wish for lots of flowers," said the bees.   34
    "Please tell us why," said Owl.   40
    "The flowers will help us make honey for other   49
animals," said the bees.   53
    "That is a good wish," said Owl.   60
    Then the turtles told Owl their wish. "We wish   69
for lots of rain," they said.   75
    "Please tell us why," said Owl.   81
    "The rain will fill the ponds and lakes," said the   91
turtles. "Then all the animals will have water to   100
drink and places to swim."   105
    "That is a fine wish," said Owl.   112
    Then the birds told Owl their wish. "We wish   121
for lots of berry bushes. Then we will have   130
berries to eat, and we will chirp all day. The   140
other animals like to hear birds chirp."   147
    "I like that wish," said Owl.   153
    Finally, one little bird asked Owl what she   161
wished for. "I wish that all of your wishes come   171
true!" said Owl.   174
    "Thank you, Owl! We love you!" cried all   182
the animals.   184

MONITOR PROGRESS   • Check Fluency
   • Cause and Effect

Conventions
Plural Nouns That Change Spelling

Review

Remind children that some plural nouns are formed by a change in spelling. Have them give several examples of these nouns.

Guide practice

Write the following sentences. Have children fill each blank with a plural noun that changes its spelling.

> 1. **There are too many books on the _____.**
>
> 2. **_____ hunt in packs led by one wolf.**
>
> 3. **I went to the dentist to get my _____ cleaned.**
>
> 4. **That cow had two _____ last spring.**

Connect to oral language

Have children locate pictures or photographs in their student books that show plural nouns that change spelling, such as *men, women, mice,* and *children*. Then have children share these illustrations and complete this sentence frame orally.

> **Look at the _____.**

On their own

Use *Let's Practice It!* p. 96 on the *Teacher Resource DVD-ROM*.

Objectives
- Identify plural nouns that change spelling.
- Understand and use plural nouns in writing.
- Understand and use plural nouns when speaking.

Daily Fix-It

9. donkey humed with Dog.
   Donkey hummed with Dog.

10. what fun they had.
    What fun they had!

Discuss the Daily Fix-It corrections with children. Review sentence capitalization and punctuation and rules for doubling the final consonant when an ending is added.

Let's Practice It!
TR DVD•96

Objectives

• Edit a draft for spelling, punctuation, and capitalization.
• Use plural nouns correctly.
• Create a final draft and present.

Writing—Fairy Tale
Writer's Craft: Plural Nouns

Review Revising

Remind children that yesterday they revised their fairy tales. They may have added phrases to make the sequence of events clearer. Today they will proofread their fairy tales.

MINI-LESSON

Proofread for Plural Nouns

Teach In our fairy tales, if we spell words correctly, readers will know what we mean. When we proofread, we check to make sure the words are correct. We can check to make sure that all plural nouns are spelled correctly. Some nouns change spelling when we make them plural. Other nouns require *-s* or *-es* at the end of the word.

Writing Transparency 9C
TR DVD

Model Let us look at my fairy tale about the girl and the elves. Display Writing Transparency 9C. Explain that you will look at the plural nouns to make sure they are spelled correctly. Show how you would change *elfs* to *elves* and *bushs* to *bushes*. Show how you would change any misspellings (such as *idear* to *idea*). Quickly show how to check a word's spelling in a classroom dictionary or word list. Model how you would change a letter at the beginning of a sentence if it were not capitalized or add a period if one were missing at the end of a sentence or if it were in the wrong place.

Proofread

Display the Proofreading Tips. Have children proof-read their fairy tales to correct any misspellings, missing capital letters, or errors with periods. Circulate to assist children with plural nouns or other words.

Proofreading Tips

✔ Did I spell all plural nouns correctly?

✔ Did I spell all other words correctly?

✔ Do my sentences begin with a capital letter?

✔ Did I use periods and other end punctuation correctly?

Present

Have children make a final draft of their fairy tales, with their revisions and proofreading corrections. Help as appropriate.

Choose an option for children to present their fairy tales.

They might make a picture book of their fairy tale, writing the beginning, middle, and end on separate pages and illustrating each part.	They might choose a favorite part of their fairy tale and read it aloud to the class or to a small group.

When they have finished, help them complete a Self-Evaluation form.

ROUTINE Quick Write for Fluency — Team Talk

1. **Talk** Have partners take one minute to find plural nouns (such as *elves*, *children*, or *mice*) in each of their fairy tales.
2. **Write** Each child writes a new short sentence using one of the plural nouns.
3. **Share** Partners trade sentences and read them aloud.

Routines Flip Chart

Teacher Note

Self-Evaluation Make copies of the Self-Evaluation form from the *Teacher Resource DVD-ROM,* and hand them out to children.

English Language Learners
Support Editing
As you review a child's draft, focus on the ideas he or she expressed more than the errors. If you find consistent spelling errors, select one or two skills for the child to focus on during editing.

Objectives

- Review concept: working together can help everyone in the group.
- Organize information.
- Create poster.
- Present results of an inquiry project.

Research and Inquiry
Communicate

Teach

Tell children that today they will organize the facts and examples they found by showing them in illustrations on a poster. Then they will share. They will tell about the illustrations and how people or animals work together.

Model

Think Aloud Display your completed chart. I will review the information I found and think about how birds benefit from working together. I wrote that birds signal each other when there is food. I think other birds benefit from those signals because they learn when it is safe to come and eat. I'll write that on my chart. Continue using other information from the chart.

Guide practice

Ask children why it would be helpful to write their topic as a poster title. Give them time to review their information and then make their posters.

On their own

Have children share their posters in small groups. Remind them how to be good speakers and listeners:

- Good speakers share information and ideas in complete sentences, not too fast and not too slow.

- Good listeners ask questions about something the speaker presents but they don't completely understand.

Wrap Up Your Week!

Question of the Week

Why is it a good idea to work together?

Think Aloud This week we talked about why working together is a good idea. In the drama *The Bremen Town Musicians,* we read about a donkey, a dog, a cat, and a rooster that combined their strengths to solve a problem. In *From Me to You,* we read about another group of animals. We learned how miserable Rat was without contact from his friends. Then we read about how a special letter from a friend inspired Rat to work together with Frog and Mouse to help Bat feel better. **Have children recall their Amazing Ideas about why it is a good idea to work together. Then have children use these ideas to help them demonstrate their understanding of the Question of the Week.**

Amazing Words

You've learned **0 0 8** words this week!

You've learned **0 7 2** words this year!

ELL

English Language Learners

Poster Preview Prepare children for next week by using Week 5 ELL Poster 10. Read the Poster Talk-Through to introduce the concept and vocabulary. Ask children to identify and describe objects and actions in the art.

Selection Summary Send home the summary of *One Good Turn Deserves Another,* in English and the child's home language if available. Children can read the summary with family members.

Preview NEXT WEEK

Tell children that next week they will read about how anybody can be of help no matter how small they are.

Weekly Assessment

Use pp. 49–54 of *Weekly Tests* to check:

✔ **Phonics** Plurals

✔ 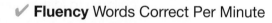 **Comprehension Skill** Cause and Effect

✔ **High-Frequency Words**

bought	scared
people	shall
pleasant	sign
probably	

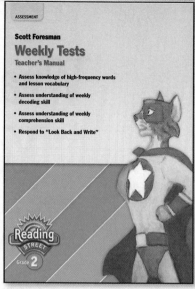

Weekly Tests

Advanced

On-Level

SI

Strategic Intervention

Differentiated Assessment

Use pp. 49–54 of *Fresh Reads for Fluency and Comprehension* to check:

✔ **Comprehension Skill** Cause and Effect

✔ Review **Comprehension Skill** Compare and Contrast

✔ **Fluency** Words Correct Per Minute

Fresh Reads for Fluency and Comprehension

Managing Assessment

Use *Assessment Handbook* for:

✔ **Weekly Assessment Blackline Masters for Monitoring Progress**

✔ **Observation Checklists**

✔ **Record-Keeping Forms**

✔ **Portfolio Assessment**

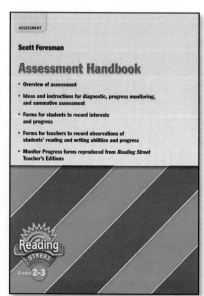

Assessment Handbook

Jobs with Zoo Animals

Mr. and Mrs. Chavez are volunteers at the zoo. They think it's fun to help the animals. At the zoo, they have different jobs.

Mrs. Chavez works in the nurseries with the animal babies. First, she cleans cages. The fox pups are in glass cages. Visitors can watch them play. The camel calves have messy cages! Mrs. Chavez's favorite part of her job is feeding the babies their lunches. Today she feeds the panda cubs and zebra colts.

At this zoo, visitors can ride tour buses. They learn more about large animals, such as giraffes and buffaloes. On some days, Mr. Chavez drives a bus and gives speeches about the animals. On other days, he visits schools. He teaches students facts about animals. He knows a lot about wolves and foxes.

Daniel and Hector Chavez are their sons. They hear many exciting stories from their parents. Daniel is thirteen years old, and now he can become a volunteer. Today Daniel met with Mr. Greenlee, who chooses volunteers. Daniel hopes he can help with the ponies or the elephant calves. Daniel wants to try many different tasks. But most of all, Daniel wants to help the animals at the zoo stay healthy and happy.

Advanced Selection 9   **Vocabulary:** volunteers, nurseries

Small Group Time

Pacing Small Group Instruction

5 Day Plan

DAY 1	• Phonemic Awareness/ Phonics • Decodable Reader
DAY 2	• High-Frequency Words • Leveled Reader
DAY 3	• Phonics • Leveled Reader
DAY 4	• High-Frequency Words • Decodable Reader
DAY 5	• Phonics Review • Comprehension Review

3 or 4 Day Plan

DAY 1	• Phonemic Awareness/ Phonics • Decodable Reader
DAY 2	• High-Frequency Words • Leveled Reader
DAY 3	• Phonics • Leveled Reader
DAY 4	• High-Frequency Words • Decodable Reader

3 Day Plan: Eliminate the shaded box

SI *Strategic Intervention* **DAY 1**

Phonemic Awareness • Phonics

■ **Substitute Initial Phonemes** Reteach p. 280–281 of the Teacher's Edition. Model substituting initial phonemes in these words. Then have children substitute initial phonemes on their own.

> **cats** Change /k/ to /h/.   **peaches** Change /p/ to /b/.
> **noses** Change /n/ to /r/.

■ ◉ **Plurals -s, -es, -ies** Reteach p. 281a of the Teacher's Edition. Then have children spell *sands* using letter tiles. Monitor their work.

• Change the first *s* in *sands* to *b*. What is the new word?

• Change the *b* in *bands* to *br*. What is the new word?

• Change the *br* in *brands* to *st*. What is the new word?

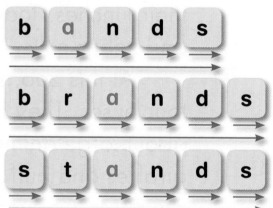

Decodable Practice Reader 9A

■ **Review** Review words with the plurals -s, -es, and -ies and the high-frequency words *are, go, together, after, give,* and *won't*. Then have children blend and read these words from the story: *lots, notes, bases, classes, puppies*.

> **If...** children have difficulty with any of these words, **then...** reteach the word by modeling. Have children practice the words, with feedback from you, until they can read them independently.

Have children reread the text orally. To achieve optimal fluency, children should reread the text three or four times.

Decodable Practice Reader 9A

Objectives
• Decode words by applying knowledge of common spelling patterns.

 SI Strategic Intervention

DAY 2

High-Frequency Words

■ **Review** Point to *love, mother, father, straight, been, couldn't,* and *build* on the Word Wall. As you point to each word, say the word, spell it, and say it again. Have children say and spell each word, first with you and then without you. Allow time for children to practice reading these high-frequency words using the word cards.

For a complete literacy instructional plan and additional practice with this week's target skills and strategies, see the **Leveled Reader Teaching Guide.**

Concept Literacy Leveled Reader

■ **Preview and Predict** Read the title and the author's name. Have children look at the cover and ask them to describe what they see. Help children activate their prior knowledge by asking them to look through the book and to use the photos to predict things that might take place.

■ **Set a Purpose** Remind children that setting a purpose for reading can help them better understand what they read. Guide children to pay attention to how the children are working together.

Concept Literacy

■ **Read** Provide corrective feedback as children read the book orally. During reading, ask them if they were able to confirm any of the predictions they made prior to reading.

> **If...** children have difficulty reading the book individually,
> **then...** read a sentence aloud as children point to each word. Then have the group reread the sentences as they continue pointing. Continue reading in this way until children read individually.

■ **Retell** Have children take turns retelling the selection. Help them identify how the children are working together by asking, What are the children doing together at the park? What are some of the things the children are picking up? What do you think they will do with all the things they pick up?

More Reading
Use Leveled Readers or other text at children's instructional level.

Objectives
• Use ideas to make predictions.
• Read at least 300 high-frequency words from a commonly used list.

Small Group Time

Phonics

■ ◎ **Plural -s, -es, -ies** Reteach p. 302d of the Teacher's Edition. Have children blend and read these words to help them practice the target phonics skill.

| parks | bills | faces | dishes | copies | misses |

For a complete literacy instructional plan and additional practice with this week's target skills and strategies, see the **Leveled Reader Teaching Guide.**

Below-Level Leveled Reader

■ **Preview and Predict** Read the title and the author's name. Have children look at the cover and ask them to describe what they see. Help children activate their prior knowledge by asking them to look through the book and to use the photos to predict what will happen.

■ **Set a Purpose** Remind children that setting a purpose for reading can help them better understand what they read. Guide children to pay attention to how the sheep react as the border collie does its job.

■ **Read** Provide corrective feedback as children read the book orally. During reading, ask them if they were able to confirm any of the predictions they made.

If... children have difficulty reading the book individually,
then... read a sentence aloud as children point to each word. Then have the group reread the sentences as they continue pointing.

■ ◎ **Story Structure** Have children explain the job that border collies have. Then prompt them to tell what happens in the beginning, middle, and end of the selection.

Below-Level

Objectives
• Decode words by applying knowledge of common spelling patterns.
• Use ideas to make predictions.

DI•66 Working Together • Unit 2 • Week 4

 eReaders

DAY 4

High-Frequency Words

■ **Review** Write *remember, people, bought, door, probably,* and *seemed* on the board. Give children copies of the word cards. Provide clues for each word meaning, such as pointing to a *door*, drawing stick figures of *people* on the board, or pointing to your head and nodding to show you *remember*. Then ask children to hold up the appropriate word card as you present the clues. Model saying and spelling each word. Then have children say each word, spell the word as you point to each letter, and then say the word again.

Decodable Practice Reader 9C

■ **Review** Use the word lists to review the plurals *-s, -es,* and *-ies.* Be sure children understand that the plurals can make the /s/, /es/, or /ez/ sounds. Have children blend and read the words. Then have children reread the text orally.

If... children have difficulty reading the story individually, **then...** read a sentence aloud as children point to each word. Then have the group reread the sentences as they continue pointing. Continue reading in this way until children read individually.

Check comprehension by having children retell the story including the characters, plot, and setting. Have children locate words in the story that have the plurals *-s, -es,* and *-ies.* List the words children identify. Then have them sort the words in a chart with columns labeled *-s, -es,* and *-ies.*

Decodable Practice Reader 9C

More Reading
Use Leveled Readers or other text at children's instructional level.

-s	-es	-ies
cards	lunches	babies
lamps	switches	
notes	elves	
things	dishes	

Objectives
• Decode words by applying knowledge of common spelling patterns.
• Identify at least 300 high-frequency words from a commonly used list.

Small Group Time

 SI Strategic Intervention

More Reading
Use Leveled Readers or other text at children's instructional level.

Phonics Review

■  **Plurals *-s, -es, -ies*.** Write these sentences on the board. Have children read them aloud as you track the print. Then call on individuals to blend and read the underlined words.

> The <u>puppies</u> played in the <u>bushes</u>.
>
> Two <u>robins</u> made their <u>nests</u>.
>
> There were many <u>places</u> for the <u>boys</u> to go.
>
> Sara and Michelle ate <u>bunches</u> of <u>berries</u>.

Comprehension Review

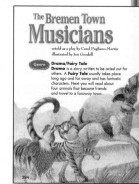

The Bremen Town Musicians

■ **Cause and Effect** Review that authors often tell what happens and why it happens in a story. This is called cause and effect. Words such as *so* and *because* help readers figure out what happens in the story and why.

■ **Read** Have children reread this week's main selection, *The Bremen Town Musicians*.

- As you read, think about some of the things that happen in the play.

- Ask yourself "Why did this happen?"

- Notice clues such as the words *so* and *because* to help you figure out what happens and why.

After reading, have children point out clues that helped them determine cause and effect.

Objectives
- Decode words by applying knowledge of common spelling patterns.
- Understand the elements of drama.

On-Level   DAY **1**

Phonics • Spelling

- 🔊 **Plurals -s, -es, -ies** Write the following words on the board and have children practice reading words with plurals -s, -es, and -ies.

times	lunches	switches	babies

Then have children identify the base word of each and tell whether the word ends with the -s, -es, or -ies.

- **y changed to i, f changed to ve** Remind children that when a noun ends in y, the y may change to i when you make it plural, for example, *baby, babies*. Sometimes f changes to ve when plural: *shelf, shelves*. Clarify the pronunciation and meaning of each word. For example, say: *That bookcase has three shelves to hold books.* Have children identify the letters and sounds in words such as *caddy, caddies; belly, bellies; elf, elves;* and *self, selves.*

Objectives
- Decode words by applying knowledge of common spelling patterns.
- Use phonological knowledge to match sounds to letters to construct unknown words.

On-Level   DAY **2**

High-Frequency Words

- **High-Frequency Words** Hold up this week's High-Frequency Word Cards and review proper pronunciation. Continue holding the cards and have children chorally read each word. To help children demonstrate their understanding of the words, give pairs of children copies of the cards. Have one child choose a card and provide his or her partner with a verbal clue. For example:

This word means I most likely will do something. (probably)

High-Frequency/Tested Word Cards

Objectives
- Understand new vocabulary and use it correctly.
- Identify at least 300 high-frequency words from a commonly used list.

Pacing Small Group Instruction

20–30 min.

5 Day Plan

DAY 1	• Phonics • Spelling • Decodable Reader
DAY 2	• High-Frequency Words • Decodable Reader
DAY 3	• Leveled Reader
DAY 4	• Conventions • Leveled Reader
DAY 5	• Phonics Review • Leveled Reader

3 or 4 Day Plan

DAY 1	• Phonics • Spelling • Decodable Reader
DAY 2	• High-Frequency Words • Decodable Reader
DAY 3	• Leveled Reader
DAY 4	• Conventions • Leveled Reader

3 Day Plan: Eliminate the shaded box

Decodable Practice Readers

Small Group Time

For a complete literacy instructional plan and additional practice with this week's target skills and strategies, see the **Leveled Reader Teaching Guide.**

On-Level Leveled Reader

■ **Preview and Predict** Read the title, the author's name, and the illustrator's name. Have children look at the cover, and ask them to describe it in detail. Help children preview the story by asking them to look through the story and use the illustrations to predict things that might take place.

On-Level

■ ◉ **Cause and Effect** Before reading, remind children that *cause* and *effect* refers to what happened and why it happened. Guide children to pay attention to the events in the story and why they happen.

■ **Read** During reading, monitor children's comprehension by providing higher-order thinking questions. Ask:

• Why do you think Jun is afraid of the puppy?

• What are some of the ways both Jun and Pepper changed as they grew up?

To help children gain a better understanding of the text, build upon their responses with a group discussion.

■ ◉ **Story Structure** In small groups, ask children to think about the structure of the story: where the story takes place, who is in the story, and what happens in the beginning, middle, and end of the story. Then have them work together to:

• Describe each of the characters in the story. Where does this family live? Who is this story mainly about?

• Find the most important events in the story.

■ **Text to Self** Help children make personal connections to the story. Ask:

• Have you ever been afraid of something? What? What happened to help you get over your fear?

Objectives
• Comprehend texts drawing on useful strategies as needed.
• Make inferences about the elements of fiction.

 DAY 4

Conventions

- ■ **Plural Nouns That Change Spelling** Remind children that some nouns change spelling when they are plural.

  - If there is one goose, we say *goose*. What if there are two? Write the word *geese* on the board. There is one *goose* but two *geese*.

  - Draw one mouse and then draw two mice together. Point to the first picture. This is one *mouse*. Point to the next picture. This shows two *mice*. Write the appropriate words underneath each picture.

  Continue modeling the same way with other plural nouns that change spelling such as *half (halves), man (men),* and *foot (feet).* In small groups, children can come up with plural nouns that change spelling. Have each group share their plural nouns. Then ask children to use the plural nouns in oral sentences.

Objectives
- Understand and use nouns (plural) in the context of reading, writing, and speaking.

More Reading
Use Leveled Readers or other text at children's instructional level.

 DAY 5

Phonics Review

- ■ **Plurals *-s, -es, -ies*** Have children practice blending and reading words that contain this week's target phonics skills. Write the following words on the board, and say and sound out each word with the children.

legs	stones	stories	branches	houses
kitties	cars	inches	patties	pushes

Then have children sort the words ending in *-s, -es,* and *-ies* into different groups.

Objectives
- Decode words by applying knowledge of common spelling patterns.

Small Group Time

5 Day Plan

DAY 1	• Phonics • Comprehension
DAY 2	• Comprehension • Main Selection
DAY 3	• Leveled Reader
DAY 4	• Comprehension • Paired Selection
DAY 5	• Fluency • Comprehension

3 or 4 Day Plan

DAY 1	• Phonics • Comprehension
DAY 2	• Comprehension • Main Selection
DAY 3	• Leveled Reader
DAY 4	• Comprehension • Paired Selection

3 Day Plan: Eliminate the shaded box

A — Advanced — DAY 1

Phonics • Comprehension

■ **Plurals -s, -es, -ies, -ves** Write the words *ponies, pets, ranches, calves,* and *countries* on the board and ask children to tell what was added to make the words plural. Then have them form plurals with the following words.

reply	watch	nursery	scarf	wish
buffalo	student	beauty	speech	wolf

■ **Advanced Selection 9** Before reading, have children identify these words from the story: *volunteers* and *nurseries*. If they do not know the words, provide oral sentences with the words in context. After reading, have children recall the two most important ideas of the story.

Advanced Selection 9

Objectives
• Decode words by applying knowledge of common spelling patterns.

A — Advanced — DAY 2

Comprehension

■ **Comprehension** Have children silently read this week's main selection, *The Bremen Town Musicians*. Have them retell the story, focusing on what happens and why it happens. Talk about what makes *The Bremen Town Musicians* a fairy tale. (It has animals that act like people.)

■ **Text to Text** Have children identify other stories they have read that are fairy tales and explain why.

The Bremen Town Musicians

Objectives
• Make inferences about text using textual evidence to support understanding.

A Advanced

DAY 3

For a complete literacy instructional plan and additional practice with this week's target skills and strategies, see the **Leveled Reader Teaching Guide.**

Advanced Leveled Reader

■ **Activate Prior Knowledge** Read the title, the author's name, and the illustrator's name. Have children look at the cover and ask them to describe in detail what they see. Ask them what they think the title *Stripes and Silver* refers to. Then activate children's prior knowledge by asking them to identify different characteristics of squirrels and chipmunks.

■ **Cause and Effect** Before reading, remind children that cause and effect describes something that happens and why it happens. Guide children to pay attention to events in the story and what caused them to happen.

Advanced Leveled Reader

■ **Read** During reading, monitor children's comprehension by providing higher-order thinking questions. Ask:

• Why do you think Stripes and Silver are looking for food? What will happen if they don't find food to store before winter?

• Describe how working together will help the animals before winter comes.

Build on children's answers to help them gain a better understanding of the text.

■ **Story Structure** Have children think about how most stories involve a problem and a solution to that problem. Have pairs of children figure out the conflict of the story and how the characters resolve the conflict. Ask:

• What is the conflict between Stripes and Silver? What is Tess's problem in the story?

• How is the conflict between Stripes and Silver resolved? How do the other animals help Tess with her problem?

■ **Text to World** Help children make connections to the story. Ask:

• Think about how other living things prepare for winter. What are some ways plants, animals, and people might get ready for winter?

More Reading
Use Leveled Readers or other text at children's instructional level.

Objectives
• Comprehend texts drawing on useful strategies as needed.

Small Group Time

More Reading
Use Leveled Readers or other text at children's instructional level.

A Advanced **DAY 4**

Comprehension

■ **Comprehension** Have children silently read this week's paired selection, "A Fool Goes Fishing." Have them retell the story identifying characters, setting, and sequence of events. Then have them summarize what they think were the most important ideas from the story.

Talk about what makes "A Fool Goes Fishing" a folk tale. (Parts of the story are repeated, there is a conflict, and there is a lesson.) Then have the children find examples in the story to help them explain why it is a folk tale.

A Fool Goes Fishing

■ **Text to Text** Have children identify other stories they have read that are folk tales and explain why.

Objectives
• Identify moral lessons as themes in well-known fables, legends, myths, or stories.

A Advanced **DAY 5**

Fluency • Comprehension

■ **Fluency** Using the first few sentences of Advanced Selection 9, model reading with expression. Then have children read the selection to a partner as you listen. Provide corrective feedback as needed.

■ **Comprehension** After they have finished reading the selection, have children retell the main events in the story, focusing on the sequence of events. Then, on the back of the selection page, have them write three sentences that describe what job they would like to do most at the zoo.

Advanced Selection 9

Objectives
• Read aloud grade-level appropriate text with fluency.

Support for English Language Learners

The ELL lessons are organized by strands. Use them to scaffold the weekly lesson curriculum or during small-group time.

Concept Development

 Why is it a good idea to work together?

- **Activate Prior Knowledge** Write the Question of the Week and read it aloud. Underline the words *work together* and have children say them with you. When people work together, a group of people help each other get a job done. Show a picture of a group of musicians. These musicians are working together to play music. How do you think the music would sound if one of these musicians were not there? (wouldn't sound the same; wouldn't sound good)

- **Connect to New Concept** Have children turn to pp. 278–279 in the Student Edition. Read the title and have children track the print as you read it. Point to the pictures one at a time and use them to guide a discussion about how working together helps get the job done. For example, point to the boys rowing a canoe. What are these boys doing? (rowing a canoe) These boys are working together to row their canoe. It's easier to row when everybody is working together.

- **Develop Concepts** Display ELL Poster 9 and have children identify the setting of the poster. (park, wintertime) What are the people doing? Have children point to the people's activities on the poster. (building a snowman, making a snow angel, swinging, shoveling, walking) Use the leveled prompts below to assess understanding and build oral language. Point to pictures on the poster as you guide discussion.

  Beginning Ask yes/no questions, such as Does the snowman have a carrot nose? Is the snowman tall?

  Intermediate Ask children questions that can be answered with simple sentences. What are the snowman's arms made of? What is the snowman holding? Why is it holding an umbrella?

  Advanced/Advanced-High Have children answer the Question of the Week by giving specific examples from the poster and their own experiences.

- **Review Concepts and Connect to Writing** Review children's understanding of the concept at the end of the week. Ask them to write in response to these questions: How does working together help get the job done? What English words did you learn this week? Write and display key ideas from the discussion.

Content Objectives
- Describe solving problems.

Language Objectives
- Share information orally.
- Use basic vocabulary for discussing working together.

Daily Planner

DAY 1
- Frontload Concepts
- Preteach Comprehension Skill, Vocabulary, Phonemic Awareness/Phonics, Conventions/Writing

DAY 2
- Review Concepts, Vocabulary, Comprehension Skill
- Frontload Main Selection
- Practice Phonemic Awareness/Phonics, Conventions/Writing

DAY 3
- Review Concepts, Comprehension Skill, Vocabulary, Conventions/Writing
- Reread Main Selection
- Practice Phonemic Awareness/Phonics

DAY 4
- Review Concepts
- Read ELL/ELD Readers
- Practice Phonemic Awareness/Phonics, Conventions/Writing

DAY 5
- Review Concepts, Vocabulary, Comprehension Skill, Phonemic Awareness/Phonics, Conventions/Writing
- Reread ELL/ELD Readers

*See the ELL Handbook for ELL Workshops with targeted instruction.

Concept Talk Video

Use this week's Concept Talk Video to help children build background knowledge about working together. See the Concept Talk Video Routine (*ELL Handbook*, p. 464) for suggestions.

Support for English Language Learners

Language Objectives

- Substitute initial phonemes.
- Identify and pronounce plural forms of words.
- Use linguistic support to enhance understanding.

 **Transfer Skills**

In Chinese and Vietnamese, nouns do not have a plural form. Adjectives indicate whether a noun is singular or plural. Have children practice by talking about real objects, such as *one pen, two pens*.

ELL Teaching Routine

For more practice with plurals, use the Sound-by-Sound Blending Routine (*ELL Handbook*, p. 457).

Phonemic Awareness: Substitute Initial Phonemes

■ **Preteach**

- Have children open to pp. 280–281. What are these red animals? (foxes) Say the word *foxes* emphasizing the initial sound. I am going to say the sounds in *foxes*. Listen for the first sound: /f/ /o/ /ks/ /ez/. The first sound I hear is /f/. Say the beginning sound with me: /f/. Now what happens if we change the first sound in the word *foxes* to /b/? What word do we have now? (boxes) Say the new word with me: *boxes*.

- Point out other pictures on the pages and guide children in substituting initial phonemes to make new words. For example, *house/mouse, sticks/chicks, skunks/trunks*.

■ **Practice** Listen again to hear how changing the beginning sound in a word can make a new word: *trees, bees*. Say the following word pairs and ask children to identify the pairs in which only the initial sound has changed:

hat/hot	saw/straw	lakes/bakes	fits/kits	run/ran

Phonics: Plurals

■ **Preteach** Display Sound-Spelling Card 139. This word is *peaches*. To make the plural form of most nouns you add an *s*. If the noun ends in *s, ch, th, tch, or x*, you add *-es*. To get the plural form of the word peach you add *-es*. The new word is *peaches*. Say the word with me: *peaches*. Display Sound-Spelling Card 142. This word is *babies*. If a word ends in *y*, you make the plural form by changing *y* to *i* and adding *-es*. *Babies* is the plural form of the word *baby*. Say the word with me: *babies*.

■ **Listen and Write** Distribute Write and Wipe Boards.

- Write the word *inches* on the board. Copy this word. As you write *-es*, say the sound to yourself: /ez/. Now say the sound aloud. (/ez/) Underline *es* in *inches*. We add *-es* to words ending in *ch* to make them plural.

- Repeat the instruction for *-ies* using the word *babies*. For words that end in *y*, we replace the *y* with *i* and add *-es* to make them plural.

Objectives

- Use visual, contextual, and linguistic support to enhance and confirm understanding of increasingly complex and elaborated spoken language. Learn relationships between sounds and letters of the English language and decode (sound out) words using a combination of skills such as recognizing sound-letter relationships and identifying cognates, affixes, roots, and base words.

Reteach and Practice

- Write *-s, -es,* and *-ies* as headings for a three-column chart as children do the same on their own paper. Then write the following nouns next to the chart: *bunny, kiss, expert, basket, brush, puppy, order, scratch, circus, army, story, quarter*.

- Have children read each base word and check for a possible spelling change before they spell the plural in their own chart. Then blend and read the plural as a group. Monitor children's work. For corrective feedback, model the correct spelling and have children correct their writing.

Beginning/Intermediate Have children say the plural forms of the words. Monitor for accurate pronunciation.

Advanced/Advanced-High Have children say and write the plural forms of the words. Monitor for accurate spelling and pronunciation.

Vocabulary: Homophones

■ **Preteach** Have children turn to p. 286 in the Student Edition.

- Remember that some words in English are pronounced the same but have different spellings and meanings. Let's look at some words on this page. Look at the word *no* in this sentence: *He could no longer work hard.* Write the word *no* on the board.

- What is another word that sounds like *no* but is spelled differently? That's right, *know*, as in to *know something*. Write the word *know* underneath *no*. These two words sound the same but have different meanings and spellings. They are homophones.

■ **Practice** Focus on other homophones throughout the selection, such as *heard/herd, be/bee, hear/here, weak/week, road/rode*. Have children say the words aloud and discuss the meaning of the word in the selection and its homophone. Then have children use the homophones in oral sentences.

Content Objectives

- Identify and define homophones.

Language Objectives

- Associate endings *-s, -es,* and *-ies* with the plural forms of words.

Catch Up

A base word is a word to which other word parts can be added to make a new word.

Transfer Skills

In Spanish, plurals are formed by adding *-s* to words ending in a vowel *(padre/padres)* and *-es* to words ending in a consonant *(pared, paredes)*. Spanish speakers may thus add *-es* to any words ending in a consonant *(girles* instead of *girls)*.

Objectives

- Speak using grade-level content area vocabulary in context to internalize new English words and build academic language proficiency.
- Learn relationships between sounds and letters of the English language and decode words using a combination of skills such as recognizing sound-letter relationships and identifying cognates, affixes, roots, and base words.
- Learn relationships between sounds and letters of the English language to represent sounds when writing in English.

Content Objectives

- Monitor and adjust oral comprehension.

Language Objectives

- Discuss oral passages.
- Understand general meaning of spoken language.
- Use a graphic organizer to take notes.

Graphic Organizer

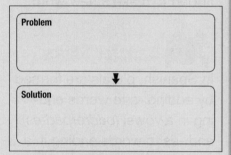

ELL Teacher Tip

Organize children into pairs. Have children use the graphic organizer to retell the story to their partner in their own words.

Language Opportunity

Understanding General Meaning Have children demonstrate comprehension of the reading on pp. 284–303 of the Student Edition by using the graphic organizer to take notes on its general meaning and important details.

ELL English Language Learners

Listening Comprehension

The Big Orange Cat

Once upon a time, there were three little mice. They lived in a beautiful park in the city. One day a big orange alley cat moved in. All of the mice in the park feared the cat. The mice thought the cat could swallow a mouse whole!

The three little mice needed a solution to their problem. They worked together. They decided to find a place to hide.

The three little mice thought and thought. They looked around the park. Finally the third little mouse spotted a small hole in the bottom of a drinking fountain. "Let's hide there," he yelled. They worked together again. They gathered old bottle caps, twigs, and small pieces of broken clay. They used these things to hide the opening to their new home.

At last, their new home was ready. "It's lovely," said one of the three little mice. "And just in time. Hurry! Here comes the alley cat!"

The three little mice hurried into their new home. They peeked at the cat from behind the new door. They giggled to themselves as the big alley cat walked away. The three little mice lived happily ever after.

Prepare for the Read Aloud The modified Read Aloud above prepares children for listening to the oral reading "Three Little Mice" on p. 283b.

- **First Listening: Listen to Understand** Write the title of the Read Aloud on the board. I am going to read a story about three mice who work together to find a safe place from a big cat. Listen to learn how they work together to find a solution to their problem. After reading, ask children to recall the characters and the events in the story. What is the problem facing the three mice? (the big orange cat) How do they solve their problem? (build a new safe house)

- **Second Listening: Listen to Check Understanding** Using a Problem and Solution graphic organizer (*ELL Handbook*, p. 477), work with children to recall the characters and the events. Ask questions as you fill in the graphic organizer. Have pairs support each other's understanding of the story.

Objectives

- Understand the general meaning, main points, and important details of spoken language ranging from situations in which topics, language, and contexts are familiar to familiar.
- Use visual and contextual support from peers and teachers to read grade-appropriate content area text, enhance and confirm understanding, and develop vocabulary, grasp of language structures, and background knowledge needed to comprehend increasingly challenging language.

English Language Learners

High-Frequency Words

- **Preteach** Give each pair of children one or more of the Word Cards. Provide clues for each high-frequency word's meaning, such as acting *scared,* pointing to a *sign* in the classroom, or drawing several stick *people* on the board.

- **Practice** Have children hold up the appropriate Word Cards as you present clues.

  Beginning Model the correct pronunciation of each word. Have students say the high-frequency word as you present each clue.

  Intermediate Have students read and repeat the words aloud. Have each pair of students create a clue for one or two words.

  Advanced/Advanced-High Monitor children as they take turns reading each word to a partner. Then have children make a clue for each word.

- **Speaking/Writing with High-Frequency Words**

  - **Teach/Model** Write the sentences on the board. Model filling in the missing word from the first sentence. 1. I ___ a hat to keep my head warm. (bought) 2. It was crowded at the fair. There were lots of ___. (people) 3. My sister and I had a ___ day at the park. (pleasant) 4. It will ___ snow tonight. (probably) 5. I was ___ when I heard a noise outside. (scared) 6. What ___ we do after school? (shall) 7. The ___ tells us to cross the street. (sign)

  - **Practice** Give each pair of children a set of the Word Cards. Have them work together to find the correct word for each sentence you read.

  Beginning Read the sentences aloud, filling in a gesture for each missing word. Have children hold up the correct Word Card for each sentence, then write each word.

  Intermediate Have children write the missing words. Have them use the Word Cards as a spelling resource.

  Advanced/Advanced-High Have children write the high-frequency words. Children can make up a sentence with a partner.

Language Objectives
- Understand and use high-frequency vocabulary.
- Expand initial vocabulary by learning routine classroom language.

Beginners Support
Have children draw and label a drawing using their word. Then have them dictate a sentence. Have them copy their sentence on their paper below their drawing.

ELL Workshop
Children can use the selection art to retell stories or information in selections. Support children with *Retell or Summarize* (*ELL Handbook,* pp. 406–407).

Objectives
- Internalize new basic and academic language by using and reusing it in meaningful ways in speaking and writing activities that build concept and language attainment.
- Expand and internalize initial English vocabulary by learning and using high-frequency words necessary for identifying and describing people, places, and objects, by retelling simple stories and basic information represented or supported by pictures, and by learning and using routine language needed for classroom communication.

Support for English Language Learners

Content Objectives
- Identify cause and effect.
- Use cause and effect to aid comprehension.

Language Objectives
- Discuss evidence of cause and effect.
- Retell causes and effects from reading.
- Write causes and effects.

ELL Workshop
Encourage children to ask questions to monitor their understanding of instruction of comprehension skills. Use *Ask Clarifying Questions* (*ELL Handbook*, pp. 402–403) for practice.

ELL English Language Learners

Guide Comprehension
Cause and Effect

■ **Preteach** Model by pantomiming as you define *cause* and *effect*. A cause explains why something happened, and an effect explains what happened. Set a book on your desk and then knock it over. What happened? (the book fell over) Why did it happen? (because I hit the book with my hand)

■ **Practice** Have children turn to Envision It! on p. El•3 in the Student Edition. Discuss the pictures with children. Have them point to the effect when you ask what happened, and point to the cause when you asked why this happened.

■ **Reteach/Practice** Distribute copies of the Picture It! (*ELL Handbook*, p. 78). Have children look at the images. Choral read the passage with the students. Why did Pig offer Cat a ride on his back? Write *cause* and *effect* on the board. Guide the children in identifying the cause and effect and recording it on the board. Repeat by asking: Why did Cat leave Pig? (**Answers** 1. b 2. b)

Beginning Read the story to the children as they follow along. Have children look at the pictures and retell the story to a partner. Guide the children in understanding the cause-and-effect relationships by asking why each of the actions is happening.

Intermediate/Advanced/Advanced-High Have the children read the passage with a partner. Write the following sentences on the board: *Cat was tired so ___. Cat left Pig because ___.* Have children work with their partner to complete each sentence frame. Discuss as a group and guide children in understanding the cause-and-effect relationship.

MINI-LESSON

Academic Language

Have children use cause and effect to talk about school-related topics. If the weather is nice, we can go outside for recess. Nice weather is the cause, and going outside is the effect. If the weather is bad, we will stay inside. What is the cause? (bad weather) What is the effect? (staying inside)

Objectives
- Internalize new basic and academic language by using it and reusing it in meaningful ways in speaking and writing activities that build language attainment.
- Develop and expand repertoire of learning strategies such as reasoning inductively or deductively, looking for patterns in language, and analyzing sayings and expressions commensurate with grade-level learning expectations.

ELL English Language Learners

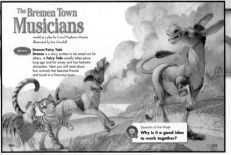
Student Edition pp. 284–285

Reading Comprehension
The Bremen Town Musicians

■ **Frontloading**

- **Background Knowledge** Read the title aloud and discuss it. Do you know how to play an instrument? Do you know someone who is a musician?

- **Preview** Guide children on a picture walk through the story, asking them to identify people, places, and actions. Reteach these words using visuals in the Student Edition: *owner* (p. 286), *friend* (p. 288), *whispered* (p. 296), *feast* (p. 299).

- **Predict** What do you think will happen to the Bremen town musicians?

Sheltered Reading Ask questions such as the following to guide children's comprehension:

- p. 286: Point to the donkey. Who is this? (a donkey) What is he doing? (carrying heavy bags of grain to the mill)

- p. 291: Point to the cat. Who is this? (a cat) What kind of song does a cat have? Read the sentence that tells you the answer.

- p. 296: Point to the picture of the animals working together to look in the window. How do the animals work together to look in the window? (They stood on each other's backs.)

- p. 300: Why did the robbers run away? (They thought there were monsters in the house.)

■ **Fluency: Expression** Remind children that reading with expression means to read like you are speaking when you talk to a friend. Read the Donkey's lines on p. 287, modeling the excitement in your voice when you read "People will love me!" Point out that punctuation like exclamation points and question marks give clues on how to read expressively. Have pairs choose a paragraph on p. 288. Have children narrate expressively as their partners listen and offer feedback. For more practice, use the Fluency: Oral Rereading Routine (*ELL Handbook*, p. 461).

After Reading Help children summarize the text with the Retelling Cards. Ask questions that prompt children to summarize the important parts of the text.

Content Objectives
- Monitor and adjust comprehension.
- Make and adjust predictions.

Language Objectives
- Read grade-level text with expression.
- Express ideas.
- Summarize text using visual support.

Graphic Organizer

Animal	Animal's Song

Audio Support
Children can prepare for reading *The Bremen Town Musicians* by using the eSelection or the AudioText CD. See the AudioText CD Routine (*ELL Handbook*, p. 464).

English Summary
Read the English summary of *The Bremen Town Musicians* (*ELL Handbook*, p. 79). Children can ask questions about ideas or unfamiliar words. Send copies home for children to read with family members.

Objectives
- Express opinions, ideas, and feelings ranging from communicating single words and short phrases to participating in extended discussions on a variety of social and grade-appropriate academic topics.

ELL Reader   ELD Reader

For additional leveled instruction, see the **ELL/ELD Reader Teaching Guide.**

Comprehension:
Big News in the Barn

■ **Before Reading** Distribute copies of the ELL and ELD Readers, *Big News in the Barn*, to children at their reading level.

- **Preview** Read the title aloud with children: This is a story about animals in a barn who hear some big news. Activate prior knowledge. This story takes place on a farm. What do you know about farms?

- **Set a Purpose for Reading** Let's read to find out what the big news is.

■ **During Reading** Follow this Reading Routine for both reading groups.

1. Read the entire Reader aloud slowly as children follow along and finger point.

2. Reread the Reader one sentence at a time, having children echo read after you.

■ **After Reading** Use the exercises on the inside back cover of *Big News in the Barn* and invite children to share drawings and writing. In a whole-group discussion, ask children to identify what happened after the animals learned the big news. How did working together help them get the job done?

ELD Reader   Beginning/Intermediate

■ **pp. 4–5** Why was the barn still messy after the animals started cleaning? (They weren't working together.)

■ **pp. 6–7** Point to the hens. What animal is this? (hen) What are the hens doing? (picking up corn)

Writing Draw and label a picture or write a sentence about a time you worked together with other people to get something done.

ELL Reader   Advanced/Advanced-High

■ **pp. 2–3** What big news does Dog have? (A baby pig is coming to live in the barn.)

■ **pp. 4–5** What do the animals decide to do? (clean the barn)

Study Guide Distribute copies of the ELL Reader Study Guide (*ELL Handbook*, p. 82). Scaffold comprehension by prompting children to point to pictures in the book that show the barn before, during, and after being cleaned. Review their responses together. (See *ELL Handbook*, pp. 209–212.)

Objectives

- Ask and give information ranging from using a very limited bank of high-frequency, high-need, concrete vocabulary, including key words and expressions needed for basic communication in academic and social contexts, to using abstract and content-based vocabulary during extended speaking assignments.

 English Language Learners

Conventions
Plural Nouns That Change Spelling

■ **Preteach** Remind children that a noun is a person, place, thing, or animal. Explain that in English you can make most nouns plural by adding an *s, es, ies,* or *ves.* Offer the following examples: dog/dogs, wish/wishes, baby/babies, and shelf/shelves. Then tell children that some plural nouns are irregular because the spelling of the word changes. Write and say the following examples. Use gestures or visual support to communicate meaning. *Foot/feet, goose/geese, mouse/mice, man/men.*

■ **Practice** Use the Student Edition to provide practice for children at their language proficiency level.

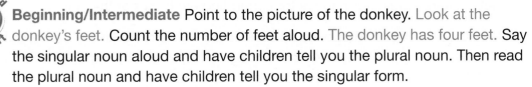 Leveled LS Support

Beginning/Intermediate Point to the picture of the donkey. Look at the donkey's feet. Count the number of feet aloud. The donkey has four feet. Say the singular noun aloud and have children tell you the plural noun. Then read the plural noun and have children tell you the singular form.

Advanced/Advanced-High Have children write sentences using irregular plural nouns based on pictures in the Student Edition.

■ **Reteach**

• Use visual support, such as pictures or photographs, to demonstrate using plural nouns that change spelling. For example, hold up a picture of a group of children. There are many children in this picture. This child is the tallest.

• Write the words *children* and *child* on the board. Which word is singular? Which word is plural? Repeat this task several times using different pictures and nouns.

■ **Practice** Provide practice at children's language proficiency level.

Leveled LS Support

Beginning/Intermediate In pairs, ask children to make a list of three plural nouns that change spelling. Then ask children to make the nouns singular. Monitor spelling and pronunciation.

Advanced/Advanced-High Have children write two sentences that use plural nouns that change spelling.

Content Objectives
• Identify and use plural nouns that change spelling.
• Correctly use plural nouns that change spellings.

Language Objectives
• Speak using plural nouns that change spellings.
• Write phrases and sentences with plurals that change spellings.

 ## Transfer Skills
If children have literacy skills in Spanish, compare how some English and Spanish nouns change their spelling when forming the plural. For example, *pez* (*fish*) in Spanish becomes *peces* (*fishes*, or the plural *fish*).

Grammar Jammer
For more practice with plural nouns, use the Grammar Jammer for this target skill. See the Grammar Jammer Routine (*ELL Handbook*, p. 465) for suggestions on using this learning tool.

Support for English Language Learners

Content Objectives

- Identify words that indicate parts of a story.
- Identify the characteristics of a fairy tale.

Language Objectives

- Write sentences showing the beginning, middle, and end of a story.
- Explain with increasing detail.
- Share feedback for editing and revising.

 **Transfer Skills**

Fairy tales are found in all cultures. Instead of the story starter, you may choose to ask children to retell a fairy tale that they know from their own culture and heritage.

ELL Teaching Routine

For practice spelling words related to working together, use the Spelling Routine (*ELL Handbook*, p. 463).

Language Opportunity

Explaining With Detail Have children practice explaining with increasing detail as a prewriting activity to the writing assignment on the Student Edition p. 304. Instruct students to include a variety of sentence lengths in their writing.

Write a Fairy Tale

- **Introduce Terms** Write *fairy tale* on the board. Explain the meaning of *fairy* by briefly describing the fairy tale elements of *The Bremen Town Musicians*. A fairy tale is a made up story. Many fairy tales begin, *Once upon a time . . .* and end, *They lived happily ever after.*

- **Describe Story Parts** Explain that fairy tales have a beginning, middle, and end. Write these sentences on the board:

  Beginning: Once upon a time there was a girl named Emily.

  Middle: Emily met a prince.

  End: Emily and the prince lived happily after ever.

  Help children brainstorm ideas for expanding each part of the story.

- **Model** Draw three large boxes on connected with arrows on the board. Label them *Beginning, Middle,* and *End*. Engage children in thinking of how Emily and the prince meet. Write sentences in the boxes.

Beginning	→	Middle	→	End

- **Write** Have children copy this story starter: *Once upon a time there was a lonely dog.* Have them draw three large boxes under the sentence and label them *Beginning, Middle,* and *Last*. Have partners work together to imagine what will happen in this story.

Beginning Supply the graphic organizer. Write the words *Beginning, Middle,* and *End* in your boxes. Think of what might happen to this lonely dog. Draw something that happens in the beginning, the middle, and the end. Have children tell about their pictures. Supply vocabulary if necessary and have children copy sentences in the appropriate boxes.

Intermediate Guide children's writing. Assist children as they brainstorm ideas. Help them with spelling and vocabulary choices.

Advanced/Advanced-High Have children use the boxes for prewriting. Then have them write their sentences in paragraph form.

Objectives

- Narrate, describe, and explain with increasing specificity and detail as more English is acquired.
- Use visual and contextual support from peers and teachers to read grade-appropriate content area text, enhance and confirm understanding, and develop vocabulary, grasp of language structures, and background knowledge needed to comprehend increasingly challenging language.

This Week on Reading Street!

Question of the Week
How can we work together to solve problems?

Working Together

Daily Plan

Don't Wait Until Friday

Whole Group
- ◉ Vowel Patterns *a, ai, ay*
- ◉ Compare and Contrast
- • Fluency
- • Vocabulary

MONITOR PROGRESS | **Success Predictor**

Day 1 Check Word Reading	Day 2 Check High-Frequency Words	Day 3 Check Retelling	Day 4 Check Fluency	Day 5 Check Oral Vocabulary

Small Group

Teacher-Led
- • Reading Support
- • Skill Support
- • Fluency Practice

Practice Stations

Independent Activities

Customize Literacy More support for a Balanced Literacy approach, see pp. CL•1–CL•45.

Customize Writing More support for a customized writing approach, see pp. CW•11–CW•20.

Whole Group
- • Writing: Folk Tale
- • Conventions: Possessive Nouns
- • New Literacies

Assessment
- • Weekly Tests
- • Day 5 Assessment
- • Fresh Reads

You Are Here! Unit 2 Week 5

Week 5

This Week's Reading Selections

Main Selection
Genre: **Folk Tale**

Paired Selection

Decodable Practice Readers

Leveled Readers

ELL and ELD Readers

Resources on Reading Street!

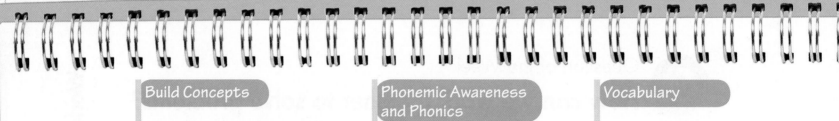

	Build Concepts	Phonemic Awareness and Phonics	Vocabulary
Whole Group	 Student Edition pp. 314–315 Sing with Me	 Student Edition pp. 316–319 Sound-Spelling Cards	 Student Edition p. 319
Go Digital	• Concept Talk Video • Sing with Me Animations	• Interactive Sound-Spelling Cards • Decodable eReaders	• Vocabulary Activities • Journal Word Bank
Small Group and Independent Practice	 Practice Station Flip Chart Leveled Readers ELL and ELD Readers	 Practice Station Flip Chart Decodable Practice Readers	 Practice Station Flip Chart Student Edition p. 319
Go Digital	• eReaders	• Decodable eReaders • Letter Tile Drag and Drop	• Journal Word Bank • Vocabulary Activities
Customize Literacy	• Leveled Readers	• Decodable Practice Readers	• High-Frequency Word Cards
Go Digital	• Concept Talk Video • Big Question Video • eReaders	• Interactive Sound-Spelling Cards • Decodable eReaders	• Sing with Me Animations • Vocabulary Activities

Question of the Week
How can we work together to solve problems?

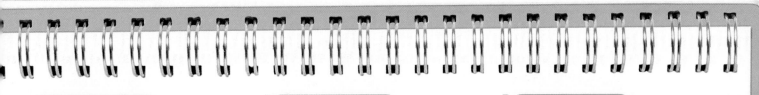

Comprehension	Fluency	Conventions and Writing
 Student Edition pp. 320–335	Decodable Practice Readers	 Student Edition pp. 338–339
• Envision It! Animations • eSelections	• eSelections • eReaders	• Grammar Jammer
Practice Station Flip Chart Leveled Readers ELL and ELD Readers	Practice Station Flip Chart Decodable Practice Readers	Practice Station Flip Chart Reader's and Writer's Notebook
• eReaders • Story Sort	• Decodable eReaders	• Grammar Jammer
• Envision It! Skills and Strategies Handbooks • Leveled Readers	• Leveled Readers	*Reader's and Writer's Notebook*
• Envision It! Animations • eReaders	• eReaders	• Grammar Jammer

Week 5

You Are Here!
Unit 2
Week 5

My 5-Day Planner for Reading Street!

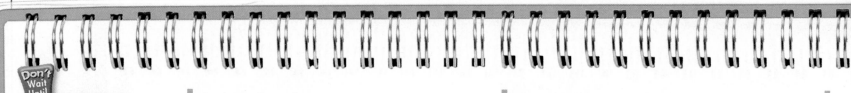

Don't Wait Until Friday
SUCCESS PREDICTOR

	Check Word Reading **Day 1** pages 314j–319f	Check High-Frequency Words **Day 2** pages 320a–335f

Get Ready to Read	**Concept Talk,** 314j–315
	Oral Vocabulary, 316a–316b *conflict, pursue, resolve*
	Phonemic Awareness, 316–317
	  Substitute Final Phonemes
	Phonics, 317a–318a
	  ◉ Vowel Patterns *a, ai, ay*
	READ Decodable Practice Reader 10A, 318b–318c
	Spelling, 318d Pretest
		Concept Talk, 320a–320b
		Oral Vocabulary, 320b
		  deserve
		Review **Phonics,** 320c
		  ◉ Vowel Patterns *a, ai, ay*
		Spelling, 320d Practice

Read and Comprehend	**High-Frequency Words,** 319
	  Introduce *behind, brought, door, everybody, minute, promise, sorry*
	Listening Comprehension, 319a–319b
	  ◉ Compare and Contrast
		High-Frequency Words, 320e
		  Build Fluency *behind, brought, door, everybody, minute, promise, sorry*
		Story Words, 320f
		  Introduce *armadillo, creature, grateful, groaned, snorted*
		Vocabulary, 320f Unfamiliar Words
		Build Background, 320g
		READ Main Selection—First Read, 320h–335
		  One Good Turn Deserves Another
		Literary Text, 335a Setting, Character, and Plot

Language Arts	**Conventions,** 319c Possessive Nouns
	Writing, 319d–319e
	  Folk Tale
	Research and Inquiry, 319f
	  Identify and Focus Topic
		Conventions, 335b Possessive Nouns
		Writing, 335c–335d Folk Tale
		  Writer's Craft: Know Your Purpose
		Handwriting, 335e
		  Manuscript *q, Q, v, V:* Letter Spacing
		Research and Inquiry, 335f
		  Research Skill: Reading a Web Page

You Are Here!
Unit 2
Week 5

Check Retelling	Check Fluency	Check Oral Vocabulary
Day 3 pages 336a–339b	**Day 4** pages 340a–343f	**Day 5** pages 344a–345k
Concept Talk, 336a–336b **Oral Vocabulary,** 336b *mope* **Phonics,** 336c ◉ Vowel Patterns *a, ai, ay* **READ Decodable Practice Passage 10B,** 336d **Spelling,** 336e Dictation	**Concept Talk,** 340a–340b **Oral Vocabulary,** 340b *coax, ramp, startle* `Review` **Phonics,** 340c Plurals `Review` **Fluent Word Reading,** 340d **READ Decodable Practice Reader 10C,** 340e–340f **Spelling,** 340g Partner Review	**Concept Wrap Up,** 344a `Review` **Oral Vocabulary,** 344b `Review` **Phonics,** 344c Vowel Patterns *a, ai, ay* **Spelling,** 344d Test
Fluency, 336f Accuracy `Review` **High-Frequency Words,** 336g *behind, brought, door, everybody, minute, promise, sorry* `Review` **Story Words,** 336g *armadillo, creature, grateful, groaned, snorted* **READ Main Selection—Second Read,** 320–335, 336h–337a	**Social Studies in Reading,** 340h **READ Paired Selection,** 340–343 "The Lion and the Mouse" **Fluency,** 343a Accuracy	**Vocabulary,** 344–345 Unfamiliar Words **Fluency,** 345a Accuracy **Listening and Speaking,** 345a Give and Follow Instructions `Review` **Comprehension,** 345b Compare and Contrast `Review` **Vocabulary,** 345b High-Frequency and Story Words **Literary Text,** 345c Idioms **Assessment,** 345d–345f Monitor Progress
Conventions, 337b Possessive Nouns **Writing,** 338–339a Folk Tale Writing Trait: Sentences **Research and Inquiry,** 339b Gather and Record Information	**Conventions,** 343b Possessive Nouns **Writing,** 343c–343d Folk Tale Revising Strategy **Listening and Speaking,** 343e Give and Follow Instructions **Research and Inquiry,** 343f Review and Revise Topic	`Review` **Conventions,** 345g Possessive Nouns **Writing,** 345h–345i Folk Tale **Research and Inquiry,** 345j Communicate **Wrap Up Your Week,** 345k ❓ How can we work together to solve problems?

Grouping Options for Differentiated Instruction
Turn the page for the small group time lesson plan.

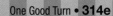

Week 5

Planning Small Group Time on Reading Street!

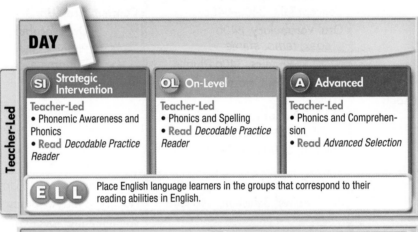

SMALL GROUP TIME RESOURCES

Look for this Small Group Time box each day to help meet the individual needs of all your children. Differentiated Instruction lessons appear on the DI pages at the end of each week.

DAY 1

Teacher-Led

SI Strategic Intervention

Teacher-Led
• Phonemic Awareness and Phonics
• Read *Decodable Practice Reader*

OL On-Level

Teacher-Led
• Phonics and Spelling
• Read *Decodable Practice Reader*

A Advanced

Teacher-Led
• Phonics and Comprehension
• Read *Advanced Selection*

ELL Place English language learners in the groups that correspond to their reading abilities in English.

Practice Stations
• Listen Up
• Word Work

Independent Activities
• *Reader's and Writer's Notebook*
• Concept Talk Video

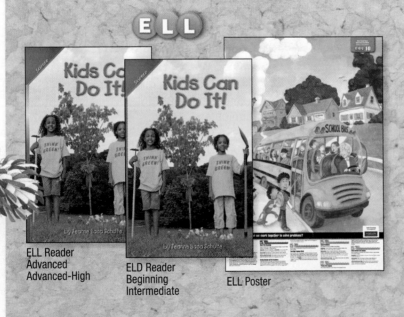

ELL

ELL Reader
Advanced
Advanced-High

Kids Can Do It!

ELD Reader
Beginning
Intermediate

Kids Can Do It!

ELL Poster

You Are Here!
Unit 2
Week 5

Day 1

SI Strategic Intervention	**Phonemic Awareness and Phonics,** DI•85 Read **Decodable Practice Reader 10A,** DI•85
OL On-Level	**Phonics and Spelling,** DI•90 Read **Decodable Practice Reader 10A,** DI•90
A Advanced	**Phonics and Comprehension,** DI•93 Read **Advanced Selection,** DI•93
ELL English Language Learners	DI•96–DI•105 **Concepts and Oral Vocabulary** **Listening (Read Aloud)**

Reading Street Response
to Intervention Kit

Reading Street Leveled
Practice Stations Kit

SI Strategic Intervention

Below-Level Reader

Decodable Practice Readers

Concept Literacy Reader

OL On-Level

On-Level Reader

A Advanced

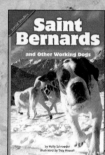

Advanced
Reader

Advanced Selection

Small Group Weekly Plan

Day 2	Day 3	Day 4	Day 5
High-Frequency Words, DI•86 **Read Concept Literacy Leveled Reader,** DI•86	**Phonics,** DI•87 **Read Below-Level Leveled Reader,** DI•87	**High-Frequency Words,** DI•88 **Read Decodable Practice Reader 10C,** DI•88	**Phonics and Comprehension,** DI•89 **Reread Main Selection,** DI•89
High-Frequency Words, DI•90 **Reread Decodable Practice Reader 10A,** DI•90	**Read On-Level Leveled Reader,** DI•91	**Conventions,** DI•92 **Read Leveled Reader,** DI•92	**Phonics Review,** DI•92 **Read On-Level Leveled Reader,** DI•92
Comprehension, DI•93 **Read Main Selection,** DI•93	**Read Advanced Leveled Reader,** DI•94	**Comprehension,** DI•95 **Read Paired Selection,** DI•95	**Fluency and Comprehension,** DI•95 **Reread Advanced Selelction,** DI•95
DI•96–DI•105 Concepts Vocabulary **Phonics and Spelling** **Conventions**	DI•96–DI•105 Concepts Vocabulary **Comprehension Skill** **Main Selection**	DI•96–DI•105 Concepts Vocabulary **ELL/ELD Readers** **ELL Workshop**	DI•96–DI•105 Concepts Vocabulary

Week 5

Practice Stations for Everyone on Reading Street!

Listen Up!
Substitute initial phonemes.

Objectives
• Substitute initial phonemes.

Materials
• *Listen Up!* Flip Chart
• paper
• pencils

Differentiated Activities

 Write the word *mend.* Circle the *m.* Now change the /m/ to another letter sound to make a new word. Do it again to make another word ending in *-end.* Quietly say each word.

▲ Write the word *brand.* Circle the *br.* Change the /b/ /r/ to another letter sound to make a new word. Do it twice more to make three new words ending in *-and.* Quietly say each word.

■ Divide your paper in four columns with the headings *-ing, -eat, -ick,* and *-ore.* Say a letter sound before each phoneme to make all the words you can.

Technology
• Modeled Pronunciation Audio CD
• Interactive Sound-Spelling Cards

Word Work
Make plurals by adding the endings -s, -es, and -ies.

Objectives
• Make plurals by adding the endings *-s, -es,* and *-ies.*

Materials
• *Word Work* Flip Chart
• Teacher-made word cards *puppy, candy, butterfly, berry, address, buzz, scratch, tax, coat, orange, bird,* and *crayon.* Include all 12 spelling words, too.
• paper, pencils, crayons

Differentiated Activities

Group 1: Words ending in -y
         sounding like *e* in deep.   ADD *-ies.*
Group 2: Words ending in
         -s, -ch, -tch, -z, or *-x.*   ADD *-es.*
Group 3: Words ending in other
         letters (except *-o*)   ADD *-s.*

● Take one word card to fit each group. Say it quietly. Draw a picture of it. Write the singular and plural by the picture. Circle the singular word's plural ending. Use a new color for each.

▲ Fold your paper in two columns. Label the left column *Singular* and the right *Plural.* Choose two word cards to fit each group. Write them in the *Singular* column. Then write the correct plurals.

■ Fold your paper in two columns. Label the left column *Singular* and the right *Plural.* Complete the chart by writing all the word card words that fit the groups. Then write their plurals.

Technology
• Interactive Sound-Spelling Cards

Words To Know
Identify homophones.

Objectives
• Identify homophones.
• Choose the correct homophone in context.

Materials
• *Words to Know* Flip Chart
• Teacher-made word cards: *dear/deer, eye/I, ad/add, one/won, read/red, be/bee, too/two, sum/some, write/right, would/wood*
• paper, pencils, crayons

Differentiated Activities

• **Homophones** are words that sound the same but have different meanings.

● Choose one homophone card. Quietly say the words. Think about the meaning of each word. Draw a picture showing the difference in meaning. Write a sentence using each word.

▲ Choose three homophone cards. Pronounce each pair. Write three sentences that each uses *both* words of a homophone pair. Make a poster showing the different meanings of the words in one pair.

■ Use the homophone cards to write a funny story or scene using as many homophone pairs as you can. Underline all of the homophones.

Technology
• Online Tested Vocabulary Activities

You Are Here! Unit 2 Week 5

Use this week's materials from the
Reading Street Leveled Practice Stations
Kit to organize this week's stations.

Key

● Below-Level Activities
▲ On-Level Activities
■ Advanced Activities

Practice Station
Flip Chart

Let's Write!
Write a fairy tale.

Objectives
• Write a fairy tale.
• Organize the story so it has a beginning, middle, and end.

Materials
• *Let's Write!* Flip Chart
• paper
• pencils

Differentiated Activities

• A **fairy tale** is a story in which magical events take place. Fairy tales may have fantastic beings, like talking animals and fairies.

● Write a short fairy tale in which characters work together. Think about your fairy tale's setting. Use pictures to show the beginning, the middle, and the end.

▲ Write a fairy tale in which characters work together. Think about your fairy tale's setting. Give the story a beginning, a middle, and an end.

■ Write a fairy tale in which fantastic characters work together to achieve a common goal. Think about your fairy tale's setting. Organize the story so it has a beginning, a middle, and an end.

Read For Meaning
Identify cause and effect in a story.

Objectives
• Identify cause and effect in a story.

Materials
• *Read for Meaning* Flip Chart
• 2.2.4 Leveled Readers
• cause-and-effect graphic organizer
• paper
• pencils
• crayons

Differentiated Activities

• A **cause** is an event or situation that brings about another event.
• An **effect** is an event brought about by an earlier event (*cause*).

● Think about the causes and effects in *Working Dogs.* Fill in the graphic organizer with one example.

▲ Think about examples of causes and effects in *Growing Up.* Fill in the graphic organizer with two examples. Then add a new example taken from your own experience.

■ Think about examples of causes and effects in *Stripes and Silver.* Fill in the graphic organizer with two examples. Then write a paragraph showing how a different effect might have changed the story.

Technology
• Online Student Edition
• Leveled eReaders

Get Fluent
Practice fluent reading.

Objectives
• Read aloud with expression (characterization).

Materials
• *Get Fluent* Flip Chart
• 2.2.4 Leveled Readers

Differentiated Activities

• **Expression** is how the voice shows emotion or sets a mood.
• **Characterization** is how a writer or speaker shows a character.

● Work with a partner. Take turns reading pages from *Working Dogs.* Read with expression. Pay attention to punctuation. Give your partner feedback.

▲ Work with a partner. Take turns reading pages from *Growing Up.* Read with expression. Pay attention to punctuation. Give your partner feedback.

■ Work with a partner. Take turns reading pages from *Stripes and Silver.* Read with expression. Pay attention to punctuation. Give your partner feedback.

Technology
• Reading Street Readers CD-ROM

My Weekly Work Plan

week 5

Objectives
- Introduce concept: working together to solve problems.
- Share information and ideas about the concept.

Today at a Glance

Oral Vocabulary
conflict, pursue, resolve

Phonemic Awareness
Substitute Final Phonemes

Phonics and Spelling
◉ Vowel Patterns *a, ai, ay*

Fluency
Oral Rereading

High-Frequency Words
behind, brought, door, everybody, minute, promise, sorry

Comprehension
◉ Compare and Contrast

Conventions
Possessive Nouns

Writing
Folk Talk: Introduce

Research and Inquiry
Identify and Focus Topic

Concept Talk

Question of the Week

How can we work together to solve problems?

Introduce the concept

To build concepts and to focus children's attention, tell them that this week they will talk, sing, read, and write about how working together solves problems. Write the Question of the Week and track the print as you read it.

ROUTINE **Activate Prior Knowledge** **Team Talk**

 Think Have children think for a minute about how we can work together to solve problems.

 Pair Have pairs of children discuss the question.

 Share Call on a few children to share their ideas with the group.

Guide discussion and encourage elaboration with prompts such as:
What problem have we solved in class by working together?

Routines Flip Chart

Anchored Talk

Develop oral language

Have children turn to pages 314–315 in their Student Editions. Read the title and look at the photos. Use these questions to guide discussion and create the "How can we work together to solve problems?" concept map.

- Find the picture on page 314. What are the people doing? (They are chasing a remote-controlled car.) *Pursuing* is another word for *chasing*. Let's add *We pursue things* to our map.

- The boys in the picture at the top of the next page are arm wrestling. Sometimes people arm wrestle to resolve conflicts. What sort of conflict could the boys resolve? (Possible response: The boys could have argued over who goes first in a game.) Let's add *We resolve conflicts* to our map.

- What do you think the boys are doing with the bicycle? (Possible response: They are working to fix it.) Let's add *We fix things* to our map.

Objectives
● Listen closely to speakers and ask questions to help you better understand the topic. ● Share information and ideas about the topic. Speak clearly and at a correct pace.

Oral Vocabulary

Let's **Talk** About

Solving Problems
● Share information about solving problems.
● Share ideas about helping those in need.

READING STREET ONLINE
CONCEPT TALK VIDEO
www.ReadingStreet.com

● **You've learned**
0 7 2
Amazing Words
so far this year!

Student Edition pp. 314–315

Amazing Words

You've learned **0 7 2** words so far.

You'll learn **0 0 8** words this week!

conflict	mope
pursue	coax
resolve	ramp
deserve	startle

 **Writing on Demand**

Develop Writing Fluency
Ask children to write about what they know about solving problems by working together. Have them write for two to three minutes. Children should write as much as they can. Tell them to try to do their best writing. You may want to discuss what children wrote during writing conferences.

Connect to reading

Explain that this week, children will read about a coyote that works to save a mouse in need of help. Let's add *We help those in need* to our map.

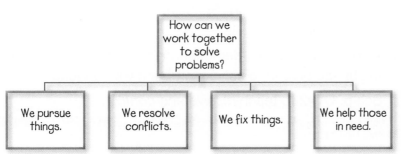

```
            How can we
            work together
            to solve
            problems?
   ┌──────────┬──────────┬──────────┐
We pursue   We resolve  We fix things.  We help those
things.     conflicts.                  in need.
```

ELL **Preteach Concepts** Use the Day 1 instruction on ELL Poster 10 to assess and build background knowledge, develop concepts, and build oral vocabulary.

ELL Poster 10

ELL

English Language Learners

ELL Support Additional support and modified instruction is provided in the *ELL Handbook* and in the ELL Support lessons on pp. DI•96–DI•105.

Visual Support English learners will benefit from additional visual support to understand the key terms in the concept map. Use the pictures on pages 314–315 to scaffold understanding. For example, when talking about pursuing things, point to the picture of the people pursuing the car.

Objectives

- Build oral vocabulary.
- Discuss the concept to develop oral language.
- Share information and ideas about the concept.

Oral Vocabulary
Amazing Words

Introduce Amazing Words

Display p. 10 of the *Sing with Me* Big Book. Tell children they are going to sing about how working together can solve problems. Ask children to listen for the Amazing Words *resolve*, *conflict*, and *pursue* as you sing. Sing the song again and have children join you.

 Sing with Me Big Book Audio

Sing with Me Big Book p. 10

Teach Amazing Words

Amazing Words · Oral Vocabulary Routine

1 Introduce Relate the word *pursue* to the song: The song says that talking it out is a step you can *pursue* when you have a problem with a friend. Supply a child-friendly definition: *Pursue* means "to keep on doing or trying to do something." It can also mean to chase something or someone. Have children say the word.

2 Demonstrate Provide examples to show meaning: I'm going to *pursue* my plan to learn Spanish. Max *pursued* his love of fishing while he was at the lake.

3 Apply Have children demonstrate their understanding: What steps might you *pursue* to solve a problem with a friend?

See p. OV•2 to teach *resolve* and *conflict*.

Routines Flip Chart

Check understanding of Amazing Words

Have children look at the picture on p. 10. It looks like these boys in the picture at the top of the page are arguing. What *conflict* might they have? Use *conflict* in your answer. (Possible response: The boys might have a conflict over whether the soccer ball is inside the goal.)

In the picture at the bottom, the boys look happy. What did they do about their conflict? Use *resolve* in your answer. (Possible response: The boys look like they resolved their conflict.)

Talking it out is a good way to resolve a conflict. When is it something you would want to *pursue?* (Possible response: It is good to pursue talking out a problem when you have an argument.)

Teach Amazing Words

Have children demonstrate their understanding of the Amazing Words by completing these sentences orally.

Carlos and Guillermo want to **resolve** their _____.

The neighbors have a **conflict** over _____.

Carissa **pursues** her interest in _____ by taking lessons.

Corrective feedback

If... children have difficulty using the Amazing Words, **then...** remind them of the definitions. Then provide opportunities for children to use the words in sentences.

Preteach Academic Vocabulary

Write the following on the board:

- **compare and contrast**
- **folk tale**
- **possessive nouns**

Have children share what they know about this week's Academic Vocabulary. Use children's responses to assess their prior knowledge. Preteach the Academic Vocabulary by providing a child-friendly description, explanation, or example that clarifies the meaning of each term. Then ask children to restate the meaning of the Academic Vocabulary in their own words.

Amazing Words

resolve	mope
conflict	coax
pursue	ramp
deserve	startle

ELL

English Language Learners
Pronunciation Spanish-speaking children hear no final consonant blends in Spanish but do hear initial blends such as *bl* in *blanco.* Clarify that English also has consonant blends at the end of words as the sound of /kt/ for the letters *ct* at the end of *conflict.* If children have difficulty pronouncing the /kt/ in *conflict,* say the word slowly, emphasizing the position of the tongue on the roof of the mouth, and have children repeat.

Cognates The words *conflict* and *resolve* may have cognates in children's home languages. Invite Spanish speakers to identify cognates *conflicto* and *resolución.* Point out how this prior knowledge can help children with learning new words.

Objectives

- Recognize the phoneme /ā/ in spoken words.
- Change final phonemes in spoken words.
- ◎ Associate the spellings *a*, *ai*, and *ay* with the long *a* sound.
- ◎ Read words with *a*, *ai*, and *ay*.
- Recognize and divide syllabication patterns to decode words including open syllable (CV).

Skills Trace

◎ **Vowel Patterns:** *a, ai, ay*
Introduce U2W5D1
Practice U2W5D2; U2W5D3; U2W5D4
Reteach/Review U2W5D5; U3W1D4
Assess/Test Weekly Test U2W5
Benchmark Test U2

Key:
U=Unit   W=Week   D=Day

Student Edition pp. 316–317

Phonemic Awareness
Substitute Final Phonemes

Introduce
Have children look at the picture on pages 316–317 of the Student Edition. Read the first bulleted point. We see a beach of an ocean bay. The sound /ā/ is at the end of the word *bay*: /b/ /ā/. What sound is in the middle of the word *snail*? (/ā/) Yes, the sound /ā/ is in *snail*: /s/ /n/ /ā/ /l/, *snail*. Have children identify other things in the picture that have the sound /ā/. (train, sailboats, sail, pail, braid, highway) Now we will make new words by changing the last sound in a word.

Model
Read the second bulleted point. *Pail* has the sounds /p/ /ā/ /l/. Let's change /l/ in *pail* to /n/: /p/ /ā/ /n/, *pain.*

Guide practice
Read aloud the other points on the page and guide children in identifying the final phoneme in *train* (/n/) and *sail* (/l/). Help them find and say other words that end with /l/ *(pail, nail, snail, toenail)*. Have children substitute final phonemes: /l/ in *snail* to /k/ *(snake)*, /n/ in *pain* to /d/ *(paid)*, /l/ in *sail* to /m/ *(same)*, /p/ in *grape* to /d/ *(grade)*, /d/ in *trade* to /n/ *(train)*.

Corrective feedback
If... children make an error,
then... model by segmenting and blending the starting word and have them repeat. Do the same for the changed word. Then say both words.

Phonics—Teach/Model
 Vowel Patterns *a, ai, ay*

ROUTINE

Blending Strategy

1 Connect Write *trade.* Ask children what they know about the vowel sound in this word. (The vowel sound is /ā/, long *a*, spelled *a_e.*) Explain that today they will learn how to spell and read words with the long *a* sound spelled *a, ai,* and *ay.*

2 Use Sound-Spelling Cards Display Card 54. Point to *ai.* The long *a* sound, /ā/, you hear in the word *snail* can be spelled *ai.* Have children say /ā/ several times as you point to *ai.* Repeat with Card 59 for the spelling *ay.*

3 Model Write *snail.* In this word, the letters *ai* stand for the long *a* sound, /ā/. Segment and blend *snail;* then have children segment and blend with you: /s/ /n/ /ā/ /l/, snail. Follow this procedure to model *hay.*

Write *basic.* You can blend a longer word like this if you divide it into syllables. When a word has a vowel-consonant-vowel pattern and you divide it after the first vowel, that vowel often has a long sound. In this word, *ba* is the first syllable, and *a* has the long *a* sound. Blend each syllable and then read them together: /b/ /ā/ - /s/ /i/ /k/, *basic.*

4 Guide Practice Continue the process in step 3. This time have children blend with you. Remind children that /ā/ can be spelled *a, ai,* and *ay.*

aid	play	basin	pain	clay	paper
snail	gray	crater	braid	spray	wafer

5 Review What do you know about reading these words? (The sound /ā/ can be spelled *a, ai,* and *ay.*)

Sound-Spelling Card 54

Sound-Spelling Card 59

Sound-Spelling Card 73

Routines Flip Chart

Differentiated Instruction

SI Strategic Intervention

Reading Two-Syllable Words Remind children that words such as *basin* and *crater* have a VCV pattern, and that when syllables are divided after the first vowel, it usually has a long sound. Have children practice reading such words one syllable at a time and then blending them.

Vocabulary Support

You may wish to explain the meaning of these words.

basin a wide shallow dish; bowl

crater a hole in the ground shaped like a bowl

English Language Learners

Pronunciation Point out that the tongue stays up when saying words with the long *a* sound, such as *snail, hay,* and *basic.*

Language Transfer Spanish speakers may pronounce *ai* and *ay* as these vowel patterns sound in Spanish, producing a long *i* sound. If so, the word *tail* may be pronounced *tile;* the word *bay, by.* Help children recognize these differences between English and Spanish.

Phonics—Build Fluency
⟲ Vowel Patterns *a, ai, ay*

Model

Envision It!

Have children turn to page 318 in their Student Editions. Look at the pictures on this page. I see pictures of *hay* and a *snail*. The word *hay* has the long *a* sound, /ā/, in it. When I say *hay,* I hear /ā/ at the end. Continue with the Envision It! picture of a snail, stressing the long *a* sound.

Guide practice

For each word in *Words I Can Blend,* ask for the sound of each letter or group of letters. Make sure that children identify the correct sound for each long *a* vowel pattern and consonant. Then have children blend the whole word.

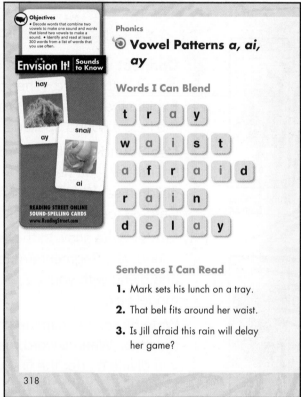
Student Edition p. 318

Corrective feedback

If... children have difficulty blending a word,
then... model blending the word, and then ask children to blend it with you.

Blend and Read

Decode words independent of context

After children can successfully segment and blend the words on page 318 in their Student Editions, point to words in random order and ask children to read them naturally.

Decode words in context

Have children read each of the sentences on page 318. Have them identify words in the sentences that have the long *a* sound.

Team Talk Pair children and have them take turns reading each of the sentences aloud.

On their own

Use *Reader's and Writer's Notebook* p. 145.

Reader's and Writer's Notebook, p. 145

Don't Wait Until Friday

MONITOR PROGRESS   Check Word Reading   Vowel Patterns *a, ai, ay*

Write the following words and have the class read them. Notice which words children miss during the group reading. Call on individuals to read some of the words.

strain	gray	trail	paper	basin	**Spiral Review** Row 2 reviews long *a* spelled *a_e*.
flake	state	grade	place	maze ←	
spray	cracker	chain	sharp	match ←	Row 3 contrasts short *a* and *r*-controlled *ar* with long *a* spellings.

If... children cannot blend words with *a, ai, ay* at this point,

then... use the Small Group Time Strategic Intervention lesson, p. DI•85, to reteach vowel patterns *a, ai, ay*. Continue to monitor children's progress using other instructional opportunities during the week. See the Skills Trace on p. 316–317.

Day 1 Check Word Reading	**Day 2** Check High-Frequency Words	**Day 3** Check Retelling	**Day 4** Check Fluency	**Day 5** Check Oral Vocabulary

Differentiated Instruction

 Advanced

Extend Blending Provide children who can segment and blend all the words correctly with more challenging words such as *explain, display, maintain, raisin,* and *waiter.*

Spelling Pattern

/ā/ *ai, ay* The sound /ā/ may be spelled *ai* within a word or syllable or *ay* at the end of a word or syllable.

Professional Development

Syllable Patterns Words with a VCV pattern may have a closed or an open initial syllable, depending on where the syllables are divided. If they are divided after the first vowel, the first syllable is open, with a long vowel sound (e.g., *pa/per*). If the syllables are divided after the consonant, the first syllable is closed, with a short vowel sound (*tal/ent*). Tell children that when they see a word with a VCV pattern, they can try dividing it before and after the consonant, giving the first vowel its long and short sounds, and see which produces a word they know. Give practice with lists of words.

Success Predictor

Word Reading

Objectives
- Apply knowledge of sound-spellings to decode unknown words when reading.
- Decode and read words in context and independent of context.
- Practice fluency with oral rereading.

Decodable Practice Reader 10A
Vowel Patterns a, ai, ay

Decode words independent of context

Have children turn to the first page and decode each word.

Read high-frequency words

Have children identify and read the high-frequency words *horse*, *main*, *problem*, *visit*, and *how* on the first page.

Decodable Practice Reader 10A

Preview Decodable Reader

Have children identify and read the title and preview the story. Tell them they will decode words with the long a sound spelled *a*, *ai*, and *ay*.

Decode words in context

Pair children for reading and listen as they decode. One child begins. Children read the entire story, switching readers after each page. Partners reread the story. This time the other child begins.

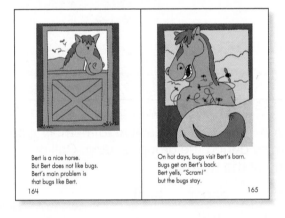

Bert is a nice horse.
But Bert does not like bugs.
Bert's main problem is
that bugs like Bert.
164

On hot days, bugs visit Bert's barn.
Bugs get on Bert's back.
Bert yells, "Scram!"
but the bugs stay.
165

Bert swishes his tail.
Those bugs think Bert
wants to play with them.
How will Bert make them go?
166

This makes Bert mad.
He uses his brain
to come up with a basic plan.
167

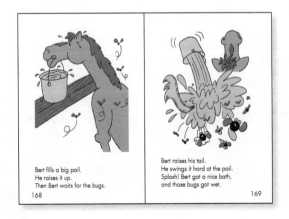

Bert fills a big pail.
He raises it up.
Then Bert waits for the bugs.
168

Bert raises his tail.
He swings it hard at the pail.
Splash! Bert got a nice bath,
and those bugs got wet.
169

Now the bugs stay away.
That's how Bert likes it.
170

Corrective feedback

If... children have difficulty decoding a word,

then... refer them to the Sound-Spelling Cards to identify the sounds in the word. Then prompt them to blend the word.

- What is the new word?
- Is the new word a word you know?
- Does it make sense in the story?

Check decoding and comprehension

Have children retell the story to include characters, setting, and events. Then have children find words that have the long *a* sound spelled *a, ai,* and *ay*. For each word, have children identify the letter(s) that spell the sound /ā/. Children should supply *stay, away, main, days, tail, play, basic, brain, pail, raises,* and *waits*.

Review print awareness

On the first few pages of the story, point out the capital letter that begins each sentence. Remind children that every sentence begins with a capital letter. Have children count the sentences on a page and point out the capital letter that begins each sentence.

Reread for Fluency

Have children reread Decodable Practice Reader 10A to develop automaticity decoding words with the long *a* sound spelled *a, ai,* and *ay*.

 ROUTINE **Oral Rereading**

1. **Read** Have children read the entire book orally.
2. **Reread** To achieve optimal fluency, children should reread the text three or four times.
3. **Corrective Feedback** Listen as children read. Provide corrective feedback regarding their fluency and decoding.

Routines Flip Chart

 **ELL**

English Language Learners
Vowel Patterns *a, ai, ay*
Beginning After reading, have children look at the sentences on the last two pages of the story. Have them identify words with the long *a* sound and say each word aloud, emphasizing the sound /ā/. (*raises, tail, pail, stay, away*)

Intermediate After reading, have children find sets of rhyming words with the long *a* sound spelled *ai* and *ay*, and say them aloud. For example: *main, brain; stay, play, away;* and *tail, pail*. Then have them think of another rhyming word for each set.

Advanced/Advanced-High After reading, have children find words in the story with the long *a* sound spelled *a, ai* and *ay*, such as *main, stay, tail,* and *crazy*, and ask questions that use those words. For example: *Where do the bugs like to stay?* Have other children answer the questions.

Objectives
- Segment and spell words with the sound /ā/ spelled *ai* and *ay*.
- Read high-frequency words.

Spelling Pretest
Vowel Digraphs *ai, ay*

Dictate spelling words

Dictate the spelling words and read the sentences. Have children write the words. If needed, segment the words for children, clarify the pronunciations, and give meanings of words. Have children check their pretests and correct misspelled words.

1. **main**	Look for the **main** idea in the story.
2. **wait**	I can't **wait** until Saturday's game!
3. **say**	Did you **say** you were having a party?
4. **away***	My uncle's wedding is two weeks **away**.
5. **play**	I like to **play** T-ball with my friends.
6. **raise**	**Raise** your hand if you have a question.
7. **brain**	Your **brain** is located inside your head.
8. **paint**	He bought a can of blue **paint**.
9. **stay**	Please **stay** away from the railroad tracks.
10. **today**	It is even colder **today** than yesterday.
11. **tray**	Rita set her **tray** on the table.
12. **tail**	A kangaroo has a strong **tail**.

*Word marked with asterisk comes from the selection *One Good Turn Deserves Another.*

Let's Practice It!
TR DVD•103

On their own   Use Let's Practice It! p. 103 on the *Teacher Resource DVD-ROM.*

Small Group Time

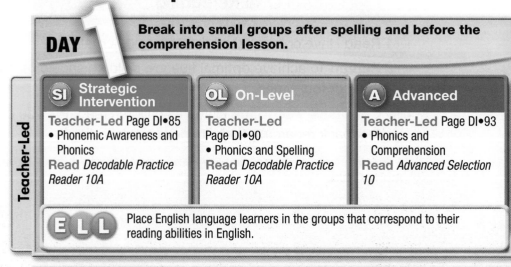

DAY 1 Break into small groups after spelling and before the comprehension lesson.

Teacher-Led

SI Strategic Intervention
Teacher-Led Page DI•85
- Phonemic Awareness and Phonics
Read *Decodable Practice Reader 10A*

OL On-Level
Teacher-Led Page DI•90
- Phonics and Spelling
Read *Decodable Practice Reader 10A*

A Advanced
Teacher-Led Page DI•93
- Phonics and Comprehension
Read *Advanced Selection 10*

ELL Place English language learners in the groups that correspond to their reading abilities in English.

Practice Stations
- Listen Up
- Word Work

Independent Activities
- Read independently/Reading Log on
- *Reader's and Writer's Notebook* p. RR2
- Concept Talk Video

High-Frequency Words

Introduce

ROUTINE **Nondecodable Words**

1 **Say and Spell** Look at page 319. Some words we have to learn by remembering the letters rather than saying the sounds. We will say and spell the words to help learn them. **Point to the first word in the High-Frequency Words list.** This word is *behind*. The letters in *behind* are b-e-h-i-n-d, *behind*. **Have children say and spell each word, first with you, and then without you.**

2 **Identify Familiar Letter-Sounds** Point to the first letter in *behind*. This letter stands for a sound. What is the letter and what is its sound? (*b/b/*) Repeat with *h, n* and *d*.

3 **Demonstrate Meaning** Tell me a sentence using the word *behind*. Follow this routine with the other High-Frequency Words.

Routines Flip Chart

Read words independent of context

Have children read the high-frequency words on page 319 aloud. Add the words to the Word Wall.

Read words in context

Chorally read the **I Can Read!** passage along with the children. Then have them read the passage aloud to themselves. When they are finished, ask children to reread the high-frequency words.

On their own

Use *Reader's and Writer's Notebook,* p. 146.

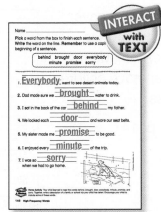

Reader's and Writer's
Notebook p. 146

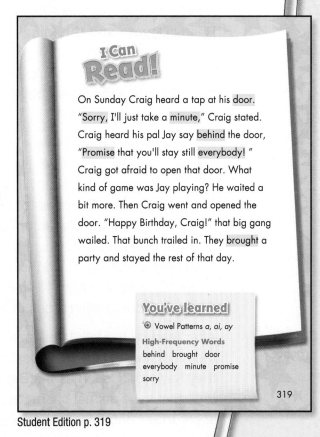

I Can Read!

On Sunday Craig heard a tap at his door. "Sorry, I'll just take a minute," Craig stated. Craig heard his pal Jay say behind the door, "Promise that you'll stay still everybody! " Craig got afraid to open that door. What kind of game was Jay playing? He waited a bit more. Then Craig went and opened the door. "Happy Birthday, Craig!" that big gang wailed. That bunch trailed in. They brought a party and stayed the rest of that day.

You've learned
- Vowel Patterns a, ai, ay
- High-Frequency Words
behind brought door
everybody minute promise
sorry

319

Student Edition p. 319

Differentiated Instruction

SI **Strategic Intervention**
Check Spelling Have children complete each spelling word by writing *ai* or *ay*. For example: *br__n, brain.*

A **Advanced**
Extend Spelling Challenge children who spell words correctly to spell more difficult words such as: *holiday, raisin, explain, daily, nation,* and *display.*

Phonics/Spelling Generalization

Each spelling word has the long *a* vowel sound spelled *ai* or *ay.*

ELL

English Language Learners
Spelling Clarify the meaning of each spelling word with examples, such as saying: *Your brain is inside your head. You use your brain to learn, think, and remember.* For *raise,* raise your hand and say, *I can raise my hand.*

Frontload for Read Aloud Use the modified Read Aloud in the *ELL Support Lessons* to prepare students to listen to "Coyote and the Mice" and "The Ungrateful Tiger" (page 319b).

DAY 1

Read and Comprehend

30~35 min.

Objectives
◎ Make inferences to compare and contrast.

Skills Trace

◎ **Compare and Contrast**

Introduce U2W5D1; U3W3D1; U6W1D1

Practice U2W5D2; U2W5D3; U2W5D4; U3W3D2; U3W3D3; U3W3D4; U6W1D2; U6W1D3; U6W1D4

Reteach/Review U1W4D3; U2W4D3; U2W5D5; U3W3D5; U6W1D5; U6W5D3

Assess/Test Weekly Tests U2W5; U3W3; U6W1 Benchmark Test U2

Key:
U=Unit   W=Week   D=Day

Listening Comprehension
🔊 Compare and Contrast

Introduce

When we tell how things are alike, we **compare**. When we tell how they are different, we **contrast**. Good readers use what they have read and what they know about real life to compare and contrast.

Envision It!

Have children turn to page EI•5 in their Student Editions. These pictures show how to compare and contrast. Discuss these questions using the pictures:

Student Edition EI•5

- How are these children alike? (They are both wearing striped shirts, gym shoes, and holding a baseball.)

- How are they different? (The girl is wearing long pants and a baseball glove; the boy is wearing short pants and holding a bat.)

Model

Today we will read two folk tales and look for likenesses and differences. Read **"Coyote and the Mice"** and **"The Ungrateful Tiger."** Use Graphic Organizer 17 to model compare and contrast. Write the titles above the two non-intersecting parts.

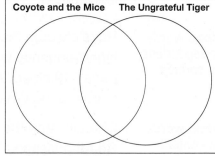

Graphic Organizer 17

Think Aloud When I read, I look for likenesses. Both of these stories are folk tales so I will write *folk tales* in the part of these circles that overlap. Add *folk tales* to the center part. Continue adding likenesses; for example, *animal characters* and *smaller animal tricks bigger one.* Then I look for differences. "Coyote and Mice" is a Native American folk tale and "The Ungrateful Tiger" is a Korean folk tale. I will write *Native American* under "Coyote and Mice" and *Korean* under "The Ungrateful Tiger." Continue adding differences in the non-intersecting parts.

Guide practice

After reading the folk tales, pair children and have them compare these folk tales with other stories they have read, such as the Big Book *From Me to You,* that have animal characters. Then have children share their comparisons with the class.

On their own

Use *Reader's and Writer's Notebook,* p. 147.

Reader's and Writer's Notebook p. 147

Coyote and the Mice

A Native American Folk Tale

Not many animals liked Coyote. He was always causing conflict. One day Coyote was out walking. He saw a group of mice running around under a tree, tying bags to the ends of ropes that hung over the tree's branches. Coyote asked the mice what they were doing. They replied, "The North Wind is coming. He is going to throw hailstones at us. We must pull ourselves up under the branches to be safe."

Coyote wanted to be safe from the North Wind too. He got a bag and a rope and climbed in. "Pull me up under the branches!" he ordered the mice. The mice tied his bag tightly shut and pulled him up. Then they threw stones at Coyote. "Ow, my head! Ow, my tail! These hailstones hurt!" cried Coyote. Finally the mice said, "North Wind is gone. We can come down now." When Coyote climbed out of his bag moaning in pain, the mice laughed, "We tricked you!" Then they scurried back to their holes.

The Ungrateful Tiger
A Korean Folk Tale

Once there was a tiger that hunted people and animals in a village and scared them. One day the villagers decided to trap the tiger.

They dug a hole, hid it under branches and dirt, and that very night, the tiger fell into it.

"Help! Help!" he cried to a man passing by. The man was afraid to help the tiger, but the tiger promised to behave. So the man placed a long log into the hole and the tiger climbed out. "Thank you," said the tiger, as he walked closer to the human and growled.

"But you gave your word that you would be nice!" cried the man. "We must ask a judge to resolve our problem." First they asked a cow. "Humans make animals work, and they are mean to them," said the cow. "Humans are not nice." The man wanted to ask another judge. They came upon a tree. "Humans cut trees down and then build their houses with them," said the tree. "Humans are very thoughtless." Scared, the man asked if they could pursue one more opinion. They came upon a rabbit.

"I don't understand how you fell into the hole," said the rabbit. The three of them went back to the hole. The tiger jumped in. "See?" he asked. "This is how I fell in."

Grinning, the rabbit hopped away. The man hurried back to the village. The tiger roared in anger at being tricked.

Academic Vocabulary

compare tell how two or more things are alike

contrast tell how two or more things are different

Objectives
- Identify and use possessive nouns.
- Understand and recognize the features of a folk tale.

MINI-LESSON

5 Day Planner
Guide to Mini-Lessons

DAY 1	Read Like a Writer
DAY 2	Know Your Purpose
DAY 3	Varied Sentence Beginnings
DAY 4	Revising Strategy: Vary Sentences
DAY 5	Proofread for Possessive Nouns

Conventions
Possessive Nouns

Model

Explain that a **possessive noun** shows who or what owns something. *Dog's, students', and teacher's* are possessive nouns.

Display Grammar Transparency 10. Read aloud the definition, the instructions for forming singular and plural possessive nouns, and the examples beside each picture. Then read the directions and model number 1.

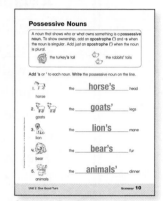

Grammar Transparency 10
TR DVD

- Look at the picture. I see there is one horse, so the noun is singular. To finish the phrase, I need a singular possessive noun. To make a singular noun possessive, I add an apostrophe and *s*.

- I write *horse's* on the line.

Guide practice

Continue with items 2–5, having children identify whether the noun in each sentence is singular or plural. Then have them explain how to make it possessive.

Connect to oral language

Have the class complete these sentence frames orally using possessive nouns.

> 1. The _____ tail got caught in the mousetrap.
>
> 2. All of the _____ keys hang in the front office.
>
> 3. A _____ fur is orange with black stripes.

On their own

Team Talk Write these nouns on the board: *cats, girl, students, toy*, and *donkeys*. Pair children and have them take turns telling how they would form the possessive of each noun. Then have them use each possessive noun in an oral sentence.

Writing—Folk Tale
Introduce

Read Like a Writer

■ **Introduce** This week you will write a folk tale. A folk tale is like a story that has come down through years of storytelling.

Prompt	Think about problems that happen when we don't work together. Now write a folk tale about animals that won't work together.
Trait	Sentences
Mode	Narrative

Reader's and Writer's Notebook, p. 148

■ **Examine Model Text** Let's listen to a folk tale. Track the print as you read aloud "The Little Red Hen" on *Reader's and Writer's Notebook* p. 148. Have children follow along.

■ **Key Features** Who are the characters in the folk tale? (Little Red Hen, Dog, Pig, Cat) Have children find and circle the characters' names. Then have them underline the sentence that tells why Dog, Pig, and Cat didn't help Little Red Hen plant the wheat. (But they were too busy to help.) Next, have children circle the sentence that tells why Dog, Pig, and Cat didn't help her bake the bread. (But they were too tired to help.) Then have them underline the sentence that tells what Dog, Pig, and Cat said when they smelled the bread. ("We would love a slice of bread!") Ask children to read aloud Little Red Hen's answer. ("I don't need your help now! I did all the work by myself. Now I will enjoy this bread by myself!")

In this folk tale, good ways of acting are rewarded. That is why Little Red Hen gets to eat her bread. Bad ways of acting are punished. That is why Dog, Pig, and Cat don't get any bread.

Write Guy
Jeff Anderson

Let's Use Books

Let's use books to solve problems! If a child wants to write dialogue, she can look at how the author of a recently read story wrote dialogue. Have the student ask herself, "What do I like about how these characters speak?" Young writers need models—and the books in your classroom are brimming with lessons to learn.

Academic Vocabulary

possessive noun a noun that shows who or what owns something

Daily Fix-It

1. The dog had pant on his tal. The dog had pa<u>i</u>nt on his tai<u>l</u>.

2. He wantted to wash it awae. He <u>wanted</u> to wash it awa<u>y</u>.

Discuss the Daily Fix-It corrections with children. Review the *ai* and *ay* patterns for the long *a* sound in *paint, tail,* and *away,* and the spelling of *wanted*.

English Language Learners
Options for Conventions Support To provide children with practice with possessive nouns, use the modified grammar lessons in the *ELL Handbook*.

Objectives

- Understand and recognize the features of a folk tale.
- Identify a topic connected to this week's concept.
- Narrow the focus of the topic by formulating inquiry questions related to the topic.
- Discuss solving problems in communities.

Writing—Folk Tale
Introduce, continued

Review key features

Review key features of a folk tale with children. You may want to post these key features in the classroom to allow children to refer to them as they work on their folk tales.

Key Features of a Folk Tale

- It is like a story from long ago.
- Good ways of acting usually are rewarded.
- Bad ways of acting usually are punished.

Connect to familiar texts

Use examples from the fable (a type of folk tale), *The Ant and the Grasshopper*, or another folk tale that children have read. In *The Ant and the Grasshopper*, the ant's behavior is rewarded and the grasshopper's behavior is punished. At the beginning of the story, it is summer, and the ant is working hard to gather food for winter. The grasshopper, on the other hand, spends his days playing. When fall comes, the ant works harder, but the grasshopper continues to play. At the end of the story, winter arrives with a blizzard. The ant is in his cozy home with plenty of food, but the grasshopper is cold and hungry. He asks the ant for food, and the ant refuses.

Look ahead

Tell children that tomorrow they will plan their own folk tales.

ROUTINE Quick Write for Fluency — Team Talk

1) **Talk** Read this question aloud, and have children respond using possessive nouns.

   Do you think the grasshopper's punishment was fair? Why?

2) **Write** Have children write persuasive statements to support their opinion. Make sure their statements include possessive nouns.

3) **Share** Partners can read their statements to one another. Have the pair judge if their partner's statements persuaded them to change their opinion.

Routines Flip Chart

Research and Inquiry
Identify and Focus Topic

Teach

Review the concept web that explores this week's question: *How can we work together to solve problems?* Help children identify that many people share the work of solving problems for people and nature in your community (such as by planting for shade, cleaning up litter, donating toys, recycling, making a park).

Model

Think Aloud I save water whenever I can. I know that my community may have a problem getting enough water for everyone, now and in the future. But I wonder what more I can do, and who else works to save water in the community. **Explain that this week you can research your topic Saving Water and record to answer** *How do people work together saving water?* What ideas about solving problems in communities would you like to learn more about?

Guide practice

Give children time to think about the topic and questions they want to research. Record children's topics and questions in a list.

Topic: Saving Water	
Question: How do people work together to save water?	
At Home	**At Work**
Catch rain for plants Turn off the faucet while brushing teeth	

Wrap Up Your Day

✔ **Phonics: Vowel Patterns *a, ai, ay*** Write *paper, mailing,* and *tray.* Ask children what sound is spelled *a, ai,* and *ay.* Have them read each word.

✔ **Spelling** Have children spell aloud *wait* and *play.*

✔ **Build Concepts** Have children recall the Read Aloud "Coyote and the Mice." How did the mice work together to solve a problem? (Possible response: They tricked Coyote into getting in a bag so they could throw stones at him.)

✔ **Homework** Send home this week's Family Times Newsletter from Let's Practice It! pp. 99–100 on the *Teacher Resource DVD-ROM.*

Let's Practice It!
TR DVD • 99–100

Preview DAY 2

Tell children that tomorrow they will read about how a coyote helps a mouse solve a problem.

Objectives
- Discuss the concept to develop oral vocabulary.
- Build oral vocabulary.

Today at a Glance

Oral Vocabulary
deserve

Phonics and Spelling
◉ Vowel Patterns *a, ai, ay*

High-Frequency Words
behind, brought, door, everybody, minute, promise, sorry

Story Words
armadillo, creature, grateful, groaned, snorted

Vocabulary
Unfamiliar Words

Comprehension
◉ Compare and Contrast
◉ Inferring

Fluency
Paired Reading

Conventions
Possessive Nouns

Writing
Folk Tale

Handwriting
Letters *Qq* and *Vv* / Letter Spacing

Research and Inquiry
Research Skill: Reading a Web Page

Concept Talk

Question of the Week

How can we work together to solve problems?

Build concepts

To reinforce concepts and to focus children's attention, have children sing "Talk It Out" from the *Sing with Me* Big Book. Why should you *pursue* talking it out with a friend? (Talking it out can resolve a conflict.)

💿 *Sing with Me* Big Book Audio

Teach Amazing Words

Display the Big Book, *From Me to You.* Read the title and identify the author and illustrator. In the story, the author uses the word *deserve* in place of the words *have a right to.* Have children listen to the story to find out who thinks he doesn't *deserve* to be admired.

Use the Oral Vocabulary routine on the next page to teach *deserve.*

From Me to You
Big Book

ELL Reinforce Vocabulary Use the Day 2 instruction on Poster 10 to reinforce the meanings of high-frequency words and discuss the lesson concept.

ELL Poster 10

Oral Vocabulary
Amazing Words

Teach Amazing Words

Amazing Words — Oral Vocabulary Routine

① **Introduce the Word** Relate the word *deserve* to the book. Rat feels he does not *deserve* the letter he received. **Supply a child-friendly definition.** *Deserve* means "have a right to" something. When you *deserve* something, you have earned it. **Have children say the word.**

② **Demonstrate** Provide examples to show meaning. My sister *deserves* a good grade because she worked hard. The talented musicians *deserve* a round of applause.

③ **Apply** Have children demonstrate their understanding. Talk about a time when you *deserved* something. Did you get it?

Routines Flip Chart

Anchored Talk

Add to the concept map

Discuss how we can work together to solve problems.

• What does "Talk It Out" say about resolving a conflict? (**Talking about a conflict helps resolve it.**) Let's add *talk it out* to our map.

• In *From Me to You,* Rat learns that Mouse has a problem with his house. What does Rat do to help? (**He helps fix the roof. They share the work.**) Let's add *share work* to our map.

• How did Rat's friends help him resolve his problem of feeling miserable? (**Rat's friends showed him they care.**) Let's add *let friends know we care* to the map.

Differentiated Instruction

SI Strategic Intervention

Amazing Words Ask children to draw a picture of something they *deserve* and label it. Remind them to draw something they have earned.

English Language Learners
Physical Response Teach the word *deserve* by acting out the part of *From Me to You* in which Rat reads his letter for the last time, says "I don't deserve it," and decides to change. Have children join you.

Objectives

• Apply knowledge of letter-sound correspondences and syllable patterns to decode words in context and independent of context.

• Spell words with vowel patterns for /ā/ spelled *a, ai, ay.*

Phonics
Contractions; Vowel Patterns *a, ai, ay*

Review Review contractions with *n't, 's, 'll,* and *'m* using Sound-Spelling Cards 110, 111, 112, and 114 and vowel patterns *a, ai, ay* using Sound-Spelling Cards 73, 54, and 59.

Decode words independent of context Display these words. Have the class blend or combine meaningful word parts to read the words. Then point to the words in random order and ask children to decode them quickly.

explain	**she's**	**stray**
isn't	**radar**	**raisin**
playing	**I'll**	**crater**

Corrective feedback Model blending or combining meaningful word parts to read the words and then ask children to blend or combine them with you.

Decode words in context Display these sentences. Have the class read the sentences.

Team Talk Then have pairs take turns reading the sentences naturally.

We'll stay at home if it starts **raining**.

He **doesn't** have any **paper** or **crayons**.

I'm going to take the **train** on **Thursday**.

Spelling
Vowel Digraphs *ai, ay*

Guide practice

Tell children that you will segment the sounds in each spelling word. They should repeat the sounds in each word as they write them. Check the spelling of each word before saying the next word.

1. /ə/ /w/ /ā/ **away**
2. /p/ /l/ /ā/ **play**
3. /w/ /ā/ /t/ **wait**
4. /b/ /r/ /ā/ /n/ **brain**
5. /r/ /ā/ /z/ **raise**
6. /s/ /t/ /ā/ **stay**
7. /t/ /ā/ /l/ **tail**
8. /t/ /ə/ /d/ /ā/ **today**
9. /t/ /r/ /ā/ **tray**
10. /m/ /ā/ /n/ **main**
11. /p/ /ā/ /n/ /t/ **paint**
12. /s/ /ā/ **say**

On their own

Use *Reader's and Writer's Notebook* p. 149.

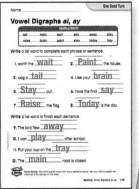

Reader's and Writer's Notebook, p. 149

Professional Development

Spelling Research has shown that spelling development usually lags behind reading development. A child can generally read a word before he or she can spell it. That is because spelling demands greater memory and visual recall than reading.

Small Group Time

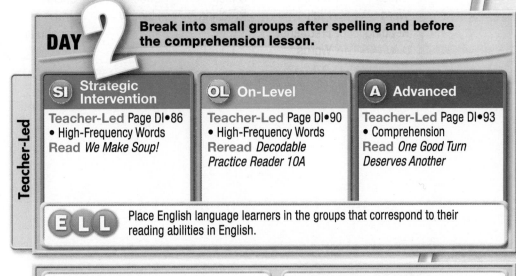

DAY 2 Break into small groups after spelling and before the comprehension lesson.

Teacher-Led

(SI) **Strategic Intervention**	(OL) **On-Level**	(A) **Advanced**
Teacher-Led Page DI•86 • High-Frequency Words **Read** *We Make Soup!*	**Teacher-Led** Page DI•90 • High-Frequency Words **Reread** *Decodable Practice Reader 10A*	**Teacher-Led** Page DI•93 • Comprehension **Read** *One Good Turn Deserves Another*

ELL Place English language learners in the groups that correspond to their reading abilities in English.

Practice Stations
• Words to Know
• Get Fluent

Independent Activities
• Read independently/Reading Log on *Reader's and Writer's Notebook* p. RR2
• AudioText of Main Selection

ELL

English Language Learners

Pronounce Words with the Sound /ā/ Spelled *ai* and *ay* Spanish does not have silent vowels, so children may pronounce vowel patterns *ai* and *ay* as two sounds. Give children additional practice with common word families, such as *ay*, *ail*, and *ain*.

Objectives

- Learn story words: *creature, grateful, armadillo, groaned, snorted.*
- Review high-frequency words.
- Use context to determine the meanings of words.

Check High-Frequency Words

SUCCESS PREDICTOR

High-Frequency Words

Read words independent of context

Point to the words *behind, brought, door, everybody, minute, promise,* and *sorry* on the Word Wall. Remind children that there are some words we learn by remembering the letters, rather than saying the sounds. Then have them read each of the high-frequency words aloud.

Team Talk Have children choose two high-frequency words and give them time to create a sentence in which both words are used properly. Then have them share their sentence with a partner.

Don't Wait Until Friday

MONITOR PROGRESS | **Check High-Frequency Words**

Point to these words on the Word Wall and have the class read them. Listen for children who miss words during the reading. Call on those children to read some of the words individually.

brought	door	behind	everybody	**Spiral Review** Rows 3 and 4 review previously taught high-frequency words.
promise	sorry	minute		
scared	sign	shall	people	
probably	bought	pleasant		

If... children cannot read these words,
then... use the Small Group Time Strategic Intervention lesson, p. DI•86, to reteach the words. Monitor children's fluency with these words during reading, and provide additional practice.

Day 1	**Day 2**	**Day 3**	**Day 4**	**Day 5**
Check Word Reading	Check High-Frequency Words	Check Retelling	Check Fluency	Check Oral Vocabulary

Success Predictor

Story Words
One Good Turn

Introduce story words

Use Vocabulary Transparency 10 to introduce this week's story words. Read each sentence as you track the print. Frame each underlined word and explain its meaning.

groaned	sound made down in the throat that shows sadness
creature	any living person or animal
armadillo	a small animal with a hard shell
snorted	forced the breath through the nose with a loud, harsh sound
grateful	feeling thankful because someone has done something for you

Vocabulary Transparency 10 TR DVD

Have children read each sentence with you.

Vocabulary
Unfamiliar Words

Model using context clues for unfamiliar words

Draw a Vocabulary Frame or display Graphic Organizer 5. Write the word *blues* in the Word box.

 Think Aloud We can figure out the meaning of an unfamiliar word by using the other words in the sentence. In *From Me to You*, we read that Rat had a case of the bathrobe *blues.* Let's figure out the relevant meaning of *blues*—the meaning that makes sense in the sentence.

Guide practice

Draw a picture of Rat's bathrobe in the *Association box* and discuss why rat stayed in his bathrobe to associate *blues* with Rat's feelings. Have children predict a definition and write it on the lines (sad or gloomy). Write the sentence from the Big Book and use context (Rat didn't want to get up) to confirm the definition.

On their own

Have children write another sentence using *blues* in context.

Use *Reader's and Writer's Notebook,* p. 150.

Reader's and Writer's Notebook p. 150

Differentiated Instruction

 Strategic Intervention

Unfamiliar Words If children have difficulty understanding how to use context clues for relevant meaning, point out additional examples in *From Me to You,* such as the word *right* in "I'll go and thank him right away."

 Advanced

Context Clues Have children use a Vocabulary Frame with another word from a book they are reading. They should verify their predicted definition in a dictionary and write their own sentence using the word.

 **ELL**

English Language Learners

Extend Language Have children draw a picture to associate the word *blues* with an emotion. Ask them to describe the picture to a small group of classmates.

Multilingual Vocabulary Lists Children can apply knowledge of their home language to acquire new English vocabulary by using the Multilingual Vocabulary Lists (*ELL Handbook,* pages 85–87).

Objectives

- Build background about fables.
- Preview and predict.
- Use key features of fables to improve understanding of text.
- Set a purpose for reading text.

Build Background
One Good Turn Deserves Another

Background Building Audio

Have children listen to the CD. Tell them to listen to learn about fables and what lesson we can learn from a fable about an eagle and a snake.

 Background Building Audio

Discuss Aesop and fables

Team Talk Have children turn to a partner and use these questions for discussion:

- Why is Aesop famous?
- Who are the characters in the fable?
- What is the lesson at the end of the fable?

Organize information in a web

Draw a web or display Graphic Organizer 15. Write *Fables* in the center circle. Help children describe characteristics of fables. Record their responses.

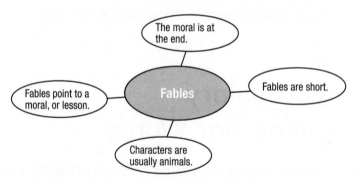

Graphic Organizer 15

Connect to selection

In the fable Aesop told, we learned about an evil snake that treated an eagle badly. In the fable we are about to read, *One Good Turn Deserves Another,* we will find out how a little mouse deals with a mean snake, and we will learn if the mouse outsmarts the snake.

Student Edition pages 320–321

 Double Day Read!

Main Selection—First Read
One Good Turn

Practice the skill

⚙ **Compare and Contrast** Remind children that when they **compare** and **contrast** they tell how things are alike and different. Use Let's Practice It! p. 107 on the *Teacher Resource DVD-ROM.*

Introduce the strategy

⚙ **Inferring** Explain that during reading, good readers use the text and what they know to figure out more than what is stated. Have children turn to page EI•20 in their Student Edition.

Envision It!

Think Aloud Look at this picture. What has happened? We can make an inference using clues in the picture. As I read *One Good Turn Deserves Another,* I will use clues in the text and pictures to help me infer things.

Introduce genre

Let's Read A **folk tale** is a story that was told long ago and passed along orally. It often has a pattern of events, repeated words, and a lesson about life. As they read *One Good Turn Deserves Another,* ask children to look for these things.

Preview and predict

Have children identify the title of the folk tale, the country from which it comes, the author, and the illustrator. Help children use the text on page 324 and the foreshadowing illustration on pages 320–321 to predict who will help the mouse.

Set a purpose

Good readers read for a purpose. Setting a purpose helps us to think and understand more as we read. Guide children to set a purpose for reading the story.

Tell children that today they will read *One Good Turn Deserves Another* for the first time. Use the Day 2 Guide Comprehension notes to help children develop their comprehension of the story.

 Double Day Read!

Continue to DAY 2
For the First Read, use **Guide Comprehension** across the top of pages 320–335.

First Read

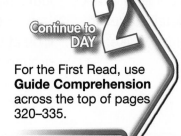

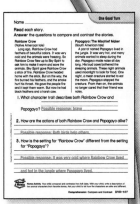
Let's Practice It!
TR DVD•107

Student Edition EI•20

INTERACT with TEXT

Strategy Response Log

Genre Have children use p. RR16 in their *Reader's and Writer's Notebook* to identify the characteristics of folk tales. Have children look for these characteristics as they read *One Good Turn Deserves Another.*

Academic Vocabulary

inferring combining background knowledge with clues in the text to determine the idea the author is trying to present. Ideas, morals, lessons, and themes are often inferred.

ELL

English Language Learners
Build Background Before children listen to the CD, build background and elicit prior knowledge. On the CD, you will hear a very good story. The characters are animals, and we learn a lesson about doing something nice for someone. How do you think stories were passed along many years ago before people knew how to print books? Use the picture on pages 324–325 to give visual support for the vocabulary words *evil* and *free*. Point out the *evil* look on the snake's face and that the mouse is not *free*.

Frontload Main Selection Take a picture walk to frontload the selection, then review the selection summary (*ELL Handbook,* p. 85). Use the Retelling Cards to provide visual support for the summary.

Objectives

◉ Use inferring to understand text in a folk tale.

◉ Make inferences to compare and contrast in a folk tale.

• Determine word meaning and use newly acquired vocabulary.

• Discuss ideas related to, but not expressed in the literature.

DAY 2

Guide Comprehension

Skills and Strategies

Connect to Concept

Working Together Look at the picture. How might the mouse and the coyote work together? (One of them might help the other solve a problem.)

Amazing Words Have children continue discussing the concept using the Amazing Words *conflict, pursue, resolve,* and *deserve* as they read.

One Good Turn Deserves Another *Mexico*

Told by Judy Sierra
Illustrated by Will Terry

Genre **Folk Tale** is a story that has been handed down over many years. Now you will read about how a coyote helps a mouse.

Question of the Week
How can we work together to solve problems?

320

321

Student Edition pp. 320–321

DAY 3

Extend Thinking

Think Critically

Higher-Order Thinking Skills

Analysis I see details in the picture that tell me where this folk tale takes place. Using these details, explain what you think the place is like.

If... children cannot explain that this looks hot and dry like a desert, **then...** provide a model: When I look at the picture, I see dry, yellow ground and cactus plants. I know that cactus grow in a desert. The sky looks bright, as if it is hot.

Strategies

Inferring Remind children that good readers use what they read and what they know about real life to figure out more than is told in the text about the characters and what happens. Use the pictures, what you have read so far, and what you know about snakes to tell what you think the snake is like.

If... children have difficulty inferring, **then...** ask them what the snake does after the mouse rolls aside the rock and what the snake says in the last sentence on page 323.

Hop, stop, sniff. Hop, stop, sniff. A mouse was going across the desert. Suddenly, she heard a voice, "Help! Help me!" The sound came from under a rock. "Pleasssse get me out of here," said the voice with an unmistakable hiss.

The mouse placed her front paws against the rock. She was small, but she brought her best to the job. The rock rolled aside like a door opening. Out slid a snake.

"Thank you sssso much," said the snake as he coiled around the mouse. "I was stuck under that rock for a long time. I am very hungry."

322

323

Student Edition pp. 322–323

Higher-Order Thinking Skills

Analysis What can you infer about the character of the mouse that she works hard to free the snake even though she knows the trapped creature is a snake? (Possible Response: The mouse is a kind-hearted creature who thinks the snake will be grateful for her help.)

Connect to Science

Force and Motion To move an object, a force must be applied to it. The force can be a push or a pull. The stronger the force is, the more the object will move.

Team Talk Have children discuss with a partner what kind of force the mouse used to move the rock and how strong the force was.

Skills and Strategies, continued

DAY 2

Skills

Compare and Contrast How are *One Good Turn Deserves Another* and "The Ungrateful Tiger" alike and different? (Both are folk tales. Both have animal characters that need help but then want to harm the helper. Only "The Ungrateful Tiger" has a human character.)

Vocabulary

Unfamiliar Words Have children locate the word *turn* on page 324. I know the word *turn* usually means "a change of direction," but here it means something else. What does *turn* mean in this sentence? (an action or a deed)

"But you wouldn't eat me," squeaked the mouse.

"Why not?" the snake asked.

"Because I moved the rock," said the mouse. "I saved your life."

"So?" hissed the snake.

"So, one good turn deserves another," the mouse said hopefully.

The snake moved his head from side to side. "You are young," he said. "You don't know much about the world. Good is often repaid with evil."

"That's not fair!" cried the mouse.

"Everybody knows I am right," said the snake. "If you find even one creature who agrees with you, I promise to set you free."

324   325

Student Edition pp. 324–325

Think Critically, continued

DAY 3

Higher-Order Thinking Skills

Evaluation What does the snake mean when he says, "Good is often repaid with evil?" Do you agree or disagree with the statement?

If… children have trouble explaining what the statement means,
then… ask them what the mouse did and what the snake intends to do.

Word Reading

Decoding Have children check their reading of new words using these questions:

- Did I blend the sounds to read the word?
- Did I put the new word in the sentence to make sure it made sense?
- Did I look for word parts to help me understand the word?

Strategies

Inferring Use what you know about crows and farmers to figure out the meaning of the crow's statement about good and evil. (Possible response: The crow thought he was doing the farmer a good turn by eating the grasshoppers, but the farmer may have thought the crow was eating the crops because he chased the crow away.)

A crow flew up behind them. "Uncle," said the snake to the crow, "help us settle an argument. I was trapped under a rock, and this silly mouse set me free. Now she thinks I shouldn't eat her."

"He should be grateful," the mouse insisted.

"Well, now," said the crow. "I've flown high and I've flown low. I've been just about everywhere. This morning, I ate some grasshoppers that were destroying a farmer's crops. Was he grateful? No, he used me for target practice! Good is often repaid with evil." And off he flew.

326

327

Student Edition pp. 326–327

Higher-Order Thinking Skills

Analysis The snake asks the crow to help settle an argument. From details in the picture, who is winning the argument at this point? (Possible response: The mouse seems to be trapped because the snake is coiled around her, so the snake must be winning.)

Evaluation How do you judge the actions of the crow when he flies away? (Possible response: I disagree with his actions; he could have saved the mouse.)

Skills and Strategies, continued

DAY 2

Skills

Compare and Contrast

Compare and contrast the animals in this folk tale with real animals. (Possible response: Unlike real animals, the animals in the folk tale talk to each other and look for someone to settle an argument. But like real animals, snakes eat mice.)

Word Reading

High-Frequency Words Point out the words *minute* and *sorry*. Have children practice reading these words.

An armadillo ambled by. "What's all the noise?" she asked.

"Merely a minute of conversation before dinner," replied the snake. "My young friend moved a rock and set me free. Now she thinks I shouldn't eat her."

"One good turn deserves another," said the mouse.

"Wait a minute," said the armadillo. "Did you know he was a snake before you moved that rock?

"I guess I did, but..."

"Sorry, a snake is always a snake," the armadillo declared as she waddled away.

"That settles it," said the snake. "Everybody agrees with me."

328

329

Student Edition pp. 328–329

Think Critically, continued

DAY 3

Higher-Order Thinking Skills

Synthesis Folk tales often include patterns. What patterns do you see through the story so far? (Possible responses: the repeated lines, the animals who come along, and the refusals to help)

Higher-Order Thinking Skills

Synthesis The word *snake* sometimes is used to mean a "sly person, or someone who should not be trusted." How can you use this other meaning of the word *snake* to create meaning for what the armadillo says?

Strategies

◉ **Inferring** What inference can you make about why the snake says that the mouse will never understand? (Possible response: The snake is impatient and doesn't want to wait any longer.)

Vocabulary

Story Words Have children locate the words *creature* and *groaned* on page 330. Who does the mouse mean when he talks about "one more *creature*"? (one more living thing) The snake *groaned.* How did he sound? (His voice was deep, and it showed disapproval and annoyance.)

"Can't we ask just one more creature?" the mouse pleaded.

"I don't think you'll ever understand," groaned the snake.

330

A coyote trotted up. "Understand what?" he asked.

"The snake was trapped under that rock," the mouse explained.

"Which rock?" asked the coyote.

"Over there. That rock," said the snake.

331

Student Edition pp. 330–331

Review Author's Purpose

Evaluation Tell why you think the author may have chosen this folk tale for retelling. (Possible response: The story is interesting, and it teaches a lesson.)

Connect to Science

Inherited Characteristics Living things are born with certain traits and qualities that come from their ancestors. These are inherited traits.

Team Talk Have children discuss with a partner how all snakes or how all armadillos are alike.

Skills and Strategies, continued

DAY 2

Skills

🔘 **Compare and Contrast** How is what happens on pages 332 and 333 similar to the beginning of the story? How does it differ?

If... children have trouble comparing and contrasting,
then... ask them where the snake was when the mouse came along in the beginning and where he is now.

"Oh," said the coyote. "The mouse was under that rock."

"No, I was under that rock!" said the snake.

"A snake under a rock? Impossible," the coyote snorted. "I have never seen such a thing."

The snake slid into the hole where he had been trapped. "I was in this hole," he hissed, "and that rock was on top of me!"

332   333

Student Edition pp. 332–333

Think Critically, continued

DAY 3

Higher-Order Thinking Skills
Analysis The coyote snorts "impossible" and seems to have a plan. Explain coyote's plan.

If... children cannot explain coyote's plan to trap the snake,
then... have them connect text and picture clues.

Higher-Order Thinking Skills
Evaluation Grade the coyote's plan to help the mouse from 1 to 5, with 1 as the best score. Explain your grade. (Possible response: I grade it with a 1 because the mouse is free from the snake.)

Strategies

⊚ Inferring What is the lesson in the folk tale? (Possible response: Someone who is helped by another should return the kindness.)

Strategy Self-Check

Have children talk about problems they encountered as they read and what they did to solve them. Then have them explain how they combined what they knew with clues in the text to figure out the lesson in the folk tale.

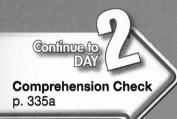
Continue to **DAY 2**
Comprehension Check p. 335a

"This rock?" the coyote asked as he lifted his paw and pushed the rock on top of the snake.

"Yess!" hissed the snake. "Now show him, little mouse! Show him how you set me free."

But the mouse was already far away. "Thank you, cousin," she called as she ran. "I'll return the favor someday."

"Yes, indeed," said the coyote. "One good turn deserves another."

334

335

Student Edition pp. 334–335

Higher-Order Thinking Skills

Analysis Classify the characters in the folk tale according to those who believe "good is repaid with evil" and those who believe "one good turn deserves another." (The snake, crow, and armadillo believe "good is repaid with evil," and the mouse and coyote believe "one good turn deserves another.")

Higher-Order Thinking Skills

Synthesis How are the endings of *One Good Turn Deserves Another* and "The Ungrateful Tiger" similar? (The evil character is tricked back into a hole and trapped, allowing the character who originally helped to escape.)

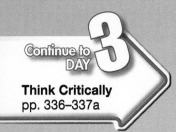
Continue to **DAY 3**
Think Critically pp. 336–337a

Objectives
- Compare different versions of a folk tale.
- Identify and use possessive nouns in writing and speaking.

Comprehension Check

Have children discuss each question with a partner and share responses.

☑ **Fable** How can you tell this story is a fable? (It is a short story that teaches a moral. The characters are animals that act like people.)

☑ **Confirm predictions** How did the illustrations help you confirm predictions? (Children may have used illustrations to confirm that the coyote helps the mouse.)

Literary Text
Setting, Character, and Plot

Compare versions of a folk tale

Use *One Good Turn Deserves Another* and "The Ungrateful Tiger" (p. 319b) to compare different versions of the same folk tale.

- How are the characters alike? (Both have animals that act like people.)
- How are the plots similar? (In both, one animal tricks another into jumping back into a trap so it won't eat a smaller animal.)
- Where are the stories set? (a Korean village and a desert)

Guide practice

Together, fill in a story comparison chart (Graphic Organizer 13). Discuss similarities and differences between the two versions of the tale.

On their own

Have small groups decide what is the most different about the stories. Have them share with the class why they think there are differences.

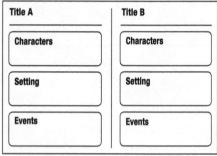

Graphic Organizer 13

Reread for Fluency

ROUTINE **Paired Reading**

1. Reread To achieve optimal fluency, have partners reread the text three or four times.

2. Corrective Feedback Listen as children read. Provide corrective feedback regarding their fluency and decoding.

Go Digital! | **Grammar Jammer**

Conventions
Possessive Nouns

Model possessive nouns

Write *coyote's friends* and *snakes' tails* on the board. Point to each word as you read it. Ask children to identify the singular possessive noun (*coyote's*) and the plural possessive noun (*snakes'*). Singular nouns and plural nouns can be *possessive*, which means they show who or what owns something. What is added to a singular noun to show possession? (apostrophe *s*) What is added to a plural noun to show possession? (apostrophe)

Guide practice

Write the following sentences on the board. Have children read the sentences, identify the possessive noun in each sentence, and tell if it is singular or plural.

1. That man's car is red.   (man's, singular)
2. Most dogs' teeth are sharp.   (dogs', plural)
3. A snake's body is long.   (snake's, singular)
4. The girls' shoes are dirty.   (girls', plural)

Connect to oral language

Have the class complete these sentence frames orally using possessive nouns.

1. This is my little _____ favorite book about trucks.
2. My mom wears my _____ gold watch.
3. That _____ tail is almost two feet long!

On their own

Use *Reader's and Writer's Notebook* p. 151.

Reader's and Writer's Notebook p. 151

Differentiated Instruction

SI Strategic Intervention

Support Conventions If children have difficulty distinguishing singular from plural possessive nouns, have them use their fingers to frame the word before the apostrophe. Explain that if the noun ends with *s*, the possessive noun is usually plural.

Daily Fix-It

3. The dog askked the cat for help?

   The dog <u>asked</u> the cat for help<u>.</u>

4. the cat told the dog to wat.

   <u>T</u>he cat told the dog to <u>wait</u>.

Discuss the Daily Fix-It corrections with children. Review sentence capitalization and punctuation, rules for doubling the final consonant when an ending is added, and the spelling of wait.

 ELL

English Language Learners

Support Conventions In many languages, speakers show possession in phrases (such as *of the cat*) rather than noun endings (like *cat's*). Help children see the difference between possessive and plural nouns. Point out the apostrophe in possessive nouns. Then provide index cards with possessive and plural nouns and have children work with a partner to sort them into two piles.

Objectives
- Generate ideas for a folk tale.
- Recognize features of a folk tale.

Writing—Folk Tale
Writer's Craft: Know Your Purpose

Introduce the prompt

Review with children the key features of a folk tale. Point out that *One Good Turn Deserves Another* is a folk tale. Assure them that they can make up a folk tale with animal characters. Explain that today children will plan their own folk tale. The folk tale will have a specific purpose: to show what happens when animals or people don't work together. Read aloud the writing prompt.

Writing Prompt

Think about problems that happen when we don't work together. Now write a folk tale about animals that won't work together.

Help children generate ideas

Sharing the Writing

Think Aloud To plan a folk tale, the first thing we will do is choose characters to write about. Let's make a chart that lists folk tales we have heard and read and their characters. **Display a T-chart.** I'll start by writing *One Good Turn Deserves Another* in the Folk Tales column and *mouse, snake,* and *coyote* in the Characters column.

Guide children in identifying other folk tales and their characters. Possible ideas are shown. Record the responses, and keep the chart, so that children can refer to it as they choose animal characters for their folk tale.

Folk Tales/Fables	Characters
One Good Turn Deserves Another	mouse, snake, coyote
The Ant and the Grasshopper	ant, grasshopper
The Little Red Hen	Little Red Hen, Dog, Pig, Cat
The Ungrateful Tiger	tiger, man, rabbit
The Three Billy Goats Gruff	goats, troll

Have each child choose animal characters to write a folk tale about. Circulate to guide them. Tell them they can select animal characters from the chart or choose other animal characters that are interesting to them.

MINI-LESSON

Know Your Purpose

■ **Introduce** Use *Reader's and Writer's Notebook* p. 152 to model story planning. To plan a folk tale, I can use a chart. I don't need a title yet, but I've decided to write about a pig and a duck. I'll use the story sequence chart to plan the beginning, middle, and end of the story. As I plan each part, I'll keep my purpose in mind: to write about animals that won't work together.

■ **Model** First, Pig and Duck walked by a river. They saw berries on the other side. I'll write that in the Beginning box. In the middle, I'll tell how they won't work together: Pig wanted to make a bridge. Duck wanted to make a raft. I'll put that in the Middle box. At the end, Pig finished his bridge and Duck finished her raft. But it took a long time. It was dark. They couldn't see the berries. So they went home with nothing. I'll write that in the End box. Now plan your folk tale. **Circulate to guide and assist children.**

INTERACT with TEXT

Name _____

Story Chart

Title _____

Beginning
Sample responses for modeling:
Pig and Duck walked by a river. They saw red berries on the other side.

Middle
Pig wanted to make a bridge to get the berries. Duck wanted to make a raft. So each animal worked alone.

End of Story
At last, Pig's bridge was finished. So was Duck's raft. It took them a long time. It was dark. They couldn't see the berries. They went home with nothing.

Reader's and Writer's Notebook, p. 152

ROUTINE — Quick Write for Fluency — Team Talk

① **Talk** Have children take two minutes to tell their story events to a partner.

② **Write** Each child briefly writes about the events and describes how the animals won't work together in the middle part of their folk tale.

③ **Share** Each child reads the story ideas to the partner.

Routines Flip Chart

Differentiated Instruction

SI Strategic Intervention

Planning Events If children find it difficult to plan events for their folk tale, make a list of "beginnings" for them to work with. For example: 1) The animals want to have a picnic. 2) The animals want to build something. 3) The animals want to play a game.

ELL

English Language Learners

Support Prewriting
Beginning Have children complete sentence frames that tell their story events. Have them read the sentences to a partner.

Intermediate Have children write phrases or simple sentences to express story events. Have them describe the plan to a partner.

Advanced/Advanced-High Have children write sentences in their story charts. Have them read their sentences to partners and expand their ideas.

Objectives

- Write legible letters with proper letter spacing.
- Understand how to use a web page to locate information.
- Understand and analyze the features of a web page.
- Apply knowledge of a web page to inquiry project.

Handwriting
Letters *Q, q,* and *V, v*/Letter Spacing

Model letter formation

Display upper- and lower-case letters: *Qq* and *Vv*. Use the stroke instructions pictured below to model proper letter formation. Have children write the letters several times and circle their best ones.

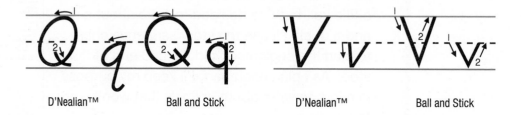

D'Nealian™   Ball and Stick   D'Nealian™   Ball and Stick

Model letter spacing

Explain that when we write a word, all the letters in that word should be evenly spaced. Write the word *quick* using correct spacing. When I write letters in a word, I need to pay attention to the spaces between each letter. Write *quick* again, with the letters too close to each other. The letters should not be so close together that they touch each other. Write *quick* a third time, with the letters too far from each other. They should not be so far apart that it's hard to tell they spell out a word. By correctly spacing letters in words, I make it easier for others to read what I write. Ask children which of the three writing examples is easiest to read and have them explain why.

Guide practice

Write the following sentence, using letter spacing that is too crowded. *Vote for Vicky and Quinn!*

Team Talk Have children work in pairs to discuss what is wrong with the sentence and how it needs to be fixed. Have children write the sentence correctly. Have them share with the class.

Research and Inquiry
Research Skill: Reading a Web Page

Teach Display Research Transparency 10. We can use a Web page like this to find information on the **Internet,** a large computer network with links to information around the world. Point out the different elements as you describe them:

Model
- The **URL** at the top of the Web page is the address for the **Web site,** a place on the Internet with a set of pages we can read on a computer.

- If I type a word into the search box, the computer will search this site for information about my word.

- I use the scroll bar to move down or back up so I can read all the text, or words, on the page.

- There are usually links to other Web pages that have more information. If I click on one of the links, I move to another Web page. Sometimes links are blue text or underlined text. Sometimes links look like buttons or shapes. Sometimes they are in pictures. If I move over a link, my cursor changes to look like a hand. Then I can click to go to the new page.

Guide practice Provide copies of Research Transparency 10. Have children point to the URL, scroll bar, search box, and Web page title. Ask them where links appear and what the new pages would be about.

Academic Vocabulary

Internet an extremely large communication system linking computer information and messages worldwide. The World Wide Web is one part of the communications.

URL the address of a Web site

Web site a place or address on the Internet where a set of pages can be placed by a computer and read by others

Research Transparency 10
TR DVD

Wrap Up Your Day

✔ **High-Frequency Words** Write: *Everybody may promise to bring something for our project.* Ask children to read the sentence. Point to *everybody* and *promise,* and have children read them.

✔ **Build Concepts** Monitor children's use of oral vocabulary as they respond. Recall *One Good Turn Deserves Another.* Ask: What conflict was in the story? (The snake wanted to eat the mouse, but the mouse didn't want to be eaten.) Did the mouse resolve the conflict? Why? (No. The coyote easily solved the problem by tricking the snake.)

Preview DAY 3

Tell children that tomorrow they will reread *One Good Turn Deserves Another.*

Objectives
- Build oral vocabulary.
- Identify details in text.
- Share information and ideas about the concept.

Today at a Glance

Oral Vocabulary
mope

Phonics and Spelling
◉ Vowel Patterns *a, ai, ay*

Fluency
Read with Accuracy

High-Frequency Words
behind, brought, door, everybody, minute, promise, sorry

Story Words
armadillo, creature, grateful, groaned, snorted

Comprehension
Author's Purpose

Conventions
Possessive Nouns

Writing
Folk Tale: Sentences

Research and Inquiry
Gather and Record Information

Concept Talk

Question of the Week

How can we work together to solve problems?

Build concepts

To reinforce concepts and to focus children's attention, have children sing "Talk It Out" from the *Sing with Me* Big Book. Why is it good to work out problems? (We can make things better.)

 Sing with Me Big Book Audio

Monitor listening comprehension

Display the Big Book, *From Me to You.* In the story, the author uses the word *mope* in place of the word *unhappy.* Review that yesterday the class listened to find out who didn't think he deserved to be admired. Have children listen today to learn how Rat changes when he stops moping around the house.

From Me to You
Big Book

ELL **Expand Vocabulary** Use the Day 3 instruction on ELL Poster 10 to expand children's use of English vocabulary to communicate about lesson concepts.

ELL Poster 10

Oral Vocabulary
Amazing Words

Teach Amazing Words

resolve	mope
conflict	coax
pursue	ramp
deserve	startle

Amazing Words Oral Vocabulary Routine

1 Introduce the Word Relate the word *mope* to the book. In *From Me to You,* Rat *mopes* around in his bathrobe all day. Supply a child-friendly definition. *Mope* means "to feel sorry for yourself." When you *mope,* you are unhappy and lose interest in things. Have children say the word.

2 Demonstrate Provide examples to show meaning. When his parents told Joseph they were moving, he was sad and *moped* around the house. When the child lost his favorite toy, he *moped* for days.

3 Apply Have children demonstrate their understanding. Show me how someone looks when they *mope.*

Routines Flip Chart

Anchored Talk

Add to the concept map

Use these questions to discuss how working together can help solve problems as you add to the concept map.

• Rat decided to change. What things did he do that were different? (Rat decided to spend time with his friends, and he wrote Bat a kind letter, like the one he received.) Let's add *spend time with friends* and *write a kind letter* to our map.

• In *One Good Turn Deserves Another,* the mouse tells the coyote that she will return his favor. What does the coyote say? (One good turn deserves another.) Let's add *return a favor* to our map.

• What kind of favor did the coyote do for the mouse? (The coyote saved the mouse from the snake.) Let's add *save someone in trouble* to the map.

Differentiated Instruction

SI Strategic Intervention

Sentence Production If children do not pronounce the sound /s/ at the end of the verb *mopes* to agree with a singular subject, say the sentence "Rat *mopes* around in his bathrobe," stressing the sound /s/. Have children repeat it.

ELL

English Language Learners
Vocabulary Help children understand that the word *mope* means "feeling sad" but also suggests feeling sorry for yourself. Have children practice using the word in oral sentences that demonstrate their understanding of the word.

Objectives
◎ Blend and read words with the sound /ā/ spelled *a*, *ai*, and *ay*.
• Decode words in context and independent of context.

Phonics
Build Words

Model word building

Now we are going to build words with the long *a* sound /ā/. Write *main* and blend it. Then have children blend it with you. Watch me change the *m* in *main* to *b*, *r*. Model blending the new word, *brain*.

Guide practice

Have children spell *brain* with letter tiles and read the word aloud. Monitor children's work.

• Change the *b* in *brain* to *t*.
Say the new word together.

| t | r | a | i | n |

• Change the *ain* in *train* to *ay*.
Say the new word together.

| t | r | a | y |

• Change the *tr* in *tray* to *p*.
Say the new word together.

| p | a | y |

• Change the *y* in *pay* to *per*.
Say the new word together.

| p | a | p | e | r |

• Change the *p* in *paper* to *t*.
Say the new word together.

| t | a | p | e | r |

• Change the *per* in *taper* to *ken*.
Say the new word together.

| t | a | k | e | n |

Corrective feedback

For corrective feedback, model the correct spelling and have children correct their tiles.

Fluent Word Reading

Model

Write *spray.* I know the sounds for *s, p, r,* and *ay.* I blend them and read the word *spray.*

Guide practice

Write the words below. Say the sounds in your head for each spelling you see. When I point to the word, we'll read it together. Allow one second per sound previewing time for the first reading.

drain	stray	waist	clay	claim	razor

On their own

Have children read the list above three or four times, until they can read one word per second.

Blend and Read

Decode words independent of context

Have children turn to page 171 in *Decodable Practice Readers* 2.1 and find the first list of words. Each word in this list has the sound /ā/ spelled *a, ai,* or *ay.* Let's blend and read these words.

Next, have children read the high-frequency words.

Critter Trail

Decodable Practice Passage 10B

Vowel patterns *a, ai, ay*

rained	April	Jay	Gail
waited	trail	explained	wait
exclaimed	main	plain	play
quails	hay	gray	snails
paying	stayed	away	tail

High-Frequency Words

| wait | minute |
| brought | main |

It had rained and rained in April! Jay and Gail had waited long to hike. May first was a perfect hiking day.

Jay gazed west. "I say hiking the west trail is the best way," explained Jay.

171

"Wait a minute!" exclaimed Gail. "April rain brought roses to the main trail. That west trail is plain."

"Then on the main trail, you must play *Spot That Critter,*" Jay said.

That's what Jay and Gail did on the main trail. Jay and Gail spotted five quails, a horse munching hay, five gray snails, and six birds paying a visit to a hole filled with rain. Jay and Gail stayed away when they spotted a white and black tail. It was a skunk!

"I can spot one more critter," smiled Gail after hiking. "You, Jay!"

Jay grinned at Gail's joke.

172

Decodable Practice Readers 2.1, pp. 171–172

Decode words in context

Chorally read the story along with children. Have children identify words in the story that have the sound /ā/ spelled *a, ai,* or *ay.*

Team Talk Pair children and have them take turns reading the story aloud to each other. Monitor children as they read to check for proper pronunciation and appropriate pacing.

Differentiated Instruction

A **Advanced**

Other Spellings for the Sound /ā/ Point out words that have unusual spellings for the long *a* sound. For example: *eight, neighbor, weigh; great, break, steak;* and *they.* Have children make up sentences that include *ai* or *ay* words as well as a word with an unusual spelling. For example: *I gave my neighbor a tray of snails.*

Objectives

• Spell words with the sound /ā/ spelled *ai* and *ay*.
• Read aloud fluently with accuracy.

Spelling
Vowel Digraphs *ai, ay*

Spell high-frequency words

Write *everybody* and *sorry* and point them out on the Word Wall. Have children say and spell the words with you and then without you.

Dictation

Have children write these sentences. Say each sentence. Then repeat it slowly, one word at a time.

> 1. **Will everybody stay and help paint the porch?**
>
> 2. **I'm sorry that I didn't wait for you today.**
>
> 3. **Everybody was away for the summer.**

Proofread and correct

Write each sentence, spelling words one at a time. Have children circle and rewrite any misspelled words.

On their own

Use *Reader's and Writer's Notebook* p. 154.

Reader's and Writer's Notebook, p. 154

Small Group Time

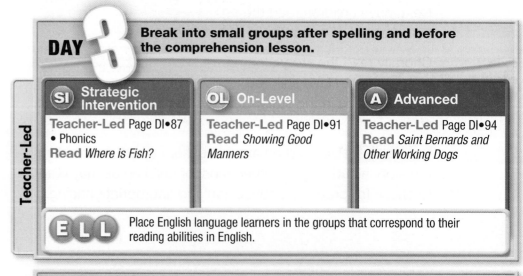

DAY 3

Break into small groups after spelling and before the comprehension lesson.

SI Strategic Intervention	OL On-Level	A Advanced
Teacher-Led Page DI•87 • Phonics **Read** *Where is Fish?*	**Teacher-Led** Page DI•91 **Read** *Showing Good Manners*	**Teacher-Led** Page DI•94 **Read** *Saint Bernards and Other Working Dogs*

ELL Place English language learners in the groups that correspond to their reading abilities in English.

Practice Stations	**Independent Activities**
• Read for Meaning • Let's Write	• Read independently/Reading Log on *Reader's and Writer's Notebook* p. RR2 • AudioText of Main Selection

Model Fluency
Read with Accuracy

Model fluent reading

Have children turn to Student Edition page 322. Follow along as I read this page. I will try to read with no mistakes.

Guide practice

Have children read the page with you. Then have them reread the page as a group without you until they read with no mistakes. Continue in the same way with pages 326–327.

Corrective feedback

If... children have difficulty reading with accuracy, **then...** prompt:

- Which word is a problem? Let's read it together.
- Read the sentence again to be sure you understand it.
- Tell me the sentence. Now read it as if you are speaking it to me.

Reread for Fluency

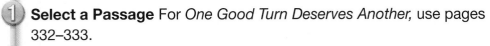 **Choral Reading**

1. **Select a Passage** For *One Good Turn Deserves Another,* use pages 332–333.
2. **Model** First, have children track the print as you read.
3. **Guide Practice** Then have children read along with you.
4. **Corrective Feedback** Have the class read aloud without you. Monitor progress and provide feedback. For optimal fluency, children should reread three to four times.

Routines Flip Chart

Check comprehension

Have children retell the fable by comparing and contrasting the characters.

Objectives
- Read high-frequency words.
- Establish purpose for reading text.
- Review key features of a folk tale.

High-Frequency and Story Words

Read words independent of context

Display and review this week's high-frequency words and story words. Have children read the words aloud.

Read words in context

Display the following sentence frames. Have children complete the sentences using high-frequency and story words. Have the children read each completed sentence with you.

1. I was *grateful* that the train arrived in one _____. (minute)

2. The horse *snorted* when I _____ him an apple. (brought)

3. An _____ is a strange looking *creature.* (armadillo)

4. _____ *groaned* when the game was called off. (everybody)

5. The big, bad wolf hid _____ the *door.* (behind)

6. Jack was _____ that he didn't keep his *promise.* (sorry)

On their own

Use *Reader's and Writer's Notebooks,* p. 155.

Reader's and Writer's
Notebook p. 155

Double Day Read!

Main Selection–Second Read
One Good Turn Deserves Another

Review Author's purpose

Recall this week's main selection, *One Good Turn Deserves Another.* Tell children that today they will read the folk tale again. Remind children that the reason or reasons that an author writes is the **author's purpose.** Identifying the author's purpose can help us better understand the events, characters, and message in the text. What are some reasons why authors write? For more practice with author's purpose, use Let's Practice It! p. 102 on the *Teacher Resource DVD-ROM*.

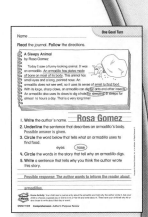

Let's Practice It!
TR DVD•102

Review Genre: folk tale

Let's Read Remind children that a folk tale is a story that was told long ago and passed on orally. It often has animal characters and teaches a lesson. Have children recall the characters in *One Good Turn Deserves Another* and the lesson in the tale.

Set a purpose

Remind children that good readers read for a purpose. Guide children to set a new purpose for reading *One Good Turn Deserves Another* today, perhaps to compare and contrast the coyote in this story with the coyote in "Coyote and Mice."

Extend thinking

Tell children they will now read *One Good Turn Deserves Another* for the second time. Use the Day 3 Extend Thinking notes to encourage children to use higher-order thinking skills to go beyond the details of the story.

 Double Day Read!

Second Read

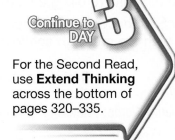 Continue to DAY 3

For the Second Read, use **Extend Thinking** across the bottom of pages 320–335.

Differentiated Instruction

 SI **Strategic Intervention**

Vocabulary Use the high-frequency words in questions for children to answer. For example, *Who is sitting behind you? What is a promise you have made this week? What have you brought in your backpack today?*

 A **Advanced**

Have children work in small groups to use the high-frequency words in a story they make up and add to in turns, round-robin fashion. Each child builds from the previous sentences and adds a new one. Start them with a sentence, such as "*Everybody* wanted to help."

Story Words

armadillo a small animal that has a hard shell

creature any living person or animal

grateful feeling thankful

groaned sound made down in the throat; it shows pain, disagreement, or annoyance

snorted a loud, harsh sound made through the nose

Academic Vocabulary

author's purpose the reason or reasons why an author writes

 E L L

English Language Learners
Words in Context Provide support by supplying a word bank for children during the sentence frames review activity on p. 336g.

Objectives

- Retell a narrative.
- ◎ Compare and contrast in a narrative text.
- ◎ Infer meaning.
- Write clear, coherent sentences.

Check Retelling
•SUCCESS PREDICTOR

Objectives
- Identify themes in well-known fables, legends, myths, or stories.
- Describe the main characters in stories, and why they feel and act the way they do.
- Read by yourself for a period of time and paraphrase what you read.

Envision It! Retell

READING STREET ONLINE
STORY SORT
www.ReadingStreet.com

336

Think Critically

1. What are other stories you have read where the animals act like people? **Text to Text**

2. What message do you think the author is trying to give you in this story? **Author's Purpose**

3. What characters think alike? What characters think differently? ◎ **Compare and Contrast**

4. Why does the coyote want to get the snake to slither back under the rock? ◎ **Inferring**

5. **Look Back and Write**
Look back at pages 324–325. What does the mouse mean by "one good turn deserves another"? Provide evidence to support your answer.

TEST PRACTICE Extended Response

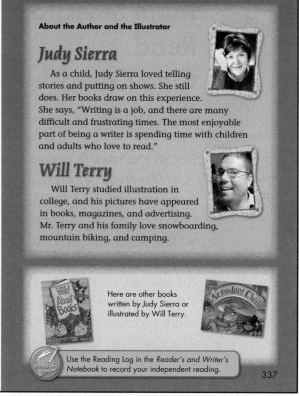

About the Author and the Illustrator

Judy Sierra

As a child, Judy Sierra loved telling stories and putting on shows. She still does. Her books draw on this experience. She says, "Writing is a job, and there are many difficult and frustrating times. The most enjoyable part of being a writer is spending time with children and adults who love to read."

Will Terry

Will Terry studied illustration in college, and his pictures have appeared in books, magazines, and advertising. Mr. Terry and his family love snowboarding, mountain biking, and camping.

Here are other books written by Judy Sierra or illustrated by Will Terry.

Use the Reading Log in the *Reader's and Writer's Notebook* to record your independent reading.

337

Student Edition pp. 336–337

Retelling

 **Envision It!** Have children work in pairs, retelling the story to one another. Remind children that their partners should include the characters, setting, and events from the beginning, middle, and end of the story. Children should use the retelling strip in the Student Edition. Monitor children's retelling.

Scoring rubric

Top-Score Response A top-score response makes connections beyond the text, elaborates on the author's purpose, and describes in detail the characters, setting, and plot.

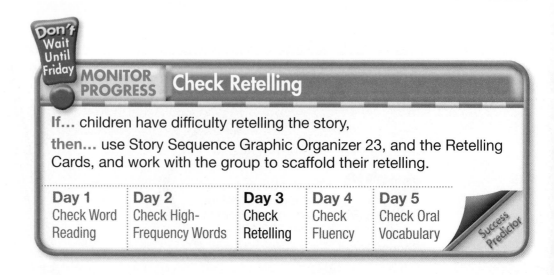

Don't Wait Until Friday

MONITOR PROGRESS | Check Retelling

If... children have difficulty retelling the story,

then... use Story Sequence Graphic Organizer 23, and the Retelling Cards, and work with the group to scaffold their retelling.

Day 1	Day 2	Day 3	Day 4	Day 5
Check Word Reading	Check High-Frequency Words	Check Retelling	Check Fluency	Check Oral Vocabulary

Success Predictor

Think Critically

Text to Text

1. Possible response: The characters in *The Bremen Town Musicians* act like people, too.

Author's Purpose

2. Possible response: The author wants us to be grateful when someone helps us and to return the favor someday.

Compare and Contrast

3. Possible response: The snake, the crow, and the armadillo think alike because they think the snake has a right to eat the mouse. The mouse and the coyote think alike because they believe the snake shouldn't eat the mouse. The mouse and the coyote think differently from the snake, the crow, and the armadillo.

Inferring

4. Possible response: Because if he slithers back under the rock, the coyote can trap the snake again, and the snake won't eat the mouse.

 Writing on Demand

5. **Look Back and Write** For writing fluency, assign a five-minute time limit. As children finish, encourage them to reread their response and proofread for errors.

Scoring rubric

> **Top-Score Response** A top-score response uses details from the text and the picture to tell what the mouse means by "one good turn deserves another." For example:
>
> The mouse set the snake free by moving the rock. The mouse believes that since he did something nice for the snake, the snake should do something nice for him and not eat him.

Meet the author and the illustrator

Read aloud page 337 as children follow along. Ask children what the author says is the best part about being a writer.

Independent Reading

After children enter their independent reading into their Reading Logs, have them paraphrase a portion of the text they have just read. Tell children that when we paraphrase, we express the meaning of what we have read using our own words.

Differentiated Instruction

A **Advanced**

Look Back and Write Ask children who show proficiency with the writing prompt to describe another situation where "One good turn deserves another."

 INTERACT with TEXT

Strategy Response Log

Inferring Have children revisit p. RR16 in their *Reader's and Writer's Notebook* where they identified the characteristics of a folk tale. After reading, have them write a sentence that describes an inference they made from what one of the animal characters said or did.

Plan to Assess Retelling

- [ ] Week 1: Strategic Intervention
- [ ] Week 2: Advanced
- [ ] Week 3: Strategic Intervention
- [ ] Week 4: On-Level
- [x] This week assess Strategic Intervention children.
- [ ] Week 6: Assess any children you have not yet checked during this unit.

Objectives
- Recognize and use possessive nouns in reading, writing, and speaking.
- Write a draft of a fairy tale.

Conventions
Possessive Nouns

Review
Possessive nouns

Remind children that possessive nouns show ownership. Singular possessive nouns are usually formed by adding *'s*. Plural possessive nouns are often formed by adding an apostrophe after the final *s*: *horse's mane, cows' tails*.

Guide practice

Write this sentence on the board and have children read it aloud.

> **The books of the boys are in the backpack of the girl.**

How would you rewrite the sentence using possessive nouns? (The boys' books are in the girl's backpack.)

Team Talk Pair children and have them brainstorm other phrases using *of* to show possession. Have them take turns restating each phrase using a possessive noun.

Connect to oral language

Have children complete these sentence frames orally using possessive nouns.

1. Tim said that is his _____ car.
2. I am going to my _____ house this weekend.
3. Those are my baby _____ toys.

On their own

Use *Let's Practice It!* p. 105 on the *Teacher Resource DVD-ROM*.

Let's Practice It!
TR DVD•105

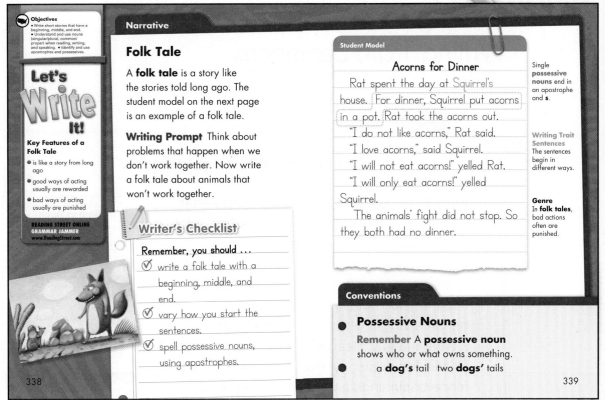

Student Edition pp. 338–339

5. The mouse find the rok.
   The mouse <u>found</u> the ro<u>ck</u>.

6. Sh'es a smat mouse.
   She<u>'</u>s a sma<u>rt</u> mouse.

Discuss the Daily Fix-It corrections with children. Review the use of the apostrophe in contractions and the spelling of *found, rock,* and *smart.*

Let's Write It!

Teach

Use pp. 338–339 in the Student Edition. Read aloud the Key Features of a Folk Tale and the definition of a folk tale. Help children better understand the Writing Prompt by reading it aloud and discussing the Writer's Checklist with children.

Review the student model

Then read "Acorns for Dinner" on page 339 to children. Point out that it is like a story from long ago, and that the characters' behavior was punished. Explain to children that the folk tale has a beginning, middle, and end. Read aloud and briefly discuss the side notes about Genre, the Writing Trait, and possessive nouns to help children understand how an author writes a folk tale.

Scoring rubric

Top-Score Response Help children understand that a top-score response sounds like a story from long ago, rewards or punishes behavior, has a beginning, middle, and end, and uses possessive nouns correctly. For a complete rubric see Writing Rubric 10 from the *Teacher Resource DVD-ROM.*

Connect to conventions

Read to children the Conventions note. Point out the possessive nouns in the model.

Objectives

- Write a draft of a folk tale.
- Use varied sentence beginnings in writing.
- Use singular and plural possessive nouns in writing.
- Gather information about a topic related to solving a community problem.

Writing—Folk Tale
Writing Trait: Sentences

MINI-LESSON

Varied Sentence Beginnings

■ **Introduce** Use your story chart from yesterday and Writing Transparency 10A to model varied sentence beginnings. When I wrote my folk tale, I used my story chart. But I wanted to begin my sentences in different ways to make my folk tale interesting to read. So I began each sentence in the first paragraph in a different way. Read aloud the first paragraph on the Transparency. Point out the varied sentence beginnings and how that helps make the writing interesting.

Pig and Duck

Pig and Duck walked by a river. They saw red berrys on the other side. "Let's get some berries!" said Pig. Duck agreed

Pig wanted to make a bridge to get the berries. duck wanted to make a raft. So each animul worked alone.

At last, Pigs bridge was finished. So was Ducks' raft. It took them a long time. It was dark outside. They couldn't see the berries. They went home with nothing.

Unit 2 One Good Turn Deserves Another   Writing Model **10A**

Writing Transparency 10A
TR DVD

■ **Explain** how children can use the story events they planned yesterday to draft their folk tale: beginning, middle, and end. Tell them to begin their sentences in different ways to make their writing interesting. Today's goal is to write the folk tale, but not to rewrite each word perfectly. They can edit later to correct the words.

Guide story writing

Now it is time to write your folk tale. Tell how your animal characters won't work together. Have children use their story charts. Help them finish the ideas. Then guide children as they draft their folk tales.

ROUTINE   **Quick Write for Fluency**   **Team Talk**

1 **Talk** Have partners take one minute to talk about how the characters in their folk tale won't work together.

2 **Write** Each child writes a sentence that tells what the characters said or did.

3 **Share** Partners point out possessive nouns in the others' sentences.

Routines Flip Chart

Research and Inquiry
Gather and Record Information

Teach

Display the topics and questions list from Day 1. Help children decide which sources might help answer their question before they gather materials.

Topic: Saving Water

Question: How do people work together saving water?

At Home	At Work
I catch rain for plants. I don't use much water at the sinks.	Fix drips Re-use water at factories.

Model

Think Aloud I think about my topic, Saving Water. It's a science topic. Next I think about sources I've already read about saving water, such as books, science magazine articles, and Web sites. I know that my family and some of our friends might know how others save water. These sound like good sources! I'll plan to start research on the Web and in science books or magazines. After school I can talk with my family.

Guide practice

Go through the list of children's topics; have children suggest relevant sources. Help with possible keywords, and post a list of challenging words that may be needed for recalling or spelling while gathering information, for example, *conservation, recycling, donations, volunteer, environment,* and *community.*

On their own

Have partners make charts and begin gathering information.

Wrap Up Your Day

✔ **Compare and Contrast** We can see how objects are the same and different. What else can we compare and contrast?

✔ **Inferring** Have children tell how things they already know can help them make inferences about story characters.

Differentiated Instruction

SI Strategic Intervention

Research Planning Remind children that their goal is to find out new facts, not just list what they already know. For example, if they have the topic recycling, they might want to find out how businesses recycle or who handles the materials after pickup.

Preview DAY 4

Tell children that tomorrow they will read about a mouse that helped a lion solve a problem.

Objectives
• Discuss the concept to develop oral vocabulary.
• Build oral vocabulary.
• Identify details in text.

Today at a Glance

Oral Vocabulary
coax, ramp, startle

Phonics and Spelling
Review Plurals

High-Frequency Words
Review

Comprehension
◉ Inferring

Fluency
Read with Accuracy

Conventions
Possessive Nouns

Writing
Folk Tale: Revise

Listening and Speaking
Give and Follow Instructions

Research and Inquiry
Review and Revise Topic

Concept Talk

Question of the Week
How can we work together to solve problems?

Build concepts

To reinforce concepts and to focus children's attention, have children sing "Talk It Out" from the *Sing with Me* Big Book. How do things get better when we work out a problem? (Possible response: We keep a friend.)

 *Sing with Me* Big Book Audio

Review
Genre: narrative nonfiction

Have children tell the key features of **narrative nonfiction:** it tells a story about an event and explains something about the real world. Explain that today you will read "A Ducky Day" by Margaret Fling about a mother duck who needs some help to solve a problem.

Monitor listening comprehension

Recall how the coyote saved the mouse in *One Good Turn Deserves Another.* Have children listen to "A Ducky Day" to find out the mother duck's problem and what caused it. Read the selection.

Read Aloud Anthology
"A Ducky Day"

ELL **Produce Oral Language** Use the Day 4 instruction on ELL Poster 10 to extend and enrich language.

ELL Poster 10

Oral Vocabulary
Amazing Words

Teach Amazing Words

Amazing Words — Oral Vocabulary Routine

1 **Introduce the Word** Relate the word *startle* to the story. The author says Mama duck *startled* a guest. Supply a child-friendly definition. *Startled* means "frightened." Have children say the word.

2 **Demonstrate** Provide examples to show meaning. The spider on the floor *startled* Luis. The dog's loud howl *startled* me.

3 **Apply** Have children demonstrate their understanding. Bugs *startle* some people. What is something that *startles* you? Show how you look when you are *startled*.

See p. OV•2 to teach *coax and ramp.*

Routines Flip Chart

Anchored Talk

Add to the concept map

Discuss how working together can solve problems.

- In the story "A Ducky Day," what was Mama's problem? (The baby ducks could not fly to get off the deck.) How did the people in the house help Mama and her baby ducks? (They showed her how to get the babies through the house and outside.)

- Let's add *help animals survive* to our concept map.

Amazing Words

conflict	mope
pursue	coax
resolve	ramp
deserve	startle

Differentiated Instruction

SI **Strategic Intervention**
Pronounce /r/ If children do not pronounce the sound /r/ in the word *startled,* say the sentence containing the word, stressing the sound /r/. Have children repeat it.

ELL

English Language Learners
Frontload Listening Comprehension Before reading "A Ducky Day," sketch a diagram of the enclosed deck that is described in the read aloud. Point to the diagram and use the language "enclosed deck," "railings," and "top railings" to help children visualize the setting.

Objectives

- Read and identify plurals with -s, -es, -ies.
- Read words fluently in context and independent of context.

Phonics Review
Plurals

Review Plurals

To review last week's phonics skill, write *trains* and *ditches.* You studied words like these last week. What do you know about the endings of these words? (The ending -s was added to *train* and the ending -es was added to *ditch* to form plurals.)

Write the word *parties.* What do you know about reading this plural? (The base word is *party.* The y was changed to i before adding -es.)

Corrective feedback

If children are unable to answer the questions about plurals, refer them to Sound-Spelling Cards 139, 141, and 142.

Guide practice

Write -s, -es, and -ies as headings in a three-column chart. I will write some words. When I write a word, read it in your head. Think about whether it ends with -s, -es, or -ies. Then tell me under what heading it belongs: *plants, stories, batches, pennies, raisins, ashes, carpets, boxes, buddies, cities, lunches, shirts.* Write each word under the appropriate heading. Then have children read the words. Have them identify the base words and plural endings and tell which base words had spelling changes.

-s	-es	-ies
plants	batches	stories
raisins	ashes	pennies
carpets	boxes	buddies
shirts	lunches	cities

On their own

Use Let's Practice It! p. 101 on the *Teacher Resource DVD-ROM.*

Let's Practice It! TR DVD•101

Fluent Word Reading
Spiral Review

Read words independent of context

Display these words. Tell children that they can blend or chunk some words on this list and others are Word Wall words. Have children read the list three or four times until they can read at the rate of two to three seconds per word.

paper	scared	people	third	probably
shiver	stay	forget	Thursday	bought
perform	shore	artist	sign	pleasant
started	board	train	painting	shall

Word Reading

Corrective feedback

If... children have difficulty reading whole words,
then... have them use sound-by-sound blending or chunking for decodable words or say and spell high-frequency words.

If... children cannot read fluently at a rate of two to three seconds per word,
then... have pairs practice the list until they can read it fluently.

Read words in context

Display these sentences. Call on individuals to read a sentence. Then randomly point to review words and have children read them. To help you monitor word reading, high-frequency words are underlined and decodable words are italicized.

> I was <u>scared</u> to *perform,* and I *started* to *shiver!*
> We <u>shall</u> not *forget* to place the *paper* on the *board.*
> <u>People</u> will see the big <u>sign</u> next to the *train.*
> If it's <u>pleasant</u> on *Thursday,* I'll <u>probably</u> *stay* at the *shore.*
> This is the *third painting* she <u>bought</u> from this *artist.*

Sentence Reading

Corrective feedback

If...children are unable to read a high-frequency word,
then...read the word for them and spell it, having them echo you.

If...children have difficulty reading a decodable word,
then...guide them in blending or combining word parts.

Differentiated Instruction

 Strategic Intervention

Reading an Exclamation Point out that the first sentence is an exclamation and ends with an exclamation mark. Remind children that we read an exclamation with excitement or strong feeling. Model how to read the sentence for children. Then have them practice reading the sentence with expression.

Spiral Review

These activities review

- previously taught high-frequency words *bought, people, pleasant, probably, scared, shall, sign.*
- vowel patterns *a, ai, ay.*
- *r*-controlled *er, ir, ur;* syllable *er.*
- *r*-controlled *ar, or, ore, oar.*
- syllable pattern VC/CV (closed syllable CVC).

E L L

English Language Learners
Fluent Word Reading Have children listen to a more fluent reader model the words or have pairs read the words together.

Objectives

- Apply knowledge of sound-spellings to decode unknown words when reading.
- Decode and read words in context and independent of context.
- Practice fluency with oral rereading.

Decodable Practice Reader 10C
Vowel Patterns *a, ai, ay*

Decodable Practice Reader 10C

Decode words independent of context

Have children turn to the first page and decode each word.

Read high-frequency words

Have children identify and read the high-frequency words *wait, thinks, brought, minute,* and *would* on the first page.

Preview

Have children read the title and preview the story. Tell them they will decode words with the long *a* sound spelled *a, ai,* and *ay.*

Decode words in context

Pair children for reading and listen as they decode. One child begins. Children read the entire story, switching readers after each page. Partners reread the story. This time the other child begins.

Caleb likes to hide and wait.
Caleb likes to jump up fast.
174

Caleb thinks it is fun
playing this way.
Mom and Dad say that it is not nice.
Caleb will not make buddies
if he plays that way.
175

One day Caleb hid behind his door.
When Kim came,
Caleb jumped out at her.
Kim got mad and started yelling.
Then Kim went back home.
176

When it rained next,
Caleb brought his best game
and asked Kim to play it with him.
Kim would not play.
Caleb felt bad.
177

Caleb sat for a minute.
"It is not the best plan
to jump out," Caleb said.
"It may make people mad at me."
178

"I'm sad about jumping out, Kim,"
Caleb said.
"I will not do it again."
179

Kim smiled.
"That's fine," Kim said.
"Let's play that game."
180

Corrective feedback

If... children have difficulty decoding a word, **then...** refer them to the Sound-Spelling Cards to identify the sounds in the word. Then prompt them to blend the word.

- What is the new word?
- Is the new word a word you know?
- Does it make sense in the story?

Check decoding and comprehension

Have children retell the story to include characters, setting, and events. Then have children find words that include the long a sound spelled *ai* and *ay* in the story. Children should supply *wait, playing, way, say, plays, day, rained, play,* and *may.*

Review print awareness

On the first two pages of the story, point out the capital letter that begins each sentence. Remind children that every sentence begins with a capital letter. Have children count the sentences on a page and point out the capital letter that begins each sentence.

Reread for Fluency

Have children reread Decodable Practice Reader 10C to develop automaticity decoding words with the long a sound spelled *a, ai,* and *ay.*

 ROUTINE **Oral Rereading**

1. **Read** Have children read the entire book orally.
2. **Reread** To achieve optimal fluency, children should reread the text three or four times.
3. **Corrective Feedback** Listen as children read. Provide corrective feedback regarding their fluency and decoding.

Routines Flip Chart

 ELL

English Language Learners
Decodable Reader
Beginning Before children read, lead them through *The Way to Play.* Preview the story, using the illustrations. Point out the two rhyming words in the story title with the long a sound: *Way* and *Play.* Then list on the board other words from the story that rhyme with *way* and *play: say, day,* and *may.* Have children read the words aloud, and then locate each word in the story.

Intermediate After reading, have children search for words with the long *a* sound, spelled *ai* and *ay.* Have children say the words as you write them in a list. Then ask questions that require children to use the words. For example: *What is your favorite day of the week?*

Advanced/Advanced-High After reading, have children look for long *a* words spelled *ai* and *ay,* and *say* them aloud. Then have children make up clues for the words and have others guess the answers. For example: *This word tells what you do with a game. (play) This word is the opposite of* night. *(day)*

Spelling
Vowel Digraphs *ai, ay*

Partner Review

Supply pairs of children with index cards on which the spelling words have been written. Have one child read a word while the other writes it. Then have children switch roles. Have them use the cards to check their spelling and correct any misspelled words.

On their own   Use Let's Practice It! p. 104 on the *Teacher Resource DVD-ROM.*

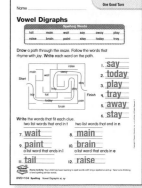

Let's Practice It!
TR DVD•104

Small Group Time

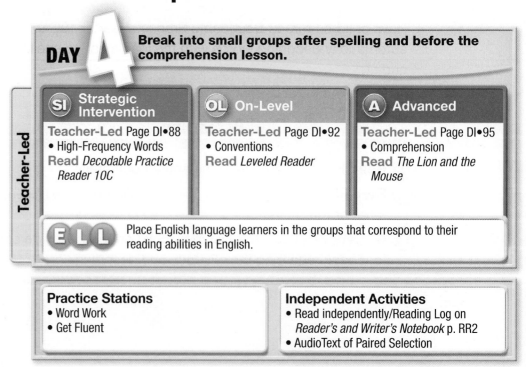

DAY 4

Break into small groups after spelling and before the comprehension lesson.

Teacher-Led

SI Strategic Intervention	OL On-Level	A Advanced
Teacher-Led Page DI•88 • High-Frequency Words **Read** *Decodable Practice Reader 10C*	**Teacher-Led** Page DI•92 • Conventions **Read** *Leveled Reader*	**Teacher-Led** Page DI•95 • Comprehension **Read** *The Lion and the Mouse*

ELL Place English language learners in the groups that correspond to their reading abilities in English.

Practice Stations	**Independent Activities**
• Word Work • Get Fluent	• Read independently/Reading Log on *Reader's and Writer's Notebook* p. RR2 • AudioText of Paired Selection

Social Studies in Reading

Academic Vocabulary

fable a very short folk tale that teaches a lesson

Preview and predict

Read the title and the first sentence of the selection on pages 340–343. Have children look through the selection and predict what they might learn. (Possible response: They might learn that doing a good deed for someone can lead to a friendship.) Ask them what clues helped them make that prediction. (Possible response: They may say the picture of the mouse chewing on the net shows a good deed. The picture of the mouse on the lion's back shows they have become friends.)

Let's Think About Genre

Folk Tale/Fable Tell children that they will read a fable. Explain that a **fable** is a kind of folk tale that is very short and teaches a lesson. Review the key features of a folk tale: It is a story that often teaches a lesson. Characters are often animals that act like people. In a fable, the lesson or theme often is directly stated at the end of the story.

Activate prior knowledge

Have children recall which character helped another in *One Good Turn Deserves Another*. (The coyote helped the mouse.)

Set a purpose

As children read "The Lion and the Mouse," use Let's Think About in the Student Edition to help them focus on the features and structure of a folk tale/fable.

Objectives

- Infer important information from text.
- Compare and contrast the characters, setting, and plot in two versions of the same folk tale.

Objectives
- Identify themes in well-known fables, legends, myths, or stories.
- Compare the characters, settings, and plots in traditional and contemporary folktales.

Social Studies in Reading

Genre
Folk Tale/Fable

- A fable is a kind of folk tale. It is a very short story that teaches a lesson.
- A fable usually states its lesson, or theme, at the end of the story.
- The characters in fables are often animals.
- Read "The Lion and the Mouse." Look for elements that make this story a fable.

The Lion and the Mouse

retold by Claire Daniel
illustrated by Dan Andreasen

One day Mouse bumped into Lion by mistake and woke him up. Lion caught Mouse and dangled him by his tail.

"Do not eat me!" Mouse cried. "One day I will return the favor."

Lion laughed so hard that he dropped Mouse. Lion said, "How can a tiny mouse ever help a mighty lion like me?"

The next day Lion fell into a hunter's trap. He was covered with a net. Lion's roars shook the ground.

Other animals heard Lion, but no one wanted to come near an angry lion. Only Mouse ran toward Lion.

Mouse said, "I will help you."

Lion roared, "You are too small to help me!"

Let's Think About...
Why do you think Mouse goes near the "angry lion"?
Folk Tale/Fable

340   341

Student Edition pp. 340–341

Guide Comprehension

Guide practice

 Inferring

Think Aloud Strong readers combine background knowledge with clues in the text to make **inferences,** or come up with their own idea about what the text means. When I read that Lion fell into a hunter's trap and started roaring, I inferred that he couldn't get out on his own. I know hunters sometimes shoot lions, so I also infer that Lion may be in great danger of losing his life.

Compare and contrast

Think Aloud When I read the first two pages of this story, it reminds me right away of *One Good Turn Deserves Another.* Both stories start with a big, scary animal trapped and asking for help from a mouse. The plots and the characters are very similar.

Let's Think About Folktale/Fable

Possible responses: Mouse goes near Lion because he is going to help him. Lion helped him once so Mouse is not afraid of him.

Let's **Think** About...
Compare these characters with the characters from the folk tale *One Good Turn Deserves Another.*
Folk Tale/Fable

Let's **Think** About...
Was Lion wrong about Mouse? How does Mouse help Lion?
Folk Tale/Fable

Mouse just said, "Lion, be quiet."

Mouse chewed the net. He chewed for a long time. Finally, Mouse made a hole. Lion was free!

Just then the hunters returned. Lion roared at the men, and they ran away.

342

One hunter looked back. He saw the proud lion walking away. The hunter rubbed his eyes. Could it be? A mouse was riding on the lion's back!

Lion and Mouse became best friends. Lion liked to say, "Little friends can make the best friends."

343

Let's **Think** About...
Compare the setting and plot with those of the folk tale *One Good Turn Deserves Another.*
Folk Tale/Fable

Let's **Think** About...
Reading Across Texts The theme of the fable is the lesson it teaches. What are the themes of "The Lion and the Mouse" and *One Good Turn Deserves Another?*

Writing Across Texts Also think about the characters and settings. Write a paragraph comparing and contrasting the tales.

Student Edition pp. 342–343

Guide Comprehension, continued

Let's Think About Folk Tale/Fable

Compare/Contrast Both tales have a small mouse and a dangerous animal—a snake in one, a lion in the other. The lion is grateful for the mouse's help, but the snake is not grateful.

Let's Think About Folk Tale/Fable

Yes, Lion was wrong. Mouse saves Lion's life by freeing him from the hunter's net.

Let's Think About Folk Tale/Fable

Compare and Contrast Both settings are outdoors; one is a desert, the other is the African grassland. In both plots, a mouse frees a dangerous animal. In one story, the freed animal wants to eat the mouse; in the other, they become friends.

Reading Across Texts Both tales have the same theme: that one good turn deserves another.

Writing Across Texts Have children compare the reactions of the snake and the lion. Although a good deed deserves to be repaid, in this world good deeds are not always rewarded.

ELL

English Language Learners
Writing Across Texts Provide sentence frames for children to complete to compare the themes of the two stories.

Objectives
- Read aloud fluently with accuracy.
- Write possessive nouns.
- Use apostrophes in possessive nouns.

Check Fluency WCPM
SUCCESS PREDICTOR

Fluency
Read with Accuracy

Guide practice

- Have children turn to pages 330–331 in *One Good Turn Deserves Another.*
- Have children follow along as you read the pages accurately.
- Have the class read the pages with you and then reread the pages as a group until they read with no hesitation and no mistakes. To provide additional fluency practice, pair nonfluent readers with fluent readers.

ROUTINE **Paired Reading**

(1) **Select a Passage** For *One Good Turn Deserves Another,* use pages 334–335.

(2) **Model** First, have children track the print as you read.

(3) **Guide Practice** Then have children read along with you.

(4) **On Their Own** For optimal fluency, have partners reread three or four times.

Routines Flip Chart

MONITOR PROGRESS **Check Fluency WCPM**

As children reread, monitor their progress toward their individual fluency goals. Current Goal: 48–58 words correct per minute. Mid-Year-Goal: 65 words correct per minute.

If... children cannot read fluently at a rate of 48–58 words correct per minute,

then... have children practice with text at their independent level.

Day 1	Day 2	Day 3	Day 4	Day 5
Check Word Reading	Check High-Frequency Words	Check Retelling	Check Fluency	Check Oral Vocabulary

Success Predictor

Conventions
Possessive Nouns

Test practice
Use *Reader's and Writer's Notebook* p. 156 to help children recognize and use possessive nouns. Recall that most singular possessive nouns are formed by adding *'s*. Most plural possessive nouns are formed by adding an apostrophe after the final *s*. Model recognizing possessive nouns by writing this sentence on the board, reading it aloud, and underlining the singular possessive noun once and the plural possessive noun twice.

I picked up the <u>twins'</u> games and the <u>baby's</u> toys.

Then read the *Reader's and Writer's Notebook* p. 156 directions. Guide children as they mark the answer for number 1.

On their own
Use *Reader's and Writer's Notebook* p. 156.

Connect to oral language
After children mark the answers to numbers 1–6, review the correct choices aloud, and have children read each sentence. Tell them to raise one hand as they read each singular possessive noun and two hands as they read each plural possessive noun.

One Good Turn

ve Nouns

of the word that completes each sentence.

1. The mouse heard the ___ voice.
   ○ A snake
   ○ B snakes
   ○ C snake's
2. Some of the ___ advice did not help the mouse.
   ○ A animals's
   ○ B animals
   ○ C animals'
3. The crow ate grasshoppers in the ___ field.
   ○ A farmers
   ○ B farmers'
   ○ C farmer's
4. The ___ dinner was the crops they ate.
   ○ A grasshoppers'
   ○ B grasshopper'
   ○ C grasshopper's
5. The ___ paw moved the rock.
   ○ A coyote
   ○ B coyotes
   ○ C coyote's
6. The ___ favor will be returned someday.
   ○ A mouse's
   ○ B mouses'
   ○ C mouse

156 Conventions Possessive Nouns

Reader's and Writer's Notebook p. 156

Differentiated Instruction

(A) Advanced
WCPM If children already read at 90 words correct per minute, allow them to read independently.

Fluency Assessment Plan

Do a formal fluency assessment with 8 to 10 children every week. Assess 4 to 5 children on Day 4, and 4 to 5 children on Day 5. Use the reproducible fluency passage, Teacher's Edition, p. 345f.

Options for Oral Rereading

Use *One Good Turn Deserves Another* or one of the week's Decodable Practice Readers.

Daily Fix-It

7. she saw the snakes tail.
   <u>S</u>he saw the snake<u>'s</u> tail.
8. That mad her run away
   That <u>made</u> her run away<u>.</u>

Discuss the Daily Fix-It corrections with children. Review sentence capitalization and punctuation, formation of possessive nouns, and spelling words with *long a*.

Objectives
• Revise a draft by changing sentences for varied sentence beginnings.

Writing—Folk Tale
Revising Strategy

MINI-LESSON

Revising Strategy: Vary Sentences

■ Yesterday we wrote folk tales about animals that won't work together. Today we will revise. We can make our stories more interesting by beginning our sentences in different ways.

Writing Transparency 10B
TR DVD

■ Display the Revising Tips. Explain that this is a time for making the folk tale interesting for anyone who will read it. Tomorrow children will proofread to correct any errors such as mis-spellings, missing capital letters, or misplaced apostrophes.

Revising Tips

☐ Make sure your tale has a beginning, a middle, and an end.

☐ Change sentences to make them begin in different ways.

■ Use Writing Transparency 10B to model changing sentence beginnings. In my folk tale, "Pig and Duck," the last paragraph has sentences that begin the same way. I can add "Now" to the sentence "It was dark outside," so that it begins in a different way than the sentence that comes before. I can change the beginning of the last sentence to say, "So Pig and Duck went home with nothing," so that two sentences don't begin with "They." **Make the changes on the transparency.** Tell children they can change sentence beginnings in their folk tale as they revise.

Peer conferencing

Peer Revision Pair up children and tell one of the pair to read the partner's folk tale. Allow one to two minutes. Then have the readers point out any sentences that begin the same way. Repeat with second partners reading and pointing out such sentences in the other folk tale. Have writers con-sider their partner's suggestions for changing sentences. Circulate to assist children planning to revise their folk tales. As appropriate, suggest changing sentences for varied sentence beginnings.

Guide practice

Have children revise their folk tales. For those not sure how to revise, have children refer to the Revising Tips or the Key Features of a Folk Tale.

Corrective feedback

Circulate to monitor and conference with children as they write. Remind them that they will have time to proofread and edit tomorrow. Today they can change their sentences to make them begin in different ways. Help them understand that beginning their sentences in different ways will make their writing more interesting. Encourage them to explain why they want to change the beginning of a particular sentence.

ROUTINE **Quick Write for Fluency** **Team Talk**

1. **Talk** Read these sentences aloud, and have children identify how one sentence might be changed so that the sentences have different beginnings.

   Jada and Susan were hungry.
   Jada and Susan went home for lunch.

2. **Write** Have children write two sentences that begin in the same way.

3. **Share** Partners can read the sentences to one another and orally change the beginning of one sentence to add variety.

Routines Flip Chart

Differentiated Instruction

 Strategic Intervention

Vary Sentence Beginnings
Point out that one way to vary sentence beginnings is to add words and phrases that show sequence. Provide children with a list of words and phrases that they can refer to as they write. For example: *then, next, after that, later on, now, so, that night,* and *the next day.*

DAY 4 Language Arts

Objectives

- Give instructions that involve a sequence of actions.
- Speak clearly at an appropriate rate.
- Listen to, restate, and follow instructions in sequence.
- Review answers to inquiry questions.

Listening and Speaking
Give and Follow Instructions

Teach how to give and follow instructions

Tell children that people often give instructions or need to listen to them.

- Good speakers speak clearly.
- When good speakers give instructions, they use sequence words such as *first, next,* and *last* to help listeners remember the steps.
- Good listeners pay close attention to instructions and restate the steps so that they can remember to follow them in order.

Model

Use the passage below to model giving instructions that involve a sequence of actions.

Here are the instructions to make pancakes. Listen to remember each step in the instructions. *First,* assemble pancake mix, milk, and 2 eggs. *Next,* mix the ingredients in a bowl. *Then,* pour some of the batter into a hot pan. *Last,* turn the pancake over to cook both sides.

Guide practice

Have children restate the steps of the instructions and then pantomime each action. Discuss other instructions that children have given or followed. Make a list of ideas on the board. Have children choose one idea and write the instructions in order using the following questions:

1. What was the first step?
2. What did you do next?
3. Then what did you do?
4. What was the last step?

On their own

Have pairs of children take turns giving and following instructions that involve a series of actions. Suggest that they use one of the ideas you have written on the board. As they follow instructions, remind children to listen carefully to the steps and restate them to help them remember the instructions.

Research and Inquiry
Review and Revise Topic

Teach
Display the Day 1 list of children's topics and questions. Tell children that the next step in the inquiry project is to review the topic to see if we are finding the new information we want. Did we find information that is recorded in just one side of our chart? We might need to focus on another part of the topic.

Model

Think Aloud I'm researching the topic Saving Water. I have learned a lot of new information about saving water at home. I need information about people at work who save water. Today I can do a Web search with the keywords Saving Water at Work.

Guide practice
Have children who have found information in only one side of their chart decide whether they need to revise their topic. If not, help them find sources for the other category. Remind them that tomorrow they will organize the information on their chart and present it to others.

On their own
Use *Reader's and Writer's Notebook* p. 153.

Wrap Up Your Day

✔ **Phonics** List *radar, vapor, snail, raisin, display,* and *spray.* Have children read each word and identify the long *a* spelling.

✔ **Fluency** Display *Gail may sketch the volcano crater behind a bay today.* Have children read the sentence three or four times until they can do so fluently.

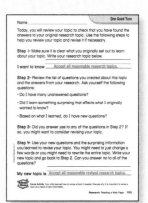

Reader's and Writer's Notebook, p. 153

Preview DAY 5

Remind children that they heard about how working together helped a duck and her babies. Tell them you will read about Mama Duck again tomorrow.

Objectives
• Review the concept: working together to solve problems.
• Build oral vocabulary.
• Identify details in text.

Today at a Glance

Oral Vocabulary
Review

Phonics
◉ Review Vowel Patterns *a, ai, ay*

Comprehension
◉ Compare and Contrast

High-Frequency Words
Review

Story Words
Review

Conventions
Possessive Nouns

Writing
Folk Tale: Edit

Research and Inquiry
Communicate

Check Oral Vocabulary
SUCCESS PREDICTOR

Concept Wrap Up

? **Question of the Week**
How can we work together to solve problems?

Review
Concept

This week we have read and listened to stories about working together to solve problems. Today you will listen to recall the family's plan to help Mama duck and her babies leave the deck. **Read the story.**

• What plan works to save the ducklings? (The family makes a ramp and coaxes Mama and ducklings to walk through the house and out the door.)

Review
Amazing
Words

Review the meaning of this week's Amazing Words. Display the concept map. Have children use Amazing Words and the concept map to answer the Question of the Week.

Read Aloud Anthology
"A Ducky Day"

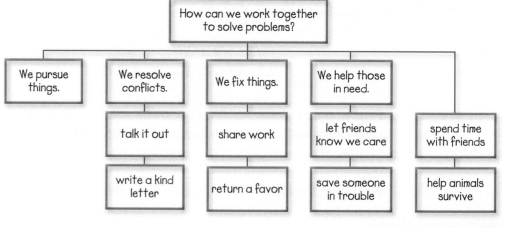

How can we work together to solve problems?

We pursue things.	We resolve conflicts.	We fix things.	We help those in need.
	talk it out	share work	let friends know we care	spend time with friends
	write a kind letter	return a favor	save someone in trouble	help animals survive

ELL **Check Concepts and Language** Use the Day 5 instruction on ELL Poster 10 to monitor children's understanding of the lesson concept.

ELL Poster 10

Oral Vocabulary
Amazing Ideas

Connect to the Big Question

Team Talk Pair children and have them discuss how the Question of the Week connects to this unit's Big Question, "How can we work together?" Tell children to use the concept map and what they've learned from this week's Anchored Talks and reading selections to form an Amazing Idea—a realization or "big idea" about **working together.** Then ask each pair to share their Amazing Idea with the class.

Amazing Ideas might include these key concepts:

• We can work together to solve problems.

• Talking things out can resolve conflicts with friends.

• We can work together to help those in need.

MONITOR PROGRESS | **Check Oral Vocabulary**

Call on individuals to use this week's Amazing Words to talk about what we can learn by working together to solve problems. Prompt discussion with the questions below. Have children respond in complete sentences. Monitor children's ability to use the Amazing Words and note which words children are unable to use.

• **How can you *resolve* a *conflict*?**

• **What solution to a problem would you like to *pursue*?**

• **How could you *coax* an animal into a cage if you didn't want to *startle* it?**

• **What kind of problem might a *ramp* solve?**

• **Does someone who *mopes* around the house *deserve* to be helped? Why or why not?**

If... children have difficulty using the Amazing Words,

then... reteach the unknown words using the Oral Vocabulary Routines, pp. 316a, 320b, 336b, 340b.

Day 1	Day 2	Day 3	Day 4	Day 5
Check Word Reading	Check High-Frequency Words	Check Retelling	Check Fluency	Check Oral Vocabulary

Success Predictor

Amazing Words

resolve	mope
conflict	coax
pursue	ramp
deserve	startle

ELL

English Language Learners

Encourage Language Production Pair and group work naturally provides a low-anxiety environment that is conducive to language acquisition. When students are in a small group, everyone gets a chance to contribute to the discussion and production is increased.

Objectives

◎ Review words with vowel patterns *a, ai, ay.*

Assess

- Spell words with vowel patterns *a, ai, ay.*
- Spell high-frequency words.

Phonics

⟳ Vowel Patterns *a, ai, ay*

Review
Target phonics skill

Write the following sentences on the board. Have children read each one, first quietly to themselves and then aloud as you track the print.

> 1. Gail paid the bills for basic things such as gas.
>
> 2. I like the painting of the bay in May.
>
> 3. The snail makes a trail on the crater.
>
> 4. We like staying in when a day is gray with rain and hail.

Team Talk Have children discuss with a partner which words have the vowel sound /ā/. Then call on individuals to share with the class.

Spelling Test

Dictate spelling words

Say each word, read the sentence, repeat the word, and allow time for children to write the word.

1. **away** — I will give **away** these old books.
2. **tray** — Dad put the food on a **tray**.
3. **say** — Can you hear what I **say**?
4. **stay** — I'll **stay** with Nan for the weekend.
5. **play** — Can you **play** after school?
6. **paint** — I want to **paint** my room yellow.
7. **brain** — You use your **brain** every day.
8. **tail** — My dog wags its **tail** a lot.
9. **today** — Jen will finish her project **today**.
10. **raise** — Did the store **raise** its prices?
11. **wait** — Will you please **wait** for me?
12. **main** — This is the **main** path to the park.

High-Frequency Words

13. **everybody** — **Everybody** likes to have a good time!
14. **sorry** — I'm **sorry** I stepped on your toe.

Differentiated Instruction

 Strategic Intervention

Check Spelling Have children complete each spelling word by writing *ai* or *ay*. For example: p__nt, p*ai*nt.

 Advanced

Extend Spelling Have children who have demonstrated proficiency in spelling individual words spell each word in a self-made sentence that is either a question or an exclamation.

Small Group Time

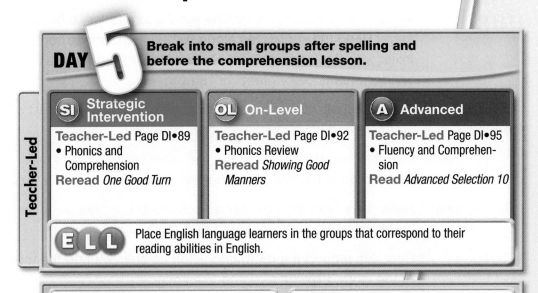

DAY 5 — Break into small groups after spelling and before the comprehension lesson.

SI Strategic Intervention
Teacher-Led Page DI•89
• Phonics and Comprehension
Reread *One Good Turn*

OL On-Level
Teacher-Led Page DI•92
• Phonics Review
Reread *Showing Good Manners*

A Advanced
Teacher-Led Page DI•95
• Fluency and Comprehension
Read *Advanced Selection 10*

ELL Place English language learners in the groups that correspond to their reading abilities in English.

Practice Stations
• Words to Know
• Read for Meaning

Independent Activities
• Read independently/Reading Log on *Reader's and Writer's Notebook* p. RR2
• Concept Talk Video

Objectives

- Determine relevant meaning of unfamiliar words.
- Read aloud fluently with accuracy.
- Give and follow instructions.
- Speak clearly.
- Listen attentively.

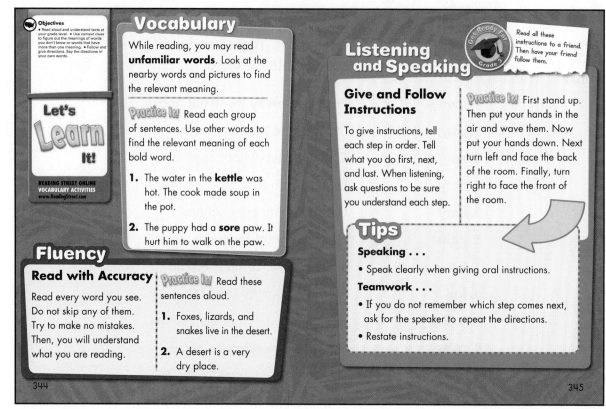

Student Edition pp. 344–345

Vocabulary
Unfamiliar Words

Teach

Read and discuss the Vocabulary lesson on page 344 of the Student Edition. Explain that we can figure out a word's meaning by looking at the words and pictures around the word for clues to the relevant meaning.

Model

Write these two sentences: *The wind was intense. It blew with very great force.* Read the sentences aloud. When I read these sentences, I am unfamiliar with the word *intense*. The words *very great* are a clue that the word *intense* means "very great" or "strong."

Guide practice

Read the instructions for the Vocabulary Practice It! activity. Then read the first item and have children repeat after you.

I want to know the meaning of the word *kettle*. When I read *The cook made soup in the pot*, I see that the meaning of *kettle* is "pot."

On their own

Have pairs read the next sentences aloud together and use the nearby words to find the relevant meaning of the word in bold.

Corrective feedback

Circulate around the room and listen as children find the relevant meaning of the word. Provide assistance as needed.

Fluency
Accuracy

Teach

Read and discuss the Fluency instructions.

Read words in context

Give children a moment to look at the sentences. Then have them read each sentence three or four times until they can read each sentence with accuracy.

Listening and Speaking
Give and Follow Instructions

Teach

Have children turn to page 345 of the Student Edition. Tell children that good speakers speak clearly when giving instructions. Remind them to listen carefully and ask questions for better understanding of the steps.

Point out that good instructions tell each step of the instructions in order. Ask children: What words could we use to help people understand each step in the order? *(first, next, and last)*

Introduce prompt

Read the Practice It! prompt with the class. Remind children to look for words that help them understand the order of the steps of the instructions.

Team Talk Have pairs take turns giving and following the instructions. Remind children to ask questions, and if they forget the order, they can ask the speaker to repeat the steps.

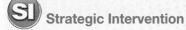 **Strategic Intervention**

Visualize Skills Help children find relevant meaning of unfamiliar words by looking for clues in pictures. Using *One Good Turn Deserves Another,* point to the word *desert* on page 322. Have children look at the pictures and tell what they think *desert* might mean. Write children's ideas on the board. Tell them that *desert* means a dry area of land covered with sand. Continue with other words in the story.

Give and Follow Directions

In addition to giving directions by telling what to do first, next, and last, children at Grade 3, should also be able to give oral instructions that involve a sequence of actions.

English Language Learners
Unfamiliar Words Write these sentences on the board:
The fuzzy cat has a lot of fur.

I flipped off my skateboard and fell on the ground.

Read the sentences aloud with children and point out the clue words *(fur; fell)* to help them understand the underlined words.

Objectives
- ◎ Use compare and contrast to understand a story.
- • Read story words.
- • Recognize idioms.

Comprehension
↻ Compare and Contrast

Review
Compare and contrast

Remember that readers can compare and contrast characters, settings, and stories. When we tell how two or more things are alike, we compare. What is it called when we tell how things are different? (contrast)

Read aloud the following story and have children answer the questions.

Irena's parents both like to fix breakfast on Saturdays. They take turns. Early one Saturday, noises in the kitchen wake Irena. She wonders who is making the racket. Dad is the early riser, but Mom gets up early only on the Saturdays she goes hiking with friends. Dad always makes eggs and sausage, but Mom makes pancakes. Then Irena smells sausage cooking.

1. How are Irena's parents alike? (They like to fix breakfast on Saturdays.)

2. What are two ways her parents are different? (Her dad is an early riser, but her mother sleeps later unless she is going hiking. Her dad cooks eggs and sausage for breakfast, but her mom makes pancakes.)

3. Explain how you can infer who Irena hears in the kitchen. (It must be her dad because she smells sausage, and he cooks eggs and sausage.)

Vocabulary
High-Frequency and Story Words

Review
High-frequency words

Review this week's high-frequency words: *behind, brought, door, everybody, minute, promise,* and *sorry.* Provide an example of two related words, having the class supply the missing word, such as *above, beside,* _____. (behind)

Team Talk Have children orally give category clues for the remaining six words and have their partner supply the missing word.

Review
Story words

Write the words *creature, grateful, armadillo, groaned,* and *snorted.* Read them aloud together. Ask questions such as: What creature would you least like to meet in a desert? For what event in the last week are you most grateful? What do you think is the most interesting thing about an armadillo? When have you groaned about something that happened? Have you ever snorted? Why?

Corrective feedback

For corrective feedback, review the definitions on p. 336h.

Literary Text
Idioms

Review Genre

Review with children that a **fable** is a story that often teaches a lesson or moral. Remind children that the characters in fables are often animals that act like people.

Teach

An **idiom** is an expression that can't be understood from the literal meaning of the words that form it. The phrase "hold your tongue" would be pretty silly if you took it literally. "Hold your tongue" is an idiom that means "be quiet" or "don't say anything."

Model

 There is an idiom in the title of the folk tale *One Good Turn Deserves Another.* The title does not mean literally that you should turn around twice. The context of the story helps me understand that *one good turn deserves another* is an idiom that means that if you do a favor for someone, that person should do a favor for you in return.

Guide practice

Ask the following questions to guide children in determining the meaning of idioms.

- When the mouse runs away, what does she mean when she says "I'll return the favor someday"? (Possible response: She means that she will do something nice for him, in return for the nice thing he did for her.)

- In "The Ungrateful Tiger," the man says to the tiger "But you gave your word that you would be nice!" What do you think the idiom "gave your word" means? (to promise)

On their own

Have children look for the phrase "good is often repaid with evil." Ask them to figure out from the pictures and text what the idiom means. (Possible response: When you do a good deed for someone, they will do something bad or mean in return.)

DAY 5 Wrap Up your Week

Assess

- Words with Vowel Patterns *a, ai, ay*
- High-Frequency Words
- Fluency: WCPM
- Compare and Contrast

Fluency Goals

Set individual fluency goals for children to enable them to reach the end-of-the-year goal.

- **Current Goal:** 48–58 WCPM
- **End-of-Year Goal:** 90 WCPM

Assessment
Monitor Progress

For a written assessment of long *a* vowel patterns *a, ai, ay;* high-frequency words; and compare and contrast, use Weekly Test 10, pp. 55–60.

Assess words in context

Sentence reading Use the following reproducible page to assess children's ability to read words in context. Call on children to read two sentences aloud. Start over with sentence one if necessary.

MONITOR PROGRESS | **Sentence Reading**

If... children have trouble reading the long *a* vowel patterns *a, ai, ay,*
then... see the Reteach Lesson in *First Stop.*

If... a child cannot read all the high-frequency words,
then... mark the missed words on a high-frequency word list and have the child practice reading the words with a fluent reader.

Assess

Fluency Take a one-minute sample of children's oral reading. Have children read the fluency passage on p. 345f.

Comprehension Have the child read the entire passage. (If the child had difficulty with the passage, you may read it aloud.) Then have the child give an example of a comparison and contrast in the passage.

MONITOR PROGRESS | **Fluency and Comprehension**

If... a child does not achieve the fluency goal on the timed reading,
then... copy the passage and send it home with the child for additional fluency practice, or have the child practice with a fluent reader.

If... a child cannot compare and contrast,
then... see the Reteach Lesson in *First Stop.*

Monitor accuracy

Record scores Have children monitor their accuracy by recording their scores using the Sentence Reading Chart and by recording the number of words read correctly per minute on their Fluency Progress Chart in *First Stop.*

Read the Sentences

1. Everybody felt bad that Jay did not stay with us.

2. Luke waited at the train stop for one more minute.

3. I promise I'll wipe that basin after playing with Jane.

4. His red apron is on a nail behind that huge desk.

5. Fern brought in her mail and paper.

6. This main door is not locked on Thursday.

7. Ray is sorry that he didn't pay his gas bill.

MONITOR PROGRESS
- Fluency
- Vowel Patterns *a, ai, ay*
- High-frequency Words

Name _____

Read the Story

The Ant and the Grasshopper

Long ago, there lived an ant and a grasshopper. The ant worked hard. Each summer morning, he woke up early. Then he gathered food for winter. The grasshopper, however, slept late each morning. Then he played all day long. Often, the grasshopper invited the ant to play. But the ant always refused. "I must gather food for winter," he said.

The grasshopper always made fun of him. "You are silly to worry about winter," said the grasshopper. "Today is such a pretty day!"

Soon fall came. The ant worked even harder. But the grasshopper kept on playing. "Winter is coming," warned the ant. But the grasshopper ignored him.

Then winter arrived with a big snowstorm. The ant rested in his cozy home. He had plenty of food. However, the grasshopper was cold and hungry. So he went to see the ant. "May I have some food?" he asked.

"I am sorry," said the ant. "I do not have enough for both of us. You played all summer while I worked. Perhaps you have learned a lesson."

9
17
26
32
41
50
58
60
68
77
83
91
99
106
108
116
126
133
144
148
158
167
175
176

MONITOR PROGRESS
• Check Fluency
• Compare and Contrast

Objectives

- Understand and use singular and plural possessive nouns in writing.
- Understand and use plural, singular, and possessive nouns when speaking.

Conventions
Possessive Nouns

Review

Remind children that a possessive noun shows ownership. Have them give several examples of possessive nouns.

Guide practice

Write the following phrases. Have children write sentences using the possessive nouns suggested by these phrases.

> 1. **branches of the tree**
> 2. **bananas of the apes**
> 3. **shirt of the boy**
> 4. **pets of the two girls**

Connect to oral language

Display and read the following sentence frame. Have children work in pairs to name as many possessive nouns as they can that could be used to complete the sentence. Then have children share their responses with the class.

> **Those are the _____ books.**

On their own

Use Let's Practice It! p. 106 on the *Teacher Resource DVD-ROM.*

Daily Fix-It

9. It wasnt' long befoe they left.
   It <u>wasn't</u> long <u>before</u> they left.

10. What fune they had
    What <u>fun</u> they had<u>!</u>

Discuss the Daily Fix-It corrections with children. Review punctuation, the use of an apostrophe in a contraction, and the CVCe generalization.

Let's Practice It!
TR DVD•106

Objectives

- Edit a draft for spelling, punctuation, and capitalization.
- Use possessive nouns correctly.
- Create a final draft and present.

Writing—Folk Tale
Writer's Craft: Possessive Nouns

Review Revising

Remind children that yesterday they revised their folk tales. They may have changed sentence beginnings to make their stories more interesting. Today they will proofread their folk tales.

MINI-LESSON

Proofread for Possessive Nouns

■ **Teach** In our folk tales, if we spell words correctly, readers will know what we mean. When we proofread, we check to make sure the words are correct. We can check to make sure that possessive nouns are spelled correctly. An apostrophe and -s is added to a singular noun to make it possessive and just an apostrophe is added to a plural noun that ends in s to make it possessive.

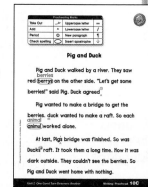

Writing Transparency 10C
TR DVD

■ **Model** Let us look at my folk tale about Pig and Duck. Display Writing Transparency 10C. Explain that you will check to make sure that possessive nouns are spelled correctly. Show how you would change *Pigs* to *Pig's* and *Ducks'* to *Duck's*. Show how you would change any misspellings (such as *berrys* to *berries* and *animul* to *animal*). Quickly show how to check a word's spelling in a classroom dictionary or word list. Model how you would change a letter at the beginning of a sentence if it were not capitalized or add a period if one were missing at the end of a sentence or if it were in the wrong place.

Proofread

Display the Proofreading Tips. Have children proofread their folk tales to correct any misspellings, missing capital letters, or errors with periods. Circulate to assist children with possessive nouns or other words.

Proofreading Tips

✔ Did I spell all possessive nouns correctly?

✔ Did I spell all other words correctly?

✔ Do my sentences begin with a capital letter?

✔ Did I use periods and other end punctuation correctly?

Present

Have children make a final draft of their folk tales, with their revisions and proofreading corrections. Help as appropriate.

Choose an option for children to present their folk tales.

They might work with a partner or a small group to dramatize the folk tale for the class.	They might draw a picture of the animal characters in their folk tale and write a caption that tells what lesson they learned.

When they have finished, help them complete a Self-Evaluation form.

ROUTINE   **Quick Write for Fluency**   **Team Talk**

1. **Talk** Have partners take one minute to find possessive nouns (such as *mouse's, bear's,* or *birds'*) in each of their folk tales.

2. **Write** Each child writes a new short sentence using one of the possessive nouns.

3. **Share** Partners trade sentences and read them aloud.

Routines Flip Chart

Teacher Note

Self-Evaluation Make copies of the Self-Evaluation form from the *Teacher Resource DVD-ROM,* and hand them out to children.

ELL

English Language Learners

Support Editing
Have children work with a partner and proofread each other's folk tale. If they find any errors, they should circle them lightly and discuss them with their partner.

Objectives

- Review concept: people work together solving problems in communities.
- Organize information.
- Create informational drawings.
- Present results of an inquiry project.

Research and Inquiry
Communicate

Teach
Tell children that today they will organize the information from their charts. They will create drawings that feature the information, and present the drawings to their classmates.

Model

Think Aloud I will use the same title for my drawing that I used for my chart topic: "Saving Water." I will include the question "How do people work together to save water?" On one side of the drawing, I can draw and label ways I found that families save water at home, such as catching rainwater in a rain barrel and brushing teeth with the faucet turned off. On the other side, I can draw and label ways people conserve water at work.

Guide practice
Have children review their charts and choose information they want to include in their drawings. Provide them with large sheets of paper and discuss ways to translate their chart information into drawings.

On their own
Give children time to think and create. Then have them present their drawings to the class or in small groups. Remind them how to be good speakers and listeners:

- Good speakers share information in clear sentences, not too fast or too slow.
- Good listeners listen carefully to speakers. They politely share additional information they know about the topic only when asked.

Wrap Up Your Week!

? Question of the Week

How can we work together to solve problems?

Think Aloud This week we talked about how working together helps solve problems. In the story *One Good Turn Deserves Another,* we read about how a coyote and a mouse worked together to solve mouse's problem with a snake. In the folk tale "The Lion and the Mouse," we read about a small mouse that solved a mighty lion's problem. Have children recall their Amazing Ideas about working together to solve problems. Then have children use these ideas to help them demonstrate their understanding of the Question of the Week.

Preview NEXT WEEK

Tell children that next week they will review this unit's skills and ideas about working together.

Weekly Assessment

Use pp. 55–60 of *Weekly Tests* to check:

✔ **Phonics** Vowel Patterns *a, ai, ay*

✔ **Comprehension Skill** Compare and Contrast

✔ **High-Frequency Words**

behind	minute
brought	promise
door	sorry
everybody	

Weekly Tests

A
Advanced

OL
On-Level

SI
Strategic
Intervention

Differentiated Assessment

Use pp. 55–60 of *Fresh Reads for Fluency and Comprehension* to check:

✔ **Comprehension Skill** Compare and Contrast

✔ Review **Comprehension Skill** Author's Purpose

✔ **Fluency** Words Correct Per Minute

Fresh Reads for Fluency and Comprehension

Managing Assessment

Use *Assessment Handbook* for:

✔ **Weekly Assessment Blackline Masters for Monitoring Progress**

✔ **Observation Checklists**

✔ **Record-Keeping Forms**

✔ **Portfolio Assessment**

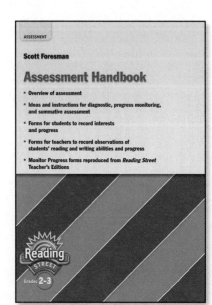

Assessment Handbook

Raising a House

Many people want to own their own home, but some need help getting one. One group of volunteers figured out a great way to help. Here's how it works. The volunteers do the main work of building the house. That saves lots of money. A family promises to pay for it little by little, and they help build it too.

The work begins on a vacant lot. The volunteers and the family work together. Some people hammer, nail, and saw wood, and others paint walls and lay carpet. Where do the basic supplies come from? One business owner may give cement for a driveway, while another may give rain gutters or drains. A store may give a stove and refrigerator. A company may donate trees. Volunteers work on sunny days and rainy days. It's so exciting to see a house go up, and the family can't wait until it's ready.

Volunteers who build the house must be adults. Some young students help by raking vacant lots, painting, or raising money for the group. These volunteers do not get paid. They say, "We want to help a family have a good place to stay." Because of volunteers like these, many people all over the world have good homes!

Advanced Selection 10   **Vocabulary:** raising, vacant

Small Group Time

Pacing Small Group Instruction

20–30 min.

5 Day Plan

DAY 1	• Phonemic Awareness/ Phonics • Decodable Reader
DAY 2	• High-Frequency Words • Leveled Reader
DAY 3	• Phonics • Leveled Reader
DAY 4	• High-Frequency Words • Decodable Reader
DAY 5	• Phonics Review • Comprehension Review

3 or 4 Day Plan

DAY 1	• Phonemic Awareness/ Phonics • Decodable Reader
DAY 2	• High-Frequency Words • Leveled Reader
DAY 3	• Phonics • Leveled Reader
DAY 4	• High-Frequency Words • Decodable Reader

3 Day Plan: Eliminate the shaded box

SI *Strategic Intervention*   **DAY 1**

Phonemic Awareness • Phonics

■ **Substitute Final Phonemes** Reteach p. 316–317 of the Teacher's Edition. Model substituting final phonemes in these words. Then have children practice substituting final phonemes on their own.

braid Change /d/ to /n/.   **trays** Change /z/ to /n/.
fate Change /t/ to /k/.

■ ◉ **Vowel Patterns a, ai, ay** Reteach p. 317a of the Teacher's Edition. Then have children spell *pail* using letter tiles. Monitor their work.

• Change the *l* in *pail* to *n*. What is the new word?

• Change the *n* in *pain* to *r*. What is the new word?

• Change the *r* in *pair* to *d*. What is the new word?

Decodable Practice Reader 10A

■ **Review** Review words with the vowel patterns *a, ai,* and *ay* and the high-frequency words *horse, main, problem, visit,* and *how*. Then have children blend and read these words from the story: *days, tail, crazy, make, brain*.

> **If...** children have difficulty with any of these words,
> **then...** reteach the word by modeling. Have children practice the words, with feedback from you, until they can read them independently.

Have children reread the text orally. To achieve optimal fluency, children should reread the text three or four times.

Decodable Practice Reader 10A

Objectives
• Decode words by applying knowledge of common spelling patterns.

 **SI** Strategic Intervention **DAY 2**

High-Frequency Words

■ **Review** Point to *brought, door, everybody, behind, promise, sorry,* and *minute* on the Word Wall. As you point to each word, say the word, spell it, and say it again. Have children say and spell each word, first with you and then without you. Allow time for children to practice reading these high-frequency words using the word cards.

For a complete literacy instructional plan and additional practice with this week's target skills and strategies, see the **Leveled Reader Teaching Guide.**

Concept Literacy Leveled Reader

■ **Preview and Predict** Read the title and the author's name. Have children look at the cover and ask them to describe what they see. Help children activate their prior knowledge by asking them to look through the book and use the photos to predict things that might take place.

■ **Set a Purpose** Remind children that setting a purpose for reading can help them better understand what they read. Guide children to pay attention to how the children work together to make the soup.

Concept Literacy

■ **Read** Provide corrective feedback as children read the selection orally. During reading, ask them if they were able to confirm any of the predictions they made prior to reading.

> **If...** children have difficulty reading the story individually, **then...** read a sentence aloud as children point to each word. Then have the group reread the sentences as they continue pointing. Continue reading in this way until children read individually.

■ **Retell** Have children take turns retelling the story. Help them identify how the children work together by asking, What are the children doing at the store? What ingredients do they buy to make the soup together?

Objectives
• Monitor comprehension using background knowledge.
• Retell important events in stories in logical order.

SI Strategic Intervention

DAY **3**

Phonics

- ◉ **Vowel Patterns *a, ai, ay*** Reteach p. 336d of the Teacher's Edition. Have children blend and read these additional words to help them practice the target phonics skill.

cape	main	say	sail	whale	clay

For a complete literacy instructional plan and additional practice with this week's target skills and strategies, see the **Leveled Reader Teaching Guide.**

Below-Level Leveled Reader

- **Preview and Predict** Read the title, the author's name, and the illustrator's name. Have children look at the cover and ask them to describe what they see. Help children activate their prior knowledge by asking them to look through the play and use the illustrations to predict things that might take place.

- **Set a Purpose** Remind children that setting a purpose for reading can help them better understand what they read. Guide children to pay attention to how this play and the story *One Good Turn Deserves Another* are alike and how they are different.

- **Read** Provide corrective feedback as children read the play orally. During reading, ask them if they were able to confirm any of the predictions they made prior to the story.

If... children have difficulty reading the play individually,
then... read a sentence aloud as children point to each word. Then have the group reread the sentences as they continue pointing.

- ◉ **Inferring** Have children identify which clues in the play helped them figure out where Fish is. Then prompt them to explain why.

Where is Fish?

by Abby Seaborne
Illustrated by George Hamblin

Below-Level

Objectives
• Decode words by applying knowledge of common spelling patterns.
• Make inferences about text using textual evidence to support understanding.

DAY 4

High-Frequency Words

■ **Review** Write *brought, door, everybody, behind, promise, minute,* and *sorry* on the board. Ask children questions about the words to check their understanding, such as "Which is longer, a second or a *minute*?, If you broke your friend's bike, would you be glad or *sorry*? Would you worry about what your friend *thinks*? Why? If you saw a monster, how long would you *wait* until you ran? What have you *brought* with you to school today?

Decodable Practice Reader 10C

■ **Review** Use the word lists to review the vowel patterns *a, ai,* and *ay*. Be sure children understand that the vowel patterns *a, ai,* and *ay* can make the long a sound. Have children blend and read the words. Then have children reread the text orally.

Decodable Practice Reader 10C

If... children have difficulty reading the story individually, **then...** read a sentence aloud as children point to each word. Then have the group reread the sentences as they continue pointing. Continue reading in this way until children read individually.

Check comprehension by having children retell the story including the characters, plot, and setting. Have children locate words in the story that have the vowel patterns of *a, ai,* and *ay*. List the words children identify. Then have children sort the words in a chart entitled *Long a sound* and columns labeled Long *a, ai,* and *ay*.

Long *A* Sound

a	*ai*	*ay*
Caleb	rained	play
	wait	playing
		way
		say
		plays
		day

More Reading
Use Leveled Readers or other text at children's instructional level.

Objectives
• Decode words by applying knowledge of common spelling patterns.

Small Group Time

More Reading

Use Leveled Readers or other text at children's instructional level.

SI Strategic Intervention

Phonics Review

■ ◉ **Vowel Patterns *a, ai, ay*** Write these sentences on the board. Have children read them aloud as you track the print. Then call on individuals to blend and read the underlined words.

> The <u>lady</u> will <u>play</u> in the <u>rain</u>!
>
> What <u>day</u> will we <u>paint</u> the <u>clay</u>?
>
> The <u>gray</u> bat flew over the <u>baker</u>.

Comprehension Review

■ ◉ **Compare and Contrast** Review that when we tell how things are alike, we **compare**. When we tell how they are different we **contrast**. We can compare and contrast things by combining information we read and what we already know.

One Good Turn
Deserves Another

■ **Read** Have children reread this week's main selection, *One Good Turn Deserves Another*.

• As you read, think about the drama we read last week, *The Bremen Town Musicians.*

• Ask yourself, "How is this story the same and how is it different from *The Bremen Town Musicians?*"

• Notice the plot, characters, and setting of each selection.

After reading, have children point out clues that helped them compare and contrast the two selections.

Objectives

• Decode words by applying knowledge of common spelling patterns.
• Make inferences about the elements of fiction.

DAY 1

Phonics • Spelling

■ 🔊 **Vowel Patterns *a, ai, ay*** Write the following words on the board and have children practice reading words with vowel patterns of *a, ai,* and *ay.*

major	spray	braid	hair

Then have children identify whether the word has the vowel pattern *a, ai,* or *ay.*

■ **Long *a* Spelled *ai, ay*** Remind children that the sound /ā/ can be spelled *ai* in the middle of a word and *ay* at the end of word; for example, *brain, main, pray,* and *stay.* Clarify the pronunciation and meaning of each word. For example, say: Chicken is the *main* ingredient in the soup. Have children identify the same letters and sounds in rhyming words such as *train, gain, rain* and *hay, day, play.*

Objectives
• Decode words by applying knowledge of common spelling patterns.

DAY 2

High-Frequency Words

■ **High-Frequency Words** Hold up this week's High-Frequency Word Cards and review proper pronunciation. Continue holding the cards and have children chorally read each word. To help children demonstrate their understanding of the words, give pairs of children one set of word cards and one set of blank cards. Have partners write a clue or draw a picture for each word on a blank card. For example, a child can draw a picture of a door on the blank card or write the clue "It is something you can open or walk through." Have them mix the word cards and clue cards together and place them face down on a table. Children take turns turning two cards over, trying to match the clue with the word card.

High-Frequency/Tested Word Cards for Grade 2

High-Frequency/Tested Word Cards

Objectives
• Read at least 300 high-frequency words from a commonly used list.

Pacing Small Group Instruction

20–30 min.

5 Day Plan

DAY 1	• Phonics • Spelling • Decodable Reader
DAY 2	• High-Frequency Words • Decodable Reader
DAY 3	• Leveled Reader
DAY 4	• Conventions • Leveled Reader
DAY 5	• Phonics Review • Leveled Reader

3 or 4 Day Plan

DAY 1	• Phonics • Spelling • Decodable Reader
DAY 2	• High-Frequency Words • Decodable Reader
DAY 3	• Leveled Reader
DAY 4	• Conventions • Leveled Reader

3 Day Plan: Eliminate the shaded box

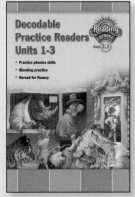

Decodable Practice Readers

On-Level

DAY 3

For a complete literacy instructional plan and additional practice with this week's target skills and strategies, see the **Leveled Reader Teaching Guide.**

On-Level Leveled Reader

■ **Preview and Predict** Read the title, the author's name, and the illustrator's name. Have children look at the cover, and ask them to describe in detail what they see. Help children preview the book by asking them to look through it and use the illustrations to predict things that might take place.

Showing Good Manners
by Stephanie Herbek
Illustrated by Jimmy Holder

On-Level

■ **Cause and Effect** Before reading, remind children that to compare and contrast is to look for similarities and differences as they read. Guide children to pay attention to the similarities and differences in ways the children act in the selection.

■ **Read** During reading, monitor children's comprehension by providing higher-order thinking questions. Ask:

• What are some of the good manners children use in the book?

• What other ways can you think of to use good manners?

To help children gain a better understanding of the text, build upon their responses with a group discussion.

■ **Inferring** Explain to children that good readers use the text, pictures, and what they already know to figure out more about the characters and events than what is stated in the text. Have partners work together to make inferences about the selection. Ask:

• How do bad manners make your classmates feel?

• How do you think good manners make them feel?

■ **Text to Self** Help children make personal connections to the story. Ask:

• What is an example of bad manners that you have experienced? What good manners could have been used instead?

Objectives
• Make inferences about the elements of fiction.

 Go Digital! eReaders

Differentiated Instruction

 OL On-Level

 OL On-Level

DAY 4

Conventions

■ **Possessive Nouns** Remind children that a noun that shows who or what owns something is a possessive noun.

- The word *dog* is a noun. The word *dog's* is a possessive noun because the apostrophe *s* shows ownership. Write the words *dog* and *dog's* on the board and use them in oral sentences. The *dog* loves to play in the park. The *dog's* owner likes to take him to the dog park.

- The word *Nikki* is a noun because it names a person. Write the name *Nikki* on the board and use it in oral sentences. *Nikki* wants to tell about her horse at show and tell. *Nikki's* horse is beautiful.

Continue modeling with other possessive nouns such as *teacher's* and *Jorge's*. Ask children to work in pairs to think of other possessive nouns. Have partners come up with sentences using the possessive nouns.

Objectives
- Use punctuation marks, including apostrophes and possessives.

More Reading

Use Leveled Readers or other text at children's instructional level.

 OL On-Level

DAY 5

Phonics Review

■ **Vowel Patterns *a, ai, ay*** Have children practice blending and reading words that contain this week's target phonics skills. Write the following words on the board. Say and sound out each word with the children.

bacon	ray	raid	stray	paper
maid	favor	later	pain	clay

Then have children sort the words with the vowel patterns *a, ai,* and *ay* into different groups.

Objectives
- Decode words by applying knowledge of common spelling patterns.

Small Group Time

Pacing Small Group Instruction

⏱ 20–30 min.

5 Day Plan

DAY 1	• Phonics • Comprehension
DAY 2	• Comprehension • Main Selection
DAY 3	• Leveled Reader
DAY 4	• Comprehension • Paired Selection
DAY 5	• Fluency • Comprehension

3 or 4 Day Plan

DAY 1	• Phonics • Comprehension
DAY 2	• Comprehension • Main Selection
DAY 3	• Leveled Reader
DAY 4	• Comprehension • Paired Selection

3 Day Plan: Eliminate the shaded box

A Advanced — DAY 1

Phonics • Comprehension

■ **Vowel Patterns *a, ai, ay*** Have children practice with longer words containing vowel patterns *a, ai,* and *ay.* Have them choose several words to use in sentences.

raise	replay	delay	waiter	raking
essay	afraid	braking	yesterday	claims

■ **Advanced Selection 10** Before reading, have children identify these words from the story: *raising* and *vacant.* If they do not know the words, provide oral sentences with the words in context. After reading, have children recall the two most important ideas of the story.

Advanced Selection 10

Objectives
• Decode words by applying knowledge of common spelling patterns.

A Advanced — DAY 2

Comprehension

■ **Comprehension** Have children silently read this week's main selection, *One Good Turn Deserves Another.* Have children identify the characters, events, and the message. Talk about what makes *One Good Turn Deserves Another* a folk tale. (The characters are animals that act like people. There is a lesson.)

■ **Text to Text** Have children identify other stories they have read that are folk tales and explain why.

One Good Turn Deserves Another

Objectives
• Make inferences about the elements of fiction.

 DAY **3**

For a complete literacy instructional plan and additional practice with this week's target skills and strategies, see the **Leveled Reader Teaching Guide.**

Advanced Leveled Reader

■ **Activate Prior Knowledge** Read the title, the author's name, and the illustrator's name. Have children look at the cover and ask them to describe in detail what they see. Then activate children's prior knowledge by asking them to predict what kinds of work these dogs might do.

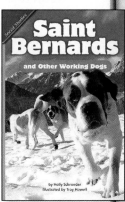

Advanced Leveled Reader

More Reading
Use Leveled Readers or other text at children's instructional level.

■ **Compare and Contrast** Before reading, remind children that to compare and contrast is to look at two or more things and notice the similarities and differences. Guide children to pay attention to how the dogs in the selection are alike and how they are different.

■ **Read** During reading, monitor children's comprehension by providing higher-order thinking questions. Ask:

• What traits do you think dogs need to be working dogs?

• Describe the similarities and differences between the Saint Bernards and the German shepherds.

Build on children's answers to help them gain a better understanding of the text.

■ **Inferring** Have partners discuss the instincts of Saint Bernards that help them rescue people. Ask:

• How do you think Saint Bernards were able to find people in the snow?

• How do you think Barry the Saint Bernard knew when a snowstorm was coming?

■ **Text to Text** Help children make connections to the story. Ask:

• How are the dogs in this story similar to and different from dogs you have previously read about? Explain.

Objectives
• Make inferences about text using textual evidence to support understanding.

Small **Group Time**

More Reading

Use Leveled Readers or other text at children's instructional level.

A Advanced

DAY 4

Comprehension

- **Comprehension** Have children silently read this week's paired selection, "The Lion and the Mouse." Have them retell the story identifying characters, setting, and sequence of events. Then have them summarize what they think were the most important ideas from the story.

    Talk about what makes "The Lion and the Mouse" a fable. (The characters are animals, and it teaches a lesson.)

- **Text to Text** Have children identify other stories they have read that are fables and explain why.

The Lion and the Mouse

Objectives
- Identify moral lessons as themes in well-known fables, legends, myths, or stories.
- Retell important events in stories in logical order.

A Advanced

DAY 5

Fluency • Comprehension

- **Fluency** Using the first few sentences of Advanced Selection 10, model reading with accuracy and an appropriate pace. Then have children read the selection to a partner as you listen to their reading. Provide correct feedback as needed.

- **Comprehension** After they have finished reading the selection, have children retell what happened by stating the events in sequence. Then, on the back of the selection page, have them write three sentences that describe a way to help the community.

Advanced Selection 10

Objectives
- Read aloud grade-level appropriate text with fluency.

Support for English Language Learners

English Language Learners

The ELL lessons are organized by strands. Use them to scaffold the weekly lesson curriculum or during small-group time.

Concept Development

 How can we work together to solve problems?

■ **Activate Prior Knowledge** Write the Question of the Week and read it aloud. Underline the word *together* and have children say it with you. *Together* means "working with other people to get a job done." Display a picture of people working together. People work together when they need to solve problems and get a job done.

■ **Connect to New Concept** Have children turn to pp. 314–315 in the Student Edition. Read the title and have children track the print as you read it. Point to the pictures one at a time and use them to guide a discussion about how people work together to solve problems.

■ **Develop Concepts** Display ELL Poster 10 and have children identify things in this neighborhood they know. (houses, street, bus, lamp post) What are the children doing? Have children point to what the children are doing on the Poster. (waiting for the bus, riding the bus, going to school) Use the leveled prompts below to assess understanding and build oral language. Point to pictures on the poster as you guide discussion.

Leveled Support

Beginning Ask yes/no questions, such as Do the children have backpacks? Is the bus going to school?

Intermediate Ask children questions that can be answered with simple sentences. How many children are waiting for the bus? Who is first in line for the bus? Why is a mom chasing the bus?

Advanced/Advanced-High Have children answer the Question of the Week by giving specific examples from the poster and their own experiences.

■ **Review Concepts and Connect to Writing** Review children's understanding of the concept at the end of the week. Ask them to write in response to these questions: How can working together help us solve problems? What English words did you learn this week? Write and display key ideas from the discussion.

Objectives

• Learn new language structures, expressions, and basic and academic vocabulary heard during classroom instruction and interactions.

Content Objectives

• Describe working together.

Language Objectives

• Share information orally.

• Use basic vocabulary for discussing working together to solve problems.

Daily Planner

DAY 1	• **Frontload Concepts** • **Preteach** Comprehension Skill, Vocabulary, Phonemic Awareness/Phonics, Conventions/Writing
DAY 2	• **Review** Concepts, Vocabulary, Comprehension Skill • **Frontload Main Selection** • **Practice** Phonemic Awareness/Phonics, Conventions/Writing
DAY 3	• **Review** Concepts, Comprehension Skill, Vocabulary, Conventions/Writing • **Reread Main Selection** • **Practice** Phonemic Awareness/Phonics
DAY 4	• **Review Concepts** • **Read ELL/ELD Readers** • **Practice** Phonemic Awareness/Phonics, Conventions/Writing
DAY 5	• **Review** Concepts, Vocabulary, Comprehension Skill, Phonemic Awareness/Phonics, Conventions/Writing • **Reread ELL/ELD Readers**

*See the ELL Handbook for ELL Workshops with targeted instruction.

Concept Talk Video

Use this week's Concept Talk Video to help children build background knowledge. See the Concept Talk Video Routine (*ELL Handbook*, p. 464) for suggestions.

Support for English Language Learners

Language Objectives

- Substitute final phonemes.
- Identify and pronounce vowel patterns *a, ai, ay*.

 **Transfer Skills**

In Spanish, words often end in vowels and the consonants found at the ends of words are *d, j, l, n, r, s,* and *z*. As a result, Spanish speakers may delete or substitute unfamiliar consonant sounds at the end of English words.

ELL Teaching Routine

For more practice with vowel patterns, use the Sound-by-Sound Blending Routine (*ELL Handbook*, p. 457).

Phonemic Awareness: Substitute Final Phonemes

■ Preteach

- Have children open to pp. 316–317. What is the girl playing with? (pail) Say the word *pail* emphasizing the final sound. I am going to say the sounds in *pail*. Listen for the final sound: /p/ /ā/ /l/. The final sound I hear is /l/. Say the final sound with me: /l/. Now what happens if we change the final sound in the word *pail* to /n/? What word do we have now? (pain) Say the new word with me: *pain*. Now what happens if we add a /t/ sound to the end of the word? What word do we have now? (paint) Say the new word with me: *paint*.

- Point out other pictures on the pages and guide children in substituting final phonemes to make new words. For example, *train/trail, rock/rod, worm/word*.

■ Practice
Listen again to how changing the final sound in a word can make a new word: *hot, hop*. Say the following word pairs and ask children to identify the pairs in which only the final sound has changed:

hat/had	pot/pat	cat/cake	tin/tip

Phonics: Vowel Patterns *a, ai, ay*

■ Preteach
Display Sound-Spelling Card 73. This is paper. What vowel sound do you hear in the first part of *paper*? (/ā/) Say it with me: /ā/. Point to *a*. The sound /ā/ is spelled *a* in *paper*. Display Sound-Spelling Card 54. This is a snail. What vowel sound do you hear in *snail*? (/ā/) Say it with me: /ā/. Point to *ai*. The sound /ā/ can also be spelled *ai* as in *snail*. Display Sound-Spelling Card 59. This is hay. What vowel sound do you hear in *hay*? (/ā/) Say it with me: /ā/. Point to *ay*. The sound /ā/ can also be spelled *ay* as in *hay*.

■ Listen and Write
Distribute Write and Wipe Boards.

- Write the word *label* on the board. Copy this word. As you write *a*, say the sound to yourself: /ā/. Now say the sound aloud. (/ā/) Underline *a* in label. The letter *a* spells /ā/ in *label*.

- Repeat the instruction for /ā/ using the words *rain* and *day*. The letters *ai* spell /ā/ in *rain*. The letters *ay* spell /ā/ in *day*.

Objectives
- Monitor oral and written language production and employ self-corrective techniques or other resources.

ELL *English Language Learners*

■ **Reteach and Practice**

Leveled Support

• Display these sentences: *If you stay, we'll play with my train. Let's paint on the paper and label the pictures.* Have children read the sentences aloud with you and identify all the words that have a long *a* sound. Create a chart on the board with the following headings: *a, ai, ay*. Have children copy the chart and then write each long *a* word from the sentences in the correct column.

Beginning/Intermediate Have children say and write the words from the board in their chart. Monitor for accurate spelling and pronunciation.

Advanced/Advanced-High Have children say and write the words from the board in their chart. Then have children write additional words with long *a* spelled *a, ai,* and *ay* in the appropriate columns on the chart. Monitor for accurate spelling and pronunciation.

Vocabulary: Unfamiliar Words

■ **Preteach** Have children turn to p. 323 in the Student Edition.

• Let's look at some words on this page. *"Thank you ssso much," said the snake as it coiled around the mouse.* What does the word *coiled* mean in this sentence? Let's see if other words in the sentence can give us a clue. *The snake coiled around the mouse.* A snake can curl its body around something. I think that *coiled* means "curled." If we want to learn the meaning of unfamiliar words we can use other words in the sentence or the sentences around it to help us figure out the meaning.

■ **Practice** Focus on other pages in the Student Edition. Choose words that might be unfamiliar to children, such as *trapped* (p. 326), *destroying* (p. 327), and *waddled* (p. 329). Then have partners work together using context clues on the page to figure out the meaning of each unfamiliar word.

Content Objectives

• Identify and define unfamiliar words.

Language Objectives

• Associate the long vowel sound /ā/ with *ai, ay*.

• Use peer support to understand language.

 Transfer Skills

Spanish speakers may pronounce *ai* and *ay* with a long *i* sound, which is the way these vowel patterns sound in Spanish. Thus *tail* may be pronounced *tile*; *day* may be pronounced *die*. Help children recognize the differences between Spanish and English pronunciation.

Practice Page

ELL Handbook p. 253 provides additional practice for this week's phonics skill.

Content Objectives

- Monitor and adjust oral comprehension.

Language Objectives

- Discuss oral passages.
- Share information and seek clarification.
- Use a graphic organizer to take notes.

Graphic Organizer

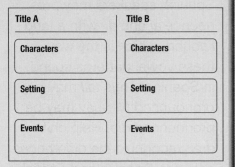

ELL Teacher Tip

Children may benefit from a third listening to confirm their answers.

 Transfer Skills

Directionality Assist children who have difficulty with directionality of English texts, especially children whose home language entails reading with a different directionality. Have children use their finger to show you how they read from left to right, top to bottom, line to line, and page to page.

ELL English Language Learners

Listening Comprehension

Two Folk Tales

A Native American Folk Tale

One day Coyote was walking. He saw a group of mice running around under a tree. They were tying bags to the ends of ropes. Coyote asked the mice what they were doing. They replied, "The North Wind is coming. He is going to throw hailstones at us. We must pull ourselves up under the branches to be safe."

Coyote wanted to be safe too. He got a bag and a rope and climbed in. The mice tied his bag tightly shut. Then they threw stones at him. Finally the mice said, "North Wind is gone. We can come down now." When Coyote climbed out of his bag moaning in pain, the mice laughed, "We tricked you!" Then they ran away.

A Korean Folk Tale

Once there was a tiger who fell into the trap. A man heard the tiger crying for help. He was afraid, but the tiger promised to behave. But after the tiger climbed out of the hole, he growled at the man.

A rabbit was passing by. "I don't understand how you fell into the hole," said the rabbit. The three of them went back to the hole. The tiger jumped in. "See?" he asked. "This is how I fell in."

Grinning, the rabbit hopped away. The tiger roared in anger at being tricked.

Prepare for the Read Aloud The modified Read Aloud above prepares children for listening to the oral readings "Coyote and the Mice" and "The Ungrateful Tiger" on p. 319b.

■ **First Listening: Listen to Understand** Write the title of the Read Aloud on the board. I am going to read two folk tales about animals. Listen to find out what the animals do. After reading, ask children to recall the names of the characters and the events. Who tricks the coyote? (the mice) How did the tiger act when the man helped him out of the hole? (ungrateful)

■ **Second Listening: Listen to Check Understanding** Using Story Comparison (*ELL Handbook*, p. 472), work with children to recall characters and events. Ask questions as you complete the graphic organizer.

Objectives

- Monitor understanding of spoken language during classroom instruction and interactions and seek clarification as needed.
- Demonstrate listening comprehension of increasingly complex spoken English by following directions, retelling or summarizing spoken messages, responding to questions and requests, collaborating with peers, and taking notes commensurate with content and grade-level needs.

 English Language Learners

High-Frequency Words

- **Preteach** Give each pair of children one or more of the Word Cards. Provide clues for each high-frequency word's meaning, such as you can open it or close it for *door,* and it means all of us for *everybody.*

- **Practice** Have children hold up the appropriate Word Cards as you present clues.

Beginning Model the correct pronunciation of each word. Have students say the high-frequency word as you present each clue.

Intermediate Have students read and repeat the words aloud. Have each pair of students create a clue for one or two words.

Advanced/Advanced-High Monitor children as they take turns reading each word to a partner. Then have children make a clue for each word.

- **Speaking with High-Frequency Words**

  - **Teach/Model** Provide clues for each word's meaning, such as sad because you did something wrong **(sorry)** and the opposite of "in front of" **(behind)**.

  - **Practice** Ask questions to check students' understanding: Who is sitting *behind* you? Which is longer, a second or a *minute?* Should you keep a *promise,* or break a *promise?* If you hurt someone's feelings, should you be glad or *sorry?* What is the opposite of *everybody?* What have you *brought* to school today?

Beginning/Intermediate Have pairs answer each question. Monitor to ensure understanding.

Advanced/Advanced-High Have children write the answers to each question. Monitor for understanding and spelling.

Language Objectives

- Understand high-frequency vocabulary.

- Describe people using basic vocabulary.

Cognates

For Spanish learners, point out that the English word *promise* is similar to the Spanish word *promesa.* Reinforce the concept these languages share many words that are the same or similar.

Beginners Support

Have children draw and label a drawing using their word. Then have them dictate a sentence. Have then copy their sentence on their paper below their drawing.

ELL Workshop

Children can use the selection art to retell stories or information in selections. Support children with *Retell or Summarize* (*ELL Handbook,* pp. 406–407).

Objectives

- Expand and internalize initial English vocabulary by learning and using high-frequency words necessary for identifying and describing people, places, and objects, by retelling simple stories and basic information represented or supported by pictures, and by learning and using routine language needed for classroom communication.
- Narrate, describe, and explain with increasing specificity and detail to fulfill content area writing needs as more English is acquired.

Support for English Language Learners

Content Objectives

- Identify compare and contrast.
- Compare and contrast to aid comprehension.

Language Objectives

- Discuss differences and similarities between two things in a reading.
- Use compare and contrast to retell a reading.
- Internalize new academic language.
- Write about compare and contrast.

ELL *English Language Learners*

Guide Comprehension
Compare and Contrast

■ **Preteach** We compare and contrast two things when we think about ways they are alike and ways they are different. Display a pencil and a marker. How are these two things alike? How are they different?

■ **Practice** Have children turn to Envision It! on p. EI•5 in the Student Edition. Discuss the pictures with children. Have them point out ways the two children are the same, and ways they are different.

■ **Reteach/Practice** Distribute copies of the Picture It! (*ELL Handbook*, p. 84). Ask children to look at the pictures and point out ways that the snake and the crow are different. Then read the text aloud twice. Prepare children for the second reading by asking them to think about how snakes and crows are alike, and how they are different. Guide children in completing the practice exercises at their language proficiency level. (*Both*: help farmers, eat things that destroy plants; *Snakes*: eat mice, smell mice with tongues, hunt at night; *Crows*: eat bugs, see bugs with eyes, hunt during the day)

Beginning Have children draw a picture of one thing that is true about crows and one thing that is true about snakes. Then they should draw a picture of one way snakes and crows are the same. Have children label their pictures.

Intermediate Read the directions aloud and have children underline sentences in the text that say what is true about crows and about snakes. Do crows help farmers? Do snakes help farmers? Where should we write "help farmers"?

Advanced/Advanced-High Have children work in pairs to complete the exercise.

MINI-LESSON

Social Language

Explain to children that *argue* and *agree* are words that can be used in solving problems. *Argue* means that ideas are different. *Agree* means to have ideas or feelings that are alike. If people agree, do they want to argue?

Objectives

- Internalize new basic and academic language by using it and reusing it in meaningful ways in speaking and writing activities that build language attainment.
- Demonstrate English comprehension and expand reading skills by employing basic reading skills such as demonstrating understanding of supporting ideas and details in text and graphic sources, summarizing text and distinguishing main ideas from details commensurate with content area needs.

Student Edition pp. 320–321

Reading Comprehension
One Good Turn Deserves Another

■ **Frontloading**

• **Background Knowledge** Read the title aloud and discuss it. One good turn deserves another—this means that if you do something good for someone, that person should do something good for you. Do you agree with this?

• **Preview** Guide children on a picture walk through the story, asking them to identify people, places, and actions. Reteach these words using visuals in the Student Edition: *coiled* (p. 323), *argument* (p. 326), *conversation* (p. 328), *pleaded* (p. 330).

• **Predict** What do you think will happen to the mouse in the story?

Sheltered Reading Ask questions such as the following to guide children's comprehension:

• p. 322: Point to the mouse. Who is this? (mouse) What is he doing? (rolling aside a stone) Point to the snake. Who is this? (snake)

• p. 324: What has happened to the mouse? (The snake has coiled around him.) What does the snake want to do with the mouse? (eat the mouse)

• p. 327: Point to the crow. Who is this? (crow) What is the crow doing? (flying) How do crows fly? Lead children in pantomiming flapping their arms like wings.

• p. 334: Is the coyote a friend of the mouse or the snake? Why? (the mouse, because the coyote helped the mouse escape)

■ **Fluency: Accuracy** Remind children that reading with accuracy means to pronounce words correctly so listeners can understand what you are reading. Read the first paragraph on p. 322. Model segmenting and blending the word *unmistakable*. Point out that children can use decoding skills when encountering unfamiliar words while reading. Have pairs choose a paragraph on p. 324. Have children read with accuracy as their partners listen and offer feedback. For more practice, use the Fluency: Word Reading Routine (*ELL Handbook*, p. 461).

After Reading Help children summarize the text with the Retelling Cards. Ask questions that prompt children to summarize the important parts of the text.

Content Objectives
• Monitor and adjust comprehension.
• Make and adjust predictions.

Language Objectives
• Read grade-level text with accuracy.
• Summarize text using visual support.

Graphic Organizer

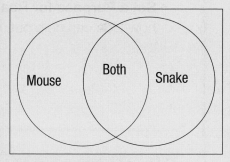

Audio Support
Children can prepare for reading *One Good Turn Deserves Another* by using the eSelection or the AudioText CD. See the AudioText CD Routine (*ELL Handbook*, p. 464) for suggestions on using these learning tools.

English Summary
Read the English summary of *One Good Turn Deserves Another* (*ELL Handbook*, p. 85). Children can ask questions about ideas or unfamiliar words. Send copies home for children to read with family members.

Objectives
• Demonstrate listening comprehension of increasingly complex spoken English by following directions, retelling or summarizing spoken messages, responding to questions and requests, collaborating with peers, and taking notes commensurate with content and grade-level needs.

ELL Reader

ELD Reader

English Language Learners

For additional leveled instruction, see the **ELL/ELD Reader Teaching Guide.**

Comprehension:
Kids Can Do It!

■ **Before Reading** Distribute copies of the ELL and ELD Readers, *Kids Can Do It!*, to children at their reading level.

• **Preview** Read the title aloud with children: This is a story about how kids can help out in their community. What do people do in your community to help others?

• **Set a Purpose for Reading** Let's read to find out how kids can help out in their community.

■ **During Reading** Follow this Reading Routine for both reading groups.

1. Read the entire Reader aloud slowly as children follow along and finger point.

2. Reread the Reader one sentence at a time, having children echo read after you.

■ **After Reading** Use the exercises on the inside back cover of *Kids Can Do It!* and invite children to share drawings and writing. In a whole-group discussion, ask children to list the different ways kids can help out in their community. Children can point to examples in the book to show different ways kids can help out.

ELD Reader Beginning/Intermediate

■ **p. 3** Point to the trash. What can kids do about trash? (pick it up and throw it away)

■ **p. 5** Point to the kids collecting food. What can kids do for people who don't have enough food? (collect food, have a food drive)

Writing Think about the different needs of your community. Draw a picture of one way you can help your community. Label your picture and share with your classmates.

ELL Reader Advanced/Advanced-High

■ **pp. 3–4** What are these kids doing? (sorting trash for recycling)

■ **p. 7** What are these people doing? (playing a game)

Study Guide Distribute copies of the ELL Reader Study Guide (*ELL Handbook*, p. 88). Scaffold comprehension by helping children look back through the Reader to complete the Study Guide. Review their responses together. (See *ELL Handbook*, pp. 209–212.)

Objectives
• Use visual, contextual, and linguistic support to enhance and confirm understanding of increasingly complex and elaborated spoken language.
• Demonstrate English comprehension and expand reading skills by employing basic reading skills such as demonstrating understanding of supporting ideas and details in text and graphic sources, summarizing text and distinguishing main ideas from details commensurate with content area needs.

 English Language Learners

Conventions
Possessive Nouns

■ **Preteach** Display and read these sentences: *The book belongs to the girl. It is the girl's book. He is the father of the two girls. He is the girls' father.* How did I show that the book belonged to one girl? (added *'s* to *girl*) How did I show that the father belonged to two girls? (added *'* to *girls*)

■ **Practice** Direct children's attention to these pages in the Student Edition and have them write possessive nouns for these sentences: *The snake has a forked tongue. It is the ___ tongue.* (p. 325) *The animals have fur. The ___ fur is hot in the desert.* (p. 332)

 Leveled LS Support

Beginning/Intermediate Write *snakes* on the board. There is only one snake. Where should I put the apostrophe? Have children point to the correct place. Have them copy the word on their own paper and then repeat this routine for the second sentence.

Advanced/Advanced-High Have children work in pairs to answer the questions.

■ **Reteach** Display the following:

the name of the dog   =   the dog's name
                          the dogs' name
the mother of the boys   =   the boy's mother
                              the boys' mother

Which one is correct? How do you know? Circle the correct possessive form and cross out the incorrect one.

■ **Practice** Have children create sentences about *One Good Turn Deserves Another*, using these possessive nouns: *the snake's life, the mouse's idea, the two animals' argument.*

 Leveled LS Support

Beginning/Intermediate Have children complete the following sentence frames: *The mouse saves ___. The snake does not agree with ___. A coyote settles ___.*

Advanced/Advanced-High Have children work in pairs to discuss their ideas and write their sentences.

Content Objectives
• Identify and use possessive nouns.
• Correctly use possessive nouns in sentences.

Language Objectives
• Speak using possessive nouns in sentences.
• Write phrases and sentences with possessive nouns.

Transfer Skills
In many languages, speakers show possession in phrases such as *the hat of the boy* rather than with noun endings. Show children how to change such phrases into possessive nouns.

Grammar Jammer
For more practice with nouns, use the Grammar Jammer for this target skill. See the Grammar Jammer Routine (*ELL Handbook*, p. 465) for suggestions on using this learning tool.

ELL Workshop
Children may need extra practice using language structures heard during classroom interactions. *Use Nouns in Your Speaking* (*ELL Handbook*, pp. 422–423) provides extra support.

Write a Folk Tale

■ **Introduce Terms** Write *folk tale* on the board. Explain the meaning of *folk tale* by briefly describing the folk tale elements of *One Good Turn Deserves Another*, which was based on a Mexican folk tale. A folk tale is a story that has been handed down over many years.

■ **Introduce Varied Sentence Beginnings** In English, we usually begin a sentence with the subject. Write this sentence on the board: *The dog chewed on a bone with delight.* Good writers like to use different sentence beginnings when they write. Varied sentence beginnings make your writing more interesting. For example, we can rewrite this sentence: *With delight, the dog chewed on a bone.*

■ **Model** Write this sentence on the board: *George took a nap even though he was not tired.* Help children think of how to rewrite the beginning of this sentence.

■ **Write** Have children write a sentence they could use as the first sentence of a folk tale. Write this model sentence on the board: *Coyote chased Road Runner every day, although he could never catch her.* This sentence can be rewritten in this way: *Although Coyote could never catch Road Runner, Coyote chased her every day.* Have partners work together to think of an opening sentence and then think of a way to rewrite the beginning of the sentence. After writing, have children trade their papers with a partner and edit for appropriate verb tenses.

Beginning/Intermediate Have children brainstorm ideas. Then have them draw a picture and dictate a sentence describing their picture. Have children copy the sentence and then help them rewrite the beginning.

Advanced/Advanced-High Have partners discuss their ideas. Then have them write their opening sentence and then rewrite the beginning of the sentence.

Content Objectives

- Identify different ways to begin sentences.
- Identify the characteristics of a folk tale.

Language Objectives

- Write story sentences with varied beginnings.
- Share feedback for editing and revising.

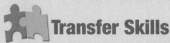 **Transfer Skills**

Folk tales are found in all cultures. You may want to ask children to retell a folk tale that they know from their own culture and heritage. They can then write an opening sentence for that tale.

ELL Teaching Routine

For practice spelling words related to working together to solve problems, use the Spelling Routine (*ELL Handbook*, p. 463).

ELL Workshop

Children can collaborate with peers to discuss their writing. *Discuss with Classmates* (*ELL Handbook*, pp. 416–417) provides assistance with discussion.

Objectives

- Edit writing for standard grammar and usage, including subject-verb agreement, pronoun agreement, and appropriate verb tenses commensurate with grade-level expectations as more English is acquired.
- Narrate, describe, and explain with increasing specificity and detail to fulfill content area writing needs as more English is acquired.

Review on Reading Street!

Working Together

Big Question
How can we work together?

Daily Plan

Review

- Concept Talk
- Oral Vocabulary
- Phonics
- Spelling
- High-Frequency Words
- Comprehension
- Fluency
- Conventions

Day 1	Day 2	Day 3	Day 4	Day 5
How can we help each other in dangerous situations?	How has working together changed history?	How can we work together to meet people's needs?	Why is it a good idea to work together?	How can we work together to solve problems?

Customize Literacy
More support for a Balanced Literacy approach, see pp. CL•1– CL•45.

Customize Writing
More support for a customized writing approach, see pp. CW•11– CW•20.

Assessment
- Unit 2 Benchmark Test
- Assessment Handbook

Review this Unit's Reading Selections

Tara and Tiree
Genre: **Literary Nonfiction**

Abraham Lincoln
Genre: **Informational Text**

Scarcity
Genre: **Expository Text**

Bremen Town Musicians
Genre: **Drama/Fairy Tale**

One Good Turn
Genre: **Folk Tale**

You Are Here!
Unit 2
Week 6

Resources on Reading Street!

	Build Concepts		Phonics and Spelling		Vocabulary
Day 1 **Review Week 1** ❓ How can we help each other in dangerous situations?	 Student Edition pp. 192–207	 Sing with Me	 Reader's and Writer's Notebook	 Sound-Spelling Cards	 Reader's and Writer's Notebook
Day 2 **Review Week 2** ❓ How has working together changed history?	 Student Edition pp. 224–239	 Sing with Me	 Reader's and Writer's Notebook	 Sound-Spelling Cards	 Reader's and Writer's Notebook
Day 3 **Review Week 3** ❓ How can we work together to meet people's needs?	 Student Edition pp. 254–267	 Sing with Me	 Reader's and Writer's Notebook	 Sound-Spelling Cards	 Reader's and Writer's Notebook
Day 4 **Review Week 4** ❓ Why is it a good idea to work together?	 Student Edition pp. 284–301	 Sing with Me	 Reader's and Writer's Notebook	 Sound-Spelling Cards	 Reader's and Writer's Notebook
Day 5 **Review Week 5** ❓ How can we work together to solve problems?	 Student Edition pp. 320–335	 Sing with Me	 Reader's and Writer's Notebook	 Sound-Spelling Cards	 Reader's and Writer's Notebook
 Go Digital	• Big Question Video • Concept Talk Video		• Interactive Sound-Spelling Cards		• Sing with Me Animations • Vocabulary Activities

Big Question

How can we work together?

Comprehension

Reader's and
Writer's Notebook

Reader's and
Writer's Notebook

Reader's and
Writer's Notebook

Reader's and
Writer's Notebook

Reader's and
Writer's Notebook

- Envision It! Animations

Fluency

Reader's and
Writer's Notebook

Reader's and
Writer's Notebook

Reader's and
Writer's Notebook

Reader's and
Writer's Notebook

Reader's and
Writer's Notebook

- Leveled eReaders

Conventions and Writing

Reader's and
Writer's Notebook

Reader's and
Writer's Notebook

Reader's and
Writer's Notebook

Reader's and
Writer's Notebook

Reader's and
Writer's Notebook

- Grammar Jammer

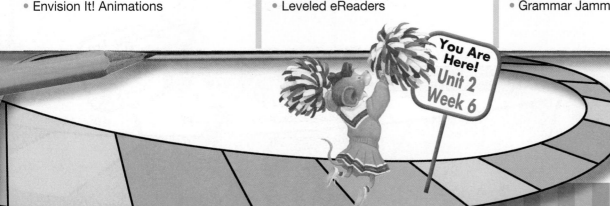

You Are
Here!
Unit 2
Week 6

Week 6

My 5-Day Planner for Reading Street!

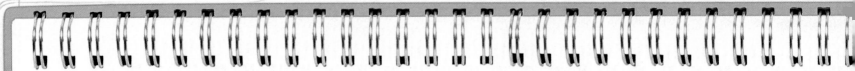

	Review Week 1 **Day 1** pages IR8–IR17	**Review Week 2** **Day 2** pages IR18–IR27
Get Ready to Read	**Concept Talk**, IR8 ❓ How can we help each other in dangerous situations? **Oral Vocabulary**, IR9 *courageous, hazard, rescue, avalanche, instinct, skittish, blustery, fast-paced* **Phonics**, IR10 ◉ Vowels: *r*-Controlled *ar, or, ore, oar* **Spelling**, IR11 Vowels: *r*-Controlled *ar, or, ore*	**Concept Talk**, IR18 ❓ How has working together changed history? **Oral Vocabulary**, IR19 *identify, participate, significant, scour, ingenious, aloft, architect, tinker* **Phonics**, IR20 ◉ Contractions **Spelling**, IR21 Contractions
Read and Comprehend	**High-Frequency Words**, IR12 *break, family, heard, listen, once, pull* **Vocabulary Skill**, IR12 Unfamiliar Words **Comprehension**, IR13–IR15 ◉ Skill: Cause and Effect ◉ Strategy: Summarize **Fluency**, IR15 Read with Accuracy and Appropriate Rate	**High-Frequency Words**, IR22 *certainly, either, great, laugh, second, worst, you're* **Vocabulary Skill**, IR22 Dictionary/Glossary **Comprehension**, IR23–IR25 ◉ Skill: Author's Purpose ◉ Strategy: Text Structure **Fluency**, IR25 Read with Expression
Language Arts	**Conventions**, IR16 Nouns **Handwriting**, IR16 Manuscript *i, I, u, U, R, r*: Letter Size **Wrap Up Your Day**, IR17	**Conventions**, IR26 Proper Nouns **Handwriting**, IR26 Manuscript *n, N, m, M*: Letter Size **Wrap Up Your Day**, IR27

You Are Here!
Unit 2
Week 6

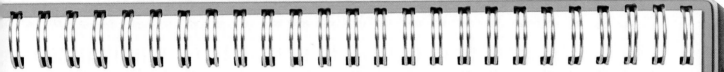

Big Question
How can we work together?

Review Week 3	Review Week 4	Review Week 5
Day 3 pages IR28–IR37	**Day 4** pages IR38–IR47	**Day 5** pages IR48–IR57
Concept Talk, IR28 How can we work together to meet people's needs? **Oral Vocabulary**, IR29 *consumers, decisions, producers, fiber, strand, extraordinary, lack, typical* **Phonics**, IR30 Vowels: *r*-controlled *er, ir, ur* **Spelling**, IR31 Vowels: *r*-controlled *er, ir, ur*	**Concept Talk**, IR38 Why is it a good idea to work together? **Oral Vocabulary**, IR39 *partnership, solution, survival, miserable, struggle, depend, familiar, insist* **Phonics**, IR40 Plurals **Spelling**, IR41 Plurals	**Concept Talk**, IR48 How can we work together to solve problems? **Oral Vocabulary**, IR49 *conflict, pursue, resolve, deserve, mope, coax, ramp, startle* **Phonics**, IR50 Vowel Patterns *a, ai, ay* **Spelling**, IR51 Vowel Digraphs *ai, ay*
High-Frequency Words, IR32 *above, ago, enough, toward, whole, word* **Vocabulary Skill**, IR32 Time and Order Words for Sequence **Comprehension**, IR33–IR35 Skill: Facts and Details Strategy: Background Knowledge **Fluency**, IR35 Read with Appropriate Phrasing	**High-Frequency Words**, IR42 *bought, people, pleasant, probably, scared, shall, sign* **Vocabulary Skill**, IR42 Homophones **Comprehension**, IR43–IR45 Skill: Cause and Effect Strategy: Story Structure **Fluency**, IR45 Read with Expression	**High-Frequency Words**, IR52 *behind, brought, door, everybody, minute, promise, sorry* **Vocabulary Skill**, IR52 Unfamiliar Words **Comprehension**, IR53–IR55 Skill: Compare and Contrast Strategy: Inferring **Fluency**, IR55 Read with Accuracy
Conventions, IR36 Singular and Plural Nouns **Handwriting**, IR36 Manuscript *j, J, p, P*: Letter Form **Wrap Up Your Day**, IR37	**Conventions**, IR46 Plural Nouns That Change Spelling **Handwriting**, IR46 Manuscript *w, W, y, Y*: Letter Slant **Wrap Up Your Day**, IR47	**Conventions**, IR56 Possessive Nouns **Handwriting**, IR56 Manuscript *q, Q, v, V*: Letter Spacing **Wrap Up Your Day**, IR57

Week 6

Turn the page for grouping suggestions to differentiate instructions.

Differentiate Instruction on *Reading Street!*

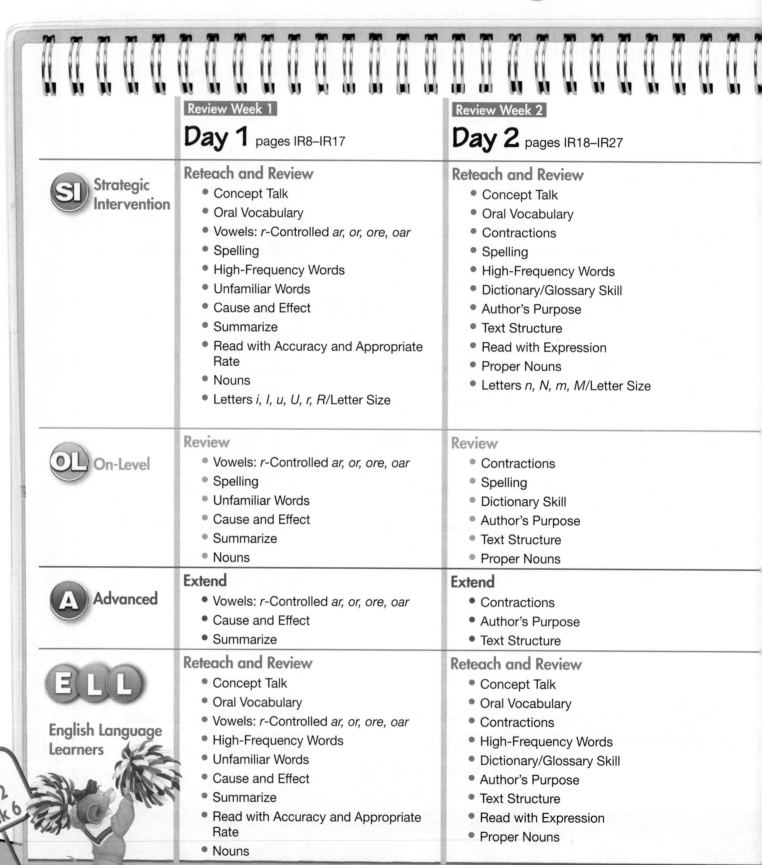

	Review Week 1 **Day 1** pages IR8–IR17	**Review Week 2** **Day 2** pages IR18–IR27
SI Strategic Intervention	**Reteach and Review** • Concept Talk • Oral Vocabulary • Vowels: *r*-Controlled *ar, or, ore, oar* • Spelling • High-Frequency Words • Unfamiliar Words • Cause and Effect • Summarize • Read with Accuracy and Appropriate Rate • Nouns • Letters *i, I, u, U, r, R*/Letter Size	**Reteach and Review** • Concept Talk • Oral Vocabulary • Contractions • Spelling • High-Frequency Words • Dictionary/Glossary Skill • Author's Purpose • Text Structure • Read with Expression • Proper Nouns • Letters *n, N, m, M*/Letter Size
OL On-Level	**Review** • Vowels: *r*-Controlled *ar, or, ore, oar* • Spelling • Unfamiliar Words • Cause and Effect • Summarize • Nouns	**Review** • Contractions • Spelling • Dictionary Skill • Author's Purpose • Text Structure • Proper Nouns
A Advanced	**Extend** • Vowels: *r*-Controlled *ar, or, ore, oar* • Cause and Effect • Summarize	**Extend** • Contractions • Author's Purpose • Text Structure
ELL English Language Learners	**Reteach and Review** • Concept Talk • Oral Vocabulary • Vowels: *r*-Controlled *ar, or, ore, oar* • High-Frequency Words • Unfamiliar Words • Cause and Effect • Summarize • Read with Accuracy and Appropriate Rate • Nouns	**Reteach and Review** • Concept Talk • Oral Vocabulary • Contractions • High-Frequency Words • Dictionary/Glossary Skill • Author's Purpose • Text Structure • Read with Expression • Proper Nouns

You Are Here! Unit 2 Week 6

Reading Street Response
to Intervention Kit

Review Week 3	Review Week 4	Review Week 5
Day 3 pages IR28–IR37	**Day 4** pages IR38–IR47	**Day 5** pages IR48–IR57

Reteach and Review	Reteach and Review	Reteach and Review
• Concept Talk • Oral Vocabulary • Vowels: *r*-Controlled *er, ir, ur* • Spelling • High-Frequency Words • Time and Order Words for Sequence • Facts and Details • Background Knowledge • Read with Appropriate Phrasing • Singular and Plural Nouns • Letters *j, J, p, P*/Letter Form	• Concept Talk • Oral Vocabulary • Plurals • Spelling • High-Frequency Words • Homophones • Cause and Effect • Story Structure • Read with Expression • Plural Nouns That Change Spelling • Letters *w, W, y, Y*/Letter Slant	• Concept Talk • Oral Vocabulary • Vowel Patterns *a, ai, ay* • Spelling • High-Frequency Words • Unfamiliar Words • Compare and Contrast • Inferring • Read with Accuracy • Possessive Nouns • Letters *q, Q, v, V*/Letter Spacing

Review	Review	Review
• Vowels: *r*-Controlled *er, ir, ur* • Spelling • Time and Order Words for Sequence • Facts and Details • Background Knowledge • Singular and Plural Nouns	• Plurals • Spelling • Homophones • Cause and Effect • Story Structure • Plural Nouns That Change Spelling	• Vowel Patterns *a, ai, ay* • Spelling • Unfamiliar Words • Compare and Contrast • Inferring • Possessive Nouns

Extend	Extend	Extend
• Vowels: *r*-Controlled *er, ir, ur* • Facts and Details • Background Knowledge	• Plurals • Cause and Effect • Story Structure	• Vowel Patterns *a, ai, ay* • Compare and Contrast • Inferring

Reteach and Review	Reteach and Review	Reteach and Review
• Concept Talk • Oral Vocabulary • Vowels: *r*-Controlled *er, ir, ur* • High-Frequency Words • Time and Order Words for Sequence • Facts and Details • Background Knowledge • Read with Appropriate Phrasing • Singular and Plural Nouns	• Concept Talk • Oral Vocabulary • Plurals • High-Frequency Words • Homophones • Cause and Effect • Story Structure • Read with Expression • Plural Nouns That Change Spelling	• Concept Talk • Oral Vocabulary • Vowel Patterns *a, ai, ay* • High-Frequency Words • Unfamiliar Words • Compare and Contrast • Inferring • Read with Accuracy • Possessive Nouns

Week 6

Objectives
- Review Week 1 concept.
- Share information and ideas about the concept.
- Review Week 1 oral vocabulary.

Today at a Glance

Oral Vocabulary
courageous, hazard, rescue, avalanche, instinct, skittish, blustery, fast-paced

Phonics and Spelling
◎ Review *r*-Controlled *ar, or, ore, oar*

High-Frequency Words
break, family, heard, listen, once, pull

Vocabulary
Skill: Unfamiliar Words

Comprehension
◎ Review Skill: Cause and Effect
◎ Review Strategy: Summarize

Fluency
Skill: Read with Accuracy and Appropriate Rate

Conventions
Nouns

Handwriting
Letters *i, I, u, U, R,r*: Letter Size

Writing
Quick Write for Fluency

Concept Talk

Question of the Week

How can we help each other in dangerous situations?

Review Week 1 selection

Today children will explore how the Question of the Week connects to *Tara and Tiree, Fearless Friends*. Read the Question of the Week above. Remind children that *Tara and Tiree, Fearless Friends* is a literary nonfiction selection about two brave dogs that save their owner's life.

ROUTINE — Activate Prior Knowledge — Team Talk

1. **Think** Have children think about a time when they or someone they know was in a dangerous situation.

2. **Pair** Have pairs of children discuss how the Question of the Week applies to the two dogs in *Tara and Tiree, Fearless Friends*.

3. **Share** Call on a few children to share their ideas with the group. Guide discussion and encourage elaboration with prompts such as: How did the dogs help Jim when he fell through the ice?

Routines Flip Chart

Connect to the Big Question

Use these questions to connect the Week 1 question and selection to the Unit 2 Big Question, **How can we work together?**

- How did Tara and Tiree know that Jim was in a dangerous situation?.
- What might have happened if Tara and Tiree had not worked together?
- What kinds of weather can cause dangerous situations? How can people work together to help others who are in danger?

ELL Reteach Concepts and Vocabulary
Use the instruction on ELL Poster 6 to assess knowledge and concepts.

ELL Poster 6

Oral Vocabulary
Amazing Words

Remind children that they have learned some Amazing Words that they can use to answer the question *How can we help each other in dangerous situations?* Display "To the Rescue!" on page 6 of the *Sing with Me* Big Book. Sing the song.

 Sing with Me Big Book Audio

Go over all the Amazing Words from Week 1. Ask children to listen as you say them: *courageous, hazard, rescue, avalanche, instinct, skittish, blustery, fast-paced.* Then say them again, and have children say each word after you.

- Would you describe someone who likes mountain climbing as *skittish* or *courageous?* (courageous)

- Would an *avalanche* be described as a *hazard* or an *instinct?* (hazard)

- Raise your hand when I name a person whose job it is to *rescue* others: *firefighter, salesperson, nurse, writer,* and *paramedic.* (firefighter, nurse, paramedic)

Have children demonstrate their understanding of Amazing Words by completing these sentences orally.

A **courageous** _____ came to **rescue** the dog from the fire.

The **blustery** _____ may have caused the **avalanche**.

A(n) _____ is a **hazard** on the beach.

George is **skittish** when he is around _____.

The dog's **instinct** helped him find the _____.

Cara enjoys living in a **fast-paced** _____.

To the Rescue!

When you see a friend who's in trouble
And facing a hazard or two,
Then run to get help on the double,
Your friend will be counting on you.

Call 9-1-1.
Or find an adult who knows what to do.
You'll be helping
To make a courageous rescue.

Sing with Me Big Book

Amazing Words

courageous	instinct
hazard	skittish
rescue	blustery
avalanche	fast-paced

Differentiated Instruction

 Strategic Intervention

Word Webs Work with children to create word webs for some of the Amazing Words. For example, write *courageous* in the center of a web and have children supply synonyms as well as other related words, such as: *brave, bold, strong, hero, daring, fearless,* and *tough.*

 Writing on Demand

Develop Writing Fluency
Ask children to write about a time when they helped someone who was hurt or in a dangerous situation or when someone helped them when they were hurt or in a dangerous situation. Have them write for two to three minutes. Children should write as much as they can. Tell them to try to do their best writing. You may want to discuss what children wrote during writing conferences.

Objectives
- Read words with /är/ spelled *ar* and /ôr/ spelled *or*, *ore*, and *oar*.
- Read multisyllabic words.
- Spell words with *r*-controlled *ar*, *or*, *ore*.

Phonics
🔊 *r*-Controlled *ar, or, ore, oar*

Review Phonics skill Review *r*-controlled *ar*, *or*, *ore*, and *oar* using Sound-Spelling Cards 55, 87, 92, and 93.

ar

Sound-Spelling Card 55

or

Sound-Spelling Card 87

or

Sound-Spelling Card 92

ore

Sound-Spelling Card 93

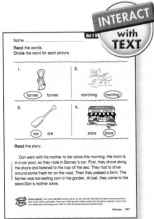

Reader's and Writer's Notebook p. 157

Read words independent of context Use *Reader's and Writer's Notebook* page 157. Point out that children know how to blend these words. Then tell children they will all read the words in each row together. Allow several seconds previewing time for the first reading.

Corrective feedback **If...** children cannot blend all the words in a row consecutively without an error,
then... return to the first word in the row, and have children reread all the words in the row. Repeat until children can read the words fluently.

Read words in context Use the passage on *Reader's and Writer's Notebook* page 157. Point out that there are many *r*-controlled *ar*, *or*, *ore*, and *oar* words in the passage that children already know how to read. Have children read the passage together.

Let's Practice It!
TR DVD•111

Corrective feedback **If...** children have difficulty reading the *r*-controlled *ar*, *or*, *ore*, and *oar* words,
then... guide them in chunking multisyllabic words and using sound-by-sound blending. Have children read each sentence. Repeat until children can read the sentences fluently.

On their own Use Let's Practice It! p. 111 on the *Teacher Resource DVD-ROM*.

Spelling
r-Controlled *ar, or, ore*

Review
Week 1
spelling
words

Write *hard, born,* and *chore.* Point out that these words have the *r*-controlled vowel sounds /är/ spelled *ar* and /ôr/ spelled *or* and *ore.* Remind children that they learned how to spell words with the /är/ and /ôr/ sounds. Use Sound-Spelling Cards 55, 92, and 93 to review how to spell words with *ar, or,* and *ore.*

Team Talk Have children review the spelling words using index cards on which the words are written. Tell them to sort the words into the ones they know and the ones they need more practice with. Partners can quiz each other on the words in the second pile.

On their own Use *Reader's and Writer's Notebook* p. 158.

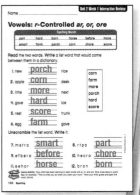

Reader's and Writer's
Notebook p. 158

Unit 2 Week 1 Spelling Words

r-Controlled *ar, or, ore*

1. part	7. smart
2. hard	8. farm
3. born	9. porch
4. horse	10. corn
5. before	11. chore
6. more	12. score

ELL

English Language Learners

Review *r*-Controlled *ar, or, ore* Remind children that /är/ is spelled *ar* as in *dark,* and /ôr/ can be spelled *or* or *ore* as in *short* and *sore.*

Beginning Write the words *arm, store, sharp, tore,* and *fork.* Have children read each word, identify the sound /är/ or /ôr/, and circle the letters that form each sound.

Intermediate Have partners write *ar, or,* and *ore* as headings, and write each spelling word under the appropriate heading.

Advanced/Advanced-High Have children write *ar, or,* and *ore* as headings, and write six words under each heading.

Objectives
- Read high-frequency words.
- Review unfamiliar words.
- Review key features of literary nonfiction.
- Preview and predict.
- Establish purpose for reading text.

High-Frequency Words

Read words independent of context

Display the Week 1 high-frequency words. Have children read the words aloud. Have children point to each word on the Word Wall.

Guide practice

Read the sentences to children. Then have children use each word in a sentence of their own.

> **break**—I can **break** the stick in half.
>
> **family**—My **family** always eats dinner together.
>
> **heard**—I **heard** the dog bark when the doorbell rang.
>
> **listen**—Dad likes to **listen** to music when he cooks.
>
> **once**—**Once** I saw a whale swimming in the ocean.
>
> **pull**—I had to **pull** on the door to open it.

Corrective feedback

If... children do not use a word correctly, then... correct the sentence, model a sentence, and have them try again.

On their own

Use *Reader's and Writer's Notebook*, page 159.

Reader's and Writer's Notebook p. 159

Vocabulary Skill
Unfamiliar Words

Review Unfamiliar words

Review that good readers often use other words in a sentence or in nearby sentences to figure out the meaning of an unfamiliar word.

- Which words in this sentence help you figure out the meaning of *gigantic?* The gigantic tree was taller than the house. **(taller than the house)**

- Which words in this sentence help you figure out the meaning of *scraped?* I fell down and scraped my knee. **(fell down, knee)**

Guide practice

Team Talk Have partners work together to write a sentence for the word *thrilled* that uses other words that give clues to its meaning.

Comprehension
Skills and Strategies

Review
Skill

 Cause and Effect Review that when we read a selection, we find out "what happens" and "why it happens." Remind children that they know how to identify events that happen and why they happen. Recall that in the selection *Tara and Tiree, Fearless Friends,* they learned, for example, that Jim became a dog trainer because he loved dogs.

Review
Strategy

Summarize Remind children that good readers can summarize what happened in a selection. When you summarize, you tell about the important events in a selection. You can summarize a selection after you have read it. You can also summarize a selection while you are reading it by telling about the important events that have happened so far.

Review
Genre

Literary Nonfiction Remind children that literary nonfiction tells about events that really happened, but tells them like a story. In literary nonfiction, the characters are based on real people or real animals. The events are also real, but they are told in story form.

Preview and predict

Have children read the title of the selection on p. 160 of *Reader's and Writer's Notebook.* Have children look through the selection and use the title to predict events that might happen in the selection. Tell them this selection is literary nonfiction.

Set a purpose

After we read "Mountain Rescues," we will talk about what happened in the selection and why it happened. Have children set a purpose for reading "Mountain Rescues."

Differentiated Instruction

 Advanced

Extend Cause and Effect After reviewing "what happens" and "why it happens" in selections, have children work with a partner to think of a scene, such as a messy kitchen or a pile of books on a table. Have them tell why the kitchen is messy or why the books are on the table. Then have them write a sentence about the scene using the word *because.* For example: The kitchen is messy because my brother and I baked a cake!

Academic Vocabulary

literary nonfiction true events that are told like a story

Objectives

- Review skill: cause and effect.
- Review strategy: summarize.
- Read aloud fluently with accuracy and appropriate rate.

Name _____   Unit 2 Week 1 Interactive Review

Read the story.
Answer the questions.

Mountain Rescues

Hiking the wooded and rocky trails of mountains can be fun, but it can also be dangerous. Hikers may get lost, because they don't follow a trail or because it gets dark, and they can't see the trail. Sometimes hikers can't see the trail, because the weather suddenly turns foggy.

It is important that hikers check what the weather will be like before they start. Hikers often get hurt or sick when the weather turns bad. They may slip on a trail, because it becomes icy. They could fall and break a bone. Sometimes a hiker gets hurt when strong winds push him or her off a trail and onto rocks. It is important that hikers be prepared for unexpected bad weather. Hikers can get sick in cold and wet weather, because they didn't wear the right clothing. Along with warm, waterproof jackets and pants, hikers should have hats, gloves, and boots.

Persons who are lost or hurt in the mountains need help. Although it is dangerous work, trained rescue workers go out to look for them. A mountain rescue team is made up of experts who know what to do, because they have hours of training. Members of a particular mountain rescue team in Colorado have to have many hours of training each year. Rescue teams are ready every day to help and will search for hikers in trouble day or night.

A team usually uses a helicopter for rescues. The helicopter flies over the mountains, trying to locate the hikers. If the rescuers

Home Activity Your child recognized causes and effects in a nonfiction story. Read a favorite story or watch a favorite children's video with your child. Pause every so often to ask about cause and effect relationships in the book or movie's story.

160 Comprehension

Name _____   Unit 2 Week 1 Interactive Review

are searching at night, they wear goggles that allow them to see in the dark. The team may have to airlift a hiker, because it's the only way to get him or her out of the mountains. For example, the hiker may be trapped on a ridge. During an airlift, the helicopter drops the rescuers on the ridge and then lowers a cable with a basket attached. The rescuers get the hiker into the basket, and the helicopter pulls the basket back up.

Rescued hikers are taken to a nearby hospital. Because brave rescue workers find lost or hurt persons as quickly as possible, they save many lives.

1. What could happen if a hiker doesn't follow a trail?

    The hiker could get lost.

2. What effect could not wearing the right clothing have on hikers?

    Hikers could get sick in cold and wet weather.

3. What is the reason rescue workers know what to do?

    Rescue workers know what to do because they have hours of training.

4. Why might a rescue team need to airlift a hurt hiker?

    It may be the only way to get the hurt hiker out of the mountains.

5. What effect do rescue workers have on lost or hurt hikers?

    Rescue workers save the lives of many lost or hurt hikers.

Comprehension 161

Reader's and Writer's Notebook pp. 160–161

Guide Comprehension
Review Cause and Effect

Have children read the selection and respond to the questions.

Corrective feedback

If... children have difficulty responding to the questions,

then... use the following to guide their responses.

1. How can hiking be dangerous? **Have children identify the sentences that tell how a hiker can get lost.**

2. Why is it important that hikers check the weather before they start out? **Have children find sentences that tell what happens when hikers are not properly dressed for the weather conditions.**

3. What happens if a hiker is trapped on a ridge? How does the rescue team rescue him or her? **Have children find the sentences that describe an airlift rescue.**

4. Why are rescue workers able to save many lives? **Have children identify the last sentence that explains that the rescue workers find lost or hurt persons as quickly as possible.**

Comprehension
Summarize

Review Strategy

Discuss strategies that children used as they read "Mountain Rescues."

Did you keep important events in mind after you read about them? What did you do to help yourself remember important events and facts? Have children identify what they did to summarize what they read.

Fluency
Accuracy and Appropriate Rate

Model fluent reading

Remind children that when they read, it is important to pay attention to each word, read with no mistakes, and read at an appropriate rate. Model reading the third paragraph of "Mountain Rescues" on *Reader's and Writer's Notebook* page 160 at an appropriate rate. Have children track the print as you read.

Guide practice

To provide additional fluency practice, pair children and have them read "Mountain Rescues."

ROUTINE **Paired Reading** **Team Talk**

1. **Reader 1 Begins** Children read the selection, switching readers at the end of each paragraph.

2. **Reader 2 Begins** Have partners reread; this time the other partner begins.

3. **Reread** For optimal fluency, children should reread three or four times.

4. **Corrective Feedback** Listen to children read and provide corrective feedback regarding their oral reading and their use of the blending strategy.

Routines Flip Chart

Differentiated Instruction

 Strategic Intervention

Comprehension and Fluency
Have children reread "Mountain Rescues" silently and then aloud. Have them think about the things that happened and why they happened. If children come to a word they don't know, remind them to chunk it into syllables. After they have read the selection, have them summarize the important events and facts.

Options for Oral Rereading

Use *Tara and Tiree, Fearless Friends* or one of the Week 1 Leveled Readers.

Objectives
- Identify nouns.
- Write letters legibly using proper size.
- Write for fluency.
- Review concepts.

Conventions

Nouns

Review Nouns

A common noun is a word that names a person, place, animal, or thing. Words like *girl, street, bird,* and *desk* are all common nouns.

Guide practice

Read the following sentences and have children identify each common noun.

> The **man** sat in his warm and cozy **house**.
>
> That **dog** likes to run around the **yard**.
>
> Look at the little **boy** dive into the **pool**!
>
> The **teacher** wrote a funny **story**.

Team Talk Pair children and have them name common nouns for items they can see in the classroom. Then have each child choose a noun and use it in a sentence. Have pairs share their sentences with the class.

On their own
Use *Reader's and Writer's Notebook*, page 162.

Reader's and Writer's Notebook p. 162

Handwriting

Letters *I, i, U, u, R, r/* Letter Size

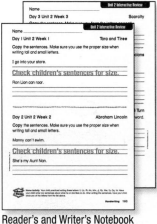

Reader's and Writer's Notebook pp. 163–164

Review Letter formation

Review the proper formation of letters *Ii, Uu,* and *Rr.* Write each letter. Have children write the letters several times and circle their best one.

Review Letter size

Review that when we write words and sentences, the letters should be the correct size. Small letters sit on the bottom line and touch the middle line. Tall letters sit on the bottom line and touch the top line.

Guide practice

Write the following sentence. Have children copy it using correct letter size. Monitor children's letter size as they write.

> **Uncle Russ ate more corn than I did at the farm.**

On their own
Use the Day 1 section on *Reader's and Writer's Notebook*, pages 163–164.

ROUTINE — Quick Write for Fluency — Team Talk

1. **Talk** Have pairs discuss what they learned about helping each other in dangerous situations.

2. **Write** Have children write a few sentences to summarize the discussion.

3. **Share** Partners can read their summaries to one another.

Routines Flip Chart

Wrap Up Your Day

Question of the Week

How can we help each other in dangerous situations?

Review
Concept and Amazing Words

Use these questions to wrap up this review of the Week 1 concept and to provide another opportunity for children to use the week's Amazing Words. Pair or group children to answer the questions. Have children share their responses with the class.

☑ Why is it helpful to be **courageous** when you are facing a dangerous **hazard** with other people?

☑ How might you **rescue** someone in a dangerous situation on a **fast-paced** river?

☑ What are some ways you could help a **skittish** animal that is caught in a small **avalanche**?

☑ How does an animal follow its **instinct** to avoid danger?

☑ How would you help someone who was lost in the woods on a **blustery** night?

Writing Workshop

Use the writing process lesson on pages CW•11–CW•20 for this week's writing instruction.

English Language Learners
Extend Vocabulary Remind children that the word *fast-paced* means "move quickly." Ask children what the opposite of *fast-paced* would be. (slow-paced or "move slowly") Then have children think of situations or environments that are fast-paced and slow-paced. For example: A fast-paced environment would be a busy city street or a crowded shopping mall. A slow-paced environment would be a country road or a library.

Homework Send home this week's Family Times Newsletter from Let's Practice It! pp. 109–110 on the *Teacher Resource DVD-ROM*.

Let's Practice It!
TR DVD•109–110

Preview DAY 2

Tell children that tomorrow they will review more skills and read "Amelia Earhart."

Objectives
• Review Week 2 concept.
• Share information and ideas about the concept.
• Review Week 2 oral vocabulary

Today at a Glance

Oral Vocabulary
identify, participate, significant, scour, ingenious, aloft, architect, tinker

Phonics and Spelling
◉ Review Contractions *n't, 's, 'll, 'm*

High-Frequency Words
certainly, either, great, laugh, second, worst, you're

Vocabulary
Skill: Dictionary/Glossary: Guide Words

Comprehension
◉ Review Skill: Author's Purpose
◉ Review Strategy: Text Structure

Fluency
Skill: Read with Expression

Conventions
Proper Nouns

Handwriting
Letters *n, N, m, M:* Letter Size

Writing
Quick Write for Fluency

Concept Talk

 Question of the Week
How has working together changed history?

Review Week 2 selection

Today children will explore how the Question of the Week connects to *Abraham Lincoln*. Read the Question of the Week above. Remind children that *Abraham Lincoln* is an informational text about the life of Abraham Lincoln and how he worked with others to end the Civil War.

ROUTINE **Activate Prior Knowledge** **Team Talk**

1 **Think** Have children think about a time when they had to work together to solve a disagreement.

2 **Pair** Have pairs of children discuss how the Question of the Week applies to President Lincoln and our country in *Abraham Lincoln*.

3 **Share** Call on a few children to share their ideas with the group.

Guide discussion and encourage elaboration with prompts such as:
How did Abraham Lincoln change history when he was president?

Routines Flip Chart

Connect to the Big Question

Use these questions to connect the Week 2 question and selection to the Unit 2 Big Question, **How can we work together?**

• Do you think Abraham Lincoln could have ended the Civil War without working with others? Why or why not?

• Why is it difficult to make big changes if you work alone?

• Can you think of other people who have changed history by working with others?

ELL **Reteach Concepts and Vocabulary** Use the instruction on ELL Poster 7 to assess knowledge and concepts.

ELL Poster 7

Oral Vocabulary
Amazing Words

Review
Week 2
Amazing
Words

Remind children that they have learned some Amazing Words that they can use to answer the question *How has working together changed history?* Display "Look at History" on page 7 of the *Sing with Me* Big Book. Sing the song.

 Sing with Me Big Book Audio

Sing with Me Big Book

Go over all the Amazing Words from Week 2. Ask children to listen as you say them: *identify, participate, significant, scour, ingenious, aloft, architect, tinker.* Then say them again, and have children say each word after you.

- Which word is another word for *clever*? (ingenious)
- In which event might a clown *participate*—a birthday party or a baseball game? (birthday party)
- Which of the following people would design a building—a doctor, an *architect*, or a chef? (architect)

Apply
Amazing
Words

Have children demonstrate their understanding of Amazing Words by completing these sentences orally.

> I decided to **participate** in the _____ .
>
> _____ is a **significant** holiday for all Americans.
>
> I told Kim that her _____ was **ingenious.**
>
> The _____ went **aloft,** and everything below looked small.
>
> Can you **identify** the _____ that the **architect** designed?
>
> We had to **scour** the _____ for my lost ring.
>
> My dad likes to **tinker** with _____ .

Amazing Words

identify	ingenious
participate	aloft
significant	architect
scour	tinker

Differentiated Instruction

SI Strategic Intervention

Make a List Have children make a list of activities and sports in which they like to *participate*. Have children share their lists with a partner and tell why they enjoy participating in these activities.

Writing on Demand

Develop Writing Fluency Ask children to write about a time when they worked with others to get something important done. Have them write for two to three minutes. Children should write as much as they can. Tell them to try to do their best writing. You may want to discuss what children wrote during writing conferences.

Objectives

- Read contractions ending in *n't, 's, 'll,* and *'m.*
- Spell contractions ending in *n't, 's, 'll,* and *'m.*

Phonics

🔊 Contractions *n't, 's, 'll, 'm*

Review
Phonics skilll

Review contractions ending in *n't, 's, 'll,* and *'m* using Sound-Spelling Cards 110, 111, 112, and 114.

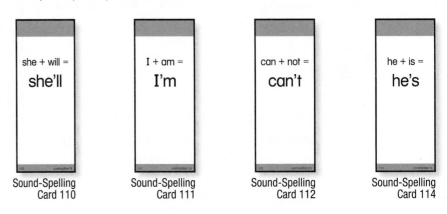

Sound-Spelling Card 110	Sound-Spelling Card 111	Sound-Spelling Card 112	Sound-Spelling Card 114
she + will = **she'll**	I + am = **I'm**	can + not = **can't**	he + is = **he's**

Reader's and Writer's
Notebook p. 165

Read words independent of context

Use *Reader's and Writer's Notebook* page 165. Point out that children know how to read these words. Then tell children they will all read the words in each row together. Allow several seconds previewing time for the first reading.

Corrective feedback

If... children cannot read all the words in a row consecutively without an error,
then... return to the first word in the row, and have children reread all the words in the row. Repeat until children can read the words fluently.

Read words in context

Use the passage on *Reader's and Writer's Notebook* page 165. Point out that there are many contractions that end in *n't, 's, 'll,* and *'m* in the passage that children already know how to read. Have children read the passage together.

Corrective feedback

If... children have difficulty reading the contractions that end in *n't, 's, 'll,* and *'m,*
then... guide them in chunking multisyllabic words and using sound-by-sound blending. Have children read each sentence. Repeat until children can read the sentences fluently.

Let's Practice It!
TR DVD•112

On their own Use Let's Practice It! p. 112 on the *Teacher Resource DVD-ROM.*

Spelling
Contractions *n't, 's, 'll, 'm*

Review
Week 2 spelling words

Write *didn't, it's, I'll,* and *I'm*. Point out that these words are contractions. Remind children that they learned how to spell contractions that end with *n't, 's, 'll,* and *'m*. Use Sound-Spelling Cards 110, 111, 112, and 114 to review how to spell these contractions.

Team Talk Have children review the spelling words using index cards on which the words are written. Tell them to sort the words into the ones they know and the ones they need more practice with. Partners can quiz each other on the words in the second pile.

On their own   Use *Reader's and Writer's Notebook*, p. 166.

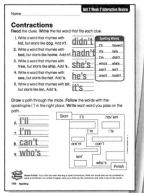

Reader's and Writer's
Notebook, p. 166

Unit 2 Week 2 Spelling Words

Contractions *n't, 's, 'll, 'm*

1. didn't	7. can't
2. it's	8. isn't
3. aren't	9. she's
4. he's	10. haven't
5. I'm	11. I'll
6. who's	12. hadn't

E L L

English Language Learners

Review Contractions Remind children that a contraction is a shortened form of two words. An apostrophe replaces any letters that are dropped from the words.

Beginning Have partners write the contractions *I'll, haven't,* and *can't*. Next to each, have them write the two words that form the contraction.

Intermediate Have partners write the contractions for these sets of words: *was not; we will; does not;* and *it is*.

Advanced/Advanced-High Have children write sentences that include the following contractions: *you'll, don't, let's,* and *that's*.

Objectives

- Read high-frequency words.
- Review dictionary/glossary guide words.
- Review key features of informational text.
- Preview and predict.
- Establish purpose for reading text.

High-Frequency Words

Read words independent of context

Display the Week 2 high-frequency words. Have children read the words aloud. Have children point to each word on the Word Wall.

Guide practice

Read the sentences to children. Then have children use each word in a sentence of their own.

> **certainly**—I will **certainly** come to your party.
>
> **either**—It will **either** rain or snow tomorrow.
>
> **great**—We had a **great** time at the picnic.
>
> **laugh**—The clown made everyone **laugh.**
>
> **second**—I was the **second** person in line.
>
> **worst**—That was the **worst** movie I have ever seen!
>
> **you're**—**You're a** very good artist.

Corrective feedback

If... children do not use a word correctly,
then... correct the sentence, model a sentence, and have them try again.

On their own

Use *Reader's and Writer's Notebook*, page 167.

Reader's and Writer's
Notebook, p. 167

Vocabulary Skill
Dictionary/Glossary
Guide Words

Review
Guide words

Review that good readers often use a dictionary or glossary to look up the meaning of an unfamiliar word. The guide words at the top of each dictionary or glossary page help you locate a word.

- What do the guide words show you? (They show the first and last entry words on a page.)

- How are the entry words listed on a page? (They are listed in alphabetical order.)

Guide practice

Team Talk Have partners look up the meaning of the word *certainly* in a dictionary. Remind them to use the guide words to find the word.

Comprehension
Skills and Strategies

Review Skill

 Author's Purpose Review that authors have different reasons for writing a selection. Some authors may write in order to entertain. Others may write in order to provide information. Remind children that they know how to identify an author's purpose. Recall that in the selection *Abraham Lincoln,* they learned information about Abraham Lincoln's life and the Civil War.

Review Strategy

Text Structure Remind children that good readers can recognize how the important ideas in a selection are organized. In an informational text, the events are usually told in their correct sequence in time. The selection *Abraham Lincoln,* begins in Ms. Grant's second grade class. Then Ms. Grant gives information about Abraham Lincoln's life and the Civil War in sequence. The selection ends back in Ms. Grant's second grade class.

Review Genre

Informational Text Remind children that an informational text gives facts and information about real people, places, and events. An informational text often helps us understand our history as well as our traditions.

Preview and predict

Have children read the title of the selection on p. 168 of *Reader's and Writer's Notebook.* Have children look through the selection and use the title to predict information they might learn in the selection. Tell them this selection is an informational text.

Set a purpose

After we read "Amelia Earhart," we will talk about the author's purpose for writing the selection. Have children set a purpose for reading "Amelia Earhart."

Differentiated Instruction

A Advanced

Extend Author's Purpose After reviewing author's purpose, have partners create a T-chart with the headings *Entertain* and *Inform.* Have children discuss books and stories they have recently read and categorize them by whether the author's purpose was to entertain or inform. Have children share their lists with the class.

Academic Vocabulary

informational text gives facts about real people, places, and events that reflect history or the traditions of communities

Objectives

• Review skill: author's purpose.
• Review strategy: text structure.
• Read aloud fluently with expression.

Unit 2 Week 2 Interactive Review

Name _____

Read the story.
Answer the questions.

Have you ever heard of Amelia Earhart? She was a great pilot. She did many amazing things.

As a child, Amelia didn't like flying. But then she went to an air show. She watched the planes. She got very excited about what she saw. She wanted to learn to fly.

So Amelia took flying lessons. Then she bought her own plane. It was bright yellow. Amelia named it *Canary* after yellow canary birds.

Soon, people heard about Amelia. They heard she was a good pilot. One day, she got a phone call. Some people wanted her to fly across the Atlantic Ocean. Amelia said yes.

She flew in a plane with two other pilots. Amelia was the only woman. The plane made it across the Atlantic Ocean. The pilots had set a new record. They were famous!

Then Amelia decided to fly across the Atlantic a second time. This time, she wanted to fly alone. She barely made it. She had many problems during the flight. She had to land her plane in a field!

Still, Amelia had done something amazing. She was the first woman to fly alone across the Atlantic. Now she was even more famous. She received many awards.

Home Activity Your child read a biography and identified the author's purpose in writing it. Have your child tell you why he or she thinks the author told readers about Amelia Earhart's life before she became famous.

168 Comprehension

Unit 2 Week 2 Interactive Review

Name _____

Amelia wasn't done flying. She wanted a bigger challenge. So she decided to fly around the world. She almost made it. She flew across the Atlantic Ocean to Europe. Then she flew from Europe to Asia. Now she had only one part left. She needed to fly over the Pacific Ocean. She would do it in two flights, or legs.

Amelia took off on the first leg of her trip. She was supposed to land on a Pacific island, but she never made it. No one knows what happened. Her plane has never been found.

1. What do you think was the author's purpose in writing this story? Circle the answer below.

to tell a funny story
(to give information about someone)
to explain something

2. Why do you think the author told the reader that Amelia Earhart didn't like flying as a child?

Possible answer: The author wanted to show that people can

change as they grow up.

3. What did you learn as you read the story? Tell three things that you learned about Amelia Earhart.

Children should write facts from the story.

Comprehension 169

Reader's and Writer's Notebook pp. 168–169

Guide Comprehension
↻ Review Author's Purpose

Have children read the selection and respond to the questions.

Corrective feedback

If... children have difficulty responding to the questions,
then... use the following to guide their responses.

1. Do you think the author wrote this selection to make you laugh, to teach you about a person, or to explain an idea to you? **Have children find sentences that support the idea that the author wrote the selection to give information about someone.**

2. How did Amelia's feelings about flying change as she got older? **Have children identify the sentences that tell how Amelia changed.**

3. Who is this mainly about? What important things did Amelia Earhart do in her life? **Have children reread to find facts about Earhart's life.**

Comprehension
 Text Structure

Review
Strategy

Discuss strategies that children used as they read "Amelia Earhart."

Did you notice that the events of Amelia Earhart's life were told in the order in which they occurred? What did you do to remember the important events of her life? Have children identify what they did to keep the text structure in mind as they read.

Fluency
Read with Expression

Model fluent reading

Remind children that when they read, it is important to read with expression. Explain that reading with expression is using your voice to express feeling. For example, you can read louder and faster to show strong feeling, or you can read softer and slower to show sadness or seriousness. Model reading the first paragraph of "Amelia Earhart" on *Reader's and Writer's Notebook* page 168 with expression. Have children track the print as you read.

Guide practice

To provide additional fluency practice, pair children and have them read "Amelia Earhart."

ROUTINE **Paired Reading** **Team Talk**

1. **Reader 1 Begins** Children read the selection, switching readers at the end of each paragraph.

2. **Reader 2 Begins** Have partners reread; this time the other partner begins.

3. **Reread** For optimal fluency, children should reread three or four times.

4. **Corrective Feedback** Listen to children read and provide corrective feedback regarding their oral reading and their use of the blending strategy.

Routines Flip Chart

Differentiated Instruction

 Strategic Intervention
Comprehension and Fluency
Have children reread "Amelia Earhart" aloud with expression. Have them think about the author's purpose as they read and raise their hand if they need help with a word. After they have read the selection, have them retell the important events of Amelia Earhart's life.

Options for Oral Rereading
Use *Abraham Lincoln* or one of the Week 2 Leveled Readers.

Objectives
- Identify proper nouns.
- Write letters legibly using proper size.
- Write for fluency.
- Review concepts.

Conventions
Proper Nouns

Review
Proper nouns

A proper noun names a particular person, place, animal, or thing. Proper nouns such as *Al, Bay Street, Duke,* and *Statue of Liberty* begin with capital letters.

Guide practice

Read the following sentences and have children identify each proper noun.

> I went to visit the **Lincoln Memorial** in **Washington, D.C.**
>
> **Jake** has a cute cat named **Fluffy**.
>
> **Ann Parker** is moving to **Dallas**.
>
> **Jefferson Elementary School** is located on **South Street**.

Team Talk Pair children and have them name one or two proper nouns for each category: people, places, animals, and things. Have pairs share their proper nouns with the class.

On their own Use *Reader's and Writer's Notebook*, page 170.

Reader's and Writer's Notebook, p. 170

Handwriting
Letters N, n, M, m/ Letter Size

Review
Letter formation

Review the proper formation of letters *Nn* and *Mm*. Write each letter. Have children write the letters several times and circle their best one.

Review
Letter size

Review that when we write words and sentences, the letters should be the correct size. Small letters sit on the bottom line and touch the middle line. Tall letters sit on the bottom line and touch the top line.

Write the following sentence. Have children copy it using appropriate letter size. Monitor children's letter size as they write.

> **I'm going to the game at noon, but Mark and Nan aren't coming.**

On their own Use the Day 2 section on *Reader's and Writer's Notebook*, pages 163–164.

ROUTINE — Quick Write for Fluency — Team Talk

1. **Talk** Have pairs discuss what they learned about how people can change history by working together.
2. **Write** Have children write a few sentences to summarize the discussion.
3. **Share** Partners can read their summaries to one another.

Routines Flip Chart

Wrap Up Your Day

Question of the Week
How has working together changed history?

Review
Concept and Amazing Words

Use these questions to wrap up this review of the Week 2 concept and to provide another opportunity for children to use the week's Amazing Words. Pair or group children to answer the questions. Have children share their responses with the class.

- ☑ Can you **identify** some examples of people working together to change history? Who were the people and what did they do?

- ☑ What are some **significant** ways citizens can **participate** in their communities to make them better?

- ☑ What **ingenious** invention takes people **aloft** so that they can move quickly from place to place?

- ☑ Why do people often have to **tinker** with an idea in order to get it just right?

- ☑ Why might an **architect** and the mayor of a town work together?

- ☑ In the past, why might people work together to **scour** for firewood?

E L L
English Language Learners
Extend Vocabulary Remind children that they learned that the word *scour* means "move quickly in search of something." Explain that the word *scour* also has another meaning: "clean or polish by hard rubbing." Have children make up sentences for each meaning of the word *scour*.

Preview DAY 3

Tell children that tomorrow they will review more skills and read "Hot Air Balloons."

Objectives
- Review Week 3 concept.
- Share information and ideas about the concept.
- Review Week 3 oral vocabulary.

Today at a Glance

Oral Vocabulary
consumers, decisions, producers, fiber, strand, extraordinary, lack, typical

Phonics and Spelling
◎ Review *r-controlled er, ir, ur*

High-Frequency Words
above, ago, enough, toward, whole, word

Vocabulary
Skill: Time and Order Words for Sequence

Comprehension
◎ Review Skill: Facts and Details
◎ Review Strategy: Background Knowledge

Fluency
Skill: Read with Appropriate Phrasing

Conventions
Singular and Plural Nouns

Handwriting
Letters *j, J, p, P:* Letter Form

Writing
Quick Write for Fluency

Concept Talk

Question of the Week

How can we work together to meet people's needs?

Review Week 3 selection

Today children will explore how the Question of the Week connects to *Scarcity.* Read the Question of the Week above. Remind children that *Scarcity* is an expository text about the choices people make when the things they want are scarce.

ROUTINE **Activate Prior Knowledge** **Team Talk**

1. **Think** children think about a time when they had to share or go without because there wasn't enough of something.

2. **Pair** Have pairs of children discuss how the Question of the Week applies to the girls who wanted oranges in *Scarcity.*

3. **Share** Call on a few children to share their ideas with the group.

   Guide discussion and encourage elaboration with prompts such as:

   What might have happened to make food like oranges scarce?

   What happens to the price when something is scarce?

Routines Flip Chart

Connect to the Big Question

Use these questions to connect the Week 3 question and selection to the Unit 2 Big Question, **How can we work together?**

- What choice did Ben have to make when the toy he wanted to buy was scarce?

- How would you help Ben decide which choice to make?

- What choice would you make if an item you wanted to buy was scarce?

ELL Reteach Concepts and Vocabulary Use the instruction on ELL Poster 8 to assess knowledge and concepts.

ELL Poster 8

Oral Vocabulary
Amazing Words

Amazing Words

consumers	strand
decisions	extraordinary
producers	lack
fiber	typical

 Review
Week 3
Amazing
Words

Remind children that they have learned some Amazing Words that they can use to answer the question *How can we work together to meet people's needs?* Display "Shopping Day Decisions" on page 8 of the *Sing with Me* Big Book. Sing the song.

 Sing with Me Big Book Audio

Shopping Day Decisions

All producers try and try
To make things we want to buy.
Then they ship them to the store
For consumers to explore.
A decision must be made.
Then the final bill gets paid.

Sing with Me Big Book

Go over all the Amazing Words from Week 3.
Ask children to listen as you say them: *consumer(s), decision(s), producer(s), fiber, strand, extraordinary, lack, typical.* Then say them again, and have children say each word after you.

- Would an actor rather be *typical* or *extraordinary*? (extraordinary)
- Which one goes to the supermarket to buy food—a *consumer* or a *producer*? (consumer)
- Which is made from *strands* of *fiber*—a sweater or a computer? (sweater)

**Apply
Amazing
Words**

Have children demonstrate their understanding of Amazing Words by completing these sentences orally.

Mary had to make a(n) _____ **decision**.

A _____ is a **producer,** and someone who _____ goods is a **consumer**.

Everyone said the singer's _____ was **extraordinary**.

Suki's dress was made with _____ **fiber**.

A **lack** of _____ can hurt plants.

A **typical** _____ is soup and a sandwich.

The cat chased a **strand** of _____.

Differentiated Instruction

 Strategic Intervention

Producers Have children discuss how two kinds of producers, farmers and car makers, are alike and different. Then have partners draw a Venn Diagram and write at least two ways in which they are the same and different.

Writing on Demand

Develop Writing Fluency
Ask children to write about a time when they couldn't find something they wanted at the store or it was too expensive and what they choices they made. Have them write for two to three minutes. Children should write as much as they can. Tell them to try to do their best writing. You may want to discuss what children wrote during writing conferences.

Objectives

- Read words with /ėr/ spelled *er, ir,* and *ur.*
- Read multisyllabic words.
- Spell words with *r*-controlled *er, ir, ur.*

Phonics

r-Controlled *er, ir, ur*

Review
Phonics skill

Review *r*-controlled *er, ir,* and *ur* using Sound-Spelling Cards 67, 72, and 104. Review closed syllable pattern VCCV using Sound-Spelling Card 147.

| Sound-Spelling Card 67 | Sound-Spelling Card 72 | Sound-Spelling Card 104 | Sound-Spelling Card 147 |

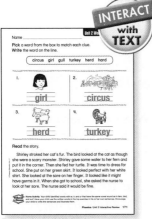

Reader's and Writer's
Notebook p. 171

Read words
independent
of context

Use *Reader's and Writer's Notebook* page 171. Point out that children know how to blend these words. Then tell children they will all read the words in the row together. Allow several seconds previewing time for the first reading.

Corrective
feedback

If... children cannot blend all the words consecutively without an error, **then...** return to the first word in the row, and have children reread all the words. Repeat until children can read the words fluently.

Read words
in context

Use the passage on *Reader's and Writer's Notebook* page 171. Point out that there are many *r*-controlled *er, ir, ur,* and VCCV words in the passage that children already know how to read. Have children read the passage together.

Corrective
feedback

If... children have difficulty reading the *r*-controlled *er, ir, ur,* or VCCV words,
then... guide them in chunking multisyllabic words and using sound-by-sound blending. Have children read each sentence. Repeat until children can read the sentences fluently.

Let's Practice It!
TR DVD•113

On their own

Use Let's Practice It! p. 113 on the *Teacher Resource DVD-ROM.*

Spelling
r-Controlled *er, ir, ur*

Review Week 3 spelling words

Write *her, dirt,* and *turn.* Point out that these words have the r-controlled vowel sound /ėr/ spelled *er, ir* and *ur.* Remind children that they learned how to spell words with the /ėr/ sound. Use Sound-Spelling Cards 67, 72, and 104 to review how to spell words with *er, ir,* and *ur.*

Team Talk Have children review the spelling words using index cards on which the words are written. Tell them to sort the words into the ones they know and the ones they need more practice with. Partners can quiz each other on the words in the second pile.

On their own Use *Reader's and Writer's Notebook* p. 172.

Reader's and Writer's
Notebook p. 172

Unit 2 Week 3 Spelling Words
r-Controlled *er, ir, ur*

1. her	7. serve
2. person	8. curb
3. nurse	9. curl
4. dirt	10. skirt
5. turn	11. purse
6. birth	12. turtle

ELL

English Language Learners
Review *r*-Controlled *er, ir, ur*
Remind children that /ėr/ can be spelled *er* as in *fern, ir* as in *girl,* and *ur* as in *fur.*
Beginning Write the words *serve, stir,* and *burn.* Have children act out each word and then say a sentence that describes what they are doing.

Intermediate Have partners write *er, ir,* and *ur* as headings, and write each spelling word under the appropriate heading.

Advanced/Advanced-High Have partners list five words that rhyme with *turn* and *dirt.* Have them circle the letters that stand for the sound /ėr/.

Objectives

- Read high-frequency words.
- Review time and order words for sequence.
- Review key features of expository text.
- Preview and predict.
- Establish purpose for reading text.

High-Frequency Words

Read words independent of context

Display the Week 3 high-frequency words. Have children read the words aloud. Have children point to each word on the Word Wall.

Guide practice

Read the sentences to children. Then have children use each word in a sentence of their own.

> **above**—I can see the sun **above** the mountains.
>
> **ago**—John got a dog two weeks **ago**.
>
> **enough**—Kate has **enough** money to buy a sandwich.
>
> **toward**—Dad and I walked **toward** the lake.
>
> **whole**—We ate the **whole** bowl of cherries.
>
> **word**—Rita knew how to spell every **word**.

Corrective feedback

If... children do not use a word correctly,
then... correct the sentence, model a sentence, and have them try again.

On their own

Use *Reader's and Writer's Notebook*, page 173.

Reader's and Writer's Notebook p. 173

Vocabulary Skill
Time and Order Words for Sequence

Review
Time and order words for sequence

Review that good readers look for time and order words to help them understand a sequence or when things are happening. Ask children to identify words in the following sentences that are time and order words.

- A hurricane hit our town three years ago. **(three years ago)**
- Toward the end of the week, the weather warmed up. **(toward the end of the week)**

Guide practice

Team Talk Have partners work together to write sentences about something that happened *a long time ago* and something that happened *yesterday*.

Comprehension
Skills and Strategies

**Review
Skill**

 Facts and Details Review that many facts and details are included in nonfiction selections. Facts are pieces of information that can be proven to be true. Details are small pieces of information. Remind children that they know how to identify facts and details. Recall that in the selection *Scarcity,* one of the facts they learned was that all countries, rich and poor, have scarcity.

**Review
Strategy**

Background Knowledge Remind children that good readers use their background knowledge to help them understand the information in a selection. When you use background knowledge, you use the information you already know about a topic. You can also use your own experiences to help you make sense of the text.

**Review
Genre**

Expository Text Remind children that an expository text explains a topic by giving facts and details about it. An expository text often includes headings that organize the text and make it easier to understand. It also may include photographs, drawings, and charts to help readers understand the topic.

**Preview and
predict**

Have children read the title of the selection on p. 174 of *Reader's and Writer's Notebook.* Have children look through the selection and use the title and headings to predict what information they might learn in the selection. Tell them this selection is an expository text.

Set a purpose

After we read "Hot Air Balloons," we will talk about the facts and details we learned in the selection. Have children set a purpose for reading "Hot Air Balloons."

Differentiated Instruction

A Advanced

Extend Facts and Details After reviewing facts and details in the selection, have children work with a partner to write several facts and details about their class. For example, they might tell the name of their teacher, the number of children in the class, and describe what they do on a typical morning. Have children share their writing with the class.

Academic Vocabulary

expository text explains a topic by giving facts and details about it

Objectives

- Review skill: facts and details.
- Review strategy: background knowledge.
- Read aloud fluently with appropriate phrasing.

Name _____

Read the text.
Answer the questions.

Hot Air Balloons

Imagine floating high above the ground. People down below look like ants. You see green fields and roofs of houses.
No, you're not in an airplane. You're in a hot air balloon.

How a Hot Air Balloon Works

Balloons are very different from planes. How does a hot air balloon work? Hot air weighs less than cold air. So the air inside the balloon is heated. As it heats, the balloon goes up. As it cools, the balloon comes down.

Parts of a Hot Air Balloon

What do balloons look like? They have several parts. There is the balloon itself. Then there is the basket. This is where the people stand. There is also the burner. The burner is used to heat the air inside the balloon.

Operating a Hot Air Balloon

Unlike airplanes, you can't turn hot air balloons. They go wherever the wind takes them. You can only make them go up or come down. You can heat the air inside to make the balloon rise. To make it fall, you can cool the air.

Hot Air Balloon Pilots

Balloon pilots know the best time for a hot air balloon ride. Most rides happen in the morning or evening. That's when the wind is

 Home Activity Your child used subheads to locate facts and details in a text about hot air balloons. Reread the text with your child. Have your child tell you one fact or detail provided under each subhead.

174 Comprehension

Name _____

the calmest. Strong winds are bad for balloon rides.
Would you like to be a hot air balloon pilot someday? You might have to wait a while. Balloon pilots have to be 16 years old or older. They must spend a lot of time in hot air balloons. They need to learn how to do everything. Until then, watching balloons float in the sky is exciting enough.

1. Where would you look to find out what a hot air balloon looks like?

   under the heading Parts of a Hot Air Balloon

2. What makes a hot air balloon work?

   heating and cooling the air inside the balloon

3. What is a hot air balloon basket?

   It is where the people riding in the balloon stand.

4. If you were operating a hot air balloon, what could you not make it do?

   I could not turn the balloon.

5. How old must a hot air balloon pilot be?

   16 years old or older

Comprehension 175

Reader's and Writer's Notebook pp. 174–175

Guide Comprehension
Review Facts and Details

Have children read the selection and respond to the questions.

Corrective feedback

If... children have difficulty responding to the questions,
then... use the following to guide their responses.

1. Finding out what a hot air balloon looks like can be found by looking at its parts. Which heading would you look under to find out the parts of a hot air balloon? **Have children find the heading "Parts of a Hot Air Balloon."**

2. What happens when the air inside a balloon is heated? What happens as the air cools? **Have children find the sentences that describe what hot air and cool air do to the balloon.**

3. What is the basket used for? **Have children find the sentence that tells how the basket is used.**

4. What decides the direction the balloon travels? **Have children find the sentences that tell how a balloon moves.**

5. What is the key word in the question? **Have children scan the headings to find the word *pilot*.**

Comprehension
 ## Background Knowledge

**Review
Strategy**

Discuss strategies that children used as they read "Hot Air Balloons."

Did you use information that you had learned about balloons to help you understand the selection? Did you use your own experiences? Have children identify how using what they know helped them understand the selection.

Fluency
Read with Appropriate Phrasing

Model fluent reading

Remind children that when they read, it is important to read words that go together in a sentence. Explain that when we read this way, it sounds natural—like the way we talk. If we read word-by-word, it doesn't sound natural. Model reading the first paragraph of "Hot Air Balloons" on *Reader's and Writer's Notebook* page 174 with appropriate phrasing. Have children track the print as you read.

Guide practice

To provide additional fluency practice, pair children and have them read "Hot Air Balloons."

ROUTINE **Paired Reading** **Team Talk**

1. **Reader 1 Begins** Children read the selection, switching readers at the end of each paragraph.

2. **Reader 2 Begins** Have partners reread; this time the other partner begins.

3. **Reread** For optimal fluency, children should reread three or four times.

4. **Corrective Feedback** Listen to children read and provide corrective feedback regarding their oral reading and their use of the blending strategy.

Routines Flip Chart

Differentiated Instruction

 Strategic Intervention

Comprehension and Fluency
Have children reread "Hot Air Balloons" aloud with appropriate phrasing. Have them think about the facts and details as they read and sound out any words they don't know. After they have read the selection, have them tell any other facts they may know about balloons.

Options for Oral Rereading

Use *Scarcity* or one of the Week 3 Leveled Readers.

30–35 min.

Objectives
- Identify plural nouns that change spelling.
- Write letters legibly using proper slant.
- Write for fluency.
- Review concepts.

Conventions
Singular and Plural Nouns

Review
Singular and plural nouns

A singular noun names one person, place, animal, or thing. A plural noun names more than one person, place, animal, or thing.

Guide practice

Read the following sentences and have children identify each noun as singular or plural.

> My **mom** likes to ride her **bike**. (singular, singular)
>
> **Giraffes** have very long **necks**. (plural, plural)
>
> Ten **birds** flew to the **forest**. (plural, singular)
>
> Lots of **books** are on the **table**. (plural, singular)

Team Talk Have one partner say a sentence that uses either a singular or plural noun. The other partner must change the sentence to use the other kind of noun. Have pairs share their sentences with the class.

On their own

Use *Reader's and Writer's Notebook*, page 176.

Reader's and Writer's Notebook p. 176

Handwriting
Letters *J, j, P, p*/Letter Form

Review
Letter formation

Review the proper formation of letters *Jj* and *Pp*. Write each letter. Have children write the letters several times and circle their best one.

Review
Letter form

Review that when we write letters that have descenders, such as *j* and *p*, we should use correct letter form. Letters with descenders have tails that go down under the bottom line and touch the line below.

Guide practice

Write the following sentence. Have children copy it using appropriate letter form. Monitor children's formation of letters as they write.

> **Pam put her purse on the porch and went jogging with Jane.**

On their own

Use the Day 3 section on *Reader's and Writer's Notebook*, pages 163–164.

 Envision It! Animations

ROUTINE Quick Write for Fluency — Team Talk

1. **Talk** Have pairs discuss what they learned about how we can work together to meet people's needs.

2. **Write** Have children write a few sentences to summarize the discussion.

3. **Share** Partners can read their summaries to one another.

Routines Flip Chart

Wrap Up Your Day

 Question of the Week

How can we work together to meet people's needs?

Review
Concept and Amazing Words

Use these questions to wrap up this review of the Week 3 concept and to provide another opportunity for children to use the week's Amazing Words. Pair or group children to answer the questions. Have children share their responses with the class.

- ☑ What is one **decision** a group of people could make to help a needy person?

- ☑ How do food **producers** and store owners work together?

- ☑ How can **consumers** work together to get the products and services they need?

- ☑ Who uses **strands** of **fiber** to make clothing for others?

- ☑ If an **extraordinary** storm damaged many homes in a town, how could the townspeople work together to help those who **lack** food and shelter?

- ☑ Do you think it is **typical** for people to work together to meet other people's needs? Why or why not?

Writing Workshop
Use the writing process lesson on pages CW•11–CW•20 for this week's writing instruction.

 E L L

English Language Learners
Extend Vocabulary Point out that the word *extraordinary* is made up of two words, *extra* and *ordinary,* and that *extraordinary* means "beyond what is ordinary; unusual or special." Have children think of extraordinary people, places, and things they have encountered and describe them to the class.

 **Preview DAY 4**

Tell children that tomorrow they will review more skills and read "Best Friends."

Objectives

- Review Week 4 concept.
- Share information and ideas about the concept.
- Review Week 4 oral vocabulary.

Today at a Glance

Oral Vocabulary
partnership, solution, survival, miserable, struggle, depend, familiar, insist

Phonics and Spelling
◉ Review Plurals *-s, -es, -ies*

High-Frequency Words
bought, people, pleasant, probably, scared, shall, sign

Vocabulary
Skill: Homophones

Comprehension
◉ Review Skill: Cause and Effect
◉ Review Strategy: Story Structure

Fluency
Skill: Read with Expression

Conventions
Plural Nouns That Change Spelling

Handwriting
Letters *w, W, y, Y:* Letter Slant

Writing
Quick Write for Fluency

Concept Talk

Question of the Week

Why is it a good idea to work together?

Review Week 4 selection

Today children will explore how the Question of the Week connects to *The Bremen Town Musicians*. Read the Question of the Week above. Remind children that *The Bremen Town Musicians* is a drama and fairy tale about four animals that work together to become successful musicians.

ROUTINE   Activate Prior Knowledge   Team Talk

1. **Think** Have children think about a time when they or someone they know needed help to get something done.

2. **Pair** Have pairs of children discuss how the Question of the Week applies to the four animals in *The Bremen Town Musicians*.

3. **Share** Call on a few children to share their ideas with the group. Guide discussion and encourage elaboration with prompts such as: What was each animal's problem at the beginning of the drama? How did joining the other animals help solve each animal's problem?

Routines Flip Chart

Connect to the Big Question

Use these questions to connect the Week 4 question and selection to the Unit 2 Big Question, **How can we work together?**

- How did the animals scare the robbers out of the house?

- How would you have helped the animals get rid of the robbers?

- How can you work together with others to succeed on a task?

ELL Reteach Concepts and Vocabulary Use the instruction on ELL Poster 9 to assess knowledge and concepts.

ELL Poster 9

Oral Vocabulary
Amazing Words

Review
Week 4
Amazing
Words

Remind children that they have learned some Amazing Words that they can use to answer the question *Why is it a good idea to work together?* Display "A Partnership with You" on page 9 of the *Sing with Me* Big Book. Sing the song.

 Sing with Me Big Book Audio

A Partnership with You

Had a problem,
Had a problem.
Tried to solve it on my own.
Couldn't find a good solution,
So I called you on the phone.

Solved my problem,
Solved my problem.
Thank you, Friend, for all you do.
What is good for my survival
Is a partnership with you.

Sing with Me Big Book

Go over all the Amazing Words from Week 4. Ask children to listen as you say them: *partnership, solution, survival, miserable, struggle, depend, familiar, insist.* Then say them again, and have children say each word after you.

- Would you rather be with someone who is *miserable* or *familiar*? (familiar)

- Which word means "an answer to a problem"? (solution)

- Would you *struggle* to carry something that was light or heavy? (heavy)

Apply Amazing Words

Have children demonstrate their understanding of Amazing Words by completing these sentences orally.

My friend and I have a _____ **partnership**.

Sammy felt **miserable** as she continued to **struggle** with her _____.

I can **depend** on _____ when I need help.

Jeff and Tina **insist** the _____ is true.

My mom and I came up with a _____ **solution**.

He brought lots of _____ to ensure his **survival** in the woods.

Katrina thought the _____ looked **familiar**.

Amazing Words

partnership	struggle
solution	depend
survival	familiar
miserable	insist

Differentiated Instruction

SI Strategic Intervention

Synonyms Have partners make a list of synonyms for the word *miserable*. For example, *sad, unhappy, glum, low,* and *blue.* Then have them make up a sentence about one of the characters from *The Bremen Town Musicians,* using the word *miserable* or one of its synonyms.

Writing on Demand

Develop Writing Fluency
Ask children to write about a time when they worked together with their family to clean their home or make their home better and why working together made the job easier. Have them write for two to three minutes. Children should write as much as they can. Tell them to try to do their best writing. You may want to discuss what children wrote during writing conferences.

Objectives

- Read plurals with *-s, -es,* and *-ies.*
- Spell plurals with *-s, -es,* and *-ies.*

Phonics

Plurals -s, -es, -ies

Review
Phonics skill

Review plurals with *-s, -es,* and *-ies* using Sound-Spelling Cards 139, 141, and 142.

Sound-Spelling
Card 139

Sound-Spelling
Card 141

Sound-Spelling
Card 142

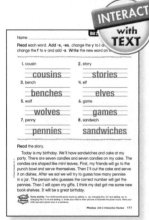

Reader's and Writer's
Notebook p. 177

Read words independent of context

Use *Reader's and Writer's Notebook* page 177. Point out that children know how to read these words. Then tell children they will all read the words in the first activity together. Allow several seconds previewing time for the first reading.

Corrective feedback

If... children cannot read all the words consecutively without an error, then... return to the first word in the row, and have children reread all the words in the row. Repeat until children can read the words fluently.

Read words in context

Use the passage on *Reader's and Writer's Notebook* page 177. Point out that there are many plurals with *-s, -es,* and *-ies* in the passage that children already know how to read. Have children read the passage together.

Let's Practice It!
TR DVD•114

Corrective feedback

If... children have difficulty reading plurals with *-s, -es,* and *-ies,* then... guide them in chunking multisyllabic words and using sound-by-sound blending. Have children read each sentence. Repeat until children can read the sentences fluently.

On their own

Use Let's Practice It! p. 114 on the *Teacher Resource DVD-ROM.*

Spelling
Plurals -s, -es, -ies

Review
Week 4 spelling words

Write *notes, lunches,* and *stories.* Point out that these words are plurals. Remind children that they learned how to spell plurals with *-s, -es,* and *-ies*. Use Sound-Spelling Cards 139, 141, and 142 to review how to spell these plurals.

Team Talk Have children review the spelling words using index cards on which the words are written. Tell them to sort the words into the ones they know and the ones they need more practice with. Partners can quiz each other on the words in the second pile.

On their own   Use *Reader's and Writer's Notebook,* p. 178.

Reader's and Writer's Notebook p. 178

Unit 2 Week 4 Spelling Words

Plurals *-s, -es, -ies*

1. note	7. tune
2. notes	8. tunes
3. lunch	9. switch
4. lunches	10. switches
5. story	11. baby
6. stories	12. babies

 ELL

English Language Learners

Review Plurals Remind children that plurals are words that mean "more than one." The endings *-s, -es,* and *-ies* are added to a word to make it plural.

Beginning Have partners make a list of all the spelling words that are plural. Have them underline each plural ending.

Intermediate Have partners write the plurals for these words: *class, park, fox,* and *puppy.*

Advanced/Advanced-High Have children write *-s, -es,* and *-ies* as headings. Have them write five plurals under each heading.

Objectives

- Read high-frequency words.
- Review homophones.
- Review key features of drama/fairy tale.
- Preview and predict.
- Establish purpose for reading text.

High-Frequency Words

Read words independent of context

Display the Week 4 high-frequency words. Have children read the words aloud. Have children point to each word on the Word Wall.

Guide practice

Read the sentences to children. Then have children use each word in a sentence of their own.

> **bought**—I **bought** two bottles of water.
>
> **people**—Many **people** went to see the parade.
>
> **pleasant**—We spent a **pleasant** day in the park.
>
> **probably**—I will **probably** go to the baseball game.
>
> **scared**—The big dog **scared** our cat.
>
> **shall**—We **shall** visit Uncle David tomorrow.
>
> **sign**—The **sign** said the store was having a big sale.

Corrective feedback

If... children do not use a word correctly, **then...** correct the sentence, model a sentence, and have them try again.

On their own

Use *Reader's and Writer's Notebook*, page 179.

Reader's and Writer's Notebook p. 179

Vocabulary Skill
Homophones

Review Homophones

Review that homophones are words that are pronounced the same way, but have different meanings and usually have different spellings. Write the following sets of homophones on the board: *ant, aunt; here, hear.*

- Which homophone names a relative? (aunt) Which homophone names an insect? (ant)

- Which homophone means *this place?* (here) Which homophone means *listen?* (hear)

Guide practice

Team Talk Have partners make up sentences for each set of homophones and share them with the class.

Comprehension
Skills and Strategies

Review Skill

 Cause and Effect Review that when we read a story, we find out "what happens" and "why it happens." Remind children that they know how to identify story events and the reasons why they happen. Recall that in the drama/fairy tale *The Bremen Town Musicians,* they find out, for example, that the donkey runs away because he learns that his owner is going to get rid of him.

Review Strategy

Story Structure Remind children that good readers can recognize story structure by identifying the important parts of a story: the characters, setting, and sequence of events. Stories usually have a beginning, a middle, and an end, and often each event leads to the next one. In *The Bremen Town Musicians,* there is a chain of events, as each animal joins the group that is traveling to Bremen Town.

Review Genre

Drama/Fairy Tale Remind children that a drama is written to be performed by actors for an audience. A fairy tale is a story that takes place long ago and far away. A fairy tale has fantastic characters that are usually all good or all bad. *The Bremen Town Musicians* is a drama because it is written to be performed by actors, but it is also a fairy tale in which the animals are the good characters and the robbers are the bad characters.

Preview and predict

Have children read the title of the story on p. 180 of *Reader's and Writer's Notebook.* Have children look through the story and use the title to predict events that might happen in the story. Tell them this story is a fairy tale.

Set a purpose

After we read "Best Friends," we will talk about what happened in the story and why it happened. Have children set a purpose for reading "Best Friends."

Differentiated Instruction

A Advanced

Extend Cause and Effect After reviewing "what happens" and "why it happens" in stories, have children think of something they did last night or this morning before they came to school. Have them write a few sentences that tell what they did and the reason(s) why they did it. Then have them share their writing with the class.

Academic Vocabulary

drama a drama is written to be performed by actors for an audience

fairy tale a fairy tale is set in the distant past and has fantastic characters that are usually all good or all bad

Objectives
• Review skill: cause and effect.
• Review strategy: story structure.
• Read aloud fluently with expression.

Name _____   **Unit 2 Week 4 Interactive Review**

Read the story.
Finish the sentences.

Best Friends

Prince Thad was sad. He was very, very sad. Why was Thad so sad? Thad had no friends. He lived in a castle with his parents, the king and queen. There were no other people around.

One day, Thad was playing outside the castle. He saw a bunny. It was sitting on the castle wall. "I shall ask the bunny to be my friend," thought Prince Thad.

"Bunny," asked Prince Thad, "can we be friends?"

"We can't be friends," said the bunny. "I am just a bunny. But I know a boy who can be your friend. His name is Fred. He lives in the forest. There's just one thing. Fred must come back to the forest every night."

"Okay," said Thad. He could hardly wait to meet Fred.

The next day, Fred came to play. It was fun. He came every day after that. But at five o'clock, Fred would always leave. He would go back to the forest. This made Thad sad again.

After a few days, Thad decided to follow Fred. He waited until Fred went into the forest. Then he crept along behind him.

Fred disappeared behind some trees and bushes. Thad wasn't scared. He sat down on some leaves and waited for his friend to come out. But his friend didn't come out. After a long wait, a bunny came out from behind the trees.

Home Activity Your child read a story to see what happened and answered questions about the cause of each event. Talk to your child about the events of the day, and what happened and why.

180 Comprehension

Name _____   **Unit 2 Week 4 Interactive Review**

Now Thad understood. The bunny wanted to be Thad's friend. So he turned himself into a boy each day. Finally, Thad was happy. He had a true friend at last. He knew he and Fred the Bunny would be best friends forever.

1. Prince Thad was sad because

    he had no friends.

2. The Prince talked to the bunny because

    Possible answers: he was lonely; wanted a friend.

3. The bunny turned himself into a boy each day because

    he wanted to be Thad's friend.

4. Prince Thad was finally happy because

    he had a friend.

Comprehension 181

Reader's and Writer's Notebook pp. 180–181

Guide Comprehension
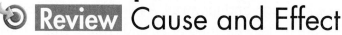
⟳ Review Cause and Effect

Have children read the story and respond to the questions.

Corrective feedback

If... children have difficulty responding to the questions,

then... use the following to guide their responses.

1. Prince Thad was very, very sad. What caused him to feel that way? **Have children reread the first paragraph of the story.**

2. What does the Prince do when he sees the bunny? **Have children find the sentences that tell what happened when Prince Thad saw the bunny.**

3. What do we learn about Fred at the end of the story? Who is Fred? **Have children find the sentences that tell who Fred is.**

4. What did Prince Thad always want? What did he finally get? **Have children find the sentences that tell what Prince Thad finally got that caused him to feel happy.**

Comprehension
 Story Structure

Review Strategy

Discuss strategies that children used as they read "Best Friends."

Did knowing how stories are organized help you follow the sequence of events in this story? What was Prince Thad's problem? How did he solve it? Have children identify how understanding story structure helped them understand and follow the events in the story.

Fluency
Read with Expression

Model fluent reading

Remind children that when they read, it is important to read the words a character says in the way that character would say them. Explain that when we read with expression, it makes the character and the story come alive. Model reading the second paragraph of "Best Friends" on *Reader's and Writer's Notebook* page 180 with expression. Have children track the print as you read.

Guide practice

To provide additional fluency practice, pair children and have them read "Best Friends."

ROUTINE **Paired Reading** **Team Talk**

1. **Reader 1 Begins** Children read the story, switching readers at the end of each paragraph.

2. **Reader 2 Begins** Have partners reread; this time the other partner begins.

3. **Reread** For optimal fluency, children should reread three or four times.

4. **Corrective Feedback** Listen to children read and provide corrective feedback regarding their oral reading and their use of the blending strategy.

Routines Flip Chart

Differentiated Instruction

SI Strategic Intervention

Comprehension and Fluency
Have children reread "Best Friends" aloud with expression. Have them think about what each character is like as they read what he says. After they have read the story, have them tell what happened in the beginning, in the middle, and at the end of the story.

Options for Oral Rereading

Use *The Bremen Town Musicians* or one of the Week 4 Leveled Readers.

DAY **4** UNIT 2 • WEEK 4 — **Interactive Review**
30–35 min.

Objectives
- Identify singular and plural nouns.
- Write letters with descenders legibly using proper form.
- Write for fluency.
- Review concepts.

Conventions
Plural Nouns That Change Spelling

Review
Plural nouns that change spelling

Most plural nouns are made by adding *-s* or *-es* to a singular noun. However, some nouns like *mouse/mice* change spelling in the plural form.

Guide practice

Read the following sentences and have children identify each plural noun.

> Some **children** like to play **sports**.
>
> The book has **pictures** of **geese** on the cover.
>
> Three **men** were packing the **boxes**.
>
> The **farmers** led their **oxen** to market.

Reader's and Writer's Notebook p. 182

Team Talk Pair children and have them name the plurals for these nouns: *woman, tooth,* and *foot.* Then have them use each plural noun in a sentence. Have pairs share their sentences with the class.

On their own Use *Reader's and Writer's Notebook,* page 182.

Handwriting
Letters *W, w, Y, y*/Letter Slant

Review
Letter formation

Review the proper formation of letters *Ww* and *Yy.* Write each letter. Have children write the letters several times and circle their best one.

Review
Letter slant

Review that when we write words and sentences, the letter slant should be consistent. All letters may slant to the right, to the left, or be straight up and down.

Guide practice

Write the following sentence. Have children copy it using consistent letter slant. Monitor children's letter slant as they write.

> **Why did Yasmin read two stories about a whale with yellow whiskers?**

On their own Use the Day 4 section on *Reader's and Writer's Notebook,* pages 163–164.

Use the writing process lesson on pages CW•11–CW•20 for this week's writing instruction.

ROUTINE **Quick Write for Fluency** Team Talk

1. **Talk** Have pairs discuss what they learned about why it is a good idea to work together.

2. **Write** Have children write a few sentences to summarize the discussion.

3. **Share** Partners can read their summaries to one another.

Routines Flip Chart

Wrap Up Your Day

Question of the Week
Why is it a good idea to work together?

Review
Concept and Amazing Words

Use these questions to wrap up this review of the Week 4 concept and to provide another opportunity for children to use the week's Amazing Words. Pair or group children to answer the questions. Have children share their responses with the class.

☑ When have you found a **solution** to a problem by working in a **partnership**? What was the problem?

☑ How can working with other climbers help increase a mountain climber's chances for **survival**?

☑ If you feel **miserable**, what can another person do to help you?

☑ What kind of task might you **struggle** to complete by yourself that would be easier with others?

☑ What are things a worker can do so that his or her coworkers can **depend** on him or her?

☑ Can you work with people you are not **familiar** with?

☑ Should teachers **insist** that students always work on schoolwork alone? Why or why not?

ELL

English Language Learners
Extend Vocabulary Remind children that the word *solution* means "the solving of a problem." Have children talk about stories they have read, such as *The Bremen Town Musicians,* in which the characters had a problem to solve. Have them tell what solutions characters in different stories came up with.

Preview **DAY 5**

Tell children that tomorrow they will review more skills and read "The Fox and the Goat."

Objectives
• Review Week 5 concept.
• Share information and ideas about the concept.
• Review Week 5 oral vocabulary.

Today at a Glance

Oral Vocabulary
conflict, pursue, resolve, deserve, mope, coax, ramp, startle

Phonics and Spelling
◎ Review Vowel Patterns *a, ai, ay*

High-Frequency Words
behind, brought, door, everybody, minute, promise, sorry

Vocabulary
Skill: Unfamiliar Words

Comprehension
◎ Review Skill: Compare and Contrast
◎ Review Strategy: Inferring

Fluency
Skill: Read with Accuracy

Conventions
Possessive Nouns

Handwriting
Letters *q, Q, v, V:* Letter Spacing

Writing
Quick Write for Fluency

Concept Talk

Question of the Week

How can we work together to solve problems?

Review Week 5 selection

Today children will explore how the Question of the Week connects to *One Good Turn Deserves Another.* Read the Question of the Week above. Remind children that *One Good Turn Deserves Another* is a folk tale about a mouse and a coyote that work together to solve a problem.

ROUTINE **Activate Prior Knowledge** Team Talk

1) **Think** Have children think about a time when they or someone they know had a problem that they could not solve by themselves.

2) **Pair** Have pairs of children discuss how the Question of the Week applies to the mouse and coyote in *One Good Turn Deserves Another.*

3) **Share** Call on a few children to share their ideas with the group. Guide discussion and encourage elaboration with prompts such as *What was the mouse's problem? How did she try to solve it?*

Connect to the Big Question

Use these questions to connect the Week 5 question and selection to the Unit 2 Big Question, **How can we work together?**

• Why did the mouse need somebody's help to solve her problem?

• What would you have told the mouse to do if you were a desert creature?

• How have you helped someone solve a problem?

ELL Reteach Concepts and Vocabulary Use the instruction on ELL Poster 10 to assess knowledge and concepts.

ELL Poster 10

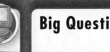
Oral Vocabulary
Amazing Words

Remind children that they have learned some Amazing Words that they can use to answer the question *How can we work together to solve problems?* Display "Talk It Out" on page 10 of the *Sing with Me* Big Book. Sing the song.

 Sing with Me Big Book Audio

Talk It Out

Problems can come up.
Bring them to an end.
What can you do with a conflict or two?
Resolve them with a friend.

Try to talk it out,
A step you can pursue.
Work together to make it better.
That's what you can do.

Sing with Me Big Book

Go over all the Amazing Words from Week 5. Ask children to listen as you say them: *conflict, pursue, resolve, deserve, mope, coax, ramp, startle.* Then say them again, and have children say each word after you.

- Which word describes what you want to do about a *conflict—pursue* or *resolve*? (resolve)

- Which word describes something a sad person might do? (mope)

- Raise your hand when I name something that might *startle* you—a bell, a rug, a dog's bark, a sandwich. (bell, dog's bark)

Have children demonstrate their understanding of Amazing Words by completing these sentences orally.

The _____ were happy to **resolve** their conflict.

_____ news causes Robert to **mope** around all day.

The police officers drove down the **ramp** to **pursue** the _____.

My teacher says I **deserve** a _____ grade.

We used _____ to **coax** the kitten out from under the car.

The _____ always seems to **startle** me.

Amazing Words

conflict	mope
pursue	coax
resolve	ramp
deserve	startle

Differentiated Instruction

SI Strategic Intervention

Resolve a Conflict Have partners discuss different ways to resolve a conflict and list the ways. For example: *talk things over; take turns; ask another person to help.* Have partners share their lists with the class.

Writing on Demand

Develop Writing Fluency Ask children to write about a time when they worked with others to solve a problem. Have them write for two to three minutes. Children should write as much as they can. Tell them to try to do their best writing. You may want to discuss what children wrote during writing conferences.

Interactive Review

Objectives

- Read words with vowel patterns for /ā/ spelled *a*, *ai*, and *ay*.
- Read multisyllabic words.
- Spell words with vowel patterns *ai* and *ay*.

Phonics
Vowel Patterns *a*, *ai*, *ay*

Review
Phonics skill

Review vowel patterns for long *a* spelled *a*, *ai*, and *ay* using Sound-Spelling Cards 54, 59, and 73. Review open syllable pattern V/CV using Sound-Spelling Card 149.

Sound-Spelling Card 54   Sound-Spelling Card 59   Sound-Spelling Card 73   Sound-Spelling Card 149

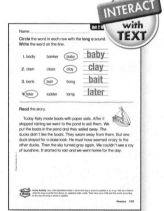

Reader's and Writer's Notebook p. 183

Read words independent of context

Use *Reader's and Writer's Notebook* page 183. Point out that children know how to blend these words. Then tell children they will all read the words in each row together. Allow several seconds previewing time for the first reading.

Corrective feedback

If... children cannot blend all the words in a row consecutively without an error,
then... return to the first word in the row, and have children reread all the words in the row. Repeat until children can read the words fluently.

Read words in context

Use the passage on *Reader's and Writer's Notebook* page 183. Point out that there are many words with vowel patterns *a*, *ai*, *ay*, and V/CV words in the passage that children already know how to read. Have children read the passage together.

Let's Practice It!
TR DVD•115

Corrective feedback

If... children have difficulty reading the words with vowel patterns *a*, *ai*, *ay*, or V/CV words,
then... guide them in chunking multisyllabic words and using sound-by-sound blending. Have children read each sentence. Repeat until children can read the sentences fluently.

On their own   Use Let's Practice It! p. 115 on the *Teacher Resource DVD-ROM*.

Spelling
Vowel Patterns *ai, ay*

Review
Week 5 spelling words

Write *tail* and *say.* Point out that these words have the long *a* sound spelled *ai* and *ay.* Remind children that they learned how to spell words with vowel patterns *ai* and *ay.* Use Sound-Spelling Cards 54 and 59 to review how to spell words with *ai* and *ay.*

Team Talk Have children review the spelling words using index cards on which the words are written. Tell them to sort the words into the ones they know and the ones they need more practice with. Partners can quiz each other on the words in the second pile.

On their own   Use *Reader's and Writer's Notebook,* p. 184.

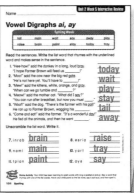

Reader's and Writer's
Notebook p. 184

Unit 2 Week 5 Spelling Words

Vowel Patterns ai, ay

1. tail	7. raise
2. main	8. brain
3. wait	9. paint
4. say	10. stay
5. away	11. today
6. play	12. tray

English Language Learners

Review Vowel Patterns *a, ai, ay* Remind children that the long a sound can be spelled *a* as in *bacon, ai* as in *rain,* and *ay* as in *clay.*

Beginning Write the words *rain* and *clay.* Have partners find two spelling words that rhyme with *rain* and six spelling words that rhyme with *clay.*

Intermediate Have partners write *a* and *ay* as headings. Have them write as many words as they can under each heading.

Advanced/Advanced-High Have partners write riddles for at least four spelling words. For example: *I use this part of my body to think. What is it?* (brain).

Objectives
- Read high-frequency words.
- Review unfamiliar words.
- Review key features of a folk tale.
- Preview and predict.
- Establish purpose for reading text.

High-Frequency Words

Read words independent of context

Display the Week 5 high-frequency words. Have children read the words aloud. Have children point to each word on the Word Wall.

Guide practice

Read the sentences to children. Then have children use each word in a sentence of their own.

> **behind**—I hid **behind** a big tree.
>
> **brought**—Laura **brought** her puppy to the vet.
>
> **door**—Please shut the **door** behind you.
>
> **everybody**—**Everybody** had a good time at the party.
>
> **minute**—I'll be ready in one **minute.**
>
> **promise**—I **promise** that I will go to bed on time.
>
> **sorry**—I'm **sorry** that you're not feeling well.

Corrective feedback

If... children do not use a word correctly,
then... correct the sentence, model a sentence, and have them try again.

On their own

Use *Reader's and Writer's Notebook*, page 185.

Reader's and Writer's
Notebook p. 185

Vocabulary Skill
Unfamiliar Words

Review

Unfamiliar words

Review that good readers often use other words in a sentence or in nearby sentences to figure out the meaning of an unfamiliar word.

- Which words in this sentence help you figure out the meaning of *liquid?* Ann poured the liquid into the glass.
  (poured, glass)

- Which words in this sentence help you figure out the meaning of *complained?* The food was bad, so I complained to the waiter.
  (food was bad)

Guide practice

Team Talk Have partners work together to write a sentence for the word *sly* that uses other words that give clues to its meaning.

Comprehension
Skills and Strategies

A Advanced

Extend Compare and Contrast After reviewing the meanings of *compare* and *contrast,* have children work with a partner to discuss how their favorite activities are alike and different. Then have children record their thoughts using a Venn diagram.

Review Skill

 Compare and Contrast Review that compare means "to explain how things are alike" and contrast means "to explain how things are different." Remind children that they know how to compare and contrast two stories. Recall that they compared and contrasted the folk tales, *One Good Turn Deserves Another* and *The Ungrateful Tiger.*

Review Strategy

Inferring Remind children that good readers infer what a story is trying to teach by using their own background knowledge as well as clues in the text. You can use what you already know along with the clues an author presents to understand the ideas and lessons that a story is trying to teach.

Academic Vocabulary

folk tale a story that has come down through years of storytelling from a particular culture, or group of people

Review Genre

Folk Tale Remind children that a folk tale is a story that has come down through years of storytelling from a particular culture, or group of people. Folk tale characters are usually animals or people who are trying to solve a problem. At the end of a folk tale, a character usually learns a lesson.

Preview and predict

Have children read the title of the selection on p. 186 of *Reader's and Writer's Notebook.* Have children look through the story and use the title to predict events that might happen in the story. Tell them this story is a folk tale.

Set a purpose

After we read "The Fox and the Goat," we will compare and contrast it with other folk tales we have read. Have children set a purpose for reading "The Fox and the Goat."

Objectives
- Review skill: compare and contrast.
- Review strategy: inferring.
- Read aloud fluently with accuracy.

Name _____   Unit 2 Week 5 Interactive Review

Read the story. **Answer** the questions.

The Fox and the Goat
A Tale from India

Dabbu the fox was happy. And full. He had just eaten a large meal. Now he was walking home in the moonlight. He sang as he walked. He was filled with happy thoughts.

Whoa! Suddenly the fox felt himself falling. He reached out to stop himself. But it was too late. Dabbu the fox had fallen into a shallow well. He often passed the well on his way home. Normally, he would never fall in it. But tonight he had been too happy. He had been singing and not paying attention. Now he was sorry.

Dabbu felt around the well. There wasn't much water in it. That was good. But how was he going to get out? Dabbu tried climbing out. But the walls were muddy and slippery. He couldn't get out. He tried again and again. Finally, he got tired. He sat down to rest. He had to think of a plan.

Not a minute later, he heard a voice. "What are you doing inside that well?" the voice asked.

Dabbu looked up. Standing above him was Laadla the goat. Dabbu studied the goat. He began to make a plan.

"Haven't you heard?" Dabbu asked Laadla. "There is a drought coming. No one will have water. So I jumped into the well to be sure to have some water near me. Why don't you jump down, too?"

The goat looked unsure. "What if you harm me when I jump down?" he asked.

Home Activity Your child compared and contrasted several stories. Read two stories with your child. Have your child tell how the stories are alike and how they are different.

186 Comprehension

Name _____   Unit 2 Week 5 Interactive Review

"Oh, I promise I won't," the fox said.

"Okay," said Laadla the goat. He jumped into the well.

Suddenly, Dabbu jumped on Laadla's back and leaped out of the well. "So long," he shouted.

Now Laadla was stranded. "Wait!" the goat cried. "You promised not to hurt me!"

The fox laughed as he left. "But I didn't promise to help you, either!"

1. How is this story like "One Good Turn Deserves Another" and "The Ungrateful Tiger"?

Possible answer: The stories are about animals that fall into a

hole and about animals not being nice to one another.

2. How is this story different from "One Good Turn Deserves Another" and "The Ungrateful Tiger"?

Possible answers: The story is about different animals. The story

is from a different country. The fox doesn't want to eat the goat.

3. How is this story alike and different from "The Lion and the Mouse"?

Both stories are about animals. The animals in the stories are

different. In this story the animals don't help each other.

Comprehension 187

Reader's and Writer's Notebook pp. 186–187

Guide Comprehension
⟳ Review Compare and Contrast

Have children read the story and respond to the questions.

Corrective feedback

If... children have difficulty responding to the questions,
then... use the following to guide their responses.

1. What is *One Good Turn Deserves Another* about? What is "The Ungrateful Tiger" about? What is "The Fox and the Goat" about? What is the same in each of these stories? Have children tell how the three stories are similar.

2. Do all three stories have the same characters? Are all three stories from the same country? Have children tell how the three stories are different.

3. Are the characters in "The Fox and the Goat" and "The Lion and the Mouse" animals or people? Do the characters in both stories help each other? Have children tell how "The Fox and the Goat" is similar to and different from "The Lion and the Mouse."

Comprehension
 Inferring

Review Strategy

Discuss strategies that children used as they read "The Fox and the Goat."

Did you use what you know about folk tales to help you figure out more about the characters and events in this folk tale? Have children explain how parts of the text as well as their knowledge of folk tales helped them understand more than what was stated in the story.

Fluency
Read with Accuracy

Model fluent reading

Remind children that when they read, it is important to pay attention to the words they are reading and to read without mistakes. Model reading the first paragraph of "The Fox and the Goat" on *Reader's and Writer's Notebook* page 186 with accuracy. Have children track the print as you read.

Guide practice

To provide additional fluency practice, pair children and have them read "The Fox and the Goat."

ROUTINE **Paired Reading** [Team Talk]

1. **Reader 1 Begins** Children read the story, switching readers at the end of each paragraph.

2. **Reader 2 Begins** Have partners reread; this time the other partner begins.

3. **Reread** For optimal fluency, children should reread three or four times.

4. **Corrective Feedback** Listen to children read and provide corrective feedback regarding their oral reading and their use of the blending strategy.

Routines Flip Chart

Differentiated Instruction

 Strategic Intervention

Comprehension and Fluency Have children reread "The Fox and the Goat," using a whisper-level voice. As they read, have them think about how different the two characters are. Tell children to raise their hand if they need help with a word. After children have read the story, have them describe each character in a sentence or two.

Options for Oral Rereading

Use *One Good Turn Deserves Another* or one of the Week 5 Leveled Readers.

Objectives
- Identify possessive nouns.
- Write letters legibly using proper spacing of letters in a word.
- Write for fluency.
- Review concepts.

Conventions
Possessive Nouns

Review
Possessive nouns

A noun that shows who or what owns something is a possessive noun. To show ownership, add an apostrophe and *s* to a singular noun, as in *dog/dog's,* and just an apostrophe to a plural noun, as in *dogs/dogs'.*

Guide practice

Read the following sentences and have children identify each possessive noun.

> My **cat's** dishes are kept in the kitchen.
>
> The **chicks'** feathers are soft and fluffy.
>
> The **kite's** string got tangled in the **tree's** branches.
>
> I saw two **birds'** nests in the park.

Team Talk Have one partner say a possessive phrase, such as *the boy's shoes.* Have the other partner complete the sentence by adding words before or after the phrase. Then have partners switch roles.

On their own

Use *Reader's and Writer's Notebook,* page 188.

Reader's and Writer's Notebook p. 188

Handwriting
Letters Q, q, V, v/Letter Spacing

Review
Letter formation

Review the proper formation of letters *Qq* and *Vv.* Write each letter. Have children write the letters several times and circle their best one.

Review
Letter spacing

Review that the letters in a word should be evenly spaced. The letters should not be written too close together or too far apart.

Guide practice

Write the following sentence. Have children copy it using appropriate letter spacing. Monitor children's spacing of letters as they write.

> **Val and Quinn gave five quacking quail some food today.**

On their own

Use the Day 5 section on *Reader's and Writer's Notebook,* pages 163–164.

Quick Write for Fluency

Team Talk

1. **Talk** Have pairs discuss what they learned about working together to solve problems.

2. **Write** Have children write a few sentences to summarize the discussion.

3. **Share** Partners can read their summaries to one another.

Routines Flip Chart

Wrap Up Your Day

Question of the Week

How can we work together to solve problems?

Review
Concept and Amazing Words

Use these questions to wrap up this review of the Week 5 concept and to provide another opportunity for children to use the week's Amazing Words. Pair or group children to answer the questions. Have children share their responses with the class.

☑ What is a **conflict** you have been able to **resolve** by working with other people?

☑ Why is it helpful to work as a group in order to **pursue** a solution to a problem that **startles** you?

☑ If you think you **deserve** to be the leader of a group, what would you say to the members of the group?

☑ If someone **mopes** around instead of working with the group, what should the other members do?

☑ What could you say to a person in order to **coax** him or her into working with you to solve a problem?

☑ How could a group of people work together to move a heavy object, such as a piano, up a **ramp**?

Writing Workshop

Use the writing process lesson on pages CW•11–CW•20 for this week's writing instruction.

ELL

English Language Learners
Visual Learning: Poster Preview Prepare children for next week by using Week 1, ELL Poster 11. Read the Poster Talk-Through to introduce the concept and vocabulary. Ask children to identify and describe objects and actions in the art.

Selection Summary Send home the summary of *Pearl and Wagner: Two Good Friends* in English and the child's home language if available. Children can read the summary with family members.

Preview Next Week

Tell children that next week they will read a story about two animal friends with a creative idea.

UNIT **2**

Unit Wrap-Up

 The Big Question

How can we work together?

Question of the Week

 How can we help each other in dangerous situations?

Concept Knowledge

Children will understand that:

- there are many dangerous situations in the world
- there are many ways that each of us can help

Question of the Week

How has working together changed history?

Concept Knowledge

Children will understand that working together:

- has changed history
- involves many people
- has made many positive changes

Understanding By Design

*Grant Wiggins, Ed.D
Reading Street Author*

"A big idea is not necessarily vast in the sense of a vague phrase covering lots of content. Nor is a big idea a 'basic' idea. Rather, big ideas are at the 'core' of the subject; they need to be uncovered; we have to dig deep until we get to the core."

Discuss the Big Question

Help children relate the concept question for this unit to the selections and their own experiences. Write the question and prompt discussion with questions such as the following.

How did the characters in the selections work together? Possible answers:

- *Tara and Tiree* The dogs and their owner worked together to save each other's lives.
- *Abraham Lincoln* Abraham Lincoln worked to put our country back together.
- *Scarcity* Producers and consumers work together to make, sell, and buy things.

Question of the Week

How can we work together to meet people's needs?

Concept Knowledge

Children will understand that meeting the needs of people:

• requires many decisions

• requires the work of many people

Question of the Week

Why is it a good idea to work together?

Concept Knowledge

Children will understand that working together:

• solves problems

• provides safety and protection

• helps us survive

• helps get the job done

Question of the Week

How can we work together to solve problems?

Concept Knowledge

Children will understand that when we work together, we:

• resolve conflicts

• share responsibility and work

• spend time with others

• help those in need

• *The Bremen Town Musicians* A team of animals worked together to overpower robbers.

• *One Good Turn* The mouse and coyote work together to trick the snake.

Why does working together make solving a problem easier? Possible answer:

• When we work with others on a problem, we can find a solution together and share the work.

Unit Assessment

Use Unit 2 *Benchmark Test* to check:

✔ **Passage Comprehension**

✔ **Writing Conventions**

✔ **Phonics**

✔ **Vocabulary**

✔ **Writing**

✔ **Fluency**

Unit and End-of-Year Benchmark Tests

Managing Assessment

Use *Assessment Handbook* for:

✔ **Weekly Assessment Blackline Masters for Monitoring Progress**

✔ **Observation Checklists**

✔ **Record-Keeping Forms**

✔ **Portfolio Assessment**

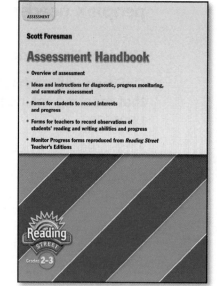

Assessment Handbook

Directions

Writing Prompt

Write about how to make or do something with a friend.

Purpose Explain the steps it takes to make or do something

Audience A friend

Introduce genre and prompt

Tell children that in this lesson they will learn about a kind of writing called directions. Directions tell how to make or do something in step-by-step order. When you write directions, you tell others exactly what they must do to make or do something.

Introduce key features

Key Features of Directions

- explain a specific task or activity using a series of steps
- use numerals or words such as *first, next,* and *last* to show the order of the steps
- provide all the necessary information and details
- use clear sentences with strong verbs to guide readers

Academic Vocabulary

directions step-by-step instructions in either paragraphs or a numbered list that others can easily follow to make or do something

ELL

English Language Learners
Introduce Genre Point out that directions tell how to make or do something using steps that are in a certain order. Explain that the writer may use words such as *first, next,* and *last* or numerals such as 1, 2, and 3 to show the order of steps. Discuss with children the key features of directions that appear on this page.

Objectives

- Understand and identify the key features of directions.
- Generate ideas for writing by listing ideas, drawing pictures, and discussion.
- Select a topic.

① Plan and Prewrite

MINI-LESSON

Read Like a Writer

■ **Examine Model Text** Let's look at an example of directions. Display and read aloud to children "How to Make a Terrarium" on Writing Transparency WP7. Point out the words *First, Next, Now, Then,* and *Last.* Explain that these are time-order words that help make the order of the steps clear. Read aloud the sentences that begin with a time-order word. Ask children how these words help them understand when to do each step.

How to Make a Terrarium

Making a terrarium isn't hard. You and a friend can make one in an afternoon. You need pebbles, charcoal chips, soil, a glass container, plants, and a plastic jar cover. After you have gathered these things, take turns reading and following these directions.

First, spread a layer of charcoal chips on the bottom. This will keep the terrarium smelling fresh. Next, spread pebbles over the chips. This will help water drain from the soil. Now put a layer of soil on the pebbles. Then poke holes in the soil and put in the plants. Last, put the cover over the container.

You and your friend can make your terrarium special. Add bugs, moss, and lizards.

Writing Transparency WP7
TR DVD

■ **Evaluate Model Text** Display "Traits of Good Directions" on Writing Transparency WP8. Discuss each trait with children. First read the name of the trait and remind children what it means. Then read aloud the statement, explaining any unfamiliar words. Finally, help children understand how the statement applies to the model directions. For Sentences, point out that most sentences in the model are commands. Explain that commands are common in directions because the writer is telling readers what to do.

Traits of Good Directions

Focus/Ideas	Directions stick to the topic and give details.
Organization	Writer tells steps in order and includes all important details.
Voice	Writer is clear and direct.
Word Choice	Writer uses time-order words, such as first and next, to show the order of the steps.
Sentences	Most sentences are commands.
Conventions	Writer uses good spelling, capitalization, punctuation, and grammar.

Writing Transparency WP8
TR DVD

Generate ideas for writing

Reread the writing prompt on p. CW11 to children. The writing prompt asks you to write about how to make or do something with a friend. Encourage children to generate ideas for writing directions using these strategies:

✔ Draw pictures of group activities they like to do. Explain how to do each activity.

✔ In a group, share ideas about foods and crafts they know how to make.

✔ Make a list of their best ideas for directions.

Corrective feedback

If... children have difficulty thinking of a topic to write about, **then...** help them recall activities they do every day or every week in school with their classmates.

Narrow topic

Have children ask themselves questions about the ideas on their list. They might ask: *How well do I know this topic? Can I explain how to make or do it in several steps?* Model how to narrow the choices on a list to one topic using the example list shown.

 I thought of three ideas. Now I will choose one. I don't think directions for tag would be interesting because the game is very simple and most kids know how to play it. Painting a mural is a big topic. I don't think I could explain it in three or four steps. I really enjoy making scratch-art pictures with my friends. I know I can give clear directions about how to do that.

Topic Ideas

playing tag

painting a mural

making a scratch-art picture

 **Write Guy**
Jeff Anderson

Use Mentor Text

Have children look back at the unit selection *Tara and Tiree.* Discuss with them the steps that the dogs take to save their owner's life. Point out why the order of these steps is important. Explain that these steps could be written as directions. Ask children to think of something they can make or do with a friend. Tell them they will be writing directions about this activity.

Differentiated Instruction

 Strategic Intervention

Alternative Writing Prompt
Think of something you know how to do, such as make your bed or brush your teeth. Write the steps in a list. Put a number next to each step. Make sure the steps are in the right order.

 Advanced

Alternative Writing Prompt
Think of a craft or game that involves four to six steps. Write directions to explain this activity. Include a brief introduction to involve your reader. Add a concluding sentence.

Objectives

- Understand the criteria for effective directions.
- Plan directions by organizing ideas.
- Sequence ideas in sentences to prepare to write a first draft.

 Plan and Prewrite

MINI-LESSON

Planning a First Draft

■ **Use a Directions Chart** Display Writing Transparency WP9 and read it aloud to children.

 Think Aloud I write sentences that tell step-by-step directions in order on my directions chart. I write the first direction in the Step 1 box, the second direction in the Step 2 box, and so on. I think of a good title and write that on the line at the top. Now I can start writing a first draft.

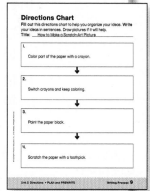

Writing Transparency WP9
TR DVD

■ Have children use the Directions Chart graphic organizer on *Reader's and Writer's Notebook*, p. 189, to help them sequence the steps in their directions and think of a title. Before you begin writing, decide what steps you need to tell about and write sentences for the steps in order. If it will help you, draw small pictures to show how the directions can be followed. Also, think of a good title that tells what your directions are about.

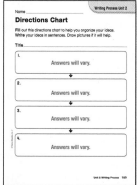

Reader's and Writer's
Notebook, p. 189

② Draft

Display rubric

Display Scoring Rubric WP2 from the *Teacher Resource DVD-ROM*. Read aloud and discuss with children the traits and criteria that you choose. Encourage children to think about these criteria as they develop drafts of their directions. Tell them that rubrics such as this one are often used to evaluate and score writing.

Scoring Rubric: *Directions*

	④	③	②	①
Focus/Ideas	Reader can understand the directions	Reader can understand some of the directions	Reader cannot understand the directions very well	Reader cannot understand the directions
Organization	Steps organized in correct order	Steps mostly in correct order	Some steps out of order or missing	No order of steps
Voice	Clearly shows how you feel about topic	Shows your interest in the topic a little	Does not show your interest in the topic very well	Does not show you are interested in the topic
Word Choice	Has strong verbs and time-order words	Has some strong verbs and time-order words	Has few strong verbs or time-order words	Has no strong verbs or time-order words
Sentences	Sentences clear; most are commands	Sentences clear; some are commands	Sentences are not clear; few commands	Sentences are not clear; no commands
Conventions	Uses good punctuation and grammar	Uses fair punctuation and grammar	Uses poor punctuation and grammar	Uses very poor punctuation and grammar

Prepare to draft

Have children look at the directions charts they worked on earlier. Ask them to make sure that their charts are complete. If their charts are not complete, have children finish them now. Use your directions chart as you write a draft of your directions. You will have a chance to revise your draft later.

Corrective feedback

If...children do not understand how the Scoring Rubric can be used to evaluate writing,
then... show them how you can use the Scoring Rubric to evaluate and score one or more traits of the model directions on Writing Transparency WP7.

Differentiated Instruction

SI Strategic Intervention

Plan a First Draft Let children dictate to you the process they want to explain in their directions. Record their steps and circle key words or concepts. Ask them questions about these key elements. Help them write an opening sentence.

ELL

English Language Learners

Prepare to Draft Have children tell you what steps they want to include in their directions. Help them restate their ideas as complete sentences. Provide a framework of partial sentences on the board and have children fill in the blanks.

Objectives

- Choose strong verbs that tell exactly what to do in directions.
- Write a first draft of directions.
- Revise a draft of written directions.

 **Draft**

MINI-LESSON

Writing Trait: Word Choice

▪ **Use Strong Verbs** Write the strong verbs below on the board. Explain that each step in directions tells an action and uses a verb. Show how verbs that are precise give readers a clearer picture of what they are supposed to do.

Weak Verb Put the beans in the dirt.
Strong Verb Press the beans into the dirt.

▪ Act out a direction using each of the remaining verbs. Have children name the correct strong verb.

Reader's and Writer's
Notebook, p. 190

Strong Verbs

cut

press

remove

attach

glue

▪ Have children use *Reader's and Writer's Notebook* page 190 to practice using strong verbs in directions.

Develop draft   Remind children that when they write their first drafts, they want to get their ideas down on paper. Suggest that they try these drafting strategies:

✔ List action verbs that tell what to do in their steps. Use the list to write the sentences in their directions.

✔ Organize their steps either in short paragraphs with time-order transition words, such as *first, next,* and *last,* or in a list with numerals followed by periods.

③ Revise

Writer's Craft: Adding Words, Phrases, and Sentences

■ Explain to children that when good writers revise, they often add words, phrases, or sentences. They may add more details to better describe or explain something. Discuss with children how the details added to the following sentence make a clearer direction.

Decorate the sock puppet.
Decorate the sock puppet using felt and colored markers.

■ Have children practice adding a word, phrase, and sentence on *Reader's and Writer's Notebook*, p. 191. Then together discuss how these revisions make the original sentence more interesting.

Reader's and Writer's Notebook, p. 191

Revise model   Use Writing Transparency WP10 to model how to revise directions.

Think Aloud In the fourth sentence, I replaced *it* with *the paper* to clearly identify what is being colored. I changed *Do it* to *Press,* a more specific direction that gives the reader a clearer picture of what to do. To give more details about a step in the process, I added this sentence: *Keep switching crayons until the whole sheet is colored.*

Writing Transparency WP10
TR DVD

Teacher Tip

Remind children that putting steps in order will make their directions clear and easy to follow, and adding time-order words to the steps will make the order even clearer. Help children make a list of time-order words. Begin with *first, next, then*, and *last*. Encourage children to find other time-order words in their reading and to add the words to the list. (*now, later, second, third, finally*)

ELL

English Language Learners
Revise for Details To improve details in their writing, work with children to add words, phrases, and sentences to their directions. Ask children questions about their writing and prompt them for more details. Demonstrate where to add these details in their sentences.

3 Revise

Revise draft

We have written first drafts of our directions. Now we will revise our drafts. When we revise, we try to make our writing clearer and easier to read.

Peer conferencing

Peer Revision Write the questions that you choose from the Revising Checklist on the board. If you elect to use peer revision, help pairs of children exchange and read each other's drafts. Read aloud the checklist, one question at a time. Ask children to answer each question about their own draft or their partner's draft. Remind them to think about where words, phrases, or sentences could be added to give more details.

Help children revise their directions using their own ideas or their partner's comments as well as what they have learned about writing directions to guide them.

Revising Checklist

✔ Do the directions tell how to make or do something?

✔ Are the steps in the correct order?

✔ Does the writer use time-order words or numerals to help show the order?

✔ Does the writer use strong verbs that tell readers exactly what to do?

✔ Are there places where the writer could add words, phrases, or sentences to give more details?

④ Edit

Editing Strategy: Work with a Partner

■ Explain this editing strategy to children: With a partner, read each other's directions and look for errors. Circle possible errors and discuss them with your partner. Model this strategy using Writing Transparency W11. If you elect to teach proofreading marks, explain what they mean and how they are used as you discuss the errors on the transparency.

Think Aloud When I proofread, I look for missing or incorrect punctuation, misspelled words, and words that need uppercase letters. I see a sentence that needs a period added at the end. The sentence that begins with *First* begins the steps of the process, so a new paragraph should start there. The word *swich* doesn't look right. It needs a *t*. I correct the spelling.

Writing Transparency WP11
TR DVD

■ Have children edit the sentences on *Reader's and Writer's Notebook*, p. 192. Encourage them to use proofreading marks.

■ Help children edit their own drafts. Make a simple rubric to help them check their spelling, grammar, punctuation, and capitalization.

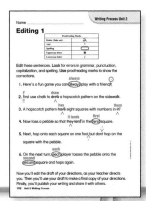

Reader's and Writer's Notebook, p. 192

Technology Tips

Children who type their directions on computers may find these tips useful as they edit:

✔ If their program has a thesaurus, they can look up verbs in their steps and see if they can find stronger verbs to use.

✔ If their program has a print preview or a page layout feature, they can use it to see how their work will appear on a page before they print it.

Differentiated Instruction

 Advanced

Apply Editing Skills As they edit their work, children can consider these ways to improve it.

• Check that each sentence has a subject and a predicate.

• Make sure each sentence ends with the correct punctuation mark.

• Look up words in a dictionary to see whether they are spelled correctly.

 Write Guy
Jeff Anderson

Experiment!

Encourage children to experiment with spelling, punctuation, and grammar. Although they shouldn't "worry" about these things when they are drafting, they should attempt to do the best they can. The time to really focus on whether or not they use conventions correctly in their drafts is in the editing step.

ELL

English Language Learners

Support Editing When reviewing a child's draft, focus on ideas more than errors. If you find consistent spelling errors, choose one or two skills for attention during editing. Use the appropriate lessons in the *ELL Handbook* to explicitly teach the English conventions.

Objectives
- Write and present a final draft of directions.
- Evaluate one's own writing.

(5) Publish and Present

Present

Remind children of the writing process steps they read about on *Reader's and Writer's Notebook*, p. 192. After they have revised and edited their directions, have children write a final draft. Explain that it is time for them to share their writing with others. Offer children two ways to present their work:

Demonstrate the process they explained in their directions. Use props and visual aids.	Illustrate or make their products. Display the illustrations and products in the classroom.

MINI-LESSON

Evaluating Writing

■ Prepare children to evaluate their directions. Display and read aloud Writing Transparency WP12. Model the self-evaluation process.

Think Aloud My directions tell about making a scratch-art picture with friends. My steps are in the right order, and I used time-order transition words to show the order. Strong verbs such as *press, switch,* and *scratch* in commands tell exactly what to do. My punctuation and grammar are good. But I wish I had listed the materials you need at the beginning. That would have been helpful to readers.

How to Make a Scratch-Art Picture

Would you like to make a very different picture? Make scratch-art with your friends. Start by giving each person a sheet of paper and a different color of crayon.

First, color part of the paper. Press hard so that the color is dark. Next, switch crayons with another person and color another part of your paper. Keep switching crayons until the whole sheet is colored. Then paint the paper black.

Last, when the paint is dry, take toothpicks and scratch off some black paint so you can see the colors. Make a design or draw a picture with your scratch-art. Be creative!

Unit 2 Directions • PUBLISH   Writing Process 12

Writing Transparency WP12
TR DVD

■ Help children use the Scoring Rubric to evaluate their directions. They can save their work in a portfolio to help them monitor their development as writers. Encourage them to build on their skills and to note areas for improvement.

Contents

Pacing Guide

This chart shows the instructional sequence from *Scott Foresman Reading Street* for Grade 2. You can use this pacing guide as is to ensure you are following a comprehensive scope and sequence. Or, you can adjust the sequence to match your calendar, curriculum map, or testing schedule.

Grade 2

REVIEW WEEK

READING	UNIT 1					UNIT 2	
	Week 1	Week 2	Week 3	Week 4	Week 5	Week 1	Week 2
Phonics	Short Vowels	Long Vowels CVC*e*	Consonant Blends	Inflected Endings	Consonant Digraphs	*r*-Controlled *ar, or, ore, oar*	Contractions
High-Frequency Words	*someone, somewhere, friend, country, beautiful, front*	*everywhere, live, work, woman, machines, move, world*	*couldn't, love, build, mother, bear, father, straight*	*water, eyes, early, animals, full, warm*	*together, very, learn, often, though, gone, pieces*	*family, once, pull, listen, heard, break*	*laugh, great, you're, either, certainly, second, worst*
Comprehension Skill	Character and Setting	Main Idea and Details	Character and Setting	Main Idea and Details	Facts and Details	Cause and Effect	Author's Purpose
Comprehension Strategy	Monitor and Clarify	Text Structure	Story Structure	Important Ideas	Predict and Set Purpose	Summarize	Text Structures
Fluency	Appropriate Rate	Read with Accuracy	Accuracy and Appropriate Rate	Attend to Punctuation	Read with Expression/ Intonation	Accuracy and Appropriate Rate	Read with Expression/ Intonation

REVIEW WEEK

	UNIT 4					UNIT 5	
	Week 1	Week 2	Week 3	Week 4	Week 5	Week 1	Week 2
Phonics	Syllables C + *le*	Vowels *oo, u* (as in *book*)	Diphthongs *ou, ow/ou/*	Syllables CV, CVC	Vowels *oo, ue, ew, ui* (as in *moon*)	Suffixes -*ly, -ful, -er, -ish, -or*	Prefixes *un-, re-, pre-, dis-*
Comprehension Skill	Draw Conclusions	Sequence	Fact and Opinion	Plot and Theme	Plot and Theme	Fact and Opinion	Cause and Effect
Comprehension Strategy	Background Knowledge	Important Ideas	Questioning	Visualize	Monitor and Clarify	Important Ideas	Visualize
Vocabulary Strategy/Skill	Context Clues/Multiple-Meaning Words	Context Clues/ Antonyms	Word Structure/ Suffixes	Context Clues/ Multiple-Meaning Words	Word Structure/ Prefixes	Word Structure/ Suffixes	Dictionary/ Unfamiliar Words
Fluency	Accuracy and Appropriate Rate	Read with Accuracy	Appropriate Phrasing	Characterization	Read with Expression/ Intonation	Read with Accuracy	Accuracy and Appropriate Rate

Are you the adventurous type? Want to use some of your own ideas and materials in your teaching? But you worry you might be leaving out some critical instruction children need? **Customize Literacy** *can help.*

REVIEW WEEK · **UNIT 3** · **REVIEW WEEK**

Week 3	Week 4	Week 5
r-Controlled er, ir, ur	Plurals	Long a: a, ai, ay
enough, toward, above, ago, word, whole	people, sign, shall, bought, probably, pleasant, scared	door, behind, brought, minute, promise, sorry, everybody
Facts and Details	Cause and Effect	Compare and Contrast
Background Knowledge	Story Structure	Inferring
Read with Appropriate Phrasing	Express Characterization	Accuracy

Week 1	Week 2	Week 3	Week 4	Week 5
Long e: e, ee, ea, y	Long o: o, oa, ow	Compound Words	Long i: i, ie, igh, y	Comparative Endings
science, shoe, won, guess, village, pretty, watch	picture, school, answer, wash, parents, company, faraway	today, whatever, caught, believe, been, finally, tomorrow	their, many, alone, buy, half, youngest, daughters	only, question, clothes, money, hours, neighbor, taught
Author's Purpose	Draw Conclusions	Compare and Contrast	Sequence	Fact and Opinion
Questioning	Visualize	Summarize	Predict and Set Purpose	Inferring
Read with Appropriate Rate	Accuracy and Appropriate Rate	Express Characterization	Attend to Punctuation	Read with Expression and Intonation

REVIEW WEEK · **UNIT 6** · **REVIEW WEEK**

Week 3	Week 4	Week 5
Silent Consonants	ph, gh/f/, ck, ng	Vowels aw, au, augh, al
Plot and Theme	Character and Setting	Main Idea and Details
Background Knowledge	Story Structure	Inferring
Dictionary/Classify and Categorize	Word Structure/Compound Words	Word Structure/Suffixes
Read with Expression/Intonation	Express Characterization	Appropriate Phrasing

Week 1	Week 2	Week 3	Week 4	Week 5
Inflected Endings	Abbreviations	Syllables -tion, -ture, -ion	Suffixes -ness, -less, -able, -ible	Prefixes mis-, mid-, micro-, non-
Compare and Contrast	Author's Purpose	Draw Conclusions	Sequence	Facts and Details
Monitor and Clarify	Summarize	Questioning	Text Structure	Predict and Set Purpose
Context Clues/Homophones	Context Clues/Multiple-Meaning Words	Context Clues/words from other languages	Context Clues/Unfamiliar Words	Dictionary/Multiple-Meaning Words
Accuracy and Appropriate Rate	Read with Accuracy	Appropriate Phrasing	Accuracy and Appropriate Rate	Appropriate Phrasing

Pacing Guide

Grade 2 — LANGUAGE ARTS

UNIT 1

	Week 1	Week 2	Week 3	Week 4	Week 5
Speaking, Listening, and Viewing	Why We Speak/ Why We Listen	Be a Good Speaker/Listen Attentively	Recognize Purposes of Media	Narrate in Sequence	Dramatize
Research and Study Skills	Media Center/ Library	Reference Sources	Personal Sources	Parts of a Book	Maps
Grammar	Sentences	Subjects	Predicates	Statements and Questions	Commands and Exclamations
Weekly Writing; Trait of the Week	Personal Narrative/ Conventions	Expository Paragraph/ Sentences	Realistic Story/ Organization	Brief Report/ Word Choice	Play Scene/ Conventions
Writing	Keyboarding/Personal Narrative				

REVIEW WEEK

UNIT 2

	Week 1	Week 2
Speaking, Listening, and Viewing	Give and Follow Directions	Explain Purposes of Media
Research and Study Skills	Notes	Time Line
Grammar	Nouns	Proper Nouns
Weekly Writing; Trait of the Week	Narrative Nonfiction/ Voice	Biography/ Focus/Ideas

UNIT 4

	Week 1	Week 2	Week 3	Week 4	Week 5
Speaking, Listening, and Viewing	Media Techniques	Make an Announcement	Speak Well	Media Techniques	Give an Oral Summary
Research and Study Skills	Thesaurus	Personal Sources	Diagram	E-mail	Natural and Personal Sources
Grammar	Adjectives and Our Senses	Adjectives for Number, Size, and Shape	Adjectives That Compare	Adverbs That Tell When and Where	Adverbs That Tell How
Weekly Writing; Trait of the Week	Friendly Letter/ Organization	Expository Nonfiction/ Word Choice	Short Expository Report/ Sentences	Narrative Poem/ Voice	Thank-You Note/ Focus/Ideas
Writing	E-Newsletter/Description				

REVIEW WEEK

UNIT 5

	Week 1	Week 2
Speaking, Listening, and Viewing	Identify Cultural Characteristics in Media	Give a Demonstration
Research and Study Skills	Online Directory	Bar Graph
Grammar	Pronouns	Singular and Plural Pronouns
Weekly Writing; Trait of the Week	Narrative Nonfiction/ Word Choice	Realistic Story/ Organization

REVIEW WEEK

Week 3	Week 4	Week 5
Ask and Answer Questions	Explain Purposes of Media	Give and Follow Directions
Chapter Headings	Encyclopedia	Read a Web Page
Singular and Plural Nouns	Plural Nouns That Change Spelling	Possessive Nouns
Expository Nonfiction/Word Choice	Fairy Tale/Organization	Folk Tale/Sentences

Electronic Pen Pal/Directions

UNIT 3 — REVIEW WEEK

Week 1	Week 2	Week 3	Week 4	Week 5
Make Introductions	Solve Problems	Summarize Information	Give a Description	Describe Media Technique
Picture-Graph	Newspaper and Periodicals	Interview	Alphabetized Index	Search Internet
Verbs	Verbs with Singular and Plural Nouns	Verbs for Past, Present, and Future	More About Verbs	Verbs: *Am, Is, Are, Was,* and *Were*
Animal Fantasy/Voice	Friendly Letter/Focus/Idea	Narrative Poem/Conventions	Realistic Story/Word Choice	Review/Organization

Story Starters/Compare and Contrast Essay

REVIEW WEEK

Week 3	Week 4	Week 5
Listen for Facts and Opinions	Maintain Focus in a Narrative Presentation	Speak to Your Audience
Online Reference Sources	Tables	Evaluate Online Sources
Using *I* and *Me*	Different Kinds of Pronouns	Contractions
Journal Entry/Voice	Animal Fantasy/Conventions	Humorous Story/Sentences

Community Interview/Persuasive Letter

UNIT 6 — REVIEW WEEK

Week 1	Week 2	Week 3	Week 4	Week 5
Use Vocabulary to Express Ideas	Evaluate Ads	Listen to a Description	Identify Conventions	Listen for Speaker's Purpose
Globe	Chart	Interview a Natural Source	Schedules	Interview a Natural Source
Capital Letters	Quotation Marks	Prepositions	Commas	Commas in Compound Sentences
Realistic Story/Organization	Descriptive Poem or Song/Voice	Invitation or Letter/Sentences	Compare-Contrast Text/Focus/Ideas	Persuasive Statement/Word Choice

Blogging/Research Report

Teaching Record Chart

This chart shows the critical comprehension skills and strategies you need to cover. Check off each one as you provide instruction.

Reading/Comprehension	DATES OF INSTRUCTION		
Use ideas (e.g., illustrations, titles, topic sentences, key words, and foreshadowing) to make and confirm predictions.			
Ask relevant questions, seek clarification, and locate facts and details about stories and other texts and support answers with evidence from text.			
Establish purpose for reading selected texts and monitor comprehension, making corrections and adjustments when that understanding breaks down (e.g., identifying clues, using background knowledge, generating questions, re-reading a portion aloud).			
Identify moral lessons as themes in well-known fables, legends, myths, or stories.			
Compare different versions of the same story in traditional and contemporary folktales with respect to their characters, settings, and plot.			
Describe how rhyme, rhythm, and repetition interact to create images in poetry.			
Identify the elements of dialogue and use them in informal plays.			
Describe similarities and differences in the plots and settings of several works by the same author.			
Describe main characters in works of fiction, including their traits, motivations, and feelings.			
Distinguish between fiction and nonfiction.			
Recognize that some words and phrases have literal and non-literal meanings (e.g., take steps).			

Tired of using slips of paper or stickies to make sure you teach everything you need to? Need an easier way to keep track of what you have taught, and what you still need to cover? **Customize Literacy** can help. **"**

Reading/Comprehension	DATES OF INSTRUCTION		
Read independently for a sustained period of time and paraphrase what the reading was about, maintaining meaning.			
Identify the topic and explain the author's purpose in writing the text.			
Identify the main idea in a text and distinguish it from the topic.			
Locate the facts that are clearly stated in a text.			
Describe the order of events or ideas in a text.			
Use text features (e.g., table of contents, index, headings) to locate specific information in text.			
Follow written multi-step directions.			
Use common graphic features to assist in the interpretation of text (e.g., captions, illustrations).			
Establish purposes for reading selected texts based upon content to enhance comprehension.			
Ask literal questions of text.			
Monitor and adjust comprehension (e.g., using background knowledge, creating sensory images, re-reading a portion aloud, generating questions).			
Make inferences about text using textual evidence to support understanding.			
Retell important events in stories in logical order.			
Make connections to own experiences, to ideas in other texts, and to the larger community and discuss textual evidence.			

Cause and Effect

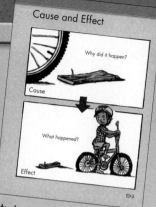

Student Edition p. EI•3

Objectives

- Children answer *What happened?* and *Why did that happen?*
- Children identify cause-and-effect relationships.
- Children understand that cause-and-effect relationships can be signaled by clue words.

What is it? A **cause** is why something happens. An **effect** is the result of the cause. Not all causal relationships are stated directly or signaled by clue words, such as *because*, *so*, and *since*. In these cases, children must infer either cause or effect, using information in the text and their prior knowledge. At Grade 2, readers are identifying causal relationships by answering the questions: *What happened? Why did it happen?*

How Good Readers Use the Skill Children experience cause-and-effect relationships every day. To be successful, they need to recognize these relationships in fiction as well as in all content areas. The ability to do so will help them increase their understanding when dealing with longer, more difficult texts. Readers begin their understanding of causal relationships by asking: *What happened? Why did it happen?* Children then learn that a cause may have multiple effects and one effect can have many causes and that sometimes clue words signal causal relationships.

Texts for Teaching

Student Edition
- *Tara and Tiree, Fearless Friends*, 2.1, pages 193–207
- *The Bremen Town Musicians*, 2.1, pages 284–301
- *Carl the Complainer*, 2.2, pages 230–247

Leveled Readers
- See pages 22–27 for a list of Leveled Readers.

Mini-Lesson 1

Teach the Skill
Use the **Envision It!** lesson on page EI•3 to visually review cause and effect.

Remind children that as they read they should:
- think about **what happens.**
- think about **why** that thing happens.

Practice
Write these sentences on the board and read them with children.
a. It was raining and I got wet.
   Ask: What happened? (I got wet.) Why did that happen? (It was raining.)
b. Christie dropped a book and there was a loud noise.
   Ask: What happened? (There was a loud noise.) Why did that happen? (Christie dropped a book.)
If... children have difficulty identifying what happened and why it happened,
then... provide additional physical examples and ask *What happened?* and *Why did that happen?*

Apply
As children read, have them ask themselves: *What happened? Why did it happen?*

Writing
Children can work in pairs to write what happened and why sentences.

 **ini-Lesson 2**

Teach the Skill
Use the Envision It! lesson on page EI•3 to visually review cause and effect.

Remind children that as they read they should:
- think about **what happens.**
- think about **why** that thing happens.
- look for words such as *because* and *so* that can make it easier to understand what happened and why.

Practice
Read aloud the following and have children listen for what happened and why it happened.

It rained all day yesterday, so it was very muddy. I took my dog on a walk. I walked on the sidewalk, but he walked in the mud. When we got home, I took off my boots. Since my dog doesn't have any boots, he tracked mud into the house. He made the floor very messy with his paws.

Ask: What happened? (It was muddy; the dog made the floor messy.) Why? (It rained; the dog walked in the mud and then on the floor.) Record their ideas on a chart.

What happened?	Why did it happen?

If... children have difficulty identifying it what happened and why, **then...** have children visualize the events in the story and ask specific what happened and why questions as you reread the passage.

Apply
As children read, have them think about what happens and why.

Writing
Have children complete a chart like the one here for a familiar story.

 **ini-Lesson 3**

Teach the Skill
Use the Envision It! lesson on page EI•3 to visually review cause and effect.

Remind children that as they read they should:
- think about **what happens.**
- think about **why** that thing happens.
- look for words such as *because* and *so* that can make it easier to understand what happened and why.

Practice
Tell children that some words are clues to helping them figure out why things happened. Two of these words are *because* and *so*. On strips of paper, write things that happened. Then have students complete them using *because* or *so*. Use everyday happenings, such as the following: It poured; The cat yowled; The fence fell down; Marie beamed; The snowman melted. Have children share their ideas.

If... children have difficulty finishing a sentence, **then...** provide a clue word as a prompt.

Apply
As children read the assigned text, have them think about what happens and why that thing happens.

Writing
Children can take one of the finished sentences and write more about what happened and why it happened.

Instruction

Compare and Contrast

Objectives
- Children define *compare* and *contrast*.
- Children identify some clue words that can help them see comparisons.

Student Edition p. EI•5

What is it? **Comparing and contrasting** means finding likenesses and/or differences between two or more people, places, things, or ideas. At Grade 2, children use the terms *compare* and *contrast*. They learn to use clue words such as *like, but, unlike,* and *as* to help them identify likenesses and differences in text.

How Good Readers Use the Skill Comparing and contrasting are basic reasoning devices. We try to understand an unknown using the known—i.e., a likeness or difference. At first, students notice likenesses and differences. Older children begin to use clue words as signals for comparisons. They learn about similes, which are literary comparisons. Children also learn that authors sometimes use comparison and contrast as a way to organize an entire piece of writing.

Texts for Teaching

Student Edition
- *One Good Turn Deserves Another,* 2.1, pages 320–335
- *Anansi Goes Fishing,* 2.1, pages 424–443
- *Just Like Josh Gibson,* 2.2, pages 368–381

Leveled Readers
- See pages 22–27 for a list of Leveled Readers.

Teach the Skill
Use the **Envision It!** lesson on page EI•5 to visually review compare and contrast.

Remind children that:
- to **compare** means to tell how things are the same or almost the same.
- to **contrast** means to tell how things are different.
- they can group things by comparing and contrasting.

Practice
Show a picture of a classroom long ago or remind children of a story about a classroom they have read. Draw a Venn diagram (two overlapping circles) on the board with these labels: *Our School, Both Schools, The Other School.* Work together to list qualities that are unique to each and then list the qualities the two schools share. Help get children started by asking: How are the two classes alike? How are they different?

If... children have difficulty identifying likenesses and differences of two classes,

then... give answer choices and have the child choose.

Apply
As children read on their own, have them think about how places and people they read about are alike and different.

Writing
Children can write some sentences about how the classrooms are the same or different.

Mini-Lesson 2

Teach the Skill
Use the Envision It! lesson on page EI•5 to visually review compare and contrast.

Remind children that:
- to **compare** means to tell how things are the same or almost the same.
- to **contrast** means to tell how things are different.
- clue words in text can help them see when an author is comparing or contrasting people, places, things, or ideas.

Practice
Write the following paragraph on the board and read it with children. Both Juan and Jamie are in the same grade. Juan goes to North School, but Jamie goes to West School. They both like sports, although neither plays on a team yet. Juan likes baseball, while Jamie prefers soccer. Both are learning how to play. Unlike Juan, however, Jamie practices every day.

Circle the words *both, but, neither, while,* and *unlike*. Explain that these are clues to comparisons. Reread the sentences together and use the clue words to complete a Venn diagram.

If... children have difficulty identifying likenesses,

then... have them ask themselves: *Are they alike in this way? Are they different?*

Apply
As children read on their own, have them think about how places and people they read about are alike and different.

Writing
Have children write finish these sentences: *[name] and I are alike because we both _____.*

Mini-Lesson 3

Teach the Skill
Use the Envision It! lesson on page EI•5 to visually review compare and contrast.

Remind children that:
- to **compare** means to tell how things are the same or almost the same.
- to **contrast** means to tell how things are different.
- clue words in text can help them see when an author is comparing or contrasting people, places, things, or ideas.

Practice
With children, think of two things to compare, for example, two characters from a story, two settings, two books, two animals, and so on. As a class, create a Venn diagram, deciding on specific qualities for each thing you are comparing and deciding on qualities they share. Qualities might include shape, size, color, talents, and so on. Then have partners write sentences using the qualities. Review the clue words that will help their readers see comparisons (*like, also, as, but, unlike, neither, both*). Have partners share their sentences. Talk about how finding likenesses and differences (comparisons and contrasts) as they read will help them better understand what they read.

If... children have difficulty writing sentences with clue words,

then... provide sentence starters, for example, *The king loved gold, but the queen loved _____.*

Apply
As children read on their own, have them look for places authors make comparisons.

Writing
Children can turn their sentences into a paragraph or short story.

Instruction

Objectives

- Children recognize that stories are organized in order from beginning to middle to end.
- Children identify a problem and a solution in a story.

Texts for Teaching

Student Edition

- *Henry and Mudge and the Starry Night,* 2.1, pages 88–103
- *The Bremen Town Musicians,* 2.1, pages 284–301
- *Horace and Morris but mostly Dolores,* 2.2, pages 296–313

Leveled Readers

- See pages 22–27 for a list of Leveled Readers.

Story Structure

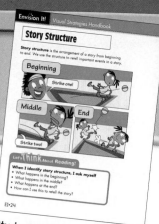

Student Edition p. EI•24

Understand the Strategy

Story structure refers to how a story is arranged. This means understanding the basic elements of a story—characters, setting, and plot—and how the author presents them. Recognizing story structure helps readers understand, recall, and appreciate stories.

Teach

Use the **Envision It!** lesson on page EI•24 to visually review story structure.

Remind children that stories are alike in some ways. Stories tell about events in order. In a story, there is a beginning, a middle, and an end. Most have a problem that characters work to solve. Ask children to name some favorite stories. Choose one and talk about who is in the story and what happens in the beginning, middle, and end. Model, if necessary, by thinking aloud.

A story I like is *Charlotte's Web*. The story is all about how Charlotte the spider saves Wilbur the pig. At the beginning, Fern raises the little pig and gets to know all the animals in the barn. In the middle, we learn about the problem and Charlotte goes about solving it. She writes things about Wilbur in her spider web. In the end, Wilbur goes back to live on the farm. He makes friends with Charlotte's children.

Story Sequence Chart
Beginning
Fern saves Wilbur and gets to know the barn animals.
Middle
Charlotte writes words about Wilbur in her web and everyone thinks he is a very special pig.
End
Wilbur goes back to the farm and he befriends all her children.

Show what happens on a Story Sequence Chart. Talk about the problem and solution. Work to write a statement of the problem and how it is solved.

Practice

Have pairs of children choose a story and reread or retell it to each other. They can fill in a Story Sequence Chart and use it to retell the story to the class.

If... children have difficulty recognizing story structure,

then... have them use stickies and number the events as they read.

Apply

Ask children to read a short story and record the events in order. They can check their order by retelling the story.

Anchor Chart

Anchor charts help children make their thinking visible and permanent. Display anchor charts so readers can use them as they read. Here is a sample chart for story structure.

Story Structure

1. Look over the story before you read. Ask yourself:
   What will this be about?
   Do I recognize any characters?
   What is going on in the pictures?

2. Read the story.

3. Think about the story. Ask yourself:
   What happens in the beginning?
   What happens in the middle?
   What happens at the end?

4. Write down the events on a Story Sequence Chart.

5. Use your chart to retell the story. Is it in the right order?

6. Think about the problem and solution. Write a sentence that states these two things.

Anchor Chart

Using Multiple Strategies

Good readers use multiple strategies as they read. You can encourage children to read strategically through good classroom questioning. Use questions such as these to help children apply strategies during reading.

Questioning

- Who or what is this question about?

- Where can you look to find the answer to this question?

- What do you want to know about _____?

- What questions to do you have about the _____ in this selection? Use the words *who, what, when, where, why* and *how* to ask your questions.

- Do you have any questions after reading?

Graphic Organizers

- What kind of graphic organizer could you use to help you keep track of the information in this selection?

Monitor and Clarify

- Does the story or article make sense?

- What don't you understand about what you read?

- Do you need to reread, review, read on, or check a reference source?

- Do you need to read more slowly or more quickly?

- What is a _____? Where could you look to find out?

Predict and Set Purpose

- What do you think this story or article will be about? Why do you think as you do?

- What do you think you will learn from this selection?

- Do the text features help you predict what will happen?

- Based on what has happened so far, what do you think will happen next?

- Is this what you thought would happen?

- How does _____ change what you thought would happen?

Preview

- What do the photographs, illustrations, or graphic sources tell about the selection?

- What do you want to find out? What do you want to learn?

Background Knowledge

- What do you already know about _____?
- Have you read stories or articles by this author before?
- How is this selection like others that you have read?
- What does this remind you of?
- How does your prior knowledge help you understand _____?
- Did the text match what you already knew? What new information did you learn?

Story Structure

- Who are the characters in this story?
- What is the setting?
- What is the problem in this story? How does the problem get solved?
- What is the point of this story?

Summarize

- What two or three important ideas have you read so far?
- How do the text features relate to the important ideas?
- Is there a graphic organizer that can help you organize the information before you summarize?

Text Structure

- How has the author organized the writing?
- What clues tell you that the text is structured _____?

Visualize

- When you read this, what do you picture in your mind?
- What do you hear, see, or smell?
- What do you think _____ looks like? Why do you think as you do?

> " You know explicit strategy instruction is a must! But you also want children to use strategies every time they read. **Customize Literacy** shows you how to help them do this. "

Glossary of Literacy Terms

This glossary lists academic language terms that are related to literacy.
They are provided for your information and professional use.

A

alliteration	the repetition of a consonant sound in a group of words, especially in poetry
allusion	a word or phrase that refers to something else the reader already knows from history, experience, or reading
animal fantasy	a story about animals that talk and act like people
answer questions	a reading strategy in which readers use the text and prior knowledge to answer questions about what they are reading
antonym	a word that means the opposite of another word
ask questions	a reading strategy in which readers ask themselves questions about the text to help make sense of what they read
author's point of view	the author's opinion on the subject he or she is writing about
author's purpose	the reason the author wrote the text
autobiography	the story of a real person's life written by that person

B

background knowledge	the information and experience that a reader brings to a text
biography	the story of a real person's life written by another person

C

cause	why something happens
character	a person, an animal, or a personified object in a story
chronological order	events in a selection, presented in the order in which they occurred
classify and categorize	put things, such as pictures or words, into groups
climax	the point in a story at which conflict is confronted
compare	tell how things are the same
comprehension	understanding of text being read—the ultimate goal of reading
comprehension strategy	a conscious plan used by a reader to gain understanding of text. Comprehension strategies may be used before, during, or after reading.
conclusion	a decision or opinion arrived at after thinking about facts and details and using prior knowledge
conflict	the problem or struggle in a story
context clue	the words, phrases, or sentences near an unknown word that give the reader clues to the word's meaning
contrast	tell how things are different

Instruction

details	small pieces of information
dialect	form of a language spoken in a certain region or by a certain group of people that differs from the standard form of that language
dialogue	written conversation
diary	a day-to-day record of one's activities and thoughts
draw conclusions	arrive at decisions or opinions after thinking about facts and details and using prior knowledge

D

effect	what happens as the result of a cause
etymology	an explanation of the origin and history of a word and its meaning
exaggeration	a statement that makes something seem larger or greater than it actually is
expository text	text that contains facts and information. Also called *informational text.*

E

fable	a story, usually with animal characters, that is written to teach a moral, or lesson
fact	piece of information that can be proved to be true
fairy tale	a folk story with magical characters and events
fantasy	a story that could not really happen
fiction	writing that tells about imaginary people, things, and events
figurative language	the use of language that gives words a meaning beyond their usual definitions in order to add beauty or force
flashback	an interruption in the sequence of events of a narrative to include an event that happened earlier
folk tale	a story that has been passed down by word of mouth
foreshadowing	the use of hints or clues about what will happen later in a story

F

generalize	make a broad statement or rule after examining particular facts
graphic organizer	a drawing, chart, or web that illustrates concepts or shows how ideas relate to each other. Readers use graphic organizers to help them keep track of and understand important information and ideas as they read. Story maps, word webs, Venn diagrams, and KWL charts are graphic organizers.
graphic source	a chart, diagram, or map within a text that adds to readers' understanding of the text

G

H

historical fiction	realistic fiction that takes place in the past. It is an imaginary story based on historical events and characters.
humor	writing or speech that has a funny or amusing quality
hyperbole	an exaggerated statement not meant to be taken literally, such as *I'm so hungry I could eat a horse.*

I

idiom	a phrase whose meaning differs from the ordinary meaning of the words. *A stone's throw* is an idiom meaning "a short distance."
imagery	the use of language to create beautiful or forceful pictures in the reader's mind
inference	conclusion reached on the basis of evidence and reasoning
inform	give knowledge, facts, or news to someone
informational text	writing that contains facts and information. Also called *expository text.*
interview	a face-to-face conversation in which someone responds to questions
irony	a way of speaking or writing in which the ordinary meaning of the words is the opposite of what the speaker or writer is thinking; a contrast between what is expected and what actually happens

J

jargon	the language of a special group or profession

L

legend	a story coming down from the past about the great deeds of a hero. Although a legend may be based on historical people and events, it is not regarded as historically true.
literary elements	the characters, setting, plot, and theme of a narrative text

M

main idea	the big idea that tells what a paragraph or a selection is mainly about; the most important idea of a text
metacognition	an awareness of one's own thinking processes and the ability to monitor and direct them to a desired goal. Good readers use metacognition to monitor their reading and adjust their reading strategies.
metaphor	a comparison that does not use *like* or *as,* such as *a heart of stone*
meter	the pattern of beats or accents in poetry

Instruction

monitor and clarify	a comprehension strategy by which readers actively think about understanding their reading and know when they understand and when they do not. Readers use appropriate strategies to make sense of difficult words, ideas, or passages.
mood	the atmosphere or feeling of a written work
moral	the lesson or teaching of a fable or story
motive	the reason a character in a narrative does or says something
mystery	a story about mysterious events that are not explained until the end, so as to keep the reader in suspense
myth	a story that attempts to explain something in nature

M

narrative	a story, made up or true, that someone tells or narrates
narrator	the character or someone outside the selection who tells the story
nonfiction	writing that tells about real things, real people, and real events

N

onomatopoeia	the use of words that sound like their meanings, such as *buzz* and *hum*
opinion	someone's judgment, belief, or way of thinking
oral vocabulary	the words needed for speaking and listening
outcome	the resolution of the conflict in a story

O

paraphrase	retell the meaning of a passage in one's own words
personification	a figure of speech in which human traits or actions are given to animals or inanimate objects, as in *The sunbeam danced on the waves.*
persuade	convince someone to do or to believe something
photo essay	a collection of photographs on one theme, accompanied by text
play	a story that is written to be acted out for an audience
plot	a series of related events at the beginning, middle, and end of a story; the action of a story
poem	an expressive, imaginative piece of writing often arranged in lines having rhythm and rhyme. In a poem, the patterns made by the sounds of the words have special importance.
pourquoi tale	a type of folk story that explains why things in nature came to be. *Pourquoi* is a French word meaning "why."

P

P

predict	tell what a selection might be about or what might happen in a text. Readers use text features and information to predict. They confirm or revise their predictions as they read.
preview	look over a text before reading it
prior knowledge	the information and experience that a reader brings to a text. Readers use prior knowledge to help them understand what they read.
prop	an item, such as an object, picture, or chart, used in a performance or presentation

R

reading vocabulary	the words we recognize or use in print
realistic fiction	a story about imaginary people and events that could happen in real life
repetition	the repeated use of some aspect of language
resolution	the point in a story where the conflict is resolved
rhyme	to end in the same sound(s)
rhythm	a pattern of strong beats in speech or writing, especially poetry
rising action	the buildup of conflicts and complications in a story

S

science fiction	a story based on science that often tells what life in the future might be like
semantic map	a graphic organizer, often a web, used to display words or concepts that are meaningfully related
sensory language	the use of words that help the reader understand how things look, sound, smell, taste, or feel
sequence	the order of events in a selection or the order of the steps in which something is completed
sequence words	clue words such as *first*, *next*, *then*, and *finally* that signal the order of events in a selection
setting	where and when a story takes place
simile	a comparison that uses *like* or *as*, as in *as busy as a bee*
speech	a public talk to a group of people made for a specific purpose
stanza	a group of lines in a poem
steps in a process	the order of the steps in which something is completed

S

story map	a graphic organizer used to record the literary elements and the sequence of events in a narrative text
story structure	how the characters, setting, and events of a story are organized into a plot
summarize	give the most important ideas of what was read. Readers summarize important information in the selection to keep track of what they are reading.
supporting detail	piece of information that tells about the main idea
symbolism	the use of one thing to suggest something else; often the use of something concrete to stand for an abstract idea

T

tall tale	a humorous story that uses exaggeration to describe impossible happenings
text structure	the organization of a piece of nonfiction writing. Text structures of informational text include cause/effect, chronological, compare/contrast, description, problem/ solution, proposition/support, and ask/answer questions.
theme	the big idea or author's message in a story
think aloud	an instructional strategy in which a teacher verbalizes his or her thinking to model the process of comprehension or the application of a skill
tone	author's attitude toward the subject or toward the reader
topic	the subject of a discussion, conversation, or piece of text

V

visualize	picture in one's mind what is happening in the text. Visualizing helps readers imagine the things they read about.

Instruction

Leveled Readers Skills Chart

Scott Foresman Reading Street provides more than six hundred leveled readers. Each one is designed to:

- Practice critical skills and strategies
- Build fluency
- Build vocabulary and concepts
- Develop a lifelong love of reading

Grade 2

Title	Level*	DRA Level	Genre	Comprehension Strategy
The Rescue Dogs	C	3	Narrative Nonfiction	Summarize
Country Mouse and City Mouse	D	4	Traditional Tales	Monitor and Clarify
All About Astronauts	D	4	Expository Nonfiction	Text Structure
Camping with Pup	D	4	Animal Fantasy	Story Structure
Deserts	D	4	Expository Nonfiction	Important Ideas
Too Many Rabbit Holes	D	4	Fantasy/Play	Predict and Set Purpose
A Class Play	D	4	Realistic Fiction	Text Structure
The Barn Raising	D	4	Nonfiction	Background Knowledge
Working Dogs	D	4	Expository Nonfiction	Story Structure
Where Is Fish?	D	4	Fantasy	Inferring
Our School Science Fair	D	4	Realistic Fiction	Questioning
Let's Send a Letter!	D	4	Narrative Nonfiction	Visualize
Using a Net	D	4	Expository Nonfiction	Summarize
Ana Is Shy	E	6–8	Realistic Fiction	Predict and Set Purpose
Sink or Float?	E	6–8	Narrative Nonfiction	Inferring
The Camping Trip	E	6–8	Realistic Fiction	Background Knowledge
How to Grow Tomatoes	E	6–8	How-to	Important Ideas
How a Seed Grows	E	6–8	Expository Nonfiction	Questioning
Snakeskin Canyon	E	6–8	Realistic Fiction	Visualize
Blizzard!	E	6–8	Realistic Fiction	Monitor and Clarify
The New Kid in Bali	F	10	Realistic Fiction	Monitor and Clarify
Desert Animals	F	10	Expository Nonfiction	Important Ideas
Camping at Crescent Lake	F	10	Realistic Fiction	Story Structure
An Astronaut Space Walk	F	10	Expository Nonfiction	Story Structure
Service Workers	F	10	Expository Nonfiction	Important Ideas
What Can You Do?	F	10	Narrative Nonfiction	Visualize
Sally and the Wild Puppy	F	10	Humorous Fiction	Background Knowledge
Join an Adventure Club!	F	10	Narrative Nonfiction	Story Structure
Andrew's Mistake	F	10	Realistic Fiction	Inferring
Glooskap and the First Summer: An Algonquin Tale	G	12	Folk Tale	Predict and Set Purpose

* Suggested Guided Reading Level. Use your knowledge of children's abilities to adjust levels as needed.

The chart here and on the next few pages lists titles of leveled readers appropriate for children in Grade 2. Use the chart to find titles that meet your children's interest and instructional needs. The books in this list were leveled using the criteria suggested in *Matching Books to Readers: Using Leveled Books in Guided Reading, Grades K–3* by Irene C. Fountas and Gay Su Pinnell. For more on leveling, see the *Reading Street Leveled Readers Leveling Guide.*

Target Comprehension Skill	Additional Comprehension Instruction	Vocabulary
Cause and Effect	Fact and Opinion	High-Frequency Words
Character and Setting	Fact and Opinion	High-Frequency Words
Main Idea and Details	Author's Purpose	High-Frequency Words
Character and Setting	Main Idea and Details	High-Frequency Words
Main Idea and Details	Compare and Contrast	High-Frequency Words
Facts and Details	Character and Setting	High-Frequency Words
Author's Purpose	Facts and Details	High-Frequency Words
Facts and Details	Cause and Effect	High-Frequency Words
Cause and Effect	Compare and Contrast	High-Frequency Words
Compare and Contrast	Author's Purpose	High-Frequency Words
Author's Purpose	Plot and Theme	High-Frequency Words
Draw Conclusions	Sequence	High-Frequency Words
Compare and Contrast	Draw Conclusions	High-Frequency Words
Sequence	Cause and Effect	High-Frequency Words
Fact and Opinion	Sequence	High-Frequency Words
Draw Conclusions	Character and Setting	Word Structure/Prefixes
Sequence	Fact and Opinion	Context Clues/Antonyms
Fact and Opinion	Facts and Details	Context Clues/Unfamiliar Words
Plot and Theme	Draw Conclusions	Context Clues/Multiple Meanings
Plot and Theme	Main Idea and Details	Picture Clues/Multiple Meanings
Character and Setting	Plot and Theme	High-Frequency Words
Main Idea and Details	Compare and Contrast	High-Frequency Words
Character and Setting	Main Idea and Details	High-Frequency Words
Character and Setting	Sequence	High-Frequency Words
Fact and Opinion	Author's Purpose	Word Structure/Suffixes
Cause and Effect	Facts and Details	Dictionary Skills/Unfamiliar Words
Plot and Theme	Sequence	Dictionary Skills/Unfamiliar Words
Character and Setting	Plot and Theme	Dictionary Skills/Unfamiliar Words
Main Idea and Details	Character and Setting	Word Structure/Compound Words
Facts and Details	Character and Setting	High-Frequency Words

Leveled Readers Skills Chart *Continued*

Grade 2 — Title	Level*	DRA Level	Genre	Comprehension Strategy
Be Ready for an Emergency	G	12	Narrative Nonfiction	Summarize
Let's Work Together!	G	12	Realistic Fiction	Text Structure
Farming Families	G	12	Expository Nonfiction	Background Knowledge
Growing Up	G	12	Realistic Fiction	Story Structure
Three Great Ballplayers	G	12	Autobiography/Biography	Monitor and Clarify
America's Birthday	G	12	Expository Nonfiction	Summarize
Special Chinese Birthdays	G	12	Narrative Nonfiction	Questioning
Down on the Ranch	G	12	Historical Fiction	Story Structure
Just Like Grandpa	G	12	Realistic Fiction	Predict and Set Purpose
Showing Good Manners	H	14	Nonfiction	Inferring
Dotty's Art	H	14	Realistic Fiction	Questioning
Living in Seoul	H	14	Narrative Nonfiction	Visualize
Arachnid or Insect?	H	14	Expository Nonfiction	Summarize
The International Food Fair	H	14	Realistic Fiction	Predict and Set Purpose
Thomas Adams: Chewing Gum Inventor	I	16	Biography	Inferring
Making Travel Fun	I	16	Expository Nonfiction	Background Knowledge
How Do Plants Grow?	I	16	Expository Nonfiction	Important Ideas
A Slice of Mud Pie	I	16	Realistic Fiction	Questioning
Too Many Frogs!	I	16	Humorous Fiction	Visualize
Rainbow Crow Brings Fire to Earth	J	18	Narrative Nonfiction	Monitor and Clarify
Keeping Our Community Safe	J	18	Expository Nonfiction	Important Ideas
Annie Makes a Big Change	J	18	Realistic Fiction	Visualize
Hubert and Frankie	J	18	Animal Fantasy	Background Knowledge
Everyone Can Make a Difference!	K	20	Narrative Nonfiction	Story Structure
Freda the Signmaker	K	20	Humorous Fiction	Inferring
Women Play Baseball	K	20	Narrative Nonfiction	Monitor and Clarify
American Revolution Heroes	K	20	Biography	Summarize
Country Friends, City Friends	L	24	Realistic Fiction	Monitor and Clarify
Look at Our Galaxy	L	24	Expository Nonfiction	Text Structure
At Home in the Wilderness	L	24	Historical Fiction	Story Structure

* Suggested Guided Reading Level. Use your knowledge of children's abilities to adjust levels as needed.

You know the theory behind leveled books: they let you match books with the interest and instructional levels of your children. You can find the right reader for every child with this chart.

Target Comprehension Skill	Additional Comprehension Instruction	Vocabulary
Cause and Effect	Fact and Opinion	High-Frequency Words
Author's Purpose	Facts and Details	High-Frequency Words
Facts and Details	Cause and Effect	High-Frequency Words
Cause and Effect	Compare and Contrast	High-Frequency Words
Compare and Contrast	Draw Conclusions	Context Clues/Homophones
Author's Purpose	Fact and Opinion	Context Clues/Unfamiliar Words
Draw Conclusions	Cause and Effect	Context Clues/Synonyms
Sequence	Main Idea and Details	Word Structure/Suffixes
Facts and Details	Compare and Contrast	Word Structure/Compound Words
Compare and Contrast	Author's Purpose	High-Frequency Words
Author's Purpose	Plot and Theme	High-Frequency Words
Draw Conclusions	Sequence	High-Frequency Words
Compare and Contrast	Draw Conclusions	High-Frequency Words
Sequence	Cause and Effect	High-Frequency Words
Fact and Opinion	Sequence	High-Frequency Words
Draw Conclusions	Character and Setting	Word Structure/Prefixes
Sequence	Fact and Opinion	Context Clues/Antonyms
Fact and Opinion	Facts and Details	Context Clues/Unfamiliar Words
Plot and Theme	Draw Conclusions	Context Clues/Multiple Meanings
Plot and Theme	Main Idea and Details	Context Clues/Multiple Meanings
Fact and Opinion	Author's Purpose	Word Structure/Suffixes
Cause and Effect	Facts and Details	Dictionary Skills/Unfamiliar Words
Plot and Theme	Sequence	Dictionary Skills/Unfamiliar Words
Character and Setting	Plot and Theme	Dictionary Skills/Unfamiliar Words
Main Idea and Details	Character and Setting	Word Structure/Compound Words
Compare and Contrast	Draw Conclusions	Context Clues/Homophones
Author's Purpose	Fact and Opinion	Context Clues/Unfamiliar Words
Character and Setting	Plot and Theme	Amazing Words
Main Idea and Details	Author's Purpose	Amazing Words
Character and Setting	Main Idea and Details	Amazing Words

Matching Books & Readers

Leveled Readers Skills Chart *Continued*

Grade 2

Title	Level*	DRA Level	Genre	Comprehension Strategy
A World of Birthdays	L	24	Narrative Nonfiction	Questioning
A Cowboy's Life	L	24	Historical Fiction	Text Structure
Voting Day	L	24	Realistic Fiction	Predict and Set Purpose
The First People to Fly	L	24	Realistic Fiction	Predict and Set Purpose
The Hummingbird	M	28	Expository Nonfiction	Important Ideas
Special Animal Helpers	M	28	Narrative Nonfiction	Summarize
The Hoover Dam	M	28	Expository Nonfiction	Text Structure
Many Types of Energy	M	28	Expository Nonfiction	Background Knowledge
Stripes and Silver	M	28	Play	Story Structure
Saint Bernards and Other Working Dogs	N	30	Expository Nonfiction	Inferring
Maggie's New Sidekick	N	30	Fantasy	Questioning
Communicating Then and Now	N	30	Expository Nonfiction	Visualize
How Can Animals Help?	N	30	Narrative Nonfiction	Summarize
Hank's Tortilla Factory	N	30	Realistic Fiction	Predict and Set Purpose
A Few Nifty Inventions	N	30	Expository Nonfiction	Inferring
Starting a New Life	N	30	Expository Nonfiction	Background Knowledge
Plants Grow Everywhere	O	34	Expository Nonfiction	Important Ideas
Compost: Recycled Waste	O	34	Narrative Nonfiction	Questioning
A Quiet Place	O	34	Realistic Fiction	Visualize
Hurricane!	O	34	Expository Nonfiction	Monitor and Clarify
Services and Goods	O	34	Narrative Nonfiction	Important Ideas
A Vet for All Animals	O	34	Narrative Nonfiction	Visualize
Training Peanut	O	34	Realistic Fiction	Background Knowledge
Protect the Earth	P	38	Narrative Nonfiction	Story Structure
Marty's Summer Job	P	38	Realistic Fiction	Inferring
Baseball Heroes Make History	P	38	Autobiography/Biography	Monitor and Clarify
Living in a Democracy	P	38	Expository Nonfiction	Summarize
Celebrations and Family Traditions	P	38	Narrative Nonfiction	Questioning
Living on a Ranch	P	38	Realistic Fiction	Text Structure
Happy New Year!	P	38	Realistic Fiction	Predict and Set Purpose

* Suggested Guided Reading Level. Use your knowledge of children's abilities to adjust levels as needed.

You know the theory behind leveled books: they let you match books with the interest and instructional levels of your children. You can find the right reader for every child with this chart. 99

Target Comprehension Skill	Additional Comprehension Instruction	Vocabulary
Draw Conclusions	Cause and Effect	Context Clues/Synonyms
Sequence	Main Idea and Details	Word Structure/Suffixes
Facts and Details	Compare and Contrast	Word Structure/Compound Words
Facts and Details	Character and Setting	Amazing Words
Main Idea and Details	Compare and Contrast	Amazing Words
Cause and Effect	Cause and Effect	Amazing Words
Author's Purpose	Facts and Details	Amazing Words
Facts and Details	Cause and Effect	Amazing Words
Cause and Effect	Compare and Contrast	Amazing Words
Compare and Contrast	Author's Purpose	Amazing Words
Author's Purpose	Plot and Theme	Amazing Words
Draw Conclusions	Sequence	Amazing Words
Compare and Contrast	Draw Conclusions	Amazing Words
Sequence	Cause and Effect	Amazing Words
Fact and Opinion	Sequence	Amazing Words
Draw Conclusions	Character and Setting	Word Structure/Prefixes
Sequence	Fact and Opinion	Context Clues/Antonyms
Fact and Opinion	Facts and Details	Context Clues/Unfamiliar Words
Plot and Theme	Draw Conclusions	Context Clues/Multiple Meanings
Plot and Theme	Main Idea and Details	Context Clues/Multiple Meanings
Fact and Opinion	Author's Purpose	Word Structure/Suffixes
Cause and Effect	Facts and Details	Dictionary Skills/Unfamiliar Words
Plot and Theme	Sequence	Dictionary Skills/Unfamiliar Words
Character and Setting	Plot and Theme	Dictionary Skills/Unfamiliar Words
Main Idea and Details	Character and Setting	Word Structure/Compound Words
Compare and Contrast	Draw Conclusions	Context Clues/Homophones
Author's Purpose	Fact and Opinion	Context Clues/Unfamiliar Words
Draw Conclusions	Cause and Effect	Context Clues/Synonyms
Sequence	Main Idea and Details	Word Structure/Suffixes
Facts and Details	Compare and Contrast	Word Structure/Compound Words

Matching Books & Readers

What Good Readers Do

You can use the characteristics and behaviors of good readers to help all your children read better. But what are these characteristics and behaviors? And how can you use them to foster good reading behaviors for all your children? Here are some helpful tips.

Good Readers enjoy reading! They have favorite books, authors, and genres. Good readers often have a preference about where and when they read. They talk about books and recommend their favorites.

Develop this behavior by giving children opportunities to respond in different ways to what they read. Get them talking about what they read, and why they like or dislike it.

This behavior is important because book sharing alerts you to children who are somewhat passive about reading or have limited literacy experiences. Book sharing also helps you when you select books for the class.

Good Readers select books they can read.

Develop this behavior by providing a range of three or four texts appropriate for the child and then letting the student choose.

This behavior is important because children gain control over reading when they can choose from books they can read. This helps them become more independent in the classroom.

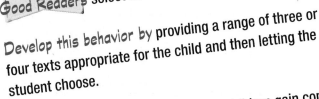

Good Readers read independently for longer periods of time.

Develop this behavior by taking note of the level of support children need during guided reading. Use this information to gauge independent reading time accordingly.

This behavior is important because children become better readers when they spend time reading many texts at their independent level.

Good Readers use text features to help them preview and set purposes.

Develop this behavior by having children use the title and illustrations in fiction texts or the title, contents, headings, and other graphic features in nonfiction texts to make predictions about what they will be reading.

This behavior is important because previewing actually makes reading easier! Looking at features and sampling the text enables readers to predict and set expectations for reading.

" Want to improve your students' performance by fostering good reading behaviors? **Customize Literacy can help.** "

Good Readers predict and ask questions before and while they read.

Develop this behavior by asking questions. After reading a passage, ask children what they think will happen next in a fiction text. Have them ask a question they think will be answered in a nonfiction text and read on to see if it is.

This behavior is important because when children predict and ask questions as they read, they are engaged. They have a purpose for reading and a basis for monitoring their comprehension.

Good Readers read meaningful phrases aloud with appropriate expression.

Develop this behavior by giving children lots of opportunities to read orally. As they read, note children's phrasing, intonation, and attention to punctuation and give help as needed.

This behavior is important because reading fluently in longer, meaningful phrases supports comprehension and ease in reading longer, more complex texts.

Good Readers read aloud at an appropriate reading rate with a high percent of accuracy.

Develop this behavior by timing children's oral reading to calculate their reading rates. You can also record students' miscues to determine a percent of accuracy. This will help identify problems.

This behavior is important because when children read fluently texts that are "just right," they find reading more enjoyable. A fluent reader is able to focus more on constructing meaning and is more likely to develop a positive attitude toward reading.

Matching Books & Readers

Good Readers use effective strategies and sources of information to figure out unknown words.

Develop this behavior by teaching specific strategies for figuring out unknown words, such as sounding out clusters of letters, using context, reading on, and using references.

This behavior is important because when readers have a variety of strategies to use, they are more able to decode and self-correct quickly. Readers who do these things view themselves as good readers.

CH-
QU-
ST-

Good Readers construct meaning as they read and then share or demonstrate their understanding.

Develop this behavior by having children retell what they read or write a summary of what they read in their own words.

This behavior is important because the ability to retell or write a summary is essential for success in reading. It shows how well a student has constructed meaning.

Good Readers locate and use what is explicitly stated in a text.

Develop this behavior by asking questions that require children to go back into the text to find explicitly stated information.

This behavior is important because the ability to recall, locate, and use specific information stated in a text enables readers to respond to literal questions, as well as to support opinions and justify their responses.

Good Readers make connections.

Develop this behavior by asking questions to help children make connections: *What does this remind you of? Have you ever read or experienced anything like this?*

This behavior is important because making connections helps readers understand and appreciate a text. Making connections to self, the world, and other texts supports higher-level thinking.

Good Readers interpret what they read by making inferences.

Develop this behavior by asking questions to help children tell or write about what they think was implied in the text: *Why do you think that happened? What helped you come to that conclusion?*

This behavior is important because the ability to go beyond the literal meaning of a text enables readers to gain a deeper understanding. When children make inferences, they use background knowledge, their personal knowledge, and the text to grasp the meaning of what is implied by the author.

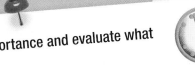

Good Readers determine importance and evaluate what they read.

Develop this behavior by always having children identify what they think is the most important message, event, or information in a text.

This behavior is important because readers must be able to sort out important from interesting information. The ability to establish and/or use criteria and provide support when making judgments is an important critical-thinking skill.

Good Readers support their responses using information from a text and/or their own background knowledge.

Develop this behavior by always asking children to give the reason(s) they identified an event, message, or ideas as most important.

This behavior is important because the ability to justify one's response is important for all learners. It enables others to know the basis for a decision and provides an opening for further discussion.

Conversation Starters

Asking Good Questions When children read interesting and thought-provoking books, they want to share! You can encourage children to think critically about what they read. Use questions such as the following to assess comprehension as well as evoke good class/group discussions.

Author's Purpose

- Why did the author write this piece?

- How does figuring out the author's purpose help you decide how to read the text?

Cause and Effect

- Why did these events happen? How might they have been different if the causes had been different?

- What clues helped you know what caused these events to happen?

Compare and Contrast

- What clue words show the author is comparing and/or contrasting in this article?

- How are the fictional characters and events in this story like and/or different from real people and events you know of?

Draw Conclusions

- Based on what you have read, seen, or experienced, what can you conclude about this event in the selection?

- This story seems to be a fantasy. Why might you conclude this?

- What conclusions can you draw about the characters?

Fact and Opinion

- Is this a statement of fact or a statement of opinion? How do you know?

- This seems to be a statement of opinion. Why is it really a statement of fact? (Alternately: This seems to be a statement of fact. Why is it really a statement of opinion?)

Graphic Sources

- How does the author use graphic sources (chart, maps, illustrations, time lines, and so on) to support ideas and opinions?

- This selection has many graphic sources. Which one or ones best help you understand the events or ideas in the selection? Why?

Literary Elements: Character, Setting, Plot, Theme

- Describe the main character at the beginning of the story and at the end of the story. How and why does he or she change?

- What is the setting of the story? How might the story be different if its time or its place were different?

- What does the main character want at the beginning of the story? How does the main character go about trying to achieve this?

- In a few sentences, what is the plot of the story?

- What is the theme of the story? Use details from the story to support your statement.

Main Idea and Details

- What is the main idea of this paragraph or article? What are some details?

- The author makes this particular statement in the article. What details does the author provide to support that statement?

Sequence

- What is the sequence of events in the text?

- Is the order of events important in this story? Why or why not?

- Based on what has already happened, what will most likely happen next?

Connecting Science and Social Studies

Scott Foresman Reading Street Leveled Readers are perfect for covering, supporting, or enriching science and social studies content. Using these books ensures that all children can access important concepts.

Grade 2 Leveled Readers

Science

Earth and Space Science

Nonfiction Books

- *All About Astronauts*
- *An Astronaut Space Walk*
- *Desert Animals*
- *Hurricane!*
- *Deserts*
- *Look at Our Galaxy*

Fiction Books

- *Blizzard!*
- *Maggie's New Sidekick*
- *Rainbow Crow Brings Fire to Earth*
- *A Slice of Mud Pie*

Life Science

Nonfiction Books

- *Arachnid or Insect?*
- *Compost: Recycled Waste*
- *Farming Families*
- *How a Seed Grows*
- *How Can Animals Help?*
- *How Do Plants Grow?*
- *How to Grow Tomatoes*
- *Plants Grow Everywhere*
- *A Vet for All Animals*

Fiction Books

- *Annie Makes a Big Change*
- *Camping at Crescent Lake*
- *Growing Up*
- *Too Many Rabbit Holes*
- *Where Is Fish?*

Physical Science

Nonfiction Books

- *Many Types of Energy*
- *Sink or Float?*

Fiction Books

- *The Hummingbird*
- *Our School Science Fair*

Grade 2 Leveled Readers

Social Studies

Citizenship

Nonfiction Books

- *America's Birthday*
- *The Barn Raising*
- *Be Ready for an Emergency*
- *Everyone Can Make a Difference!*
- *Join an Adventure Club!*
- *Keeping Our Community Safe*
- *Protect the Earth*
- *The Rescue Dogs*
- *Service Workers*
- *Special Animal Helpers*
- *Using a Net*
- *What Can You Do?*
- *Working Dogs*

Fiction Books

- *Andrew's Mistake*
- *Camping with Pup*
- *Freda the Signmaker*
- *Hubert and Frankie*
- *Let's Work Together!*
- *Marty's Summer Job*
- *Sally and the Wild Puppy*
- *Stripes and Silver*
- *Too Many Frogs!*
- *Training Peanut*

Culture

Nonfiction Books

- *Celebrations and Family Traditions*
- *Living in Seoul*
- *Showing Good Manners*
- *Special Chinese Birthdays*
- *A World of Birthdays*

Fiction Books

- *Ana Is Shy*
- *The Camping Trip*
- *Country Friends, City Friends*
- *Dotty's Art*
- *The First People to Fly*
- *Glooskap and the First Summer: An Algonquin Tale*
- *Happy New Year!*
- *The International Food Fair*
- *Just Like Grandpa*
- *Living on a Ranch*
- *The New Kid in Bali*
- *Voting Day*

Economics

Nonfiction Books

- *Services and Goods*

Fiction Books

- *Country Mouse and City Mouse*
- *A Quiet Place*
- *Snakeskin Canyon*

History

Nonfiction Books

- *A Few Nifty Inventions*
- *The Hoover Dam*
- *Living in a Democracy*
- *Making Travel Fun*
- *Saint Bernards and Other Working Dogs*
- *Starting a New Life*
- *Women Play Baseball*

Fiction Books

- *At Home in the Wilderness*
- *A Class Play*
- *A Cowboy's Life*
- *Down on the Ranch*
- *Hank's Tortilla Factory*

Government

Nonfiction Books

- *Communicating Then and Now*
- *Let's Send a Letter!*

More Great Titles

Biography

- *American Revolution Heroes*
- *Baseball Heroes Make History*
- *Thomas Adams: Chewing Gum Inventor*
- *Three Great Ballplayers*

Section 3 Matching Books and Readers

Connecting Science and Social Studies

Need more choices? Look back to Grade 1.

Grade 1 Leveled Readers

Science

Earth and Space Science

Nonfiction Books
- All About the Weather
- The Communication Story
- Over the Years
- Ready for Winter?
- Using the Telephone

Fiction Books
- Cody's Adventure
- Marla's Good Idea
- What a Detective Does

Life Science

Nonfiction Books
- All About Food Chains
- Animals Change and Grow
- Around the Forest
- Around the World
- Baby Animals in the Rain Forest
- Bees and Beekeepers
- The Dinosaur Detectives
- The Dinosaur Herds
- Fun in the Sun
- Honey
- In My Room
- Learn About Butterflies
- Learn About Worker Bees
- Let's Go to the Zoo
- Let's Visit a Butterfly Greenhouse
- Look at Dinosaurs
- A Mighty Oak Tree
- Monarchs Migrate South
- People Help the Forest
- The Seasons Change
- Seasons Come and Go
- What Animals Can You See?

Life Science

Fiction Books
- Bix the Dog
- Britton Finds a Kitten
- Carlos Picks a Pet
- Cary and the Wildlife Shelter
- Mac Can Do It!
- Mack and Zack
- Plans Change
- Sam
- The Sick Pets
- Time for Dinner
- What Brown Saw
- Which Animals Will We See?
- Which Fox?

Physical Science

Nonfiction Books
- The Inclined Plane
- Simple Machines at Work
- Simple Machines in Compound Machines

Grade 1 Leveled Readers

Social Studies

Citizenship

Nonfiction Books

- *A Class*
- *A Garden for All*
- *Great Scientists: Detectives at Work*
- *Here in My Neighborhood*
- *A New Library*
- *Puppy Raiser*
- *The Story of the Kids Care Club*
- *Ways to Be a Good Citizen*

Fiction Books

- *The Art Show*
- *At Your Vet*
- *Big Wishes and Her Baby*
- *Double Trouble Twins*
- *Fly Away Owl!*
- *Grasshopper and Ant*
- *Hank's Song*
- *Let's Build a Park!*
- *Look at My Neighborhood*
- *My Little Brother Drew*
- *On the Farm*
- *Paul's Bed*
- *A Play*
- *Rules at School*
- *Space Star*
- *Squirrel and Bear*
- *That Cat Needs Help!*

Culture

Nonfiction Books

- *Cascarones Are for Fun*
- *My Babysitter*
- *Special Days, Special Food*
- *We Are a Family*
- *What Makes Buildings Special?*

Fiction Books

- *Go West!*
- *Grandma's Farm*
- *Gus the Pup*
- *Jamie's Jumble of Junk*
- *A New Baby Brother*
- *A Party for Pedro*
- *A Visit to the Ranch*
- *Where They Live*

History

Nonfiction Books

- *School: Then and Now*
- *Treasures of Our Country*

Fiction Books

- *Loni's Town*

Government

Nonfiction Books

- *America's Home*
- *Our Leaders*

Fiction Books

- *Mom the Mayor*

Section 3 **Matching Books** and **Readers**

Connecting Science and Social Studies

Need more choices? Look ahead to Grade 3.

Grade 3 Leveled Readers

Science

Earth and Space Science

Nonfiction Books
- *The Frozen Continent: Antarctica*
- *Fun with Hobbies and Science!*
- *Gemstones Around the World*
- *Grandpa's Rock Kit*
- *How to Measure the Weather*
- *Measuring the Earth*
- *Meet the Stars*
- *Pictures in the Sky*

Fiction Books
- *What a Day!*
- *Journey Across the Arctic*

Life Science

Nonfiction Books
- *A Pet Bird*
- *All About Birds*
- *All About Penguins*
- *Animal Tracking: Learn More About It*
- *Animals of the Concrete Jungle*
- *Coral Reefs*
- *Desert Life*
- *The Field Trip*
- *Free in the Sea*
- *Growing Vegetables*
- *Ice Fishing in the Arctic*
- *Largest, Fastest, Lightest, Longest*
- *Life in the Arctic*
- *Raisins*
- *Rescuing Whales*
- *These Birds Can't Fly!*
- *Whales and Other Amazing Animals*

Life Science

Fiction Books
- *The Best Field Trip Ever!*
- *Bills and Beaks*
- *Buddy Ran Away*
- *Grape Season*
- *The Hunters and the Elk*
- *In the Fields*
- *Swimming in a School*
- *Swimming Like Buck*
- *Toby the Smart Dog*

Grade 3 Leveled Readers

Social Studies

Citizenship

Nonfiction Books
- Sweet Freedom!
- Symbols, Signs, and Songs of America

Fiction Books
- Buddy Goes to School
- Camping with Aunt Julie
- The Opposite Cousins
- Our Garden
- Puppy Problems

Culture

Nonfiction Books
- A Child's Life in Korea
- A Walk Around the City
- Celebrate Around the World
- China's Special Gifts to the World
- His Favorite Sweatshirt
- Let's Go Have Fun!
- Life Overseas
- Mixing, Kneading, and Baking
- New York's Chinatown
- The French Connection
- The World of Bread!

Fiction Books
- A Tea Party with Obâchan
- Bobby's New Apartment
- Cowboy Slim's Dude Ranch
- E-mail Friends

Culture

- Grandmother Spider Steals the Sun
- Iguana Takes a Ride
- Kapuapua's Magic Shell
- The Last Minute
- Lily's Adventure Around the World
- The Magic of Coyote
- One Forest, Different Trees
- The Road to New York
- The Three Bears and Goldilocks
- The Thunder and Lightning Men

Economics

Nonfiction Books
- It's a Fair Swap!
- It's a World of Time Zones
- Let's Make a Trade
- What's Money All About?

Fiction Books
- A Family of Collectors
- Joanie's House Becomes a Home
- Let's Surprise Mom
- The Market Adventure
- The Metal Detective
- Mr. Post's Project
- The Shopping Trip

History

Nonfiction Books
- Across the English Channel
- Celebrate Independence Day/Celebra El Día de la Independencia
- Changing Times: Women in the Early Twentieth Century
- Greek Myths
- The Statue of Liberty: A Gift From France

Fiction Books
- A Trip
- The Winning Point
- With a Twist

More Great Titles

Biography
- Extraordinary Athletes
- Great Women in U. S. History
- Thomas Hart Benton: Painter of Murals

Planning Teacher Study Groups

Adventurous teachers often have good ideas for lessons. A teacher study group is a great way to share ideas and get feedback on the best way to connect content and children. Working with other teachers can provide you with the support and motivation you need to implement new teaching strategies. A teacher study group offers many opportunities to collaborate, support each other's work, share insights, and get feedback.

Think About It

A weekly or monthly teacher study group can help support you in developing your expertise in the classroom. You and a group of like-minded teachers can form your own study group. What can this group accomplish?

- Read and discuss professional articles by researchers in the field of education.

- Meet to share teaching tips, collaborate on multi-grade lessons, and share resources.

- Develop lessons to try out new teaching strategies. Meet to share experiences and discuss how to further improve your teaching approach.

Let's Meet!

Forming a study group is easy. Just follow these four steps:

1. **Decide on the size of the group.** A small group has the advantage of making each member feel accountable, but make sure that all people have the ability to make the same commitment!

2. **Choose teachers to invite to join your group.** Think about whom you want to invite. Should they all teach the same grade? Can you invite teachers from other schools? Remember that the more diverse the group, the more it benefits from new perspectives.

3. **Set goals for the group.** In order to succeed, know what you want the group to do. Meet to set goals. Rank goals in order of importance and refer often to the goals to keep the group on track.

4. **Make logistical decisions.** This is often the most difficult. Decide where and when you will meet. Consider an online meeting place where group members can post discussion questions and replies if people are not able to meet.

What Will We Study? Use the goals you set to help determine what your group will study. Consider what materials are needed to reach your goals, and how long you think you will need to prepare for each meeting.

How Will It Work? Think about how you structure groups in your classroom. Use some of the same strategies.

- **Assign a group facilitator.** This person is responsible for guiding the meeting. This person comes prepared with discussion questions and leads the meeting. This could be a rotating responsibility dependent on experience with various topics. This person might be responsible for providing the materials.

- **Assign a recorder.** Have someone take notes during the meeting and record group decisions.

- **Use the jigsaw method.** Not everyone has time to be a facilitator. In this case, divide the text and assign each portion to a different person. Each person is responsible for leading the discussion on that particular part.

Meet Again Make a commitment to meet for a minimum number of times. After that, the group can reevaluate and decide whether or not to continue.

> " Have some great teaching tips to share? Want to exchange ideas with your colleagues? Build your own professional community of teachers. **Customize Literacy** gets you started. "

Trial Lessons

Use your colleagues' experiences to help as you think about new ways to connect content and children. Use the following plan to create a mini-lesson. It should last twenty minutes. Get the support of your colleagues as you try something new and then reflect on what happened.

Be Creative! As you develop a plan for a mini-lesson, use these four words to guide planning: *purpose, text, resources,* and *routine.*

- **Purpose:** Decide on a skill or strategy to cover. Define your purpose for teaching the lesson.

- **Text:** Develop a list of the materials you could use. Ask your colleagues for suggestions.

- **Resources:** Make a list of the available resources, and consider how to use those resources most effectively. Consider using the Leveled Readers listed on pages CL22–CL27 and CL34–CL39 of Customize Literacy.

- **Routine:** Choose an instructional routine to structure your mini-lesson. See the mini-lessons in Customize Literacy for suggestions.

Try It! Try out your lesson! Consider audio- or videotaping the lesson for later review. You may wish to invite a colleague to sit in as you teach. Make notes on how the lesson went.

How Did It Go? Use the self-evaluation checklist on page CL43 as you reflect on your trial lesson. This provides a framework for later discussion.

Discuss, Reflect, Repeat Solicit feedback from your teacher study group. Explain the lesson and share your reflections. Ask for suggestions on ways to improve the lesson. Take some time to reflect on the feedback. Modify your lesson to reflect what you have learned. Then try teaching the lesson again.

Checklist for Teacher Self-Evaluation

How Well Did I ...	Very Well	Satisfactory	Not Very Well
Plan the lesson?			
Select the appropriate level of text?			
Introduce the lesson and explain its objectives?			
Review previously taught skills?			
Directly explain the new skills being taught?			
Model the new skills?			
Break the material down into small steps?			
Integrate guided practice into the lesson?			
Monitor guided practice for student understanding?			
Provide feedback on independent practice?			
Maintain an appropriate pace?			
Assess student understanding of the material?			
Stress the importance of applying the skill as they read?			
Maintain students' interest?			
Ask questions?			
Handle student questions and responses?			
Respond to the range of abilities?			

Building Community

Books for Teachers

Children aren't the only ones who need to read to grow. Here is a brief list of books that you may find useful to fill your reading teacher basket and learn new things.

A Professional Bibliography

Adams, M. J. "Alphabetic Anxiety and Explicit, Systematic Phonics Instruction: A Cognitive Science Perspective." *Handbook of Early Literacy Research.* The Guilford Press, 2001.

Adams, M. J. *Beginning to Read: Thinking and Learning About Print.* The MIT Press, 1990.

Afflerbach, P. "The Influence of Prior Knowledge and Text Genre on Readers' Prediction Strategies." *Journal of Reading Behavior,* vol. XXII, no. 2 (1990).

Armbruster, B. B., F. Lehr, and J. Osborn. *Put Reading First: The Research Building Blocks for Teaching Children to Read.* Partnership for Reading, Washington, D.C., 2001.

Bear, D. R., M. Invernizzi, S. Templeton, and F. Johnston. *Words Their Way.* Merrill Prentice Hall, 2004.

Beck, I., M. G. McKeown, and L. Kucan. *Bringing Words to Life: Robust Vocabulary Instruction.* The Guilford Press, 2002.

Biemiller, A. "Teaching Vocabulary in the Primary Grades: Vocabulary Instruction Needed." *Vocabulary Instruction Research to Practice.* The Guilford Press, 2004.

Blachowicz, C. and P. Fisher. "Vocabulary Instruction." *Handbook of Reading Research,* vol. III. Lawrence Erlbaum Associates, 2000.

Cunningham, P. M. and J. W. Cunningham. "What We Know About How to Teach Phonics." *What Research Says About Reading Instruction,* 3rd ed. International Reading Association, 2002.

Daniels, H. *Literature Circles.* 2nd ed. Stenhouse Publishers, 2002.

Dickson, S. V., D. C. Simmons, and E. J. Kame'enui. "Text Organization: Instructional and Curricular Basics and Implications." *What Reading Research Tells Us About Children with Diverse Learning Needs: Bases and Basics.* Lawrence Erlbaum Associates, 1998.

Diller, D. *Making the Most of Small Groups: Differentiation for All.* Stenhouse Publishers, 2007.

Duke, N. K., V. S. Bennett-Armistead, and E. M. Roberts. "Bridging the Gap Between Learning to Read and Reading to Learn." *Literacy and Young Children: Research-Based Practices.* The Guilford Press, 2003.

Duke, N. K. and C. Tower. "Nonfiction Texts for Young Readers." *The Texts in Elementary Classrooms.* Lawrence Erlbaum Associates, 2004.

Ehri, L. C. and S. R. Nunes. "The Role of Phonemic Awareness in Learning to Read." *What Research Has to Say About Reading Instruction.* 3rd ed. International Reading Association, 2002.

Fountas, I. C. and G. S. Pinnell. *Guided Reading: Good First Teaching for All Children.* Heinemann, 1996.

Fountas, I. C. and G. S. Pinnell. *Matching Books to Readers: Using Leveled Books in Guided Reading,* K-3. Heinemann, 1999.

Harvey, S. and A. Goudvis. *Strategies That Work: Teaching Comprehension to Enhance Understanding.* 2nd ed. Stenhouse Publishers, 2007.

Hiebert, E. H. and L. A. Martin. "The Texts of Beginning Reading Instruction." *Handbook of Early Literacy Research.* The Guilford Press, 2001.

Indrisano, R. and J. R. Paratore. *Learning to Write, Writing to Learn. Theory and Research in Practice.* International Reading Association, 2005.

Juel, C., G. Biancarosa, D. Coker, and R. Deffes. "Walking with Rosie: A Cautionary Tale of Early Reading Instruction." *Educational Leadership* (April 2003).

National Reading Panel. *Teaching Children to Read.* National Institute of Child Health and Human Development, 1999.

Pressley, M. *Reading Instruction That Works: The Case for Balanced Teaching,* 3rd ed. The Guilford Press, 2005.

Smith, S., D. C. Simmons, and E. J. Kame'enui. "Word Recognition: Research Bases." *What Reading Research Tells Us About Children with Diverse Learning Needs: Bases and Basics.* Lawrence Erlbaum Associates, 1998.

Snow, C., S. Burns, and P. Griffin, eds. *Preventing Reading Difficulties in Young Children.* National Academy Press, 1998.

Vaughn, S., P. G. Mathes, S. Linan-Thompson, and D. J. Francis. "Teaching English Language Learners at Risk for Reading Disabilities to Read: Putting Research into Practice." *Learning Disabilities Research & Practice,* vol. 20, issue 1 (February 2006).

Building Community

Oral Vocabulary for

Let's Learn
Amazing Words

Definitions, examples, and **applications** to use with the Oral Vocabulary in each lesson.

The Bremen Town Musicians

Amazing Words Oral Vocabulary Routine

DAY 1

solution

1. **Introduce** *Solution* means "the solving of a problem."

2. **Demonstrate** I used subtraction to find the *solution* to the math problem. Mom's *solution* to missing the bus was to drive to work.

3. **Apply** Some people leave litter in a park. What could be a *solution* to this problem?

survival

1. **Introduce** *Survival* means "the act of remaining alive."

2. **Demonstrate** *Survival* is difficult in a harsh place like the desert. When the weather turns cold, *survival* for some birds means flying to another place.

3. **Apply** What things are necessary for a person's *survival*?

DAY 2

Instruction for this day can be found in the Oral Vocabulary lesson.

DAY 3

Instruction for this day can be found in the Oral Vocabulary lesson.

DAY 4

familiar

1. **Introduce** People, places, or things you know well are *familiar* to you.

2. **Demonstrate** It was nice to be home in a *familiar* place after traveling. I am *familiar* with all the characters in that story.

3. **Apply** With what tools are you *familiar*?

insist

1. **Introduce** To *insist* is to make a demand or be firm about something.

2. **Demonstrate** Mom *insisted* that I finish my homework before watching TV. The racer *insists* that she crossed the finish line first.

3. **Apply** When have you *insisted* that you were right about something? Tell me about it.

Oral Vocabulary for

Let's Learn
Amazing Words

Definitions, examples, and applications to use with the Oral Vocabulary in each lesson.

One Good Turn Deserves Another

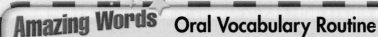 **Oral Vocabulary Routine**

 **DAY 1**

conflict

1. **Introduce** A *conflict* is a quarrel, struggle, fight, or problem.

2. **Demonstrate** My brother and I always have a *conflict* over whose turn it is to set the table. The Civil War was a *conflict* over slavery.

3. **Apply** Tell me about a *conflict* you have had with a family member or friend. Use the word *conflict* when you tell about it.

resolve

1. **Introduce** When you *resolve* something, you make a decision or solve a problem.

2. **Demonstrate** I *resolved* to study harder for the next spelling test. My dad *resolved* the argument over who would sit in the front seat of the car.

3. **Apply** Tell me about a problem you once had and how you *resolved* it.

DAY 2

Instruction for this day can be found in the Oral Vocabulary lesson.

DAY 3

Instruction for this day can be found in the Oral Vocabulary lesson.

 **DAY 4**

coax

1. **Introduce** When you gently talk someone into something, you *coax* that person.

2. **Demonstrate** My brother *coaxed* me into letting him ride my bike. Sometimes Mom has to *coax* my baby sister into eating.

3. **Apply** Think of something you want me to do and then try to *coax* me to do it.

ramp

1. **Introduce** A *ramp* is a slope or slant that connects two different levels.

2. **Demonstrate** Cars go down a *ramp* from the street to get into underground parking garages. A *ramp* helps someone in a wheelchair go up to a door.

3. **Apply** Make a *ramp* and show me how a pencil can roll down it. You can use some books to make the *ramp*.

UNIT 2 Acknowledgments

Acknowledgments

Text

Grateful acknowledgment is made to the following for copyrighted material:

Page 48: "The 1st Day of School" and "The 179th Day of School" from *Lunch Box Mail and Other Poems* by Jenny Whitehead. Copyright © 2001 by Jenny Whitehead. Reprinted by permission of Henry Holt and Company, LLC.

Page 58: From *Exploring Space with an Astronaut* by Patricia J. Murphy. Copyright © 2004 by Enslow Publishers, Inc. Published by Enslow Publishers, Inc., Berkeley Heights, NJ. All rights reserved.

Page 88: From *Henry and Mudge and the Starry Night* by Cynthia Rylant, illustrated by Suçie Stevenson. Text copyright © 1998 by Cynthia Rylant. Illustrations copyright © 1998 by Suçie Stevenson. Reprinted with permission of Simon & Schuster Books for Young Readers, an imprint of Simon & Schuster Children's Publishing Division. All rights reserved.

Page 120: From *A Walk in the Desert* by Caroline Arnold. Copyright © Alloy Entertainment and Al Jarcon. Reprinted by permission. All rights reserved.

Page 144: From www.factmonster.com from *The Columbia Electronic Encyclopedia, 6E.* Copyright © 2004 Columbia University Press. Licensed from Columbia University Press. Reprinted by permission. All rights reserved.

Page 156: "The Strongest One," from *Pushing Up the Sky* by Joseph Bruchac, copyright © 2000 by Joseph Bruchac, text. Used by permission of Dial Books for Young Readers, A Division of Penguin Young Readers Group, A Member of Penguin Group (USA) Inc., 345 Hudson Street, New York, NY 10014. All rights reserved.

Page 192: From *Tara and Tiree, Fearless Friends: A True Story* by Andrew Clements. Text copyright © 2002 by Andrew Clements. Reprinted with permission of Aladdin Paperbacks, an imprint of Simon & Schuster Children's Publishing Division. All rights reserved.

Page 254: *Scarcity* by Janeen R. Adil, copyright © 2006 by Capstone Press. All rights reserved. Used by permission.

Page 284: From *Easy-to-Read Folk and Fairy Tale Plays* by Carol Pugliano. Scholastic Inc./Teaching Resources. Copyright © 1997 by Carol Pugliano. Reprinted by permission.

Page 320: From *Silly & Sillier: Read-Aloud Tales from Around the World* by Judy Sierra and illus. by Valeri Gorbachev, copyright © 2002 by Judy Sierra. Illustrations copyright © 2002 by Valeri Gorbachev. Used by permission of Alfred A. Knopf, an imprint of Random House Children's Books, a division of Random House, Inc.

Page 354: *Pearl and Wagner, Two Good Friends* by Kate McMullan, Illustrations by R.W. Alley, copyright © 2003 by Kate McMullan, text. Used by permission of Dial Books for Young Readers, A Division of Penguin Young Readers Group, A Member of Penguin Group (USA) Inc., 345 Hudson Street, New York, NY 10014. All rights reserved.

Page 388: From *Dear Juno* by Soyung Pak, text copyright © 1999 by Soyung Pak, illustrations copyright © 1999 by Susan Kathleen Hartung. Used by permission of Viking Children's Books, a division of Penguin Young Readers Group, a member of Penguin Group (USA) Inc., 345 Hudson Street, New York, NY 10014 and Dystel & Goderich Literary Management, Inc. All rights reserved.

Page 410: From *Many Ways to Be A Soldier* by Wendy Pfeffer. Text copyright © 2008 by Wendy Pfeffer.

Page 424: *Anansi Goes Fishing.* Text copyright © 1992 by Eric A. Kimmel. Illustrations copyright © 1992 by Janet Stevens. All rights reserved. Reprinted by permission of Holiday House, Inc.

Page 448: "Do Spiders Stick to Their Own Webs?"and "Do Turtles Leave Their Shells?", from *Where Fish Go in Winter and Other Great Mysteries* by Amy Goldman Koss, copyright © 1987 by Amy Goldman Koss. Used by permission of Dial Books for Young Readers, A Division of Penguin Young Readers Group, A Member of Penguin Group (USA) Inc., 345 Hudson Street, New York, NY 10014. All rights reserved.

Page 458: *Rosa and Blanca* by Joe Hayes, illustrated by José Ortega, 1993. Reprinted by permission of Joe Hayes.

Page 474: *The Crow and the Pitcher* retold by Eric Blair. Copyright © 2004 by Compass Point Books. Used by permission of Picture Window Books. All rights reserved.

Page 486: From *A Weed Is a Flower* by Aliki. Text copyright © 1965, 1988 by Aliki Brandenberg. Reprinted with permission of Simon & Schuster Books for Young Readers, an imprint of Simon & Schuster Children's Publishing Division. All rights reserved.

Page 512: "Products Made from Corn" from Ohio Corn Marketing Program Web site, www.ohiocorn.org. Reprinted by permission of Ohio Corn Marketing Program.

Note: Every effort has been made to locate the copyright owner of material reproduced in this component. Omissions brought to our attention will be corrected in subsequent editions.

Illustrations

Cover: Scott Gustafson; **EI1–EI15** Robert Neubecker; **EI18–EI27** John Haslam; **16** Dani Jones; **26–46** Jana Christy; **48** Stephen Gilpin; **78** Gabriel Carranza; **110** Bill McGuire; **146** Nathan Hale; **156–175** David Diaz; **179** Derek Grinnell; **182** Victor Rivas; **192–206** Scott Gustafson; **214** Matt Loxich; **224, 230–236** Stephen Costanza; **244** Orlando Ramirez; **274** Ethan Long; **280–295** Jon Goodell; **307–310** Dylan T. Weeks; **308** Mick Reid; **320, 322–334** Will Terry; **340–343** Dan Andreasen; **342** Jennifer Zivoin; **368–371** Paul Eric Roca; **374** Erwin Haya; **406** Doug Holgate; **410–415** Paul Weiner; **440** Scott R. Brooks; **468** Steve Simpson; **474–477** Laura Ovresat.

530

Photographs

Every effort has been made to secure permission and provide appropriate credit for photographic material. The publisher deeply regrets any omission and pledges to correct errors called to its attention in subsequent editions.

Unless otherwise acknowledged, all photographs are the property of Pearson Education, Inc.

Photo locators denoted as follows: Top (T), Center (C), Bottom (B), Left (L), Right (R), Background (Bkgd)

18 (C) ©Stephen Frink/Corbis; **20** (B) ©Powered by Light/Alan Spencer/Alamy Images; **53** ©Deco/Alamy; **58** (BR) ©Royalty-Free/Corbis, (T, C, Bkgd) Getty Images; **59** (C) NASA; **60** (L) NASA; **61** (T, B) NASA; **62** (CC) Getty Images, (L, BR) NASA; **63** (BR) ©Joseph Sohm/ChromoSohm Inc./Corbis, (CR, C) ©Richard T. Nowitz/Corbis, (T) Corbis, (TC, BR) NASA; **64** (TR, T, B) ©Richard T. Nowitz/Corbis, (B) NASA/Roger Ressmeyer/Corbis; **65** (BR) ©Richard T. Nowitz/Corbis, NASA; **66** (TR, Bkgd) NASA; **68** (Bkgd) Getty Images, (T, C) NASA; **69** (CR, B) NASA; **70** (C) NASA; **80** (C) ©Image Source/Getty Images, (T) ©John Foxx/Getty Images; **98** (BC) ©David A. Northcott/Corbis, (TL) ©Ralph Hopkins/Lonely Planet Images; **99** (TR) ©Tim Flach/Stone; **112** (T) ©Michael S. Quinton/National Geographic/Getty Images; **123** (BR) ©Maryellen Baker/Botanica; **124** (Bkgd) Getty Images, (BL) ©Jeri Gleiter/Getty Images, (BR) ©Marco Simoni/Robert Harding Picture Library Ltd.; **125** (B) ©Robert Van Der Hilst/Getty Images; **126** (Bkgd) ©Paul McCormick/Getty Images; **127** (BR) ©Bates Littlehales/NGS Image Collection, (BL) ©David Muench/Corbis, (CR) ©Gary W. Carter/Corbis; **128** (CR) ©Charles C. Place/Getty Images, (Bkgd) Getty Images, (TC) ©Ralph Hopkins/Lonely Planet Images; **129** (TR) ©David Aubrey/Getty Images, (TC) ©Jack Dykinga/Getty Images; **130** (Bkgd) ©Arthur S. Aubry/Getty Images, (BC) Getty Images; **131** (TR) ©George D. Lepp/Corbis, (BR) ©David A. Northcott/Corbis, (CL) ©Joe McDonald/Corbis; **132** (Bkgd) Digital Vision, (BL) ©Farrell Grehan/Corbis, (BR) ©Shai Ginott/Corbis; **133** (BC) ©Tom Bean/Corbis; **134** (Bkgd) ©Joe McDonald/Corbis; **136** (CR) ©David Muench/Corbis, (BR) Getty Images, (BL) ©Jonathan Blair/NGS Image Collection; **136** (BL, Bkgd) Getty Images, (BR) ©Michael & Patricia Fogelen/Corbis; **137** (TL, BR) Getty Images, (TR) ©Mel Yates/Getty Images; **138** (BR) ©Layne Kennedy/Corbis, (BL) ©Tom Bean/Getty Images; **139** (TC) ©Matthias Clamer/Getty Images; **140** (Bkgd) ©Ira Rubin/Getty Images, (CL) ©Tim Flach/Stone/Getty Images, (CR) ©William J. Hebert/Getty Images; **141** (TR) ©Rogier Gruys, (TL) ©Royalty-Free/Corbis, (BC) ©Ira Rubin/Getty Images, (CR) ©Jean Paul Ferrero/Ardea; **142** (BR) ©Steve Maslowski/Visuals Unlimited; **156** Courtesy David Diaz; **179** (Bkgd) ©Tom Brakefield/Corbis; **180** (B) ©John H. Hofman/Bruce Coleman Inc., (T) ©Roland Seitre/Peter Arnold, Inc.; **181** (Bkgd) ©Theo Allofs/Corbis; **182** (T) Getty Images; **184** (C) ©Juniors Bildarchiv/Alamy Images; **187** ©Larry W. Smith;/epa/Corbis; **212** (Bkgd) ©Tim Davis/Corbis; **213** (TL) ©Andrea Comas/Corbis, (CL) ©Jean-Bernard Vernier/Corbis, (BL) ©Tom Nebbia/Corbis; **214** (CR) ©Armando Arorizo/Corbis, (Bkgd, B) ©Owen Franken/Corbis, (CL) ©Shanid Zhumatov/Corbis, (TR) ©Vaughn Youtz/Corbis; **215** (TL) ©Kai Pfaffenbach/Corbis, (BR) ©Ralf-Finn Hestoft/Corbis; **218** (B) ©Bernard Annebicque/Sygma/Corbis; **236** (BC) Corbis; **237** (BR) ©Bettmann/Corbis, (C) Corbis; **248** ©Peter Vadnal/Corbis, ©Stock Photos/Stock Photos/zefa/Corbis; **254** ©Wayne Eastep/Getty Images; **256** ©Chris Livingston/Getty Images; **260** ©Wayne Eastep/Getty Images; **261** ©Bill Bachman/Alamy Images; **262** Jupiter Images; **264** ©Phil Klein/Corbis; **265** ©Tom McCarthy/Unicorn Stock Photos; **268** ©Owen Franken/Corbis; **273** (R) ©Michael Newman/PhotoEdit, (L) Index Open; **274** (R) ©Jonathan Nourok/PhotoEdit, (L) ©VStock/Index Open; **275** (C) ©Felicia Martinez/PhotoEdit; **314** (B) ©David Katzenstein/Corbis; **346** (C) ©Roger Bamber/Alamy Images; **349** ©Blend Images/SuperStock; **380** (T) ©4 Eyes Photography/Getty Images, (C) Getty Images; **418** ©Fabio Colombini Medeiros/Animals Animals/Earth Scenes, (B) ©Karl Ammann/Nature Picture Library; **448** (CL) Getty Images, (BL) ©PBNJ Productions/Corbis; **449** (C) ©Mark E. Gibson/Corbis; **450** (C) ©Jupiter Images/Alamy, (T) ©Kathy Quirk-Syversen/Getty Images; **478** (T) ©Sean Justice/Corbis; **481** ©Blend Images/SuperStock; **514** (C, B) Corbis; **515** (TR, CR, BR, BL) Getty Images; **518** (TL) Corbis; **520** (BR) ©Jim Winkley/Corbis; **523** (BR) ©Haruyoshi Yamaguchi/Corbis, (TL) Getty Images; **524** (BL) ©Royalty-Free/Corbis **525** (BR) Getty Images.

531

Teacher Editions

KWL Strategy: The KWL Interactive Reading Strategy was developed and is used by permission of Donna Ogle, National-Louis University, Skokie, Illinois, co-author of *Reading Today and Tomorrow,* Holt, Rinehart & Winston Publishers, 1988. (See also the *Reading Teacher,* February 1986, pp. 564–570.)

Understanding by Design quotes: Wiggins, G. & McTighe, J. (2005). *Understanding by Design.* Alexandria, VA: Association for Supervision and Curriculum Development.

Illustrations
Cover Scott Gustafson
Running Header Steven Mach

Photographs
Every effort has been made to secure permission and provide appropriate credit for photographic material. The publisher deeply regrets any omission and pledges to correct errors called to its attention in subsequent editions.

Unless otherwise acknowledged, all photographs are the property of Pearson Education, Inc.

Teacher Resources

Looking for Teacher Resources and other important information?

In the **First Stop** on Reading Street

- Dear Second Grade Teacher
- Research into Practice on Reading Street
- Guide to Reading Street
- Assessment on Reading Street
- Customize Writing on Reading Street
- Differentiated Instruction on Reading Street

- ELL on Reading Street
- Customize Literacy on Reading Street
- Digital Products on Reading Street
- Teacher Resources for Grade 2
- Index

Teacher Resources

Looking for Teacher Resources and other important information?

In the **First Stop** on Reading Street

- **Dear Second Grade Teacher**
- **Research into Practice on Reading Street**
- **Guide to Reading Street**
- **Assessment on Reading Street**
- **Customize Writing on Reading Street**
- **Differentiated Instruction on Reading Street**

- **ELL on Reading Street**
- **Customize Literacy on Reading Street**
- **Digital Products on Reading Street**
- **Teacher Resources for Grade 2**
- **Index**